NORDIC EQUALITY AT A CROSSROADS

Nordic Equality at a Crossroads

Feminist Legal Studies Coping with Difference

Edited by

EVA-MARIA SVENSSON
University of Gothenburg, Sweden

ANU PYLKKÄNEN
University of Helsinki, Finland

JOHANNA NIEMI-KIESILÄINEN
Umeå University, Sweden

Routledge
Taylor & Francis Group
LONDON AND NEW YORK

First published 2004 by Ashgate Publishing

Reissued 2019 by Routledge
2 Park Square, Milton Park, Abingdon, Oxon, OX14 4RN
52 Vanderbilt Avenue, New York, NY 10017

Routledge is an imprint of the Taylor & Francis Group, an informa business

A Library of Congress record exists under LC control number:

ISBN 13: 978-0-8153-9073-2 (hbk)
ISBN 13: 978-1-351-15232-7 (ebk)

Contents

List of Contributors

Karoliina Ahtela, LLM, Doctoral student, Department of Law, University of Helsinki. Previously, she worked at the Office of the Ombudsman for Equality. E-mail: *Karoliina.Ahtela@kolumbus.fi*

Hege Brækhus, LLD, Associate Professor, University of Tromsø. Her professional interest, in particular, is the legal regulation of women's unpaid contributions, especially in relation to social security benefits and family law. E-mail: *Hege.Braekhus@jus.uit.no*

Monica Burman, LLM, Lecturer in Criminal Law, Umeå University. Formerly, she worked seven years as an associate judge. She is currently preparing a doctoral thesis on the Swedish legal constructions relating to men's violence against women. E-mail: *Monica.Burman@jus.umu.se*

Susanne Fransson, LLD, Lecturer, University of Uddevalla/Trollhättan. She has written a doctoral thesis (2001) on wage discrimination and several articles on labour law, for example, Collective and Individual Strategies, in Nousiainen, *et al.* (eds) *Responsible Selves. Women in the Nordic Legal Culture* (Ashgate 2001). E-mail: *Susanne.Fransson@adm.gu.se*

Åsa Gunnarsson, LLD, Professor in Tax Law, Umeå University. She has written extensively on tax law and legal theory. Currently, she is leading several research projects about tax law and social welfare law, focusing on poverty traps in family support and on the legal construction of social citizenship. E-mail: *Asa.Gunnarsson@jus.umu.se*

Kristine Helen Korsnes, LLM, Lecturer, University of Tromsø. She teaches family law and contract law. She is writing a PhD in international private law. E-mail: *Kristine.Korsnes@jus.uit.no*

Sari Kouvo, LLM, Lecturer, Department of Law, School of Economics, University of Gothenburg. She is finalizing her PhD on the concept of gender and the gender mainstreaming strategy within the international human rights framework. E-mail: *Sari.Kouvo@law.gu.se*

Johanna Niemi-Kiesiläinen, LLD, Professor of Law, Umeå University. She has published articles on Finnish and comparative bankruptcy law and legal topics related to violence against women. She was a co-editor of the previous title from the same group: *Responsible Selves. Women in the Nordic Legal Culture* (Ashgate 2001). Currently, she is leading a research project, *Violence in the Shadow of Equality: Hidden Gender in Legal Discourse.* E-mail: *Johanna.Niemi-Kiesilainen@helsinki.fi*

Kevät Nousiainen, LLD, Professor of Women's Law and Legal Theory, University of Helsinki, and Professor of Legal Theory and Comparative Law, University of Turku. She has written extensively on legal theory, feminist jurisprudence and procedural law. She was the primary co-editor of the previous title from the same group: *Responsible Selves. Women in the Nordic Legal Culture* (Ashgate 2001). E-mail: *Kevat.Nousianen@helsinki.fi*

Hanne Petersen, LLD, Professor of Greenlandic Sociology of Law, University of Copenhagen. She is national partner in an interdisciplinary EU research project *Gender Relations at the Turn of the Millennium. Women as Subjects in Marriage and Migration* with researchers from Bulgaria, Denmark, Hungary, the Netherlands and Italy. E-mail: *Hanne.Petersen@jus.ku.dk*

Anu Pylkkänen, LLD, Academy Research Fellow, University of Helsinki. Her research interests have been the legal status of women in the early modern period and the history of matrimonial law from a comparative perspective. Her current research project is on the law on person. E-mail: *Anu.Pylkkanen@helsinki.fi*

Eva-Maria Svensson, LLD, Senior Lecturer of Legal Science and Philosophy, University of Gothenburg. She has published articles on legal philosophy, gender theory and public law. Her articles discuss, for example, freedom of speech and pornography from a feminist perspective. Her current research projects deal with equality and epistemology in legal science. E-mail: *Eva-Maria.Svensson@law.gu.se*

Christer Thörnqvist, Ph.D., Lecturer, Department of Work Science, University of Gothenburg. His main research interests are industrial conflicts, collective bargaining and social exclusion. He has jointly edited *Global Redefining of Working Life – A New Nordic Agenda for Competence and Participation?* (Copenhagen 1998, with D. Fleming, P. Kettunen and H. Søborg); and *European Working Lives: Continuities and Change in Management and Industrial Relations in France, Scandinavia, and the U.K.*, (Cheltenham 2001, with S. Jefferys and F. Mispelblom Beyer). E-mail: *Christer.Thornqvist@av.gu.se*

Lena Wennberg, BA, MA in Social Work, Lecturer, Department of Law, Umeå University. She is preparing a doctoral thesis on *Solo Mothers in the Context of Active Citizenship*. E-mail: *Lena.Wennberg@jus.umu.se*

Preface

For half a century, the Nordic societies have been almost synonymous with the strong welfare state and progressive equality politics. However, this image has been challenged in the processes of privatization and globalization. These processes together with increasing multiculturalism unavoidably change the notions of what has long been understood as 'Nordic equality'. Consequently, the legal concepts are undergoing a change.

This volume is based on the work of a Nordic network of feminist legal scholars that has assembled in different institutional and non-institutional activities since the late 1980s. The group gathered at the Oñati International Institute for the Sociology of Law, from 19 to 21 September, 2001, for a workshop entitled, *Nordic Feminist Legal Studies*. The starting point was threefold: to open up a dialogue on the specific features of law and gender in the Nordic countries, to present critical analyses on the legal and social structures underpinning equality and to analyze the relationship between law and sex equality. This collection is based on the papers presented at the Oñati seminar and on the discussions that ensued.

This anthology is a sequel, though able to stand alone, of *Responsible Selves. Women in the Nordic Legal Culture*, edited by Kevät Nousiainen, et al. (Ashgate 2001) by the same network.

We warmly thank the Oñati International Institute for the Sociology of Law for financial contributions to the workshop and for helping organizing it. The city of Oñati and the Institute were the perfect surroundings for our work. We also would like to thank *Institutet för rättsvetenskaplig forskning grundat av Knut och Alice Wallenbergs stiftelse* (The Institute for Legal Research, founded by Knut and Alice Wallenberg's fund) for financial support for the editing of this book. We also would like to thank Linda Augustine MA, JD who has edited our English language in an excellent way, Tuomas Tammilehto for editorial assistance and Pekka Sirkiä for the pagesetting. We would also like to thank all the contributors to this volume and other participants in the Oñati workshop for their constructive collaboration and for sharing the joys and concerns of legal academics dealing with gender equality.

Gothenburg and Helsinki, 31 December 2003

Eva-Maria Svensson   Anu Pylkkänen   Johanna Niemi-Kiesiläinen

Chapter 1

Introduction: Nordic Feminist Legal Studies at a Crossroads

Eva-Maria Svensson, Anu Pylkkänen and Johanna Niemi-Kiesiläinen

The contributions to this collection have sprung out of an awareness that we are now at a crossroads. Nordic feminist legal scholars are currently facing a new reality where we must deconstruct the understandings we have taken for granted about the strong State, progressive equality politics and homogenous societies. Our understanding of equality seems to have been based on the assumption of a homogenous society at a level deeper than we ever could have expected. This assumption was recently challenged by the tragic death of a young immigrant woman in Sweden and in the many-faceted discussions that ensued.

Fadime Sahindal, a young Kurdish immigrant woman, was murdered in Sweden by her own father in January 2002. The murder was soon labelled an 'honour killing' because the motive of the girl's father was to protect the honour of his family. In our opinion, this event symbolizes the end of the previously held beliefs of the homogenous Nordic societies.

The discussions which followed demonstrated the complexity of the issues linked with the Nordic model of equality. The topics ranged from gendered violence, immigration and social integration to the values of Swedish society. The murder touched the Swedes in a profound way. The issue was intensely debated, not only in the media, but also among ordinary people and, in particular, among feminist academics. One of the central issues in the feminist discussion was whether the murder should be viewed as a cultural issue or as a feminist one. Was Fadime murdered because she was a woman or because she was from another culture? Why did Fadime's murder evoke such a compassionate reaction at the same time that thousands of instances of other women being battered and raped by their partners in all Nordic countries went unremarked? Why did the reports of these assaults fail to raise similar concerns?

It is our argument that the reaction to Fadime's fate did not follow from the fact that she was a woman, nor from the fact that she was an immigrant. The reaction is best explained by the fact that she was a Swede. Even before she died, although even more so afterwards, Fadime had become a new symbol for Swedish values.

Well integrated into the Swedish society and culture, at the age of 26, Fadime was an independent young woman, who lived alone and was studying to become a social worker. She had immigrated as a young girl and had become an interpreter for her father with whom she had had a good relationship. Fadime's father was a manual worker who never adjusted to Swedish society. Fadime had been engaged to a Swedish man, a non-Kurd, who had later died in a car accident. The engagement had broken Fadime's father's heart, prompting him to threaten to kill Fadime because of it. Fadime decided to go public with the alarming situation. Speaking in flawless Swedish, Fadime even brought her case before the Swedish Parliament, addressing the threats facing immigrant women in Sweden.

As an immigrant, Fadime was a symbol of solidarity. As an independent woman, she represented sex equality. With a working class background and a good education, she represented progress and equal opportunity. As an aspiring social worker, Fadime epitomized a sense of shared responsibility for persons in need. And, as the Swedish historian Yvonne Hirdman (2002) has pointed out, Fadime had publicly defended Swedish values. In short, Fadime represented everything about which Sweden is proud. So, an attack on her was an attack on the core values of Swedish society. Fadime was considered to be a member of this society, whereas her father was considered an outsider, who threatened its values.

According to this interpretation,[1] the murderer, an uneducated male of immigrant background, is constructed as the threat and as 'the alien'. But can it lead us any further in our pursuit of understanding the case? As Julia Kristeva (1988) argues, in order to learn something from the alien, we need to recognize the alien in ourselves. The challenge, therefore, of Fadime's murder goes right to the Nordic identity we have constructed for ourselves. Our understanding of a Nordic identity seem to fall short of a genuine understanding of difference and multiculturalism. To create an identity is always to relate oneself to the others, but the question remains, how reflective is this process with regard to controversy and exclusion.

The danger that we can distinguish in the discussions following Fadime's death is that the boundaries between us and them are only drawn in a new place, between the well-integrated immigrant and the 'other' immigrants. What is needed, though, is a renegotiation of the whole concept and notion of these boundaries in order to attain a genuine multiculturalism.

After some thirty years of progressive equality politics, we must now deconstruct the taken-for-granted understandings of the strong and women-friendly State, the mixed blessings of the undeniably progressive Nordic equality politics and the image of culturally homogenous societies.

Nordic equality has been founded on economic growth, progressive welfare and educational policies as well as on the presence of women in politics and in the labour force. The economic and social development of the Nordic societies has relied on a universal mobilization of human resources. Now, privatization, globalization and multiculturalism unavoidably challenge the notions of the concept that has long been understood as 'Nordic equality'. Encountering challenges from peoples and cultures dissimilar to the one cherished in Scandinavia, there are no longer any self-evident planks on which to base the policies of the Nordic welfare states. Fundamental issues with regard to subjectivity, citizenship and equality must be addressed from a new perspective. The communitarian traditions of small and ethnically homogenous societies are now being replaced by a more liberal system in which individual rights and anti-discrimination dominate over more collective patterns and values. As we will argue later, this shift poses a challenge as to how we comprehend law and legal studies.

The Nordic Equality Model

The Nordic equality model has its historical roots in the nation state formation based on egalitarian and communitarian elements. The present understanding of Nordic equality is a product of a little less than hundred years of progressive social policy characterized by social engineering. In the early 20th century, the Nordic societies were very poor. Emigration of surplus labour was extensive. In the 1920s, in Denmark and Sweden, important steps were taken to elevate society and direct it towards economic growth. One part of this politics was to enhance the social equality between men and women. Liberal marriage reforms and pro-natalist policies were one part of this process (Melby et al. 2000). Women were granted legal and economic independence, even if it was understood that most women, nevertheless, would stay at home.

In Finland, the attainment of independence in 1917 and the subsequent Civil War created much social controversy and required resources that were bereft of any constructive social policy. However, women were somewhat more active in political life and working life than in the other Nordic countries. Even today, working ethos and an emphasis on waged labour characterize the lives of women in Finland to a greater extent than in any other Nordic country.

All Nordic countries, in principle, have based their social and equality politics on economically independent individuals, irrespective of gender or family status (Kautto et al. 1999, Kalliomaa-Puha 2000). The image of socially and economically well-developed societies with a strong emphasis on substantive equality, or the equality of results, is, thus, a product of deliberation and active social planning. There have been visions of the best possible world we, as Nordic citizens, could achieve.

The downside of these developments is that the ability to recognize difference and disadvantage on an individual level is less practiced. Liberal notions of individual rights and protected privacy have only very recently come onto the agenda due to the adherence to international Human Rights conventions and the European Union. A liberal understanding of the equality of opportunities does not always fit easily into the framework of collective patterns, for example, into the trade-union regulated labour market. At this moment, under serious consideration in the Nordic societies is the question of how the requirements of individual anti-discrimination and collective egalitarian policies and norms may be accommodated.

In this book, we argue that Nordic equality has been based on sameness to such a degree that it leaves little room for politicians and lawyers to recognize and appreciate difference (Nousiainen 2004). The notion of equality as sameness is most persistently anchored in the legal system. Proactive equality politics are repeatedly hampered by legal constraints.

The authors argue that not only equality and anti-discrimination law, but also the legal system, in general, have been built upon the principles of similarity and assimilation. The authors claim that the model of the sex-neutral, self-supporting, independent individual is assumed as the basis of most fields of law. Gender-related issues are recognized only as far as they are compatible with the idea of a genderless actor. As these articles will demonstrate, people not corresponding to this model, such as care-givers, single parents or weaker parties in sexual encounters, are considered as foreign elements in the legal system. The legal system, with its formally neutral law on non-discrimination, has been unable to realize substantive equality, or the equality of results.

In the Nordic civil law countries, the statutory law system is of primary interest in legal analyses (Nousiainen and Niemi-Kiesiläinen 2001). Furthermore, law is used as a tool to direct the societies, signifying social engineering, not only as a method to resolve conflicts as in the more liberal regimes that have been called residue models. Quite paradoxically, however, the standpoint of Scandinavian legal scholarship is quite formal and seldom concerned with the societal impacts of law. The Scandinavian tradition of legal realism has not included in-depth analyses of legal constructions as such or of their intertwined connections with other than legal norms and social practice. Laws are seen as tools to attain political goals such as equality and welfare, but it has not been conceded that law and legal constructs themselves could have any impact on social life and even be discriminatory by ignoring the inequalities hidden beneath the formally neutral system. It is, therefore, of great importance for feminist lawyers to analyze the impact of the systemic structure of law and its internal lacunae and controversies that produce indirectly discriminatory effects. It will be argued in this book that despite the overtly egalitarian and gender-neutral form of the statutory system and its context in actively promoted equality politics, the outcome can often be less favourable to marginalized people.

The recognition of difference requires first recognition of a context. Legal assessments of similarity and difference, which are at the core of equality and discrimination law based on comparison, mean that law is applied in a certain context. Contextualization has been one of the debated topics in feminist legal studies, but so far it has had little impact in the North. Legal science has been extremely formal with regard to social norms and practices that intertwine with the legal discourse. While we should be aware of the context, at the same time, we should be alert to the dangers that are implied in the application of law in patriarchal contexts. As feminist lawyers, we recognize this danger in positivistic legal dogmatics, which very seldom clearly explicate the assumptions on gender.

Nordic feminist legal studies have become more critical of the possibilities of achieving equality through legal reform. While we are not unwilling to abandon legal reform as such, we want yet to explore the foundations on which such reforms are based. The contributors of this book have become more and more interested in the processes in which both legal discourses and wider societal discourses construct legal concepts and contexts. It is symptomatic that such interest has arisen only after the Nordic welfare and equality model has fallen into crisis. Public concerns are shifted to other spheres: law, market, media, private sphere of contracting.

Equality Through Labour

Since the early 20th century, the Nordic welfare model is based on individual self-support through waged labour. Thus, women's high participation in the labour market has been crucial for the quest for equality. Today, however, we are disillusioned about achieving equality in work and through work. It has been deeply disappointing to realize that the Nordic labour market is not a market of equal opportunity or equal pay. The wage gap between women and men can only be partly explained by occupational patterns. At the same time, the proportion of women in higher positions is still considerably low, also in the Academia (Husu 2001).

The Nordic equality model has been challenged from two directions. On the one hand, its own inability to fulfil the expectations has led to criticism and to the questioning of its premises. On the other hand, the Nation State as a basis for achieving political goals, such as equality, is losing ground. The states have yielded some of their sovereignty to the EU, the globalizing market and trans- or supranational bodies and organizations. The nation states are not necessarily the fora where reform is sought today. Investigations concerning power structures in society, such as the one made in Sweden in 1990, '*Demokrati och makt i Sverige*' (SOU 1990:44), show that there are many areas such as the economy and the market where women actually wield very little influence.

In this book, Susanne Fransson and Christer Thörnqvist make a claim that the failure of the traditional labour market strategies to achieve equal rights for everyone is partly due to the gendered structures within the bargaining strategies. In the chapter, *Gender, Bargaining Strategies and Strikes in Sweden,* they discover notable differences between 'male' and 'female' bargaining strategies, in particular, in the use of the strike. While occupational groups dominated by men have frequently used wildcat strikes to apply pressure to shop-floor wage negotiations, groups dominated by women have remained largely mute. Instead of saying that women are the problem since they do not use labour market strategies, Fransson and Thörnqvist argue that these strategies, as such, are gendered structures.

In the palmy days of the Swedish labour market model, typically female occupations were guaranteed a decent pay increase owing to the so-called solidaristic wage policy. The changes in the 1990s have demanded new strategies. The most important new strategy has been to use legislation for collective purposes; the systematic use of the legislation against wage discrimination in the health sector is the most obvious case. Expectations have now turned to anti-discrimination law.

The basis for the Sex Equality Acts issued in the 1970s and 1980s[2] was an equality of opportunities, signifying formal equality and anti-discrimination. The Swedish Equality Act was a compromise between two ideologies, liberal and collective, decided upon by a government with a liberal prime minister. Together with the principle of equal opportunity in the Constitution (1976 in Sweden, 1995 in Finland), the Sex Equality Acts predominantly represented a liberal model of regulation. The collective elements were an innovation of the Social Democrats, signifying that the trade unions should have an active role in the promotion of sex equality through equality planning and monitoring.

Through reforms of the Equality Acts, the equality of results policy has been more active than the liberal equality of opportunities policy. Equality of results policies, such as quota systems (SOU 1987:19), have led to an almost equal representation in politics.[3] In the legal sphere, however, it has been more difficult to pursue an active sex equality policy through anti-discrimination cases or positive action (*Jämställdhetsombudsmannen*, Annual report 2001).

Because anti-discrimination unavoidably involves litigation, lawyers could engage themselves in cases that provide arenas for an active argumentation for and application of the equality principle. Pursuing cases is a strategy vis-à-vis environmental issues and the human rights of marginalized groups. When it comes to sex equality, it does not seem to be such an efficient method. The Swedish Sex Equality Ombudsman has pursued cases related to sex equality for several years, but the office seldom ends up in a winning case, such as the one in April 2002 (ADD 45/2002). Other lawyers in Sweden have been reluctant to take on employment discrimination cases. In Finland, the Equality Ombudsmen have shown no interest in litigation. Private claimants have taken cases to court not without some success, but the compensation for discrimination is low and there is no chance of getting one's job back.

Another challenge to the Nordic equality model is the shift of power to international fora and to the European Union, in particular. When Finland and Sweden joined the EC in 1995, a strong feminist lobby argued that this membership would be detrimental to Nordic sex equality politics. Women in the Nordic countries have attained both political power and economic independence, to some extent, due to positive action policies such as quotas. It was argued that when power is shifted from nation States to the European Union, power is also shifted from women to men as the EU structures are much more male-dominated. Recent feminist legal scholarship has also shown how, for example, the EC case law relating to sex equality reproduces patriarchal structures (Lundström 2001; Shaw 2001). But we can distinguish an opposite effect as well. After the Amsterdam Treaty, the Member States are obliged to pursue policies which promote equality and remove obstacles to equality. Especially in Sweden, this new approach in EU law has coincided with active equality politics at the national level. As will be argued by Svensson and Pylkkänen, it has not been easy to translate these claims into national law.

One example of how difficult it is to implement policies that require the active promotion of equality is given by Karoliina Ahtela in the chapter, *Promoting Equality in the Workplace: Legislative Intent and Reality*. In Finland, the Equality Act of 1987 requires all major employers to establish equality plans to promote equality in the working place. The promotion of equality by these plans has not been realized as it had been intended to be upon the enactment of the Act. According to Ahtela, the reasons for the failure stem from the fact that the legislation was passed as a response to requirements from the outside, that is, the UN and later, the EU. Therefore, the equality plans, required by law, lack legitimacy in the Finnish labour market. The law and the plans are not accompanied with any insight into the construction of inequalities in the working place. Even when there is a consciousness of inequality, its structural bases are not recognized and plans are not put into effective use. Ahtela points out that a law has to be congruent with politics and society in order to be efficiently implemented. Ahtela raises important concerns about the implementation of equality law both in national and in the EU contexts.

Reproduction and Care

In the Nordic feminist studies of the 1980s and early 1990s, two fields of interest may be distinguished. In Sweden and Finland, feminist legal research was mostly interested in equality legislation and the regulation of labour relations from the women's point of view; as for examples, see Fransson and Thörnqvist in this volume. In Norway, under a new disciplinary title, 'Women's Law', new areas of law were addressed from a woman's point of view. The idea was to identify problems that were common among women, to analyze them, and to offer alternative interpretations that would lead to legal reform. The Norwegian Women's Law intersected traditional areas of law and created new fields of law, such as Housewife Law, Birth Law and Money Law (Dahl 1987). The Norwegian term *Kvinderet*, 'Women's law', has become the name used in all Nordic countries to refer to a discipline that is interested in the legal regulation of women's issues.

A mutually-held interest for both the Norwegian and the Swedish-Finnish approaches has been the regulation of care and its effects on women. For feminists, the question of how to deal with women's caring duties has long been a sensitive issue. Some of them think, quite plausibly, that home care strengthens patriarchal structures and enforces dependency. Especially in Sweden and Finland, equality politics have strived to combine work and motherhood as a feasible option within the more or less formally equal legal framework. The approach of the Norwegian women's law has been different. Its method has been to focus on women as a social category: to take up legal issues with relevance to women, such as home care, to consider alternative interpretations of law and to suggest legal reform.

While equality in the labour market has mainly concerned the similarities or differences between women and men, the politics of care also raise the issues of equality and difference among women. While caring responsibilities are not equally shared by men and women, they are not equally shared among women, either. It can be argued that this division is an artificial one. Actually, many women with or without a job choose to care for their children, old parents or sick partner at some phase in their lives.

As an author deriving her analysis from the Norwegian women's law tradition, Hege Braekhus discusses in her chapter, *Care and Social Rights,* the legal framework of financing home care in Norway. In Norway, social problems linked with caring responsibilities have been resolved with a multiplicity of measures that together build a patchwork quilt, often sewn up with concerns other than caring itself. It is not at all sure that the aim to secure women's economic independence as caregivers is secured in practice. The patchwork of regulations includes internal contradictions and gaps that reiterate the patterns of dependence rather than change them.

Furthermore, Braekhus discusses the evaluation of different occupations. Obviously the work done mostly by women is given less value than the work done mostly by men. Care is an occupation considered to have low value, no matter whether it is done as unpaid activity in the private sphere or as paid work in the labour market. Braekhus argues that care is work no matter where and no matter under what circumstances it is done. As such, care should be valued not only as a way to obtain a moderate income and social rights, but also as a ground for a better than moderate level of income. However, as long as women have little influence in the prioritized choices of national economy, such a vision may remain utopian.

If care is seen as work that should be compensated, the following questions inevitably arise: who should be obligated to pay for it and at which level: the caregiver herself or himself, the partner or the State? Politically, the fiercest controversies among the Nordic countries, nowadays, concern the care of one's own children.

The EU, as well, has become interested in this issue. The Presidency conclusions of Barcelona European Council, held on 15–16 March 2002, defined an aim to provide childcare to at least 90 per cent of children between the ages of three and the mandatory school age by 2010 and to at least 33 per cent of children under the age of three (Paragraph 32). The same concern, *viz.*, to remove disincentives for female waged labour, had been in the background of corresponding Nordic provisions since the 1970s.

The Nordic countries have chosen different policies. In Sweden and Finland, every child is assured of a day care place in a day care facility, mostly provided for by municipal day care centres. Sweden has built a comprehensive network of day care facilities. Finland has promoted alternatives and 'family choice', which has meant both municipal and state-funded day care and financial support to families who choose to care for their children in private arrangements. Norway introduced a home care allowance system in 1998. For a short period of time in 1994, even Sweden had such a system, introduced by the conservative government.[4] It was criticized as unequal and was abolished by the social democratic regime after the following election.[5]

The Norwegian allowance system has come to stay. Benefits are paid to families who have children between the ages of one and three and who are not cared for in state-subsidized day-care centres. The actual benefit, however, is low and it is impossible to live on it. It is a modest contribution to the family budget. In the chapter, *The Norwegian Home Care Allowance,* Kristine Korsnes discusses this scheme and argues that, despite the low level of compensation, the scheme, however, can be seen as highlighting the important issue of the value of care.

Family Model and Equality

The two trends in Nordic feminist law, equality through the labour market and the focus on women's problems, have both turned out to be problematic as means to obtain equality or to reveal obstacles for equality. As will be discussed below, Nordic feminist legal studies have of late turned into analysis of law itself, into asking questions about how law, legal practice and legal studies themselves construct gender and gendered structures. The latter part of this book consists of examples of this approach, starting with a discussion of about how the gendered structures of family law, tax law and social law have a combined effect on women's lives.

Nordic equality has been based on an idea of self-supporting individuals who organize reproduction in dual breadwinner families. During the 20th century, the trend in family law has been towards increasing individualism and independence in family relations. Even if marriage is still regulated as an institution, the individualism in marriage has been continuously fortified. In practice, however, personal and economic dependence is the reality for many people. The relation of dependence and self-support in family, tax and social law is the object of Monica Burman, Åsa Gunnarsson and Lena Wennberg in the chapter *Economic Dependence and Self-support in Family, Tax and Social Law*.

They show that normative and structural patterns are shaped according to divergent models in different areas of law: the nuclear family model and the individual model. They argue that tax law is based on an individual model, but social security law, on the nuclear family model. While family law is mostly based on an individual model, traces of the family model are found in the regulation of matrimonial property and support. Since women's living conditions are intertwined with family life more than men's living conditions are, women have to deal with normative and structural constraints derived from the predominance of the public side of life to the neglect of the private side in which their caring role still creates patterns of dependence. Therefore, women often encounter, to their detriment, the contradictory or competing requirements of family, tax and social laws.

Sexual Violence and Sexual Images

Violence against women and discriminatory sexual images of women were core themes in feminist legal scholarship during the 1990s. These themes have also been central in Nordic scholarship and in sex equality politics and legislation. Initiatives have been taken to integrate criminal law perspectives into social policy, both in theory and in practice. The Swedish legal reform, *Kvinnofrid,* or 'Women's peace', bears excellent witness to this trend to utilize feminist knowledge in the law drafting (Nordborg & Niemi-Kiesiläinen 2001).

Sex crime law is usually understood as manifesting the sexual difference. Johanna Niemi-Kiesiläinen points out in her chapter, *The Reform of Sex Crime Law and the Gender-Neutral Subject,* that sex crime law has been used to make distinctions among women as well: a distinction between maidens and wives, on one side, and other women on the other side or a distinction between good women and bad women. Taking a constructivist stand, Niemi-Kiesiläinen argues that law also plays a crucial role in the construction of sex and sexuality today. The Finnish reform of the law on sexual offences from the late 1990s and the gender-neutral concept of the legal subject signify a completion of a liberal project that has made sexual crimes sex-neutral and neutral in relation to expressions of sexuality. According to her, the law on sex crimes also constructs the liberal subject and a liberal notion of sexuality.

The aim to protect sexual self-determination, however, is problematic when it comes to situations and relations in which the parties would not otherwise attain the full standard of self-determination. Some sexual relations, for example, with regard to minors or in the workplace, are relations which are characterized by weak self-determination, strong dependence and inequality. The author argues that a law based on gender neutrality and a protection of liberal self-determination is inadequate to deal with such situations and, at worst, makes power imbalance invisible and difficult to recognize and assess. Niemi-Kiesiläinen suggests that the focus be shifted towards a conceptualization of integrity as the protected good in sex crime and understanding sex, sexuality and subjectivity in relational terms. This kind of understanding would make it possible to account for different victims and different types of violations.

Feminist Legal Studies

Nordic feminism, including legal feminism, has shared a faith in national politics and legal reform as a means to achieve equality. Therefore, the decline of space for national politics, where the State of our time has even been characterized as an impotent State (Therborn 2000), is a paramount question for Nordic feminist studies. Political or, rather, private activity in the non-traditional sense is on the rise and power has shifted to international fora. It is our concern that such activities seem to lack the democratic safeguards related to nation States. How do these forces deal with issues related to equality, if at all?

Throughout the process of European integration, clashes of different legal cultures have become apparent. For example, the Swedish legislation of positive action in academia[6] with a predefined political aim and a clearly defined end result, *e.g.*, that a position *shall be* filled with a competent applicant of the underrepresented sex, even if he or she is less qualified than an applicant of the overrepresented sex, has been deemed to be in conflict with EC law (ECJ C-407/98). According to the Court, one is *allowed* to advance the equality of opportunities, but not to define the *automatic outcome* of certain measures.[7]

One difficulty in adapting to the EC law concerns indirect discrimination. It is not easily accepted that formally neutral criteria or factors can produce indirectly discriminatory effects and, thus, become forbidden discrimination. Correspondingly, the role of positive action has remained inefficient and is surprisingly seldom considered legitimate.

These examples demonstrate an implicit problem in sex equality law. The principle of equality as adopted in most European Constitutions, may be an obstacle when it comes to the horizontal implementation of the equality principle. A rule can be understood as a tool for implementing the principle but at the same time, it can be claimed as violating the equality principle if and when its purpose is to change the unequal relation itself, for example, with positive action. Finally, equality issues have to be balanced with other values. When doing so, equality often remains a principle that is of a relative rather than of an absolute character.

In Nordic feminist law, this paradox of equality law, together with disillusionment with the policy of equality through labour and with the failed efforts of upgrading care work, have led to a paradigmatic shift. The approaches in Nordic feminist legal studies vary a lot today. We can no longer talk about a uniform 'Nordic Women's Law'. What seems to be a common feature, however, is the more reflective and self-critical attitude towards law itself.

This disillusionment with traditional approaches to law has led to a critical analysis of the basic concepts that, as we argue, signifies an epistemological turn in Nordic legal science. The traditional approach of legal science to look at legal norms is inadequate to address the problems of women. It is felt that the positivistic understandings of normativity must be contested as well. The interaction between legal and other societal norms needs to be incorporated into a broader analysis of legal regulation. In the Nordic countries, socio-legal studies have not been a part of mainstream legal science as they are in some other European countries.

While women's law approach originally recognized the need to construct new concepts in order to address women's legal interests and concerns, it nevertheless operated within a positivist legal framework and mode of argumentation. Recently, Nordic feminist legal scholarship has distanced itself from the previous positivistic understandings of law. It is also interested in the construction of legal concepts as well as those concepts of related societal discourses. This approach is characterized by a critical reading of the legal canon as a whole, not only by certain concepts believed to be unfavourable to women.

The turn that has taken place in Women's Law during the past ten years epitomizes an aim of questioning the current normative basics of law and arguing for new interpretations of normativity. Instead of providing a new truth to replace the old one, feminist legal scholarship is critical towards the universal normative order as such. The new feminist legal studies challenge the strong belief in the systemic coherence of the legal order, which remained strong in Nordic jurisprudence. It is argued that the universal normative order has actually been constructed from one point of view, which, in this analysis is the male point of view. There has been an 'egalitarian bias' in our understandings of law that must be opened up to critical scrutiny. The new feminist legal studies is interested in how concepts are constructed in law, jurisprudence and other legal discourses. It is also interested in reconstruction, but it has to be built on an analysis of the gendered structure of the legal system and a legal mode of argumentation.

The debates on 'sex' and 'gender' have been central to feminist legal studies. In Sweden, the historian, Yvonne Hirdman, has developed a structural conceptualization of sex and gender utilizing the concepts of '*genus*' and '*genus theory*'. She makes an effort to analyze gendered structures in society as a whole. *Genus* theory is an attempt to incorporate the unequal power relation between men and women into social analysis at all levels. In her work, Eva-Maria Svensson has considered the theoretical implications of *genus* theory in law and the implicit gendered elements of the language of the law (Svensson 1997; Svensson 2001).

The chapters by Burman, Gunnarsson and Wennberg, and Niemi-Kiesiläinen, in this volume, are examples of works in which the construction of legal concepts in the respective fields of law are analyzed from a gendered point of view. Furthermore, they consider the possibility of a power conscious de- and reconstructions. In Sweden, recent legal reforms of legal education (Burman, Svensson and Ågren 2003), positive action in the recruitment of university personnel, women's peace reform in criminal law (Nordborg & Niemi-Kiesiläinen 2001) and the criminalization of the purchase of sex (Pylkkänen and Svensson in this volume) are all examples of how the structural understanding of *genus* relation can have an impact on the law drafting.

An additional legal concept in need of a critical analysis is equality. Equality is still often understood as a static concept creating a biased standard against which claims of inequality are measured, thus dichotomizing it into 'the norm' and 'the other'. Such an understanding of concepts as predefined implies a danger in universal meanings that continue the processes of marginalization. Another approach to the concept of equality is presented in the chapter by Kevät Nousiainen, *On the limits of the Concept of Equality; Arguments for a Dynamic Reading*. Nousiainen argues that while equality and rights have for some decades had a bad name in feminist research, they, nevertheless, can include significant dynamic potential. According to her, such a dynamic understanding might avoid both denial of difference and denial of sameness.

The strong tradition of social equality, including sex equality, has been based on the ideology of sameness, whereas issues relating to multiplicity and pluralism have only very recently come onto the agenda. In fact, our traditions of liberalism are quite diluted, or, they have been intertwined with a communitarian ethos. Furthermore, discussions on legal personality have merited less scholarly interest than the equality policies of the welfare state. However, the increasingly international discourse urges the use of rights to promote the individual in the Nordic countries as well. Rights debate has also been ambiguous because it is not always clear whose rights we are talking about and what they are. Yet, it is a challenge we must face.

We are concerned about the prospective capabilities of law and public policies to handle diversity in multicultural Europe, including the Nordic countries. While we are critical about the advantages and disadvantages of the 'world's best sex equality politics', purportedly existing in Sweden, as defined by the United Nations (Pylkkänen and Svensson in this volume), we still think that the political dimension of Nordic welfarism, to promote people in vulnerable positions, is an important starting point both in feminism and in other respects. Liberalism with a lack of sensitivity towards differences in power is destructive, but rights consciousness combined with sensitivity to an uneven distribution of resources and adequate supportive structures could be the Nordic model of real multiculturalism and equality.

We analyze both the current problems and the positive values connected with the 'North' which are still worth preserving, such as the collective traditions. Focus is on equality issues related to the contemporary process of convergence in Europe. We realize that much of our understandings have been derived from certain inherent nationalistic constructions and narratives, but, at the same time, we see the Nordic countries as 'the others' in a European context dominated by the big legal cultures of the European Union. It is our hope that a dialogue between 'the European' and the 'Nordic' could be dismantled – from both sides – of certain ethnocentric biases that undoubtedly have complicated dialogues so far. The current debates on European citizenship, reinforced employment strategy or anti-racist programmes concern us in the North as much as they do scholars anywhere else.

The question of diversity must be reconciled with traditional thinking about equality and equality politics. An increasingly sharp focus on differences, pluralism, and many-faceted cultural representations and identities requires further analysis, especially, vis-à-vis, discriminatory practices. The challenges we feminists are facing today are numerous: we must learn to cope not only with diversity, but also with new actors, new relations and new ways of imposing normative order. We have to communicate with other traditions of culture and knowledge.

Promoting sex equality is an international issue and currently much focused upon in the human rights discourse. In the international context as well as in the contexts of the Nordic countries, developments have moved towards a requirement of a more actively promoted strategy. The contemporary strategy, gender mainstreaming, is the one now used in the Nordic countries, in the EU as well as in human rights instruments. The strategy and its connections to international and Nordic feminist perspectives are focused upon in the chapter, *Equality through Human Rights – International and Nordic Feminist Perspectives on Rights,* by Sari Kouvo. She points out that the international discourse is primarily based on the civil and political rights of an individual as the norm for human rights. The Nordic approach has valuable elements, *i.e.*, the priority assigned to the community and the interdependence of civil and political rights with economic and social rights.

Finally, Hanne Petersen heads for the future and the global world in the chapter, *Bringing Difference into the Classroom,* detailing her reflections on teaching an Erasmus course at the University of Copenhagen. Dealing with differences in moral and legal education requires continuous and self-conscious reflections on the part of the teacher. Diversity and difference on an individual level, such as in a teaching situation, are hard to deal with, perhaps even harder than on a general level, but diversity and difference also open up to new ways of thinking and understanding the world.

Teaching foreign students Nordic law, the issue of community and communality always emerges. In the Nordic countries, the state obviously wields a greater role in constructions of community than elsewhere. However much we still think that the State has a responsibility to support families, local unities and interest groups, we have to focus on other driving forces as well. It has been claimed that in the Nordic countries, the State has been understood as almost the same as a society or a community with shared values. But, at the same time we are conscious of the social control deployed by the State and the disability of recognizing conflicts between minority rights and individual rights, especially on the axis of gender and ethnicity. The conflicts usually arise when the rights of an individual are in conflict with the values of cultural minority communities as was the case with Fadime Sahindal.

The state could not protect her rights. Fadime knew that she was threatened. She had taken all possible precautions and Swedish society had done all it could to protect her. Fadime, however, could not bear the isolation from the family and she met up with her fate when she went to meet her mother and sister in a secret place. In her eyes, as well as in the eyes of her father, Swedish society must have been a lonely place with a dearth of community among people.

The discussions that followed Fadime's death indicates that a many-sided discourse on multiculturalism is possible. Many voices of immigrant women were heard, representing different standpoints. While it was self evident that means of protection of threatened immigrant women had to be developed, a broader discussion about the integration process and cultural encounters was also activated by the tumultuous event of Fadime´s death.

Notes

1 Eva Lundgren, Jenny Westerlund and Åsa Eldén presented a very similar analysis of the discussion after Fadime's death (5th European Feminist Research Conference: Gender and Power in the new Europe, Lund 20–24.8.2003). They, however, concluded by emphasizing

the pervasive existence of violence against women in Swedish society.

2 1976 in Iceland, 1978 in Denmark, 1979 in Norway, 1980 in Sweden, 1987 in Finland.
3 *Varannan damernas* ('Ladies by turn') was the first governmental report explicitly based on a perspective addressing gendered power structures. Cf. Lindvert 2002.
4 Lag (1994:553) om vårdnadsbidrag.
5 It was repealed after six months, 1 January 1995.
6 The so-called 'Tham Professorships', (Law 1995:936) allocating certain positions of research fellows and professors to the underrepresented sex in order to enhance sex equality.
7 There has been a discussion after the decision of the ECJ on whether or not the Swedish legislation relating to affirmative action is in accordance with EC law. The Equality Ombudsman argues that it is not in conflict with EC law, *JämO* decision nr. 848/00.

References

Burman, Monica, Svensson, Eva-Maria and Ågren, Karin (2003), 'Kunskapsbildning inom juristutbildningen – exemplet könsrelaterad kunskap', *Retfærd*, Vol 26(2), pp. 20-38.

Dahl, Tove Stang (1987), *Women's Law. An Introduction to Feminist Jurisprudence*, Universitetsforlaget AS, Oslo.

Hirdman, Yvonne (2002), 'Hon sviker det som Fadime stod för', *Dagens Nyheter*, 30 January 2002.

Husu, Liisa (2001), *Sexism, Support and Survival in Academia: Academic Women and Hidden Discrimination in Finland*. University of Helsinki.

Kalliomaa-Puha, Laura (ed.), (2000), *Perspectives of Equality. Work, women and family in the Nordic countries and EU*, Nord 200:5, Nordic Council of Ministers, Copenhagen.

Kautto, Mikko, Heikkilä, Matti, Hvinden, Björn, Marklund, Staffan and Ploug, Niels (1999), *Nordic Social Policy: Changing Welfare States*, Routledge, London.

Kristeva, Julia (1988), *Étrangers à nous-mêmes*, Fayard, Paris.

Lindvert, Jessica (2002), *Feminism som politik*, Boréa Bokförlag, Umeå.

Lundström, Karin (2001), 'The ECJ's Conditional Release of Women', in K. Nousiainen, Å. Gunnarsson, K. Lundström, and J. Niemi-Kiesiläinen (eds), *Responsible Selves. Women in the Nordic legal culture*. Ashgate, Dartmouth, pp. 263-373.

Melby, Kari et al. (2000), *The Nordic Model of Marriage and the Welfare State*, Nord 2000:27, Nordic Council of Ministers, Copenhagen.

Nordborg, Gudrun and Niemi-Kiesiläinen, Johanna (2001), 'Women's Peace. A Criminal Law Reform in Sweden', in K. Nousiainen, Å. Gunnarsson, K. Lundström, and J. Niemi-Kiesiläinen (eds.), *Responsible Selves. Women in the Nordic legal culture*. Ashgate, Dartmouth, pp 353-373.

Nousiainen, Kevät (2004), 'Against discrimination or for equality?', in V. Puuronen et al. (eds), *New Challenges for Welfare Society*, Joensuu university press, forthcoming.

Nousiainen, Kevät and Niemi-Kiesiläinen, Johanna (2001), 'Introductory remarks on Nordic Law and Gender Identities', in K. Nousiainen, Å. Gunnarsson, K. Lundström, and J. Niemi-Kiesiläinen (eds.), *Responsible Selves. Women in the Nordic legal culture*. Ashgate, Dartmouth, pp. 1-22.

Nousiainen, Kevät, Gunnarsson, Åsa, Lundström, Karin and Niemi-Kiesiläinen, Johanna (eds.), (2001), *Responsible Selves. Women in the Nordic legal culture*. Ashgate Dartmouth.

Shaw, Jo (2001), 'Gender and the Court of Justice', in Gráinne de Búrca and J.H.H. Weiler (eds.), *The European Court of Justice*, Oxford University Press, Oxford.

Svensson, Eva-Maria (1997), *Genus och rätt. En problematisering av föreställningen om rätten*. Iustus Förlag, Uppsala.

Svensson, Eva-Maria (2001), 'Sex Equality: Changes in Politics, Jurisprudence and Feminist Legal Studies', in K. Nousiainen, Å. Gunnarsson, K. Lundström, and J. Niemi-Kiesiläinen (eds.), *Responsible Selves. Women in the Nordic legal culture*. Ashgate, Dartmouth, pp. 71-104.

Therborn, Göran (2000), 'Globalizations. Dimensions, Historical Waves, Regional Effects, Normative Governance', *International Sociology*, Vol 15(2), pp. 151-179.

SOU 1987:19 *Varannan damernas*

SOU 1990:44 Demokrati och makt i Sverige

SOU 1995:60 Kvinnofrid. Huvudbetänkande av Kvinnovåldskomissionen (Women's Piece)

Jämställdhetsombudsmannen, Annual Report 2001.

EC Court of Justice Case C-407/98

Chapter 2

Contemporary Challenges in Nordic Feminist Legal Studies

Eva-Maria Svensson and Anu Pylkkänen

Introduction

The objective of this chapter is to discuss the traditions, current developments and challenges of the 'Nordic model of equality'.[1] The Nordic model usually connotes distributive justice and a substantive notion of equality.[2] Individuals are seen as basically similar and independent of family status (Sainsbury 1994; Fraser 1995; Sörensen and Bergqvist 2002). Faith in the state's ability to promote sex equality and social equality at large through legislation has been virtually unwavering, especially in Sweden. The role of social engineering has been less significant in Finland. Irrespective of the same legal framework and obligation to promote equality, there are differences in politics and legislation within the 'Nordic model'.[3] It is important, therefore, to analyze these countries from a comparative perspective, and to ask what the relation among feminism, feminist legal studies and sex equality politics is today. Furthermore, we must also look at other arenas, actors and methods to promote the democratic goal of equality when the state loses its strength in favour of other forces.

The notion of equality, however, is not unambiguous. The strong tradition of social equality, including sex equality, has been based on the ideology of sameness, whereas the issues related to multiculturalism and pluralism have only very recently come onto the agenda. Furthermore, discussions on legal personality or anti-discrimination have merited less interest than the collective equality policies of the welfare state. A liberal discourse on individual rights has been fairly weak in the Nordic countries. The tensions between these two traditions, *viz.*, the Nordic 'communitarian' tradition and the liberal tradition, are at the crux of our analysis.

The Challenges of the Nordic Feminist Legal Studies

Trust in the ability of law and politics to improve the situation of women has occurred quite naturally in the Nordic context.[4] The State has long been understood as virtually identical with society, as something good and as a promoter of the interests of its citizens. Such a 'citizen-friendly state' is often called the Nordic Model. One important characteristic of this model is faith in the State's ability *to put life in order.*[5] This ability applies to equality issues and to general social welfare. In Sweden, an all-encompassing social model was supposed to satisfy the needs of all people, irrespective of their individual situations or preferences. In a culturally homogenous society and a regime led by a social democratic majority, this notion was met with little criticism.

More recently, and concomitantly with increasing cultural multiplicity and burgeoning market-oriented individualism, this legitimacy has come into question. Still however, the government pursues active social policy through legislation and takes the initiative vis-à-vis issues of equality and anti-discrimination. In contemporary Sweden, feminism is politically correct at the governmental level, whereas the academic legal community has reacted quite recalcitrantly.

During the 1990s, Nordic Feminist Legal Studies (NFLS), especially in Sweden and Finland, has distanced itself both from the women's movement and sex equality politics. The feminist legal tradition has become more academic, more theoretical and more concerned with the internal relation between feminism and jurisprudence. Unfortunately, there is a dearth of male participants in this dialogue.[6]

Unlike in Sweden, Finnish equality politics has not become imbued with the active promotion of equality. The two most characteristic features of Finnish equality politics have been gender neutrality and a formal understanding of equality. A recognition of women's disadvantaged status, category politics or the promotion of groups claiming discrimination have not been among the priorities of Finnish policymakers. This lack of interest can be explained by referring to history: long integrative roots (Holli 2003; Pylkkänen 2001). Today, the European Union and human rights instruments challenge us to invigorate anti-discrimination policies, which we have to take even more seriously than before.

An analysis of the important challenges facing the NFLS is urgently needed:

- Is it or is it not possible to achieve equality by means of legal measures?
- What directions of sex equality politics in the future are possible and what impact do they have on law? Who are the actors and objects of equality measures?
- How is it possible to make inclusions of multiple subjects without being exclusive?
- How is it possible to acknowledge in law the unequal power relation between men and women without being trapped by such an acknowledgement? How can the law be more dynamic in issues related to equality?
- What are the roles of legal professionals and academics?

It is not irrelevant how the problems are defined, what methods are to be deployed and by whom. Should equality politics aim at improving the position of women as a group or should it invigorate anti-discrimination law and positive action on an individual basis? What are the possibilities of dealing with the pluralism of different subjectivities? Even if we do not have all the answers, we must at least pose the questions.

New Methods to 'Put Life in Order'

The Nordic countries and especially Sweden are well known throughout the world for their actively promoted sex equality politics. However, several investigations have shown that political commitment to achieving equality between men and women has not led to corresponding changes in social practice. Some disillusionment is discernible concerning the earlier trust that the people had in the State's ability to 'put life in order' and in politics as an efficient way to handle problems of inequality. The public's reliance on the State's ability to handle different social problems seems to be waning,[7] which has been characterized as the *State's impotence* (Therborn 2000). The nation State is no longer the primary source of law, but also the norms, codes and practices of the global market and different bodies across local, trans- and international levels are increasingly shaping our understandings of binding norms and the limits and boundaries of law. The methods of 'putting life in order' have changed. People's needs are no longer supposed to be interpreted by the well-meaning authorities of the welfare State. One has to take more individual responsibility in gaining and protecting rights. In other words, the importance of regulation based on individual action is increasing at the cost of welfare state regulation and the re-distributive policies typical of the earlier social-democratic welfare State.

Politics in the late or post-modern era is not the same as it used to be during modernity. The distinctions between different spheres have become subtle. Political agency no longer fulfils the predominant purpose it used to. Power cannot be bestowed upon traditional power structures, bodies and processes only, but much of the traditional power linked with politics is now indirect and exercised through media and other methods of representation. The political representation of politically organized groups is diminishing. People are represented in many other ways – as well as choosing to be represented in a spectrum of different ways. As little as there is a coherent notion of politics, there is a single coherent notion of political subjecthood. All this confusion makes it much more difficult than before to analyze, let alone formulate, political goals and methods. The closer women get to core political processes, the more power becomes elusive to them. We should also now address the market and other social and economic processes with power in shaping the lives of men and women.[8] It is important to move the focus from fixed and coherent entities and stable sources of law and morals (States, communities, persons) to processes in the market and social life in which the understandings of norm and difference are being produced and reproduced.

In Scandinavia, as well as in many other countries, there has been a shift from collective to individual remedies. Today, the good life for an individual is supposed to be achieved less through politics and general tax-funded welfare measures than through freedom of choice and individual preferences. Contrariwise to the earlier emphasis on substantive equality, it is believed that people are able to operate in the market in a rational and future-related way, irrespective of their social standing – and irrespective of the strong support of public provisions and services. The status of social rights, if they ever existed as legally protected rights,[9] is decreasing or at least changing. Moreover, many forms of support and services are being privatized and opened up to competition.

Since the early 1990s, governmental sex equality politics has basically leaned on a structural and substantive understanding of equality, while sex equality legislation is still mainly based on the liberal anti-discrimination principle, even more so in Finland than in Sweden. In that context, people are compared with each other in similar situations in a rather formal and conservative manner. The individual is responsible for taking action or demanding compensation for any breach of the equality principle. At the same time, the very same legislation also attempts to enhance actively promoted politics by leaning on collective bodies, such as trade unions. Proactive measures have earlier been based on voluntary activity, but are now compulsory. Employers are required to promote equality in the workplace, but in practice, it is almost beyond legal scrutiny whether or not this obligation is *de facto* fulfilled.[10]

Besides proactive legislation and legal policy, there have been some attempts to find new ways to obtain sex equality, especially in Sweden. One of the more recent innovative measures is a voluntary gender-equality labelling of products and services.[11] It is an attempt to encourage market actors to promote sex equality through economic and good will incentives. If a company has a competent sex equality policy, it may apply for a gender-equality label. The labelling system is supposed to influence consumers in their decisions to buy products or services. The method is, thus, comparable to environmental labelling systems. No doubt, it will be a challenge to analyze this attempt to encourage the market to improve sex equality. What difference does it make whether the market has other incentives than legal obligations or prohibitions?

Recently, an increased emphasis has been put onto the human rights discourse as a way to argue for stronger measures to promote equality. In the Nordic context, this discussion may be a double-edged sword. It is noteworthy that the human rights discourse is growing in the Nordic countries in line with reduced universal and collective welfare measures. When and if the State is seen as the actor protecting society as a whole and defending the interests of its weaker members, the defence of these interests might not require human rights arguments. It may be paradoxical that, when the welfare state is in decline, human rights are brought to light more than ever. Even if the perspective of individual rights in its traditional sense may have been less articulated in the North, the individual, nevertheless, has been strengthened through general welfare. The two models, the individualistic human rights discourse and the Nordic welfare discourse, have their pros and cons.

The human rights discourse is a tradition based on the protected privacy of the individual against State intervention. Family life is included in that privacy. The rights of the individual are strengthened at the same time as the protection and consolidation of the family as a private social institution increase. This situation is problematic, because the protected private sphere and the market can end up neglecting women's rights and obstructing equality between men and women. While women have undeniably gained a stronger position in politics, the changes in the labour market or in family life have not been unequivocally favourable. All evidence of gendered pay gaps and violence in intimate relations points to very similar situations in almost any western country.

In the Nordic countries, as everywhere else, women are often the ones with less money, less power and more responsibility for domestic duties like child care. Some of the legal measures taken in the 1990s have even further consolidated men's power in relation to children and their mothers. The universal model of joint custody and the second 'father's month' aim at the increased sharing of parental responsibilities. While promoting sex equality, these reforms may also imply a tendency to enhance the rights or power of fathers at the cost of mothers and children. These reforms have been interpreted as steps towards undermining women's hard-won social rights (Kurki-Suonio 1995; Nordborg 1998; Singer 2000).

Sex-Neutrality or Sex-Specificity?

The Nordic model of equality is, or has been, characterized by extensive and general welfare policies aiming at the reduction of differences and social inequalities in society at large. General welfare policies based on distributive justice and the ideology of sameness have been understood as the most efficient methods by which to obtain equality (Lindvert 2002; Sörensen and Bergqvist 2002). But, it is not always possible to confirm that the position of women has improved in such a context of social equality.

First, welfare and equality can exist at a relatively high level in society without altering the power structure and unequal distribution of resources between men and women. What is more, reciprocity between rights and responsibilities is seldom questioned. Even in Sweden and in Finland, where official committees are supposed to analyze the consequences of any reform in regard to equality between men and women,[12] gender impact analyses are not always actually made. However, important steps have been taken in this direction. In an appendix to the budget of 2003, the Swedish government has analyzed the economic consequences of inequality between men and women.[13] Although no measures were suggested, knowledge about economic differences is supposed to strengthen the politics of equality.

Secondly, the formal concept of equality that prevailed until the 1990s, has contributed to the belief that sex equality already exists – the myth of equality – and has made it more difficult to recognize and conceptualize discrimination (Nousiainen et al. 2001, 2). To recognize discrimination can be even more difficult in the Nordic countries where equality often has been understood in terms of sexless groups and corporations, such as trade unions. According to Pylkkänen (2001) and Lundström (2001), the distinction between masculine and feminine identity is less marked here than in many other cultures. Issues related to sex have been kept secondary to other divisive dichotomies.

Paradoxically, the distinction between masculinity and femininity does not seem to have diminished during the 1990s in fields other than in the legal arena. For example, masculine and feminine identities are being explored for more focused marketing. The media serves us traditional sex stereotypes and fundamental differences between the sexes.[14] At the same time, the media is also dealing with issues relating to sex inequality on an almost daily basis. This situation is also found in Swedish politics. Despite the great interest in the issue, there is more talk than actual deeds or profound changes in practice. Lack of sex equality is mainly an issue 'talked about instead of tackled', a method described by Yvonne Hirdman as *the speaking solution* (Hirdman 1990, 107).

The Finnish Equality Act (1986) says in its first paragraph that the aim of the law is to further equality especially by enhancing the position of women. So does the Swedish Equality Act (1980). However, this focus on women as a subordinated or 'discriminated against' social category does not seem to enjoy any legitimacy. Symptomatically, the word, equality, itself was used much more seldom than 'sexual roles' and the social problems linked to them when the debate on equality between men and women started in 1965 (Eskola 1968). The expression, 'discrimination', is used most seldom of all, because there is a strong belief that discrimination does not exist (Julkunen 1999).

The demands of the European Union to enforce anti-discrimination further by tackling sexual harassment or by fighting structural and indirect discrimination, have been met with much scepticism or criticism in Finland. Instead of specifying discriminatory practices, the Finnish solution is often to refer to collective or cultural features such as an 'inflammatory working environment' as the cause of problems. When dealing with the reform of Equality Act to meet the demands of the equality directive (2002/73/EC), the law drafting committee (KM 2002:9) was not unanimous about the necessary measures relating to pay discrimination, sexual harassment, equality planning or the level of compensation. The committee report included several dissenting opinions, among them, one of the representatives of the employer organizations in which they opposed almost any sanctioned obligations to combat discrimination or to promote equality in the workplace. In such a cultural context and in want of a conceptual framework, it is very difficult for anyone to establish that they have been discriminated against.

The definition of equality has changed from a formal equality of opportunities to a substantive equality, equality of results. Today, the latter term represents the meaning of equality in international, EU and national documents, both political and legal.[15] The objective of sex equality politics is that men and women are to be equal in the public sphere, in civil society and in the private or intimate sphere.

The scope of sex equality has become ever wider during the 20th century. Until the beginning of the 1990s, the labour market was the main focus of explicit sex equality politics. Family politics have not been seen as mainly a sex equality issue, but rather as politics related to child caring and, as such, sex neutral. Both men and women are regarded as parents on an equal basis. The parental leave provisions formally include both sexes. In the 1990s, sex equality politics came to cover matters of sexuality and sex-related violence. In many of the Swedish governmental committee reports of the 1990s, the sexual relation has been defined as unequal. This definition is especially applicable in connection with issues of who controls the areas of power in society and who can define what sex-related violence is. A famous example is the unique Swedish legislation on the unlawful purchase of sex.[16] Today, we can talk about sex equality politics as a combination of sex-neutral and sex-specific measures. In Finland, the approach is more formal and more sex-neutral than in Sweden. Inequalities are much more seldom conceptualized as structural problems.

The Historical Background – Conceptual and Political Changes

Sweden

Early sex equality politics was called family politics and based on a model of segregation and the protection of the housewife. When the welfare state was developed in the 1930s–40s, the focus was on both the productive and the reproductive spheres.[17] Yet, most of the research on the early welfare state has focused on the productive sphere and on general welfare measures such as pensions, free medical treatment, health care and health insurance. It has been shown by feminist research that one of the principal background factors behind these reforms was the declining birth rate, at that time understood to be a population crisis. Between 1934 and 1945, the government produced several official reports about pregnancy, family taxation, the legal status of working women after marriage and childbirth, child care, housing policies and other matters regarded as pertinent to the reproductive sphere (Bergqvist 1994, 156; Gunnarsson and Stattin 2001). The main purpose was probably not designed to improve the situation of women as such, but to facilitate pregnancy and child care. Pro-natalism was the dominant political discourse at that time. The population rate had to be increased and the people made healthier. Women as mothers and housewives were protected, not women as individuals or a group irrespective of their social or family status. The tasks of men and women in society were different. This difference in responsibilities was also the natural standpoint of trade union policies.

Men were seen as breadwinners and primary family supporters and, accordingly, should earn ample enough salary to provide for the whole family.

During the 1950s and 60s, the Swedish welfare scheme was complemented with income-related benefits. The income-related model was labour market-oriented with collective negotiation systems but, nevertheless, the benefits were connected to the individual more than ever before. Since the 1960s, the emphasis on self-supporting individuals has grown in importance, as also Gunnarsson, Burman and Wennberg show in this volume. In reality, however, many women are still, at least partly, dependent on men or on the state. Services have been adjusted to women's proposed needs to combine work and family. Up until very recently, there has been little fundamental criticism of the alleged primary caring responsibilities of women. All provisions have been designed according to women's 'natural' role in caring. Part-time work has been and still is typical for women in the Nordic countries, except for Finland, where the problem of child rearing is resolved mainly by extending the length of women's absence from working life up to three years (Haataja and Nurmi 2000, 14-15, 34-38).

Economist Anita Nyberg shows that women's dependence on men in general has decreased due to their increased labour force participation, whereas, on the contrary, the dependence of single parents, mostly women, has increased. The issue of dependence, however, is discussed in relation to the welfare state and not in relation to the individual man benefiting from this uneven division of resources and responsibilities (Nyberg 2001).

Sex equality was separated from general equality in the beginning of the 1970s. *Jämställdhetshetsdelegationen*, the Sex Equality Delegation, was founded by the social-democratic regime, but the liberal party had already started the debate a few years earlier. The ideological base was liberal and individualistic. Inequalities between men and women would be avoided if women changed their roles and adjusted themselves to the role of men. The formal concept of sex equality was based on an understanding of a rational and independent person who is free to choose the priorities of his or her own life and to make agreements with other persons, both in public and private life. This thesis was made explicit and turned into a democratic goal in the Constitution of 1976.[18]

The political decisions of this 'second period of equality policies' concentrated on the public sphere. Through changes in public life, relations in private life were supposed to change automatically. Even though the 1976 Constitution was generally applicable to the equal rights of men and women, the more specific legislation on sex equality, the Sex Equality Act of 1980, was limited to labour market. This separateness of applicability is typical for Sweden. In the other Nordic countries, the Equality Act was and is applicable in other fields of society too, such as education and commercial life.

The liberal non-discrimination principle was the main point in the Equality Act. Later on, certain collective policies, typically for the Social Democratic reliance on the trade unions, became increasingly important. The expectations that the trade unions would promote equality, however, turned out to be mere wishful thinking. Consequently, in the 1990s, the role of the Ombudsman for sex equality (*Jämställdhetsombudsmannen)* grew to have more clout at the cost of the trade unions. Even though the Equality Act consists of two main parts, an individual discrimination prohibition and a collective duty for positive action, the predominantly liberal framework, to a large extent, has remained unaltered.

The liberal concept of equality assumes white middle class men in a financially independent situation as the norm. The assumption defines not only the standard, but at the same time, the 'deviance'. The standard has excluded not only women as deviant, but also other groups of 'problematic' persons. Today, EC law and human rights law point out several groups in need of protection against discrimination, on the ground of sex, ethnicity, nationality, age, sexual disposition, and disability. The process tends to be the following: first, a recognition and acknowledgement of the group (cf. Taylor 1992), then protection against discrimination and, finally, gradual promotion through different programmes. At the moment, six acts prohibit discrimination in Sweden concerning sex, ethnicity, sexual disposition and disability. Sex and ethnicity are also grounds for promoting equality through positive action. The former distributive model seems to have been exchanged for the recognition model, as defined by Nancy Fraser (Fraser 1995).

From the beginning of the 1990s, the base for sex equality politics, has changed from the liberal model to an understanding of sex equality in *structural* terms. In fact, a liberal minister was in charge of the radical proposal presented to Parliament at the beginning of the 1990s: *Delad makt delat ansvar*, or, 'Shared power shared responsibility' (Prop. 1993/94:147). In the 1990s, inequality was understood as a result of an unequal power structure. Individuals are seen as parts of a system which produces and reproduces inequality between the sexes. Sex discrimination is more often a matter of discriminatory structures, such as wage policy (Fransson 2000).[19]

The measures taken by the government in the late 1990s were based on the model of the *genus* system presented by the historian Yvonne Hirdman. She was the influential figure behind the governmental report, Democracy and Power in Sweden (SOU 1990:44 *Demokrati och makt i Sverige*). The model focuses on gendered power relations in society and its institutions, the '*genus*' relations as they are called in Swedish. Women or men are not considered social categories, but rather parties in a power relation. '*Genus*' is not the same as gender. It is not only the socially constructed aspect of being a woman or a man. It is not the opposite of sex, but something more than sex and gender together. It is seen as a construction of the social and corporeal aspects of men and women embedded in both the social and legal structures and in discourses which shape the relations of men and women in society.

Sex equality perspective should be integrated, or mainstreamed, in all political and administrative decision-making, but it is not always done.[20] The method of gender mainstreaming is now universally promoted in both national and international documents,[21] but not many people seem to know what it really means and if it obligates the government to take specific action. The gap between politics and the legal sphere is also problematic. Political commitment has not been transferred to the legal profession. The legal definition of sex equality is more limited than the political definition (cf. Lerwall 2001).

Recent innovative legislation, such as the already mentioned illegal purchase of sex, is an example of active measures that are based on an understanding of the relation between men and women as unequal.[22] This legislation seems to be hard to deal with in the legal system. The law has been repeatedly criticized in several respects: it is inefficient, it fails to solve the problems of prostitutes and it helps disguise prostitution by moving it indoors. In January 2002, the media reported how the police protected men prosecuted for the illicit purchase of sex by not sending official letters about the prosecution to their home addresses. The reason was that the police wanted to protect the men from shame which might result should their wives ever find out about the grounds for prosecution. This practice is quite odd considering the explicit purpose of the law and the standard way of dealing with the accused in other criminal cases.

Sex equality *politics* in Sweden is today proactive and not merely rhetoric (Sörensen and Bergqvist 2002; Svensson forthcoming). There is considerable focus on the unequal division of power and an ambition to change the power structure to enhance the position of women. But it is not quite certain whether the chosen methods are the best ones or whether the social structures or the popular attitudes are on the road to change. The chosen methods are out of harmony with the general political development which has headed in the opposite direction. The 1980s and 1990s were the individualistic decades. Even trade unions seemed to be positively inclined towards individual wages. Individual wages do not seem to benefit women. On the contrary, the wage gap has increased since 1992. Neither of the two methods used to further sex equality, plans of positive action and individual anti-discrimination, has been particularly successful in practice. For example, the rate of women professors was 13 per cent in 2000, compared to five per cent in 1986/87 and eight per cent in 1995/96.[23] Very few cases of discrimination have been brought to the Labour Court (Annual Report of the Equality Ombudsman, *JämO Årsredovisning*, 2002).

Finland

Equality politics in Finland in the 1960s and onwards were guided by the fact that Finland had one of the highest rates of women in gainful employment in Europe. It was not necessary to engage women in the labour market because they already were there. As a natural consequence of a long tradition of shared productive labour in agriculture and in war-time industries, women were employed in the low-paying jobs of modern industries that were growing rapidly in the 1950s and 1960s. The social services and public sectors did not employ women to the same extent as they do today because the level of services was still quite low. Day care was not available to women who worked. They had to cope with the help of grandparents, temporary nannies or guarded children parks.

Quite contrary to reality, the role of the housewife was declared to be a woman's real calling and paid labour was just an economic necessity. Maybe this rhetoric was an attempt to tone down the issue of equal pay that by no means was among the prioritized goals of the trade unions (Lähteenmäki 1999). On the other hand, the women's associations of political parties held a dominant position in issues related to women and families. They were not based on a notion of equality between men and women, but rather on women's needs as mothers (Kuusipalo 1999).

In the mid-1960s, the Swedish debate spread to Finland and, especially through the influence of sociology, and a theory of social roles became a powerful way of understanding the problem. In 1965, a radical society, *Yhdistys 9* (Association 9), was founded to further sex equality. This association also included a number of men. The programme favoured policies that took both sexes into account and disfavoured the predominance of women-specific measures. Their aim was that the role of men had to change as well, although little success was achieved.

After the elections of 1966, when the parties of the Left came into the government, one committee was appointed to investigate the situation of women (KM 1970:A 8) and another to explore ways of meeting the needs of day care (KM 1967:B 46). A Parliamentary Advisory Board on the Equality Issues (TANE) was founded in 1970. In the early 1970s, legislative reforms were passed to adapt legislation to an equality model in which women were full-time waged labourers: the separate taxation of the spouses in 1974 and the law on municipal day care in 1973. However, at that time day care was means-tested and available only to the families earning the least. In Finland, the home care of children was also supported with gradually extended maternity and parental leaves and subsidized care at home. Instead of part-time work, women could stay away from the labour market for longer periods of time. This pattern exists even today. The ILO Convention 111 on Discrimination in the workplace was ratified after a long drawn-out process in 1970 at the same time as the new Contracts of Employment Act was passed with an explicit prohibition against discrimination. The outcome of this reform was modest. The Equality Act was not passed until 1986, after the signing of the Convention on the Elimination of All Forms of Discrimination against Women (CEDAW), and the sex equality clause was written into the Constitution in 1995.

At the same time, the needs of the family and the society were prioritized over the needs of women as individuals. Even though the marriage law reform, which was initiated around 1970 and came into force in 1987, was aimed at increased liberalization and the individualization of spouses, in much of the social law the nuclear family was still the starting point. For instance, the family pension was paid out only to the widow. Women's income was understood to be supplemental to the income of the primary breadwinner. Nearly all parties saw social institutions and not individuals as the primary targets of social and equality policies. Parties took as a given that women have a double role and that it was the responsibility of the State to support maternity. Only the radical Left had an explicit equality programme in which it maintained that men and women must have equal rights and opportunities in all fields of society (Turunen 1968).

In the 1980s, the Equality Act, the Surname Act and the Amendment of the Marriage Act were passed after considerable political struggle to give women more independent choices and stronger protection against discrimination. These measures have proved to be quite inefficient. The sad consequence is that the little there has been of some kind of equality politics, it almost entirely faded away in the 1990s. The role of the Finnish Equality Ombudsman is marginal. Sex-related violence has been addressed in a few projects since the late 1990s, but it is just a moderate step compared to the *Kvinnofrid* (Women's Peace) reform in Sweden. In sum, it has been difficult in Finnish culture to accept that discrimination exists and to call it by its name. Any demands of better anti-discrimination protection are usually rejected by referring to some other more prioritized needs – or to the already existing equality.

Feminism and Sex Equality Politics

The first wave of feminism in the late 19th and early 20th centuries gradually resulted in a formal equality between women and men. The 'second wave feminism' can be understood as a disappointment of the outcome of formal equality. The movement started quite actively, radically and challenging the way in which society was organized in the spirit of social engineering. The previous politics was based on a clear division of labour between men and women. Only a few radical proposals were presented. One was to create collective forms of living, such as common cooking and the common upbringing of children as advocated the legendary Alva Myrdal (Myrdal 1935 and 1957). Traditional ways of living were questioned by feminists in the 1970s and new forms of organizing life were tested. By living in collectives and engaging in free sexual relations, young people protested against paternalistic definitions of how one should live.

Today, such proposals are conspicuous by their absence. Even feminists accept nuclear family life. The nuclear family has actually become stronger in politics, in culture,[24] in media and in law, for example, in the increased use of joint custody. The regulation of heterosexual and homosexual cohabitation in Sweden in 1987 and of the registered partnership for homosexual couples, in 1994 in Sweden and in 2002 in Finland, have further strengthened the predominance of the nuclear family norm. The same emphasis on the nuclear family is visible in the Western human rights discourse. Differences among the cultures of the world become obvious when immigrants apply for permission for their relatives to immigrate. The 'family' is not the same group of people in all cultures. The difference between the norm and reality is obvious in the contemporary situation in the Nordic countries, which does not correspond to the ideal either. Single parents are quite a large group and many children live together with persons other than their parents.[25]

'Second wave feminism' was an important political force in the 1970s. The integration of feminism into general politics and into the state apparatus, however, was rather ambiguous. The strategy of emphasizing liberal, individualistic values seemed to be successful. Through individual anti-discrimination legislation, through education and through changing roles, *women*, not men, would gain equality. A symptomatic official report was *Roller i omvandling* ('Changing roles', SOU 1976:71) where women's roles were put in focus. Sex equality was to be achieved by making women self-supporting and independent, preferably in typical male jobs.

Since then, feminism has distanced itself from the liberal framework as this independent person has turned out to be an illusion, especially when it comes to intimate relations and caring. Women do the main part of the caring work either with low compensation or with none at all. What is more, care is not seen as productive work, no matter if it is done in private or with the aid of public management (Nyberg in SOU 1998:6 and Nyberg in SOU 1997:138).

In the 1990s, legal and political reforms no longer speak in neutral terms, but rather are influenced by active feminist academics. Gendered power relations are directly and openly addressed. The period from 1970 to the beginning of the 21st century has provided examples of both integration projects and segregation projects. As an efficient action at the beginning of the 1990s, a group of women challenged the political parties and founded a women's party and later registered it formally. Since then, almost every party in the Swedish Parliament, at least on a rhetorical level, has integrated feminist politics into their programmes. Most of leading politicians even call themselves feminists, which is politically correct in contemporary Sweden.

However, it is not quite clear what 'state feminism' means today. In the politics of the 1990s, we can discern two types of understandings: feminism as another word for equality and, as such, a naturally occurring phenomenon in a democratic society and, secondly, feminism as a specific understanding of women's subordination to men and the unequal power structure between the sexes. The dominant discourse is the first one, even if the second one has been the basis for sex equality politics since 1993/1994. When the unequal power structure is addressed concretely with an aim to change the relation between men and women, feminism becomes controversial. Men seem to feel that they are losing their power and prerogatives.

The Finnish 'state feminism' is characterized by the early integration of women into the citizenry. According to Anne Maria Holli, Finnish 'equality' has been understood as membership in a national community (Holli 2003, 11-12, 19). Women were active participants in the nationalistic folk movements that founded the basis of a nation state, via the temperance, cooperative and enfranchisement movements. The strong distinction of entitled men and subordinated women never really gained a foothold in Finland. Women were understood to be members of civil society, however segregated in their roles and activities of caregiving and as societal mothers.

There are many interpretations of the history of the feminist movement in Finland. In 1983, Riitta Jallinoja maintained that the movement has existed, but that it has had more active and more passive periods (Jallinoja 1983). Marja Kokko (1998 and 2000) argues that women identified most of all with political parties and did not cooperate across party lines. The social gap between elites and working women was quite significant in Finland, but on the other hand, the National Women Associations did have common statements on the legislative issues. Nowhere in Europe was the Parliament so equal in its representation of its people as in Finland in 1907, when 19 women out of 200, among them working class women, were elected to the Parliament.[26] They united in efforts to dismantle the last remains of male authority in family and society. After independence in 1917, women politicians and women's organizations of the political parties concentrated their efforts on a non-political housewife movement (Lähteenmäki 1999). Housewife ideology was more an ideal than a deeply rooted cultural pattern, but much of the early welfare legislation in the 1930s was designed to support maternity. The level of these measures was not nearly as high as in Sweden.

The Finnish second wave feminism, equality feminism, was organized at the same time as in Sweden and it can also be called state feminism. What started as voluntary organizations, for example, Association 9, was soon integrated into the State apparatus.[27] However, the faith in the State's ability to put everything right has never been as strong as in Sweden. The Finnish welfare State developed comparably late. Official equality politics have not been as proactive as in Sweden, but it can be characterized rather as a series of half-hearted responses to international obligations.

On the other hand, feminist politics has not united all women and women's organizations in the same way as it has done in Sweden. Up to the 1960s, concern for women as mothers united many women politicians. Since the 1960s, politicians have tried to gain credibility by maintaining a neutral standing and by addressing general political issues (Kuusipalo 1999). It has been characteristic of Finnish politics to aim at a broad consensus. Women have been expected to be loyal to common goals – to the neglect of bringing to light women's specific problems. As Anne Maria Holli has argued, the notion of women as a resource for society has hindered women from expressing demands that are regarded as destructive to the very idea of the community. There has been significant aversion to feminism, which has been constructed as the enemy of the Finnish nation and society (Holli 2003, 16, 19). Feminism(s) do exist, but mainly in the academic discourse. Even some academics and students are hostile towards feminist studies. Gender perspective has neither been integrated into the curricula nor into the programmes of political parties. Official bodies such as the Delegation of Equality Affairs (TANE) have pursued 'gender politics' to a limited extent whenever there has been a favourable political environment, especially a left-wing government (Holli 2003, 161-164).

Feminist Perspectives on Law

Nordic Feminist Legal Studies in the Academia

Kirsten Ketscher has launched an idea of Western and Eastern Scandinavian models, according to which, theorizing about legal systems and concepts is more typical for Sweden and Finland, whereas the Danish and Norwegian feminist law is more or less based on legal 'dogmatics' (Ketscher 2000). This idea is quite interesting because legal theory has been much appreciated in the Finnish legal tradition whereas of lesser value in Sweden. It has been easier in Finland to pursue theoretical studies on law and gender, as such analysis does, in principle, belong to 'state of the art' legal scholarship. Systemic, conceptual and principle-related issues of law are considered to be of greater significance than in Sweden. Quite another thing is that issues related to gender are often rejected as such or viewed as controversial. In Sweden, theory was rejected for a long time by the Scandinavian Realist tradition as being unnecessary 'metaphysics'.

As seen from the Finnish perspective, the Swedish academic feminism in the 1990s and its new conceptual and theoretical innovations have been tremendously successful. The governmental sex equality politics has integrated and based legal reforms on that knowledge. In Finland, the academic and political spheres are quite separate from each other. Secondly, the belief in public politics did not exist in Finland to the same extent than in Sweden. One could say that out of necessity, concerns other than social engineering have predominantly occupied politics. The notion of visionary equality politics '*à la suédeois*', thus, cannot be applied to Finland, even if some of the influences from Sweden have spread to the other side of the Gulf. Correspondingly, Finnish feminist legal studies have developed its critical analysis within the legal sphere. Only recently have feminist legal scholars more actively participated in law drafting, especially as concerns the revision of anti-discrimination law and the monitoring of the human rights of women.

Feminist jurisprudence is one of the critical approaches of law. It does not distance itself from the objects it is exploring, but rather recognizes its role as one of the actors producing this discourse. Feminist legal scholarship denies the status of law as a closed system. Feminist legal scholarship sees the statutory law as one of the social discourses and practices that are in constant interaction and that produce our understandings of the lives of human beings. The specific features of law as a discourse and a practice, of course, must be recognized. Legal texts are powerful as such when defining what is legally relevant and protected and what is not and, thus, political in a broad sense. This power also opens up the possibility of discussing legal texts as texts including a meta-text or a suppressed text, meanings that are implied but not given form or voice. In this respect, NFLS unavoidably contains a political dimension. We have an emancipatory and transformative mission and see the role of legal science as one of the factors that can shape and change social relations.

On the other hand, NFLS is not political in a traditional sense. It is not the NFLS that is the motor in politics. To the contrary, it is politics that can actively use the academic knowledge. In Finland, experiences of pursuing equality issues in the political system based on academic knowledge have been less encouraging than in Sweden. In Scandinavia, critical approaches to law and legal science have been developed outside traditional academic communities. The journal *Retfærd* and the Nordic research training schools and networks funded by all-Nordic funds such as the Nordic Academy of Advanced Study (NorFA) have provided arenas in which discussions on alternative approaches to law have been conducted. So far, these discussions have had but minor impact on mainstream legal science but they have certainly buttressed the path of young scholars into the academic world. By networking and pooling resources with the help of such cross-national financing, it has been possible to strengthen the qualities and positions of young women academics that otherwise might have experienced lack of support in their home institutions.

The recent intensified equality politics beg the question, should not the same goal permeate the legal system in its entirety? Even the explicit incorporation of the goal of equality into the law does not necessarily lead to an active application of the goal. The legal system seems to be quite resistant to change. The obstacles are of different kinds as is shown in several research projects (Lundström 1999; Schömer 1999; Fransson 2000; Svensson 1997).

Traditionally in the Nordic countries and, especially, in Sweden, the attitude towards written law and legislative preparatory works is very obedient. Law is a political decision, based on political values transformed into rules and laws. However, the prevailing attitude of obedience towards the written law and politically defined aims is not really as keen when it comes to sex equality. Sex equality politics has resulted in several fundamental rules with the purpose of obtaining sex equality. But even so, sex equality measures have been met with varying responses within the legal system. It is relevant to pose the question why the legal system, which is normally so obedient to the intentions devised by politicians, is disobedient when it comes to sex equality? Is the legal system based on principles other than those principles used in sex equality politics and legislation?

There are several explanations for this occurrence. First, written law is not as focused on positive action as is politics. The Sex Equality Act does not emphasize affirmative action. The Act is interpreted as requiring action against discrimination, as Karoliina Ahtela shows in her chapter on Finland in this volume. The legislation focuses on the individual, which often makes it difficult to discern intersecting legal constructions as symptoms of a structurally unequal relationship between men and women – however much it is highlighted in the explicit goals of equality politics (see Burman, Gunnarsson and Wennberg in this volume). The notion of indirect discrimination makes it easier, but is insufficient (Lundström 1999). Law tends to treat conflicts and situations as connected to abstract individuals defined as neutral unencumbered persons.

Gendered Constructions of Legal Subjects

Feminists have criticized the free and independent individual as the archetype of the legal subject. The conceptualization of the abstract and autonomous subject is often used as an explanation for inequalities, but yet it may not suffice as an explanation. The legal subject is often intertwined in different relationships and the legal system certainly handles a lot of unequal relations where the position of the weaker party is enhanced in different ways. Often the measure is constructed to promote some group and, thus, the individual is indirectly strengthened. Perhaps, a focus on groups rather than on individuals has been characteristic of the Nordic countries. Entities considered to be 'weaker parties' may, for example, include employees, tenants and consumers. This 'weak identity', however, is different from the weak identity of a woman. Even if women are defined as having 'a less favourable situation' than men, it is problematic to define women as a weak group in need of protection and positive action.

The judicial system is often able to see not only the very special human being, but also the complex situation of that person. In many situations, one part is seen as quite concrete and in special relation to another part. Law deals with inequalities, both in legislation with regard to the constructions of an equal relation and, in practice, through extenuating circumstances. Yet, problems do arise when the relation is based on sex – why? Becoming a legal professional presupposes a socialization into a certain way of thinking irrespective of the sex of the individual lawyers themselves. This thinking is based on a harmonious and on non-adversarial legal system and on neutrality rather than based on an open attitude towards conflicting interests and value adjustments.

Our proposed solution might be that the weakness does not have to follow the individual identity, but rather the situation. This type of argumentation is used in 'social civil law' (Wilhelmsson 1987). Conditions that are actually problematic in a contractual relation may be used in the amendments of a contract. Accordingly, conditions such as unequal power in a relation between men and women may be used as adjustments without defining women as weak as such.

Law and Other Normative Structures

Another question is the inability of the legal system to handle the focus on the 'equality of results'. Law maintains formal equality without seeing its practical implications. Law does not acknowledge the interplay of legal and other discourses that together contribute to persistent discriminatory practices. In Swedish jurisprudence, women have not been recognized as a group, and neither sex nor gender have been viewed as factors that can lead to discrimination. Despite this reluctance among legal scholars, the law has been changed, vis-à-vis, several issues in a number of areas.

In our opinion, the next step NFLS has to take is to define the situation and the aims and methods by which to obtain equality with an explanation that is suitable for human beings, both females and males. In a way, it is like going back to the early Women's law and Tove Stang Dahl; the goal of Women's law is to describe, explain and understand the legal position of women in order to improve their position in law and society (Dahl 1985, 21). But, today, we cannot study women as objects – we are subjects, varying, pluralistic and many-faceted. The distinction of women as opposed to men and the recently defined third sex, transsexuals,[28] is no longer as sharp as it has seemed to be. We cannot restrict our studies only to legal positions. We have to broaden our analysis and critically assess the possibilities of improving our position in law and society through law. Law is not the only, or maybe not even the most important, normative structure today. We are at a crossroads. We have to think dynamically and perhaps travel along new pathways. As academics, we have tools not only for analyzing and reflecting upon issues, but also for influencing the understandings held by politicians, scholars and students.

It is possible to find a starting point in women's experiences without reproducing the same pattern for women and men in the future. Hanne Petersen has maintained that we should be aware of our use of concepts. We can see our concepts either as repressive or emancipatory. We can fix them onto an individual or onto a state. We can take advantage of both the conservation and the dynamic potential of the concept. We can view concepts either as static or in a constant process of mutation. Concepts, such as equality, are constructive forces in social processes armed with progress. With an awareness of this fact, as well as of the dangers of binary oppositions, a lot of important political progress can be made. Concepts such as *emancipating equality* and *emancipating difference* could be used to extricate ourselves from a sometimes repressive or depressive discussion on equality. In Scandinavian jurisprudence especially, where the systemic character of law is less important than, e.g., in German jurisprudence, it should not be too difficult to reintroduce the concept of equality as a dynamic one. For some reason, legal science, so far, has been much more reluctant to open up its concepts to dynamic change than the political sphere. A dynamic approach to equality between the sexes characterizes the initiatives of the Swedish government, whereas these initiatives are met with much scepticism in academic legal communities or in the legal profession.

Equality Issues of the NFLS Today: Gendered Subjects and Social Rights

The increased emphasis on rights has been imported to Sweden and Finland through European integration and international conventions. We should indeed discuss whether this strategy could be used to advance women's needs. The emphasis on human rights can be a method by which the decline of social rights is disguised, which we find most alarming in the current state of affairs. Nordic societies have been more directed towards mutual solidarity and responsibility than societies with strong liberal traditions (Nousiainen et al. 2001). Our traditional notions of distributive justice are being undermined by referring to protected privacy, when the status of social rights, on the contrary, should be strengthened.

We cannot speak of equality without a profound implementation of social rights. Experiences are numerous enough to prove that the formally equal law without positive measures can leave much of the imbedded inequalities untouched. If we are going to improve the rights discussion, at the same time we have to improve the discussion about responsibilities. Responsibilities go hand in hand with social relations and, when analyzing them, power is an important issue.

In this context, justice should not be seen *only* as a matter of the morally just distribution of social benefits and obligations. Dominance and oppression, rather than distribution, ought to be the starting point for a theory of social justice (Young 1990). The Nordic model may signify a just distribution of material goods, but the gendered pattern of social institutions and relations have not yet received enough attention.

The new anti-discrimination regulations take different marginalized groups as their starting point. What is the effect of these new regulations on the feminist discourse on subjectivity? Are women only one group, among others, which are discriminated against? Does this conceptualization of women as one of many groups lead to the explosion of the whole idea of feminism? Or do the subject construction of feminism and the gendered structure of society go deeper than that? The methodologies developed in feminist studies place gendered subjects both as researchers and as objects of research. Thus, the ethical dimensions of 'responsible research' challenge us to develop methodologies that give voice to different discourses among women.

When talking about liberal or other rights constructions, we have to place them in the political and social structure of society as well as in the power structures of that society. To understand rights – and discrimination in the enjoyment of rights – a context must be specified. We cannot recognize or address discrimination if it is not understood as part of a power structure. Who are the subjects and objects within these power structures? Is the power we are talking about direct abuse of power or is it disguised in more indirect and subtle forms? How are we to investigate indirect discriminatory effects? Is it meaningful to search for an explanation of power relations or should we concentrate rather on the discursive patterns that reproduce inequalities, such as the hidden meanings of overtly neutral legal terms? In the Nordic context, the public/private split as such is not the problem, neither can women be defined as powerless objects of direct discrimination.

In addition, the traditional liberal starting point of the legal person who owns himself and his property in the Lockean sense is less adequate in the North. People are understood to be subjects in a broader community-related Hegelian sense. Interventions into the private sphere have been accepted more easily than in liberal democracies due to a wide acceptance of welfare state politics. Irrespective of sex or other social qualities, the power over one's own life is not understood as the exclusive power over some specifically defined property or qualities. The power over one's life and abilities to look after one's own rights are understood as interpersonal and produced in power-related social practices.

The basic problem in integrating multiplicity in the legal construction of person is the universal nature of that definition. In traditional liberal and positivist discourse, the definition of subjects and persons as owners of rights is formal. The existence of any antecedent natural persons as the ground for that notion has been denied. Anyone with specific personal characteristics has been supposed to 'fill' that formal legal definition, sometimes characterized as an 'empty vessel'. A liberal notion would not accept a conception that even the 'natural' person behind the legal person is constructed by law and other social discourses that interact with law (Davies and Naffine 2001, 56). The liberal idea of securing the private sphere, civil rights and liberties and the moral autonomy of independent legal persons is contested by the feminists as based on a male norm. The legal construction of subjects and persons has been a homogenous one because it was never meant to cover anything other than the fraternity of free males. The ways of depicting the universal legal person, i.e., 'reasonable man', 'proprietor', 'subject', have clearly made distinctions vis-à-vis the types of legal persons and 'others' who have not been considered reasonable or in control of themselves or their property. They have been objectified and defined as non-persons: women, children, refugees, sexual minorities. Not so long ago, even a married woman's legal independence was a debated issue. Thus, it has been easy to point out this bias and to question its universality.

But, when feminists and others, then, have demanded pluralism and multiplicity instead of the universal person of law, problems have arisen. Attempts to unite male subjectivity with a feminine one have often been seen as categorizing and exclusive as the norm, which has been challenged. Not all women want to be categorized in the group, 'women', however politically and strategically important it might be on some occasions. But a complete denial of meanings built upon sexual difference does not sound too sensible, either. The claims on equality presuppose some kind of understanding of difference. We are all different but equal, and we should be able to enjoy equal rights irrespective of differences (Gerhard 2001). If there is anything we have learnt from the theorizing and critique of law's neutrality, it is that to recognize difference and discrimination is the very first step towards equality.

To base subjecthood and rights on an understanding of different discriminated groups is not an easy solution either: people lose their status as unique individuals and are forced to adapt to a group identity in order to be heard in the legal system. There is the danger as well that it is exactly these very differences that become cemented in law if principles of equality and non-discrimination are based on a conceptualization in terms of groups (Lacey 1998). Some kind of a middle ground solution to the 'aporia of difference' has been offered by a number of writers (see e.g. Minow 1990) where neither the norm/standard nor the 'deviant' are discussed, but the focus is on the process and the relation in which this distinction is made.

The issue of legal personality seems to have merited little interest in Nordic legal scholarship. As has been discussed elsewhere (Pylkkänen 2001), the State has been an overwhelmingly dominant framework in any debates on rights, welfare, or equality. The State has not been understood as the traditional bourgeois State, but, rather, as the 'good' State, an entity that is almost the equivalent of society. This good State concept is historically constructed in a context of late modernization. The bourgeois state with its distinction between the private and the public spheres and with its liberal construction of liberties, was never fully developed. It was soon replaced by the early welfare State with an egalitarian emphasis. In other words, the State – its legislation, authorities, welfare professionals, social engineers – itself has had the prerogative to interpret 'the good', not individual subjects themselves. The 'good' has dominated over the 'right'. The rights discourse is not that well developed, either. Until as late as in the 1990s, for most Scandinavians the actual meaning of the human rights discourse has been rather vague, especially, how such a discourse affects our ways of thinking of legal persons and subjects (Scheinin, ed. 2001).

The campaign for gender equality and women's rights that has been going on during the past hundred years or more, has always been in the context of the State, the family or some other social institution, all of them considerably communitarian frameworks. Women have seldom, if ever, been allowed the moral autonomy, the protection of integrity or the privacy that were the original idea accompanying human rights. This non-realization of the key ideas of the human rights is by no means unique. The critique of the one-sided rights rhetoric applies here as it does everywhere else. But, it is quite astonishing that when thinking of the early citizenship and civil rights of women, so little discussion has been directed towards the issue of women as subjects and individuals compared to the needs of society at large. The fact that sexualized violence has come onto the agenda only recently is quite symptomatic. A new understanding of rights has been suggested in which rights in the private sphere would be based on the liberal model and all other rights on a more social and contextualized one (Nousiainen and Pylkkänen 1999).

Subjectivity, perhaps, can be described as an ability to and a command of situating the unique and pluralistic self into different relations, expressing sexuality and emotions and creating fantasies and ways of challenging the norms and standards imposed upon the self. It is a dynamic moral force, identity and integrity possessed in principle by each individual, but also easily suppressed and constrained by social and legal conventions and practices. Is it enough that we just secure liberties in the liberal sense, as 'owner of the self' or does it require more positive measures? Are we satisfied with a comprehensive system of social rights? What about sexual and reproductive rights? It is quite symptomatic how difficult it is, in fact, to recognize and protect women's authentic sexuality, irrespective of social standing.

Redefinition of the Public/Private Boundary

The distinction between public and private spheres exists in Nordic countries, but looks quite different than in most other Western cultures. Rather, the boundary between the spheres should be drawn somewhere else than in the human rights discourse. Care, for instance, is a public concern, both child-care and the care of the elderly. Women do most of this work, but it is paid. The part of caring work that is not performed in public is a matter for the family to divide among themselves, despite two months of parental leave, individually for each parent. The agreement is seen as private and voluntary and independent of any issues created by the State, law or the economic system. The result, as we all know, is that women are doing the lion´s share of unpaid caring work and have a greater responsibility for private relations and the specific needs of other people than men do. What is more, family law is based on a self-supporting and individualistic ideology, which leads to a situation where women are poorer and more dependent than men (Burman 2001; Gunnarsson, Burman and Wennberg in this volume). Especially when a marriage is dissolved, the legal mutual obligation for maintenance comes to an end and the one who has had less income and who has been the dependent one, may become a dependent of the State.

In our cultures, women's ethical responsibilities have been elevated up to the social and societal levels and made into a universal rule. In Finland, one talks about a dual citizenship model: male and female citizen(ship)s with different legitimacies and connections to the State. Women have been actors in the forging of the welfare State and have also contributed to its being shaped according to a certain gendered model. Women create a social welfare for other women and for society as a whole. This issue has been discussed in the project concerning the modernization of marriage and the welfare State in the Nordic countries (Melby et al. 2001). It was concluded that women, indeed, were subjects and actors in the making of a modern welfare State. It was not a stable hierarchical structure that women have just had to adapt to.

The flip side of the process was that issues relating to women's personal integrity were of little relevance. Because of this historical tradition, if and when women now require support for such claims, these claims may be undermined by deferring to the needs of the community in the first place. As discussions of subjectivity never really came into the public debate, one cannot imagine what such a discussion would mean for women or for anyone for that matter. The communitarian discourses dominate over the liberal ones. Or perhaps it is more appropriate to talk about equality and equal rights among groups, not among individuals.

The fundamental idea behind rights is the freedom and autonomy of individuals. Human beings were believed to have the moral standing and capability of reflecting upon and defining their situations with respect to others, as well as of honouring other people's, *i.e.*, the generalized other's, need for the same respect. Several social institutions then defined why not all individuals could possess these qualities, notably the institutions of family, slavery, nationality and so on. This notion was not described in terms of power or discrimination. Instead, some people were placed in these institutions as a 'natural' necessity. When such boundaries of institutions have gradually been removed, some new, more subtle boundaries have been created in their stead. These new boundaries are more difficult to address, because it is a question of rhetoric, images and, so on. Instead of norms, rights and institutions, NFLS should concentrate on language, speech, images, corporeal existence and other similar issues. But are we trained for this kind of an analysis?

A test question for the human rights status of women might be: on what grounds may the enjoyment of rights by women and by other people who are discriminated against be restricted either by nation states or within the communities as a result of non-intervention? The human rights discourse, itself, allows such restrictions in national law that are acceptable in a democratic society and that have been adapted to the cultural traditions of such a context (Cameron 1998, 83). Issues related to morals – family, reproduction and sexuality – are especially treated as national and cultural rather than as universal ones. There is some difficulty in identifying uniform European concepts, which leads to an attempt to find the 'lowest common denominator' in these issues. Interpretations of the boundaries of privacy have been teleological and family-related rather than formal and individualistic (Cameron 1998, 84 and 86). In other words, national legal cultures are allowed to pave the way in this development, not the universal human rights discourse.

Since the CEDAW, however, the scope of this margin of appreciation should have diminished. The basic dilemma of human rights, the fundamental and primary protection of the family institution before women's rights, is yet to be resolved. Some positive developments have taken place with regard to violence against women, viz., the CEDAW and Beijing 5+ processes and the Violence against Women Convention of the Americas but, so far, the theoretical understanding of persons and their rights remains untouched. Very little discussion about this dilemma has occurred in the Nordic countries. It can be argued that the European Court of Justice is indirectly pressing for a harmonized European law on the family. Therefore, it would be of utmost importance to raise the question of women's rights in the family in the EU context. So far, the EC law itself has not covered family law. Its impact on social rights has been indirect but, in the near future, these issues may also be inserted to the federal agenda (McGlynn 2001).

We will not go further in this direction. But in the European and Nordic contexts, it is appropriate to discuss whether the family still may be considered the 'natural' framework of women's legal status. As the other contributors in this volume argue, women in all Nordic countries are expected to be self-supporting individuals with a strong labour force connection. Nevertheless, an obvious family identity still lies in the background of much social and other legislation (see also Burman and Gunnarsson, eds 2001). We feel that more such research is needed to be able to analyze the structural discrimination and disadvantage.

The human rights discourse is problematic for women. Even if the strategy today in the United Nations and in other inter-, trans- or supranational cooperation is 'mainstreaming' and the explicit starting point is gender, equality issues are still seen as areas of concern of women and, mainly, as specific issues. The goal might be lofty, but the results are not radical.

The changes are often on a rhetorical level. For example, understanding of what kind of behaviour is 'socially acceptable' does not easily change. For example, when the EC ministers agreed on legislation against trafficking in the Spring 2001, the question of prostitution was not involved. Prostitution is seen as a voluntary activity and condemnation only pointed to explicit trafficking. This limited view is not in accordance with CEDAW, Article 6 which states that the convention States shall take all appropriate measures, including legislation, to control all kinds of trafficking of women and the exploitation of women in prostitution. This aim has obviously not been achieved in the EC agreement.

Furthermore, the focus of EU cooperation, vis-à-vis this issue is on the prostitute and not on the buyer and the demand as in Sweden. The basic assumption for this difference is that the relation between seller and buyer is unequal. The prostitute is not a free individual *in this relation*. And it is the behaviour of buying sex that is so undesirable. A Swedish professor of Finnish origin in criminal law has argued that it is an individual's right to buy sex. This right is part of the accepted sexual freedom of fundamental rights, according to professor Träskman (1998). This argumentation shows that the person who is purchased is of no consequence or value and that her freedom of sexual integrity is of no concern.[29]

The challenge for NFLS is to deal with matters of unequal power without defining individuals or groups as weak. We have to focus on the *relation* and the specific situation instead of looking at social categories of women, disabled persons, or immigrants. We should focus on the majority culture and its practices. When the standard is invisible, it does not seem to need definition. We have to combine a perspective where both the individual and the group are recognized. The individual is affected by the ways in which society is organized, but he or she is not imprisoned by them. We have to assume that a human being is both dependent and independent. Finally, one has to be more *process*-oriented and find new ways of dealing with both jurisprudence and politics.

This article has been written under the auspices of two major research projects, a national research programme, SYREENI, funded by the Academy of Finland and the project called The Fall of the Strong State financed by the Bank of Sweden Tercentenary Foundation.

Notes

1 For a detailed discussion of the Nordic model of equality, see Svensson 2001, Svensson forthcoming and Nousiainen forthcoming. See also Westerhäll 1987, Bacchi 1996, Sainsbury 1999 Bergqvist, et al. (ed.), 1999, and the thematic issue of *Kvinnovetenskaplig tidskrift* no 3/1986: *Jämställdhet – ideologi och politik.*

2 The redistributive model is considered to be the opposite of the recognition model, see Fraser 1995.

3 In this chapter the focus is on the differences between Finland and Sweden. For a comparison between Norway and Sweden, see Sörensen and Bergqvist 2002. For a comparison

between Denmark and Sweden, see Dahlerup 2002.

4 In the Nordic context, legal change is achieved mainly through legislation, not through case law. The legal profession is expected to be loyal to statutory law and its preparatory works. Law and politics are inherently intertwined, especially in Swedish legal culture. For a more explicit description of the legal systems in the Nordic countries, see Nousiainen et al. (eds) 2001.

5 This expression is taken from the famous work of the historian, Yvonne Hirdman, describing Swedish welfare politics and its utopian character in its early days during the 1930s and 1940s, Hirdman 1995.

6 There are emerging signs of reflectivity of gender among Swedish male legal scholars but so far none whatsoever in Finland. Regarding Swedish discussion, see Gustafsson 1998.

7 This issue is in focus for a contemporary research project called *The Fall of the Strong State*, financed by The Bank of Sweden Tercentenary Foundation, led by Professor Bo Rothstein and Professor Lotta Vahlne-Westerhäll.

8 Svensson forthcoming. Thomas Wilhelmsson has discussed this shift in his book *Senmodern ansvarsrätt* (2001), but he has not addressed the issue in relation to gender.

9 In the Swedish legal scholarship, such notions are actually quite new. Håkan Gustafsson has recently argued that social rights are, or should be, legally protected, see Gustafsson 2002.

10 On developments in Finland, see Ahtela in this volume.

11 The official report on the voluntary gender-equality labelling of products and services, *Märk-värdig jämställdhet* (SOU 2002:30).

12 15 § *Kommittéförordningen* (Statute on Committees) 1998:1474, which replaced a general directive 1994:124. The directive was followed up in 1997. The directive was remarked upon in one-third of the studied official reports, one-third explicitly explained why the directive had been ignored and the last third made no comments on the issue at all (Skr. 1999/2000:24, 9). According to the Sex Equality Ombudsman, *JämO*, (in an e-mail correspondence 2002-03-25) the replacement is a change for the worse. It is compulsory to analyze the consequences of legislation only if they have significance for the equality of men and women. Definitions of this kind, of course, lay themselves open for different opinions. In Finland, the Gender Impact Assessment on the Contract of Employment Act was the first one. A new one is being conducted with regard to the reform of the employment pension scheme (see *Vaikuttaako sukupuoli? Työsopimuslakiesityksen arviointia tasa-arvonäkökulmasta* (Does Gender Make a Difference? Gender Impact Assessment of the Contract of Employment Bill, 2000).

13 Prop. 2003/04:1, Appendix 4.

14 See e.g. Hirdman 1999 and 2001, Edström 1998 and Edström & Jacobsson 1994. When it comes to news distribution, the number of female and male journalists is almost the same, but the news are still very male-dominated, see e.g. www.wacc.org.uk and www.yle.fi/gender.

15 Treaty of European Union articles 2 and 3, of which the latter includes the principle of mainstreaming. The main goal for Swedish sex equality politics is a society where women and men have the same opportunities, rights and responsibilities in every essential part of life. It means an equal distribution of power and influence, the same opportunities to economic independence, equal terms and conditions concerning gainful employment, possibilities to reconcile work and family and the possibility of personal development at work. It also means equal access to education and the possibility of developing personal ambitions, interests and talents, shared responsibilities for home and children and, finally, protection

against sex-related violence (Skr. 1999/2000:24. Cf. Prop.1993/94:147, in which sex-related violence was named sexualised violence.)

16 Since 1999, it has been legally prohibited to purchase sex in Sweden. See Nordborg and Niemi-Kiesiläinen 2001. Since 1 October 2003, according to the Act on Public Order, both the sale and the procurement of sex are illegal in public places in Finland.

17 These notions are constructed from the priority of the working ideology. There, the reproductive sphere is the term for the place where children are born and reared. Under another point of view, we could call it the productive sphere, where human potential is developed.

18 *Regeringsformen* Chapter 1 § 2.

19 In 1998, the wages of women were 82 per cent of the wages of men. In 1992, the figure had been 84 per cent (Statistics Sweden 2002).

20 15 § Statute on Committees (*Kommittéförordningen*) 1998:1474, and the governmental report on equality politics (*Regeringens skrivelse om jämställdhetspolitiken*) 1999/2000:24.

21 See, for example, the homepage of the Swedish Government, www.riksdagen.se (*Näringslivsdepartementet*).

22 Prop. 1997/98:55 on Women's Peace (*Kvinnofrid*) Dir. 1993:31. The report on trafficking (SOU 1995:15 *Könshandeln*) treated the relation between men and women as more equal and suggested a criminalization of both the seller and the buyer. The final proposal, however, was a criminalization of the buyer.

23 See the annual report 2001 of the Department of Higher Education (*Högskoleverkets årsrapport 2001*) and the report on women and men in higher education in 1997 (*Kvinnor och män i högskolan, Högskoleverkets rapport* 1997:44 R).

24 This development is obvious in the study of changes in values over time by the SOM Institute (Society, Opinion and Media. Young people still highly prioritize the family, even more than earlier (Oscarsson 2002).

25 In Sweden in 1998, 35 per cent of all households were one-person households, 20 per cent were cohabitant households with children and 28 per cent without children. Five per cent of the households consisted of a single parent with one or several children, most of single parents (80 per cent) being women. Most minors live with their biological parents, but if they live with only one biological parent it is most often their mother (Statistics Sweden 2000). In Finland, the rates of cohabitant, 19 per cent, and single parent households, 13 per cent, have increased but marriage is still the predominant family form with the rate of 67.4 per cent, of which 35.7 per cent units were families with children. Single parent households were predominantly headed by the mother (Statistics Finland 2001).

26 Finland, however, was not an independent country, but an autonomous Grand Duchy of Russia.

27 On the early development of the Finnish feminist movements, see Bergman 2002.

28 Prop. 2001/02:27 *Likabehandling av studenter i högskolan* (Law proposal on the equal treatment of students in the higher education).

29 In the Finnish report on trafficking (Ministry of Justice working group report 2003:5), a similar emphasis on economic liberties to the neglect of human dignity is discernible.

References

Bacchi, Carol Lee (1996), *The Politics of Affirmative Action: Women, Equality and Category Politics,* SAGE Publications, London.

Bergman, Solveig (2002), *The Politics of Feminism: autonomous feminist movements in Finland and West Germany from the 1960s to the 1980s,* Åbo Akademi University Press.

Bergqvist, Christina (1994), *Mäns makt och kvinnors intressen,* Almqvist & Wiksell International, Stockholm.

Bergqvist, Christina et al. (1999), *Likestilte demokratier?: kjønn og politikk i Norden,* Nordiska ministerrådet. Universitetsforlaget, Oslo.

Burman, Monica and Gunnarsson, Åsa (eds) (2001), *Familjeföreställningar. Om familjens betydelse inom juridik, ekonomi och forskning,* Iustus förlag, Uppsala.

Burman, Monica (2001), 'Den farliga familjen och borgenärerna' in Monica Burman and Åsa Gunnarsson (eds), *Familjeföreställningar. Om familjens betydelse inom juridik, ekonomi och forskning,* Iustus förlag, Uppsala, pp. 55-104.

Cameron, Iain (1998), *Introduction to the European Convention on Human Rights,* Iustus Förlag, Uppsala.

Dahl, Tove Stang (ed.) 1985. *Kvinnerett I.* (English version, 1987. *Women's law. An introduction to Feminist Jurisprudence*), Universitetsforlaget, Oslo.

Dahlerup, Drude (2002), 'Er ligestillingen opnået? Ligestillingsdebattens forskellighed i Danmark og Sverige' in Anette Borchorst (ed.), *Kønsmagt under forandring,* Hans Reitzels Forlag. København, pp. 226-246.

Davies, Margaret and Naffine, Ngaire (2001), *Are Persons Property? Legal debates about property and personality,* Ashgate, Aldershot.

Edström, Maria and Jacobson, Maria (1994), *Massmediernas enfaldiga typer: kvinnor och män i mediebruset den 17 mars 1994,* Institutionen för journalistik och masskommunikation, Göteborgs universitet. Arbetsrapport 1101-4679; 38.

Edström, Maria (1998), *Drömprinsen och Glamourgullet: om könsschabloner i barnreklam,* Konsumentverket, Stockholm.

Eskola, Katarina (1968), 'Sukupuoliroolikeskustelu Suomessa' in Katarina Eskola (ed.), *Miesten maailman nurjat lait,* Tammi, Helsinki, pp. 11-37.

Fransson, Susanne (2000), *Lönediskriminering. En arbetsrättslig studie av könsdiskriminerande löneskillnader och konflikten mellan kollektivavtal och lag,* Iustus förlag, Uppsala.

Fraser, Nancy (1995), 'From Redistribution to Recognition? Dilemmas of Justice in a 'Post-Socialist' Age' in *New Left Review* July/August, pp. 68-93.

Gerhard, Ute (2001), *Debating Women's Equality. Toward a Feminist Theory of Law from a European Perspective,* Rutgers University Press, New Brunswick, New Jersey and London. Gunnarsson, Åsa and Stattin, Chris (2001), 'Jämställdhetsnormen i skatte- och socialrätten' in Monica Burman and Åsa Gunnarsson (eds), *Familjeföreställningar. Om familjens betydelse inom juridik, ekonomi och forskning,* Iustus förlag, Uppsala, pp.159-199.

Gustafsson, Håkan (1998), 'Från axiom till paradox? Om kön: rätt och makt' in *Retfaerd* 82/ 1998, pp. 51-78.

Gustafsson, Håkan (2002), *Rättens polyvalens. En rättsvetenskaplig studie av sociala rättigheter och rättssäkerhet,* Lund Studies in Sociology of Law.

Haataja, Anita and Nurmi, Kaarina (2000), Naiset työelämässä – ja sen ulkopuolella, *Tasa-arvon työraportteja 2000:3*. Tasa-arvoasiain neuvottelukunta, Sosiaali- ja terveysministeriö, Helsinki.

Hirdman, Anja (1999), Images making difference: three papers on gender, style and status in recent media history of Swedish and American popular culture, *Journalistik, medier och kommunikation, Serie 1999:1*. University of Stockholm.

Hirdman, Anja (2001), *Tilltalande bilder: genus, sexualitet och publiksyn i Veckorevyn och Fib aktuellt*, Atlas, Stockholm.

Hirdman, Yvonne (1995), *Att lägga livet till rätta – studier i svensk folkhemspolitik*, Carlssons, Eslöv.

Hirdman, Yvonne (1990), 'Genussystemet' in *Maktutredningens huvudrapport: Demokrati och makt i Sverige*. SOU 1990:44. Allmänna förlaget, Göteborg, p. 73-116.

Holli, Anne Maria (2003), Discourse and Politics for Gender Equality in Late Twentieth Century Finland, *Acta Politica* 23. Department of Political Science, University of Helsinki. Helsinki University Press.

Jallinoja, Riitta (1983), *Suomalaisen naisasialiikkeen taistelukaudet*, WSOY, Helsinki.

Julkunen, Raija (1999), 'Gender, Work, Welfare State' in *Women in Finland*, Otava, Helsinki, pp. 79-100.

Ketscher, Kirsten (2000), 'Nogle udviklingslinjer i kvinderetten' in *Normativa perspektiv, Festskrift till Anna Christensen*, Juristförlaget i Lund, pp. 169-187.

Kokko, Marja (1998), *Naisten järjestäytyminen, ryhmätietoisuus ja kansalaistuminen Jyväskylässä 1800-luvun lopulta 1930-luvulle*, Jyväskylän yliopisto, Jyväskylä.

Kokko, Marja (2000), 'The Woman Question in Finland 1850-1930: Possibilities and Limits of Political Agency' in Kari Melby et al. (eds), The Nordic Model of Marriage and the Welfare State, *Nord* 2000:27, Nordic Council of Ministers, Copenhagen, pp. 147-157.

Kurki-Suonio, Kirsti (1995), 'Gemensam vårdnad – vad döljer man med barnets bästa?' in Gudrun Nordborg (ed.), *13 kvinnoperspektiv på rätten*, Iustus förlag, Uppsala, pp. 169-195.

Kuusipalo, Jaana (1999), 'Finnish women in politics' in *Women in Finland*, Otava, Helsinki, pp. 55-78.

Kvinnovetenskaplig tidskrift, 3/1986: Jämställdhet – ideologi och praktik.

Lacey, Nicola (1998), *Unspeakable Subjects. Feminist essays in legal and social theory*, Hart Publishing, Oxford.

Lerwall, Lotta (2001), *Könsdiskriminering. En analys av nationell och internationell rätt*, Iustus förlag, Uppsala.

Lindvert, Jessica (2002), *Feminism som politik. Sverige och Australien 1960-1990*, Boréa Bokförlag, Umeå.

Lundström, Karin (1999), *Jämlikhet mellan kvinnor och män i EG-rätten. En feministisk analys*, Iustus förlag, Uppsala.

Lundström, Karin (2001), 'The ECJ's Conditional Release of Women' in Kevät Nousiainen et al. (eds), *Responsible Selves. Women in the Nordic legal culture*, Ashgate, Aldershot, pp. 263-286.

Lähteenmäki, Maria (1999), 'Responsibility fosters independence. The role of the women's movement in building Finland' in *Women in Finland*, Otava, Helsinki, pp. 39-54.

Melby, Kari, Pylkkänen, Anu, Rosenbeck, Bente and Carlsson Wetterberg, Christina (2001), 'The Nordic Model of Marriage' in The Nordic Countries and Europe II. Social Sciences, *Nord 2001:23*. Nordic Council of Ministers, Copenhagen.

McGlynn, Clare (2001), 'Families and the European Charter of Fundamental Rights: progressive change or entrenching status quo?' in *European Law Review* December 2001, pp. 582-598.

Minow, Martha (1990), *Making All the Difference: Inclusion, Exclusion, and American Law,* Cornell University Press, Ithaca.

Myrdal, Alva (1935), *Stadsbarn: en bok om deras fostran i storbarnkammare*, Kooperativa Förbundet, Stockholm.

Myrdal, Alva (1957), *Kvinnans två roller*, Tiden, Stockholm.

Nordborg, Gudrun (1998), Gemensam vårdnad – för vems skull?, *Feministiskt perspektiv* nr 2, pp. 10-15.

Nordborg, Gudrun and Niemi-Kiesiläinen, Johanna (2001), 'Women's Peace: A Criminal Law Reform in Sweden' in Kevät Nousiainen et al. (eds), *Responsible Selves. Women in the Nordic legal culture,* Ashgate, Aldershot, pp. 353-373.

Nousiainen, Kevät, Gunnarsson, Åsa, Lundström, Karin and Niemi-Kiesiläinen, Johanna (eds) (2001), *Responsible Selves. Women in the Nordic legal culture.* Ashgate, Aldershot.

Nousiainen, Kevät and Pylkkänen, Anu (1999), 'Social Citizenship – the Nordic Model?' in Mireille Azzoug and Francine Demichel (eds), The Legal Status of Women in the European Union, Le Fil d'Ariane, *Publication of the Institute of European Studies*, special issue Spring 1999. University of Paris 8, pp. 99-104.

Nousiainen, Kevät, forthcoming, 'Against Discrimination or for Equality' in Vesa Puuronen et al. (eds), *New Challenges for Welfare Society.* Joensuu University Press.

Nyberg, Anita (2001), 'Inkomstutveckling för kvinnor och män', in Lena Gonäs, Gerd Lindgren and Carina Bildt (eds), *Könssegregering i arbetslivet*, Arbetslivsinstitutet, Stockholm, pp. 57-64.

Oscarsson, Henrik (ed.) (2002), *Spår i framtiden,* SOM-institutet, Göteborgs universitet.

Pylkkänen, Anu (2001), 'The Responsible Self: Relational Gender Construction in the History of Finnish Law' in Kevät Nousiainen et al. (eds), *Responsible Selves Women in the Nordic legal culture,* Ashgate, Aldershot, pp. 105-128.

Sainsbury, Diane (1994), 'Women's and Men's Social Rights: Gendering Dimensions of Welfare States' in Diane Sainsbury (ed.), *Gendering Welfare States,* SAGE, London.

Sainsbury, Diane (1999), *Gender and Welfare State Regimes*, Oxford University Press.

Scheinin, Martin (ed.) (2001), The Welfare State and Constitutionalism in the Nordic Countries – Nordic Perspectives, *Nord* 2001:5, Nordic Council of Ministers, Copenhagen.

Schömer, Eva (1999), *Konstruktion av genus i rätten och samhället. En tvärvetenskaplig studie över svenska kvinnors rätt till jämställdhet i ett formellt jämlikt rättssystem,* Iustus förlag, Uppsala.

Singer, Anna (2000), *Föräldraskap i rättslig belysning,* Iustus förlag, Uppsala.

Svensson, Eva-Maria (1997), *Genus och rätt. En problematisering av föreställningen om rätten,* Iustus förlag, Uppsala.

Svensson, Eva-Maria (2001), 'Sex equality: Changes in politics, Jurisprudence and Feminist Legal Studies' in Kevät Nousiainen et al. (eds), *Responsible Selves, Women in the Nordic Legal Culture,* Ashgate. Aldershot, pp. 71-104.

Svensson, Eva-Maria (forthcoming), '*Omförhandling pågår – om jämställdhetsreglering*'.

Sörensen, Kerstin and Bergqvist, Christina (2002), Gender and the Social Democratic Welfare Regime. A comparison of gender-equality friendly policies in Sweden and Norway, *Arbetsliv i omvandling* 2002:5, Arbetslivsinstitutet, Stockholm.

Taylor, Charles (1992), *Multiculturalism and 'the politics of recognition',* Princeton University Press.

Therborn, Göran (2000), 'Globalizations. Dimensions, Historical Waves, Regional Effects, Normative Governance' in *International sociology* June, Vol 15(2), pp. 151-179.
Turunen, Ritva (1968), 'Keskustelun perillemeno' in Katarina Eskola (ed.) *Miesten maailman nurjat lait*, Tammi, Helsinki, pp. 38-44.
Vaikuttaako sukupuoli? Työsopimuslakiesityksen arviointia tasa-arvonäkökulmasta, *Tasa-arvo-julkaisuja* 2000:8,Tasa-arvovaltuutetun toimisto, sosiaali- ja terveysministeriö, Helsinki.
Westerhäll, Lotta (1987), 'Jämställdheten och grundlagen', *Svensk Juristtidning* 1987:3, pp. 200 – 210.
Wilhelmsson, Thomas (1987), *Social civilrätt*, Juristförbundets förlag. Helsingfors.
Wilhelmsson, Thomas (2001), *Senmodern ansvarsrätt: privaträtt som redskap för mikropolitik*, Iustus förlag, Uppsala.
Young, Iris Marion (1990), *Justice and the Politics of Difference*, Princeton University Press.

Official documents

Dir. 1993:31 Kvinnofrid.
Dir. 1994:124 till samtliga kommittéer och särskilda utredare att redovisa jämställdhetspolitiska konsekvenser.
Högskoleverkets årsrapport 2001.
JämO årsredovisning 2002.
KM 1967:B 46 Lasten päivähoitolaitostoimikunnan mietintö.
KM 1970:A 8 Naisten asemaa tutkivan komitean mietintö.
KM 2002:9 Tasa-arvolain uudistamistoimikunnan mietintö.
Kommittéförordning 1998:1474.
Kvinnor och män i högskolan, Högskoleverkets rapport 1997:44R.
Prop. 1993/94:147 *Delad makt delat ansvar*. Regeringens proposition om jämställdhetspolitiken.
Prop. 1997/98:55 *Kvinnofrid.*
Prop. 2001/02:27 *Likabehandling av studenter i högskolan.*
Prop. 2003/04:1 *Budgetpropositionen* Bilaga 4.
Skr. 1999/2000:24 *Jämställdhetspolitiken inför 2000-talet.*
SOU 1976:71 *Roller i omvandling.*
SOU 1990:44 *Demokrati och Makt i Sverige*. Maktutredningens huvudrapport.
SOU 1995:15 *Könshandeln.*
SOU 1997:138 *Familj, makt och jämställdhet.*
Statistics Sweden 2002.
SOU 1998:6 *Ty makten är din.... Myten om det rationella arbetslivet och det jämställda Sverige.* Kvinnomaktutredningen.
SOU 2002:30 *Märk-värdig jämställdhet.*
www.wacc.org.uk
www.yle.fi/gender

Chapter 3

Gender, Bargaining Strategies and Strikes in Sweden

Susanne Fransson and Christer Thörnqvist

Introduction[1]

From an international perspective, Nordic labour markets are distinctive from other labour markets by virtue of their strong corporatism or rather 'social partnership', the term preferred these days by the European Union. Collective bargaining and collective agreements play an extraordinarily strong regulatory role, stronger many times over, than labour market legislation. However, a system so heavily reliant on collective bargaining is also significantly dependent on the efficacy of its conflict resolution. In Sweden, the country which is the focus of this chapter, the preconditions for both collective bargaining and conflict resolution have changed considerably during the last few decades. In the 1950s and 1960s, bargaining was never a problem; the flourishing economy guaranteed both strong real wage increases and profits for Swedish companies and, accordingly, industrial conflicts were rare. Since then, much has changed. As was the case with most other industrialized countries, Sweden experienced an upsurge in the amount of strikes – mainly wildcats – in the 1970s and in the 1980s and in the first half of the 1990s. Many employers' organizations tried to dismantle the bargaining system. Nowadays, legislation has also assumed more of the role formerly played by collective agreements.

Yet such radical changes never affect all groups or parties equally; some suffer, while others emerge as winners. This chapter discusses the effects on women in Swedish working life. The international debate of the last few decades on industrial action has departed from such 'classics' as Shorter and Tilly (1974), Tilly et al. (1975), Clegg (1976) and Crouch and Pizzorno (1978), which all highlight the strike as the workers' strongest power resource. It is rarely mentioned, however, that no matter decade or country, strikes have been mainly used as weapons by 'male' trade unions representing occupations typically male. Strikes have, for instance, been more frequent among miners, longshoremen and metal workers than among workers in food processing, the garment industry, or service occupations (Thörnqvist 1994, 157–68).

An often forgotten aspect of industrial relations is that collective bargaining strategies are not gender-neutral.

Of course, gender is not the sole reason for these differences; many other variables have to be taken into account when occupational peculiarities are discussed and we shall meet some of them in the following sections.

Already by the mid-1970s, Clegg (1976) observed the close association between the collective bargaining structure and overall patterns of industrial conflict. Some of his main findings are still valid. For instance, the risk for strikes – official as well as wildcat – is higher the more decentralized a bargaining system is. Yet, the number of wildcat strikes can be kept in check by means of elaborate and efficient dispute procedures (Clegg 1976, 76, 82). Later studies have shown that the relation between collective bargaining and industrial conflict is much more complex than Clegg suggested. For example, the relation between collective bargaining and industrial conflict differs widely between the four larger Nordic countries, among which Norway and Denmark are the two opposite ends of the spectrum. Norway has experienced a very strong industrial peace, even during the rebellious 1970s, while unofficial strikes in the Danish private sector have become an integral and largely accepted part of the bargaining system, unaffected by business-cycle related economic factors (Stokke and Thörnqvist 2001).

In this chapter we explore the gendered patterns in bargaining strategies and the use of strikes. With the exception of a few brief Nordic outlooks, we limit our investigation in this chapter to a case study of Sweden, but not, however, to any particular sector of the Swedish economy. On the contrary, a point of departure for this chapter is that gender differences in conflict patterns and bargaining strategies exist both among and within different industries. Because this field of research has not been previously explored, we cannot claim to cover all aspects equally well and we view our findings mainly as a starting point for further, more detailed analyses.

Furthermore, we shall also stress the changes in labour market legislation. In most Western countries, labour disputes are regarded as disputes of interest, no matter if the dispute is a minor clash of opinion between an employer and his employees in a shop-floor negotiation over wage-setting or if it is a strike involving thousands of workers. The industrial relations systems in all the Nordic countries, however, are highly regulated or 'juridified', that is, disputes of interest are transformed into disputes of rights (Bruun 1994). Thus, a thorough investigation of the changes in labour legislation is necessary to understand old and new collective strategies.

Sweden has the highest rate of trade union membership in the world; accordingly, an overwhelming majority of Swedish employees are covered by collective agreements. This statement is true for both women and men; at the end of the 1990s, 52 per cent of trade union members were women (Kjellberg 1999, 66–7[2]). Still, the collective agreement is not gender-neutral. The praxis of the collective bargaining system has developed within an industrial relations system dominated by men and male-dominated organizations. Consequently, new agreements are always settled within the framework of the existing industrial relations system (Bercusson and Dickens 1996).

Yet, we have reasons to believe that this pattern is changing. Still, during the 1990s, the wage gap between men and women shrank in most EU countries, as well as in Sweden (*Eurostat* 2001). A continuing deregulation of industrial relations might very well reverse that trend, which, in that case, calls for new strategies for trade unions in occupations dominated by women; thus, we find the focus on gender differences in this chapter quite timely.

Points of Departure – the Legal Framework

The Emergence of Collective Labour Law

The old guild system left a legal vacuum behind when it disappeared. During the last decades of the 19th century, no legislation governing labour contracts existed at all in any of the Nordic countries.[3] Employment issues such as wages, working hours and other employment conditions were matters of contract. Relations between employers and employees belonged to a 'private sphere', based on a hierarchical power structure where freedom of contract was an illusion. Yet, the emergence of trade unions and employers' associations paved way for a new form of contract, the collective agreement, which filled the regulation vacuum. The deregulation of the labour market, including freedom of organization, bargaining and industrial actions, broke ground for settling collective agreements. When developing into a modern labour market system, these freedoms were transformed into collective rights.

The origins of industrial relations in Denmark, Norway and Sweden are related to the establishment of the employer's prerogative registered in the national agreements between the parties. In 1899, after an enormous, nationwide conflict in Denmark, a basic agreement, in popular parlance called the September Compromise, was agreed upon by the labour market parties. In 1906, the Swedish labour market parties, the Swedish Trade Union Confederation (LO) and the Swedish Employers' Confederation (SAF), followed the Danish example. The result was the 'December Compromise' between capital and labour, which, in 1938, was completed by the so-called Saltsjöbaden Basic Agreement. The cornerstones of the Swedish Model – centralized bargaining and collective agreements settled at peak level – were thus founded.

In Norway, the first national agreement between the labour market parties was agreed upon in 1902. Among the Nordic countries, Finland stands out as a case apart in the development of labour law. The Finnish industrial relations system is a post-war creation. In 1922, a general Employments Contracts Act was enacted, but the first Basic Agreement was not reached until 1944.

Legal Regulation of the Collective Agreement

The collective agreement emerged in an unregulated field of law. Relations between the bargaining parties, as well as disputes over the content and application of collective agreements were solved via self-regulation. Industrial actions – strikes and lock-outs – were used both to bring about agreements and to enforce them. The legal status of a collective agreement was established in Sweden by the 1928 Collective Agreement Act. At the same time, a special Labour Court was introduced. Legal disputes regarding the interpretation of law and collective agreements were to be solved by this court. Matters of interest, that is, all unregulated issues, were to be solved by the parties, with the use of industrial actions as the ultimate means. The collective agreement, however, was soon turned into an instrument for labour market peace. The Collective Agreement Act stated that the collective agreement was binding not only upon the organizations, but also upon their affiliates and individual members. Hence, no legal industrial actions could take place once an agreement was settled, with the exception of sympathetic strikes. The Labour Court's interpretation of the law, especially during the 1930s, extended the area of the collective agreement and, thereby, the ban on industrial actions (Fransson 2000a, 237–44).

Historically, trade unions and employers' associations have had considerable authority to promulgate the norms for labour law; legislation has been used mainly to codify norms set forth by the parties.

The Rights of Association and Collective Bargaining

The rights of association and of negotiation are main components in the Swedish industrial relations system. The positive rights of association were established in the 1906 December Compromise. In 1933, the Labour Court established that the right of association was a fundamental principle. Thus, the right of association was a general condition for the collective agreements settled by parties representing the labour market. In 1936, a law on the rights of association and bargaining was passed to meet the demands of white-collar workers in the private sector. Some thirty years later, in 1966, salaried employees in the public sector were also given the right to collective bargaining and to take industrial actions.

A decade later, all previous norms were codified in the 1976 Codetermination Act. The right to bargaining was declared mutual; the demand of the unions to negotiate at any level with the employer was protected by law and sanctioned by punitive damages. Yet, no clause forces the parties to sign a contract.

The Legal Framework and the Right to Strike

The law did not forbid associations, bargaining and strikes in the 19th century. However, collective actions were seen as rebellions and instigations to revolt against the established order. The legislation contained repressive clauses that forbid workers to foment others to strike. Strikes and collective actions were also regarded as a breach of the employment contract (Fransson 2000a, 232).

Today, the right to strike is a collective right. The Swedish Constitution protects collective actions sanctioned by trade unions or employers' organizations, which do not violate any existing law or agreements. Once settled, the collective agreement implies a ban on strikes and lockouts not only for the parties, but also for their affiliates and individual members. An individual is protected by virtue of his or her belonging to an organization. The employment contract is still valid during a legal strike. The distinction between a legal strike and a wildcat strike is an important one for the individual because the validity of the employment contract is not protected during a wildcat strike. A wildcat strike is not decided upon according to the union's statutes. It is thereby prohibited by law. Furthermore, Swedish law requires that conflicts of rights should be resolved through negotiations between the bargaining partners or, ultimately, by the Labour Court.

As mentioned earlier, employees in the public sector were awarded the right to strike in 1966, but with legal and contractual limitations. Peak-level agreements in the public sector limit the right to strike for such groups as policemen, fire-fighters, nurses and doctors. Such groups are required to avoid conflicts which endanger the life or health of 'ordinary' citizens and, in some cases, to take responsibility for political democracy and the exercise of public authority.

The legal framework was mainly developed as a response to the problems of blue-collar workers in the private sector, that is, a highly male collective. Yet, the legal framework also sets out a framework for women's labour market strategies and collective actions. Hence, the issue in the next section is, how do women's collective actions historically correspond to this framework?

Women's Organizations and Women's Strikes before the 1990s

Women's Trade Unions

Men and women's organizational patterns in the labour market have differed widely over the decades. Even if women did not organize to the same degree as men, several unions organized solely women workers in the early 1900s.[4] Östberg (1997, 200) found 67 such organizations. Many women found it difficult to make themselves heard within the existing unions, particularly in governmental services (Nilsson 1996; Waldemarson 1996).

The first Swedish union for women was founded in 1886 by glove seamstresses in Lund in southern Sweden. Most of the first unions for women appeared in the textile and clothing industries, where the relative number of female workers was high. In 1902, those organizations formed the Women's Union (Kvinnornas fackförbund), a confederation covering the whole textile and clothing sector. Yet, the Women's Union was initiated by men. Since women generally worked for much lower wages than men, the intention of the organization was to reduce wage competition between the sexes. Therefore, in 1904, the Women's Union was admitted as a full member into the Swedish LO. Six years later, the Women's Union split up and, ever since then, the official LO policy has been to promote mixed organizations, including both female and male members.

At the same time, however, purely female occupational organizations were founded in the public sector. By the turn of the century, women's unions were actually more common in the public sector than in the textile and clothing industries. The governmental sector appointment system strictly separated men and women into different positions. Women, therefore, founded an organization of their own, from which they derived much more power than from membership in a union, representing the interests of another, most likely male-dominated profession. Moreover, many women did not feel welcome in the male-dominated unions; some of the public sector unions even openly declared that membership was reserved for men (Nilsson 1996, 152 and 182).

Despite the LO policy to avoid separate unions for men and women, a large number of female occupational organizations with the same kinds of ambitions as unions remained in the private sector between the wars. In Stockholm alone, there were about fifty such organizations, organizing such diverse groups as female office workers, sales clerks, restaurant staff, domestic servants and dentists. All these organizations cannot be labelled as trade unions in the traditional sense. Yet their purpose was to attain collective rights through collective actions, even though these organizations were unrecognized as negotiating partners by employers and even though these organizations were not as militant as the 'male' unions.

If women's organizations were neither recognized as negotiating partners nor as militant, one must ask what power resources and strategies did they really have. Both in the private and the public sectors, a key feature was co-operation rather than confrontation, vis-à-vis contacts with employers as well as with other organizations. Women built up networks. Moreover, the goal was to negotiate with each employer separately and on an individual basis. By increasing educational levels and skills of their members, these organizations believed they could improve their member's employment conditions and wages in negotiations with employers (Waldermarsson 1996, 213).

The main flaw in this strategy, though, was that it was best suited for a highly 'gender-typed' labour market, that is, industries, businesses and enterprises where there were distinct demarcated occupational groups dominated by women. Swedish unions, however, are generally considered to be industry associations, and not occupational ones, similar to certain groups found in the U.K. The more the unions within the LO and the Swedish Confederation of Professional Employees (TCO) merged into larger unions, the harder it became to maintain separate organizations for women. As affiliates of an industry association, women's unions had to accept all employees in the industry as eligible for membership, not only workers with specific occupations (Nilsson 1996, 226–7; Östberg 1997, 140 and 157) Accordingly, women's unions disappeared at the onset of the continuous amalgamation which occurred in the inter-war period. It is worth mentioning, though, that the neighbouring country, Denmark, maintained some unions open only for women. Today, the Danish association, *Kvindeligt Arbejderforbund*, (KAD) an organization for unskilled women in all sectors of the economy, is the only union in Europe that, according to its regulations, organizes women only.

Competition or Loyalty?

As mentioned earlier, women competed with male workers in the labour market by virtue of their lower wages, which made women both dangerous and unpopular in the trade union movement, especially during periods of increasing unemployment. In Denmark, low-wage competition was an explicitly stated means for women's unions such as KAD. For instance, KAD opposed the introduction of the ILO's convention no. 100, a principle of equal pay for equal work between men and women (Olsen 1984, 237). It was not until its 50th Anniversary in 1951 that the association openly stated that equal pay for equal work between men and women was a major goal. Two years later, the Danish LO (at the time DsF) accepted the idea and urged the Danish government to accept the ILO's convention no. 100, which the government finally did in 1960 (Nielsen 1979, 223–5).

It is not likely that low-wage competition as an actively used means for women's organizations was particularly widespread in Sweden; yet the threat was very real to the traditional unions. Separate wage scales for men and women were introduced into the Swedish engineering industry in the 1920s. The employers' association, VF, had, then, for more than a decade pressed for separate wage rates, but the union, Metall, had resisted just to avoid negative competition concerning jobs. When Metall finally agreed on separate wages for women, the main argument was that because women themselves accepted lower wages and were willing to work for wages below the level prescribed by the collective agreement, maintaining equal wages would just hinder the settling of agreements (Larsson 2001, 149).

It is in these types of situations where we find the origin of women's more defensive labour market strategies. While men could actively press for higher wages or other forms of better terms, women, both individually and collectively, had to fight for the right to work at all and for the right to keep their job if they married. As in most European countries, this difference became very obvious right after the Second World War. Women had filled in for men in all labour market sectors during the mobilization, but not to the same extent as in the nations actively participating in the war. No doubt, though, the Swedish economy would have seriously suffered without the participation of women in the labour market. When the war was over, most women had to go back to homemaking or to more menial jobs they had previously held, in order to make room for the returning men. Normally, the women made no fuss about leaving their jobs; they did it out of the spirit of solidarity with their husbands, brothers and sons, who were seen as the traditional bread-winners.

Actually, most of the women had entered the labour market out of loyalty to their country. In a successful newsreel drive during the war, the Swedish government introduced the character *Fru Lojal*, 'Mrs. Loyalty'. Mrs. Loyalty represented every married woman without young children, a woman, who, in addition to her tasks as a homemaker, took place in the war industry during the state of alert. Mrs. Loyalty assumed these extra responsibilities, as her name implies, not for her own purposes, but in an altruistic manner for the benefit of her country during a very critical historical situation. Hence, it was only natural that she did not get the same pay nor gain the same rights or working conditions as an ordinary, male worker; after all, her position was only temporary. Accordingly, it was also natural that Mrs. Loyalty should not compete with the men returning after the war, notwithstanding the expanding labour market (Overud 2000).

Despite relinquishing their temporary jobs and returning to normal life, i.e. homemaking, many women still remembered the new organizational experiences they had been introduced to, experiences which could well be useful for the future. One experience was that women did not seem to count as much as men did, even when women performed the same job as men or even when women, for all intents and purposes, became the family bread-winner, as they did on many occasions during the war. Some trade unions, such as the largest public sector union for municipality workers (*Kommunal*) even refused to affiliate women because women were considered 'temporary employees' and supposed to leave their jobs as soon as the war was over (cf. Lane 1995).

Women on Wildcat Strikes

The women's organizations disappeared from the labour market in the heydays of the Swedish model and the solidaristic wage policy, but the different strategies between men and women remained. The most obvious case is the strike pattern, women did not strike! Both legal and wildcat strikes have been much more sparsely evident in 'female' occupations and unions dominated by women (Thörnqvist 1994, 175–8). Moreover, strikes in traditionally male occupations have often been of an offensive character; they have been short wildcats in the manufacturing industry, usually in connection with plant-level negotiations, aiming at gaining as much as possible from the wage drift. In other words, the typically male strike has taken place among the groups of workers who had the most to profit from the Swedish model (ibid, 295–9).

Yet, before we go on to discuss the connection between men's and women's strike patterns and the Swedish industrial relations system, it should be emphasized that the differences between men's and women's strike patterns is most likely international. For instance, already by the 1950s, Knowles (1952, 210) noticed that while skilled, male car workers could be very strike-prone, grievances among young, unskilled women in the clothing industry, on the other hand, appeared in increasing labour turnover. Even though Knowles discusses the UK half a century ago, his statement could just as well apply to Sweden today, or at least to Sweden in the 1980s.

The situation was probably the same half a century before Knowles's study, too. As implied above, though, not many studies have addressed the issue more seriously. However, the few existing investigations, dealing, for instance, with the UK, Norway and Finland, seem to all arrive at the same conclusion, the differences between men and women are rather due to structural factors than explicitly to gender. Women very often work in industries where neither men nor women are particularly active in trade unions and in sectors where there is little hope of wage drift (cf. Julkunen and Rantalaiho 1993). Not surprisingly, men and women with similar occupations seem to act in the same way. A thorough study of strike-proneness in British manufacturing during the late 1970s found no significant evidence of differences between workplaces with a high number of female workers and workplaces with only few women employed (Edwards 1981, 143).

Even though 'female' strikes are rare, there are, of course, in any country, examples of women's strikes which have been noticed and, at the time, widely publicized. Sweden is no exception. The rest of this section shall discuss three of the most important Swedish strikes with only female participants. These strikes, however, were mainly defensive; they aimed at maintaining something rather than gaining higher pay or achieving better working conditions.

One of the most remarked upon industrial conflicts in the 1970s took place among female cleaners. More correctly, the conflict consisted of five partly simultaneous and closely connected wildcat strikes, directed against the same company, ASAB, in five different places at the end of 1974. In all, some 350 women participated and the reason for the strikes was a shift from wages by the hour to work by contract, which, in practice, lowered the cleaners' pay.

The outcome of the strikes differed widely depending upon the communities where they took place. In two of the cases it is pointless to talk in terms of success or failure because the actions had the character of short sympathetic strikes. Actually, both the strikes ended up in the Labour Court and most of the participants were fined for violating the peace obligation.[5] At the time, however, the penalties of 200 Swedish Kronor were barely more than symbolic.

In two other cases, at the company Domnarvets Jernverk in Borlänge, in central Sweden and in the ore-fields in the very north, the strikers came out relatively successful, the company agreed to wage raises to compensate for the new workform. Even the strike in the ore fields ended with penalties in the Labour Court for many of the participants, but the charging of penalties does not change the impression that the result was a rather satisfactory one to the strikers.

The fifth wildcat, however, which took place at a hotel in the town of Skövde, ended in disaster for most of the participants. Already from the outset of the conflict, the company took a very harsh attitude and two spokesmen of the strikers were fired after only one day of striking. In the eyes of the employer, the two women were 'strike-leaders', which justified the dismissals. Thereafter, the strike took a different turn, the aim now was to get the company to re-engage the two 'strike-leaders'. After 17 days of continuous strike and a legally binding request of the Labour Court to return to work, the rest of the cleaners, eight women in all, were also fired. The case was brought to the Labour Court, which declared the dismissal of the 'strike-leaders' illegal and sentenced the company to pay damages and retroactive wages to the two women. Yet, the court had no objections to the dismissal of the rest of the cleaners. The court argued that even if circumstances such as the lowering of the real wages and the firing of the 'strike-leaders' in some way could make the illegal action excusable, these circumstances lost all their importance because of the length of the strike (AD 1975 no. 31).

In February 1975, while the cleaners were still on trial in the Labour Court, 38 female sewers in Gällivare in the very north of Sweden took illegal action against the introduction of a new piecework system. Even this conflict was rather widely publicized in the daily newspapers. Already at the start, the positions between the workers and the company got locked; the strikers refused to go back to work and the employer refused to negotiate as long as the workers stayed away from work. Still, the strikers could maintain the strike despite the lack of income, owing in great part to outside economic assistance. Among other things, the workers received 20,000 Swedish crowns from 'the miners' strike fund', a fund created after the great miners' strike five years earlier, with the purpose of supporting wildcat strikes. After two months of strike though, the company presented the strikers with an ultimatum, if they did not immediately return to work, the employer would consider the matter as if the workers had voluntarily given notice to quit and thus hire new workers. Sixteen sewers obeyed the employer's request, while the remaining 22 continued the strike. Yet, since the strike now had lost most of its power, even these 22 sewers gave in a few weeks later. The company refused to let them back to work though and the case was never tried in the Labour Court (Thörnqvist 1994, 125–6).

Ten years after these two conflicts, one of the involved companies, Domnarvets Jernverk in Borlänge, once again got struck by a wildcat strike, which had many close points of similarity with the previous one. The strikers were cleaners, women, hired by ASAB and the reason for the strike was a change in the work organization. Yet, while the first strike at Domnarvets Jernverk was rather successful from a striker's point of view, the strike in 1985 ended after just six weeks with the dismissals of 14 workers. After a trial in the Labour Court which took more then a year, however, the court declared that the dismissals were illegal and that the cleaners could return to their old work. According to the court, the rationale was that the strikers had intended to go back to work when they heard that the company was considering firing them. The Court ruled that the workers had been refused entry into the workplace, even though they were not yet formally given notice (Thörnqvist 1998, 53–4).

Of course, it is not possible to generalize from the few cases presented here. Yet, the cases have some items in common, which, taken together, make it clear that the conflicts are not examples worthy of imitation, the strikers were women; all the strikes were mainly defensive; and all the strikes ended with dismissals of some of the participants, even though the cleaners at Domnarvets Jernverk got their jobs back a year after the strike.

Moreover, the conflicts stress the role of tradition, both vis-à-vis militancy and vis-à-vis success. In an interview for a documentary book on the 1974 ASAB conflict, one of the cleaners explained that one reason why the strike turned out so much worse in Skövde than in the ore fields was due to the lack of support from other groups of workers. The cleaners in the ore fields had had a lot of assistance from the miners, maybe not with money, but with advice and moral support (Johansson and Grahm 1975: 130). The authors developed this observation further and noticed that the workers at Domnarvets Jernverk had very clearly taken sides during the cleaners' strike, among other things, by refusing to work in areas which were not 'cleaned up enough to be safe'. In Skövde, though, the strikers were left on their own (ibid.: 147). The importance of help from 'male' groups of workers with more militant traditions is also highlighted by the sewers' strike. True, the sewers lost the conflict, but they held out more than two months, much thanks to the financial assistance from the 'miners' strike fund'. Moreover, even if workers in the garment industry have little experience of industrial conflict, the women in Gällivare lived in an area with a history of militancy. In April 1975, when the conflicts of the cleaners and the sewers were almost over in the ore fields, another, very short, wildcat strike for higher wages broke out, involving nine female shop cleaners in the same area. One of the women explained to a local newspaper that all the strikers were married to miners; thus, they 'knew what a strike meant' (*Norrbottens-Kuriren*, 22 April 1975).

Two other wildcat strikes among women, both in 1978, might shed even more light on the issue. One of the strikes, in a food industry company located outside the town of Kristianstad in southern Sweden, runs parallel with a strike among men in the same occupation and the same area and with almost the same demands. Seemingly, the 'female' strike turned out very successful, the strikers could return to work already after five hours because the CEO of the company had promised to adjust both wages and piecework rates in line with the strikers' wishes. The other strike, among 18 sewers in Kramfors in northern Sweden, makes a glaring contrast to the first one, the strikers were given notice of dismissal after only four hours of strike. Seemingly, the notice was never carried into effect, though (Thörnqvist 1994, 176).

To sum up, this brief overview of some notable women's strikes supports our hypothesis, a successful wildcat strike from a workers' perspective should preferably take place in 'male' industries with long militant traditions, where the possibilities to wage drift are higher and where even a short stoppage can force the employer to make concessions. Accordingly, it seems that wildcats in the manufacturing industries have had a positive impact on real wages for blue collar workers in the conflict-ridden 1970s and 1980s (Thörnqvist 2001, 166–9).

Women on Legal Strikes

When it comes to legal strikes, it is more difficult to determine the impact because the parties usually arrive at a solution without open conflict. Furthermore, the opportunities of taking legal industrial action have been more restricted in the public sector, where the number of women has been high. Because public employees did not get the right to strike or take other forms of actions until 1966, they never developed any militant traditions. The only exception is the threat of collective quitting, which, for a long time, has been a means of action, particularly in the health care industry. Yet, wildcat strikes have been more frequent than official ones in the public sector, too. 'Male' occupational groups have been the most strike-prone.

Moreover, the need for outside support should not be neglected in the case of legal public sector strikes, either. We find an illuminating case if we leave our focus on Sweden for a moment and look at Finland. The industrial relations systems in the two countries are close enough to make findings from Finland interesting even from a Swedish view-point. One of the largest strikes in Finnish post-war history took place in public health care in Spring 1983. Doctors and trained nurses did not take part, but all other occupational groups in the health sector did, in all, 20,200 midwives, nurse's assistants, dental nurses and janitors, 97 per cent of them women. The action was officially legal, but because the whole health care sector got struck, the strike was declared by the Parliament to be very dangerous to the Finnish society in general. Despite this proclamation, the strikers received a collective agreement which satisfied them. According to both the strikers themselves and to contemporary commentators, to a large extent, the outcome was the result of the strong support the strike garnered from public opinion; if the general public had not found the strikers' demand fair, it would have been impossible to maintain the strike (Alasilta–Hagman and Pitko 1984).

The Turning-point, Alternative Strategies in the 1990s

Centralization and Decentralization

If strikes or the threat of strikes have not worked in typically female occupations, one must ask what 'female' strategies for collective bargaining have looked like and how they will change in the future. Although a relatively small number of negotiations end in open conflict, the threat of strikes, actions short of strikes or collective quitting is still the worker side's most important power resource.

In this section, we shall emphasize the late 1980s and the early 1990s as an historical turning-point. As mentioned earlier, male groups of workers typically benefited the most from wage drift in the palmy days of the Swedish model. At the same time, however, the solidaristic wage policy guaranteed that the wage gap did not expand too much between different occupational groups, at least not between different groups of blue collar workers. In other words, unions with a majority of female members, could accept the dominance of the male-dominated unions in the export industries; because of the centralized system, they still got their fair share. In the same way that women had been 'loyal' to the Swedish nation during the Second World War, they now had to stay 'loyal' to the Swedish model.

On some occasions, as in the 1952 bargaining rounds, the peak-level agreement between the Swedish Employers' Confederation (SAF) and the Swedish Trade Union Confederation (LO) even prescribed higher overall wage raises for women than for men in order to reduce the wage gap between the sexes. Female groups could also benefit from the principle of 'equal pay for equal work', a principle which was very much a corner-stone in the solidaristic wage policy. A very prominent expression of this policy was the abolishing of the special wage rates for women in the mid–1960s (Fransson 2000b, 145–7). The wage gap between men and women was actually reduced over the first post-war decades. If looking at the engineering industry, which is normally the leading industry in the national bargaining rounds, the wage gap shrank from 31 per cent in 1950 to 11 per cent in 1990. Yet, seemingly, the narrowing of the gap was more a result of the structure of labour supply and demand than of the solidaristic wage policy; the LO policy adapted to existing wage structure trends rather than the other way around (Svensson 1996).

The transformation of the industrial relations system, however, and the growing importance of multinational Human Resource Management strategies strongly affected collective bargaining and pay setting. From the early 1980s onwards, there has been a move towards more decentralized, or uncoordinated forms of collective bargaining in many Western countries, with Sweden as one of the most remarkable cases (Traxler et al. 2001, 116, 159). As a result of the decentralization process, traditional strategies for collective action were challenged. From a trade union perspective, a pre-condition for successful negotiations has always been the possibility to take powerful industrial action, with the strike as the most important means. Hence, when the industrial relations system changes, so does the pattern of industrial conflict; a centralized control of the strike weapon is difficult to maintain when the bargaining system decentralizes.

The main actors in the move towards decentralized bargaining in Sweden were the employers' associations in the competition-exposed industries, associations, which have always had a great say on the SAF's politics. Accordingly, in February 1990, the board of the SAF announced its decision to refrain from taking part any longer in peak-level bargaining with any union counterparts. The aim was to decentralize, even individualize wage negotiations, but also to dismantle the Swedish model (cf. SAF 1990). Yet, the system never got as decentralized as the SAF hoped, much due to the stabilization drive during the deep recession in the early 1990s and because of union resistance and co-ordination of industry-wide bargaining rounds. In 1997, the employers relinquished their decentralization offensive by signing the so-called Industry Agreement.[6]

Still, the system was, and is challenged and, today, the 'female strategy' of 'loyalty' to the Swedish model has been at stake for about a decade and a half. Moreover, at the 1986 LO Congress, the President of the Metal Workers' Union (Metall), Leif Blomberg, accused the public sector unions of pressing irresponsible wage claims, which threatened the whole economy. According to Blomberg, instead of traditional wage solidarity, it was self-evident that wages should be much higher in the 'male' profitable export industries than in the 'female' unproductive public sector. Subsequently and partly as a result of Blomberg's attack, the LO policy changed in a less favourable way to the public sector at large (Swenson 1992, 52–4).

The development was also supported by many influential economists; Professor Ingemar Ståhl argued at a SAF conference on wage formation in 1990, '– it is completely grotesque that ladies reading fairy-tales in a day-care centre should have the same pay as their husbands with hard shop-floor jobs' (*SAF–tidningen* 1990 no. 33, 3[7]).

Legislation and Individualization as Strategic Means

The 1995 bargaining rounds actualized another important issue, legislation. In our case, the interesting question is whether the individualization of labour market rights has also led to an individualization of trade union strategies. The most burning issue is the ban on discriminatory wage setting due to sex, a section inaugurated in the law of equality, that is, equality between men and women.[8] Strictly juridical, the content of the ban is very much in line with the traditional solidaristic wage policy. The only main difference is that while the main intention with the solidaristic wage policy was to equalize wage gaps between industries and companies, the purpose of the ban on discriminatory wage setting due to sex is to achieve justice among employees in the same firm.

In 1995, it became clear that some unions dominated by women had grown stronger and dared to challenge the employers for higher pay. The Swedish Association of Health Professionals (*Vårdförbundet*) explicitly stated that its members, in particular nurses and midwives, were discriminated against vis-à-vis men in health care with comparable tasks and experience. All salaries in the caring sector, *Vårdförbundet* argued, should be based on individual qualifications, which would favour the union's female members who, in general, had a high degree of formal competence (Fransson 2001). As a result of the solidaristic wage policy, the wage gap between trained and assistant nurses was very small.[9] Therefore, the trained nurses demanded that their salaries be upgraded in accordance with their skills (Olsson 1996, 37 and 63). In other words, *Vårdförbundet* claimed a general pay raise for all its members, and, additionally, the trained nurses demanded individual pay raises in line with their high competence level. The conflict was however complicated by the discrepancy between the peak-level negotiators and the members of how 'a general raise' should be interpreted. Many members believed that the claim was an increase of 5,000 Swedish crowns a month, settled at industry level; a claim far beyond what any union would ever have dreamed of. Accordingly, the result after seven weeks of continuous strike was a big disappointment to many nurses, despite the fact that the outcome was rather good compared to what other occupational groups had gained from the bargaining rounds. The union leadership had failed to make clear that most of the upgrading should take place at local level, after local and individual negotiations (ibid, 43).

To conclude, *Vårdförbundet* tried to combine the use of legislation – the prohibition of discriminatory wage setting due to sex – with the individualization of collective agreements in the public sector, which gave more room for pay according to individual competence. In the years after the strike, the union also urged its members to raise their competitive power in the labour market through further education and/or vocational training. From a retrospective view, the combination of these strategies seems to have borne fruit; from between the strike in 1995 and 2002, the members of *Vårdförbundet* have had an average annual salary raise of seven per cent.

Another advantage of the comparison with male-dominated work tasks was that it legitimated the nurses' claims in the eyes of the public. When settling a collective agreement, it is the stronger party that benefits the most from the final formulation. By also relying on labour market legislation, *Vårdförbundet* turned the focus from strength to rights; the nurses deserved much higher salaries because it was not 'fair' – either from a legal or a moral point of view – that they should be less paid than men of comparable skills, responsibility and work experience.

This appeal to 'fairness' was noticed and found reasonable by the media and the public at large, but regrettably, from a union perspective, neither by *Vårdförbundet*'s bargaining counterpart nor the appointed mediators (ibid, 121 and 144). Several of *Vårdförbundet*'s members or groups of members also took individual initiatives to press for higher salaries, but in each case, without results. One example is when, during the strike, 200 nurses in intensive care collectively reported their employer – the city of Stockholm – to the authorized governmental body, the Office of the Equal Opportunities Ombudsman (JämO), for wage discrimination. The report led to a law suit in the Labour Court, but not until 2001 (AD 2001 no. 76).

In a parallel case, a midwife in the town of Örebro in central Sweden brought her employer to the Labour Court in 1996 and also in 2001. The midwife claimed that her job was equal in all important aspects to the job of two male clinical engineers; thus, she was discriminated against due to her sex. The Court's decision, however, was that the midwife failed to prove that her work was comparable to the work of a clinical engineer. Accordingly, it remained unproven that she was discriminated against (AD 1996 no. 41). A majority of the Court's members made very high demands for evidence that the two jobs were actually equal. Despite the lack of success, though, the case was very important for the advantageous outcome of the local negotiations, which ran parallel to the trial.

In the second case, in 2001, the work tasks of the same midwife – and the work tasks of another midwife were once again compared to the work tasks of a clinical engineer. This time, however, the Court found the tasks equal; thus, it was up to the employer to justify the pay differences among the employees. Hence, to prove that the different salaries were not due to sex discrimination, the employer asserted three main arguments, first, the employer claimed, the clinical engineer had higher market value; secondly, the salaries of the two employees were regulated by two different collective agreements, thirdly, the clinical engineer, a man, was older. Accordingly, the pay discrepancy was not discriminating (AD 2001 no. 13).

The Court might be criticized for making the burden of proof too low vis-à-vis the employer's evidence. Still, the verdict was a leap forwards from the midwives' point of view. The fact that the Labour Court had established that a midwife's job was equal, in principle, to the job of a clinical engineer was a very useful argument to be used in salary negotiations to come. In a later case the same year, the Labour Court also found an intensive care nurse's work tasks equal to a clinical engineer's. The pay discrepancy between the two was not found discriminating though, due to different market positions (AD 2001 no. 76). To conclude about the two cases, the individual strategies, based on legislation, might very well be in accordance with trade union strategies and demands on re-evaluating women's tasks; to run bargaining and law suits on wage-discrimination parallel is a matter of co-operation and co-ordination: hard to achieve, yet possible.

The combination of legal and individual means was certainly a new strategy. The decentralization of collective bargaining had actually gone further in the public sector than in the private and the rounds in 1995 sped up the process (Elvander 1997). Accordingly, it was the female employees in health care and nursing who showed most interest in new forms of pay setting in the following years. They saw a chance to upgrade the status of their positions and work tasks and to achieve better salaries (Fürst 1997, 327–30). What is interesting is that this strategy was a collective one; individualization of pay setting should promote salary raises for women in health care and nursing at large. The intentions behind the individualization and the decentralization of pay setting, of course, was the opposite, to achieve higher wage spread and wage flexibility (cf. Bregn 1998, 306; Pontusson and Swenson 1996).

The collective agreement has never been systematically used as a means to achieve equality between the sexes (Dahlberg 1996). Moreover, only very few cases regarding sex discrimination in working life such as discriminatory wage setting, have been brought before the Labour Court. The Swedish Labour Court drew heavily on old preparatory works when interpreting the law against discrimination, despite several new clauses in the law of equality and the introduction of EC law from 1995 onwards. The Labour Court usually argues that the 'overall values' of the labour market parties should decide the wage-setting guidelines even at firm-level; thus, the employer seldom has to prove that individual wage discrepancies between male and female employees are discriminating.

Also, 'overall values', for instance in the collective agreements, are not gender-neutral because they are shaped and developed in a labour market which has traditionally been highly 'male dominated'. The Labour Court has found it very easy to accept the employers' argument that the male employees at large have a higher market value; male workers will find other firms which pay better if they do not get higher remuneration than their female colleagues (Fransson 2000b, 378–81). Hence, in practice it has been shown to be difficult – in fact, almost impossible – for women to gain from the combination of individualized pay setting and new legislation.

The labour market parties have made attempts to find ways to equalize the opportunities for men and women to achieve the same pay for comparable work tasks. One means has been systematic job evaluation, developed by the parties in the public sector. The attempt led to conflicts between male and female occupational groups, though. Therefore, systematic job evaluation has only been sparsely used (Fransson 2000b, 417).

Furthermore, there have been 'gendered' conflicts within some unions in the 1990s. For instance, the Municipal Workers' Union (*Kommunal*) lost many male members after the 1995 bargaining rounds, which ended in a strike, when many fire fighters showed their dissatisfaction by leaving the union. The fire fighters also came out the losers in the very extensive strike in May 2003. The Municipal Workers' Union finally settled an agreement which guaranteed better minimum wages for the union's lowest paid groups, while the fire fighters got an agreement worse than the one the Municipal Workers' Union had discontinued. It would take us, however, too far to discuss this issue more thoroughly in the limited space of this chapter.

Despite the difficulties of female workers to benefit from the reformed legislation, many important issues – such as the principle of equal pay for equal work – have no doubt been juridified. The introduction of the ban on discriminatory wage setting between men and women, in fact, is the most powerful government intervention ever in any Nordic industrial relations system (Fransson 2000b, 286–7). If the ban in the coming years proves to be more than just a paper tiger, it will most likely have an impact on conflict patterns. For instance, is it possible to strike against discriminatory wages if the wage setting has already been legally declared 'fair'? Many times before in Swedish and Nordic labour market legislation, a matter of interest has been turned into a matter of right, just like in this case. But here, there is less room for collective and individual negotiations. Moreover, the need for new strategies to be able to benefit from the new clauses has been emphasized.

Yet, even though the labour markets in the Nordic countries are highly juridified in international comparison, the juridification of wage setting is actually an adaptation to EC law. Another, more famous, Nordic characteristic is the collective agreements' strong legal status; the general government policy in Sweden has ever since the late 1930s been to leave wage setting in the main to the labour market parties. When unions such as *Vårdförbundet* tries to use the new legislation as a strategic means, they are, in fact, challenging a labour market tradition which is more than half a century old. On the other hand, *Vårdförbundet* is well aware of the problem and has made it very clear that it has no intention of systematically parading issues before the Labour Court. According to the President of *Vårdförbundet*, Eva Fernvall (2001, 6), challenging and changing existing values in collective agreements is not promoted by turning pay discrepancies into a Court issue.

Be that as it may, it is clear that union activity is of the utmost importance for the Labour Court's decisions in single cases regarding wage discrimination; if a union does not actively stress those issues in firm-level negotiations, it is very unlikely that the Labour Court will rule against an employer (Fransson 2000b, 380). Very few cases of wage discrimination have so far been brought to court, neither have the trade unions used the collective agreement as a means for equality between the sexes.

Concluding Discussion

The aim of this chapter was to present evidence for different 'male' and 'female' industrial conflict patterns and bargaining strategies. The results, however, provide no final answers; rather they should be understood as starting points for further studies of a previously neglected field of research. Our examples are too sparse to explain gender differences in labour market strategies and behaviour at large. Because the labour division between the sexes has been, and still is, strongly marked, occupational differences must first be more thoroughly researched. Yet, we believe we have rather strong evidence of some important historical trends and turning-points, which must be seriously considered to understand why trade unions dominated by women and other organized groups of women have acted and continue to act differently compared with the 'male' norm, regardless of which sector of the labour market we discuss.

Women have always had a weaker position in the labour market than men. Accordingly, occupations dominated by women have been weaker than 'male' ones. Historically, the demand for male workers has been strong in the important competition-exposed export industries, while women have mainly been found in backward industries or the public sector. Still, during the golden era of the Swedish model, the solidaristic wage policy was a guarantee of continuous pay increases, even in the backward sectors of the economy. In return, the unions in these sectors, which to a large extent were dominated by women, had to offer 'loyalty' to the system. One of the purposes of the centralized bargaining system was to avoid wage-price spirals. Workers in the lower-paid industries had to accept the negotiating framework set out by the export industries because higher collective wage claims in any single sector could risk the whole system.

When the SAF's decentralization drive took off in 1990, the 'loyalty' strategy was no longer possible to maintain. Even though the decentralization process was never taken as far as the SAF originally called for, it was obvious to everyone that the whole industrial relations system was in a state of flux. Moreover, the 'female' public sector unions could no longer rely on solidarity from the unions in the private sector, which complicated the situation in the late 1980s and early 1990s even further.

In this historical context, we distinguish two of the most interesting new collective means in the 1990s, both actually radical breaks with the traditional thinking dominated by the solidaristic wage policy. The first one is to rely on legislation rather than collective bargaining in connection with remuneration issues; the other is to use individual wage claims as a collective means.

Despite the introduction of new labour market laws in the 1970s, such as the 1974 Employment Security Act (LAS) and the 1976 Codetermination Act (MBL), the core of the Swedish model has always been the collective agreement. Thus, the systematic use of the legislation against wage discrimination to increase women's salaries in the health sector no doubt is a new means. Important unions have sanctioned it, but no union has yet systematically tried to take cases before the Labour Court.

The new strategy is not only a result of a transformation of the collective bargaining system. The shift was also facilitated by some general changes in the labour market legislation. Similarly to the other Nordic countries, Swedish labour law has moved towards a system where the individual's rights in working life are laid out in laws on discrimination rather than in clauses in a collective agreement. Since 1999, there are five such laws in the Swedish legislation.[10]

Furthermore, even if the strategy is new, the idea actually dates back to the late 1970s and early 1980s. Nordic students of law engaged in lively discussion about the opportunities to use legislation as a means for social change 'from below'. In other words, legislation is not just a means to protect people with small economic and societal power resources, but is also a means to achieve goals in the face of resistance for single individuals, groups of individuals, alternative movements or a political opposition (cf. Hydén 1982). The debate faded away by the early or mid–1980s, but in the light of the latest labour market development, it no doubt still has a bearing.[11]

Concluding from the evidence presented in this chapter, however, relying on legislation does not seem to be enough to achieve goals such as pay increases. Still, it is an interesting means in combination with other strategies. One such strategy might be labelled 'collective individualism'. If, for instance, a single nurse claims that her work should be remunerated at the same level as the work of a man with a comparable job, it is an individual strategy. If, however, a group of women simultaneously asserted the same claim and if a union sanctions the claim, it is a collective strategy.[12] Of course such a strategy is highly dependent on the use of legislation; otherwise, there would be no norm of 'comparable jobs' to refer to or to rely on. Yet, the few examples we have seen so far show that it is very difficult to combine the two strategies in practice.

In fact, it is too early to talk of 'strategies', what we have seen this far are rather tactical solutions to specific situations. Be that as it may, both the use of legislation as a means 'from below' and 'collective individualism' *might* easily develop into organized trade union strategies, which we hope this chapter has shown.

Notes

1 The authors are grateful to the editors and the other participants in the Oñati workshop for fruitful 'peer reviewing'. We also wish to thank the members of our other Nordic research network, the *NordFram* group, for their help and for comments on previous drafts.
2 Women's organization rate is slightly higher in the public sector and slightly lower in the private sector than men's.
3 A special group of rural hands who got their allowance in kind were still covered, however, by an old law, the so-called *legostadga*, until 1926.
4 We make a distinction between female and male unions on the one hand and female- and male-dominated unions on the other. Female unions were only open for women.
5 A ban on strikes is always inaugurated in the collective agreement.

6 The Industry Agreement or, more correctly, the 'Agreement on industrial development and wage formation', is an agreement signed by most SAF affiliated employers' associations within the competition-exposed sector and their trade union counterparts. In practice, the signing of the Industry Agreement signalled that the SAF had given up the struggle for decentralization of collective bargaining, provided that the export industry should remain wage leading (Elvander 2001).

7 In the original text, '*– Det är fullständigt groteskt att tanter som läser sagor på dagis ska ha lika höga löner som deras män med hårda verkstadsjobb.*'

8 Previous bans on wage discrimination have been registered in Swedish labour law since 1980 and EC law since 1957.

9 Assistant nurses are not organized by Vårdförbundet, but by the Swedish Municipal Workers' Union (*Kommunal*), which is affiliated with the blue-collar confederation LO. *Vårdförbundet* also organizes laboratory technicians, whose wage-struggle has never received much public attention, though.

10 It is interesting that it is not the unions, but the SAF that has opposed this development. To achieve a flexible labour market, the SAF argues, it is necessary to deregulate all aspects of working life. Hence, no new laws should be registered, not even to guarantee individual rights (Government Bill 1997/98 no. 177).

11 At the time for the debate, this strategy to use legislation as a means for social change got the Swedish name *legalstrategi*, which is difficult to translate, but in English would be something similar to 'legal strategy' or 'law strategy'. Because the expression is also awkward in Swedish, we have decided not to use a defined term at all.

12 Labour market legislation in the Nordic countries only permits employee representatives to speak for their clients as individuals, not as a collective of workers. A Swedish Public Investigation in 1994 asked for changes on this point, but this request has not yet resulted in any government bill.

References

AD (1975), *Arbetsdomstolens domar*, no. 31.

AD (1996), *Arbetsdomstolens domar*, no. 41.

AD (2001a), *Arbetsdomstolens domar*, no. 13.

AD (2001b), *Arbetsdomstolens domar*, no. 76.

Alasilta–Hagman, Lea and Sinikka Pitko (1984), *Naiset lakossa, Laupeudentyöstä palkkataisteluun*, Tammi, Helsinki.

Bercusson, Brian and Linda Dickens (1996), *Equal Opportunities and Collective Bargaining in Europe, 1, Defining the Issues*, European Foundation for the Improvement of Living and Working Conditions and Office for Official Publications of the European Communities, Loughlinstown, Dublin and Luxembourg.

Bregn, Kirsten (1998), 'A Silent Revolution in Denmark's Public Sector Pay System', in Daniel Fleming, Pauli Kettunen, Henrik Søborg and Christer Thörnqvist (eds), *Global Redefining of Working Life – A New Nordic Agenda for Competence and Participation?* Nordic Council of Ministers, Copenhagen, pp. 293–319.

Bruun, Niklas (1994), *The Transformation of Nordic Industrial Relations*, Swedish Institute for Work Life Research, reprint no. 4–1994, Stockholm.

Clegg, Hugh A. (1976), *Trade Unionism under Collective Bargaining, A Theory Based on Comparisons of Six Countries*, Blackwell, Oxford.

Crouch, Colin and Alessandro Pizzorno (eds) (1978), *The Resurgence of Class Conflict in Western Europe Since 1968*, Macmillan, London.

Dahlberg, Anita (1996), 'Jämställdhet och kollektivavtal i EU, Studie av förhållandena i Sverige', Europeiska fonden för förbättring av levnads- och arbetsvillkoren, Working paper WP/96/59/SV.

Edwards, P.K. (1981), 'The Strike-proneness of British Manufacturing Establishments', *British Journal of Industrial Relations*, Vol. 19, pp. 135–48.

Elvander, Nils (1997), 'The Swedish Bargaining System in the Melting Pot', in Nils Elvander and Bertil Holmlund, *The Swedish Bargaining System in the Melting Pot, Institutions, Norms and Outcomes in the 1990s*, Arbetslivsinstitutet, Solna, pp. 5–89.

Elvander, Nils (2002), 'A New Swedish Regime for Collective Bargaining and Conflict Resolution', *European Journal of Industrial Relations*, Vol. 8, pp. 197–216.

Eurostat (2001).

Fernvall, Eva (2001), 'Ansvaret vilar på parterna', *Lag & Avtal*, no. 2, p. 6.

Fransson, Susanne (2000a), ' Freedom of Contract, Parity and Collective Regulation', in Marcel van der Linden and Richard Price (eds) *The Rise and Development of Collective Labour Law*, Peter Lang, Bern.

Fransson, Susanne (2000b), *Lönediskriminering, En arbetsrättslig studie av könsdiskriminerande löneskillnader och konflikten mellan kollektivavtal och lag*, Iustus, Uppsala.

Fransson, Susanne (2001), 'Collective and Individual Strategies – Women's and Men's Wages', in Kevät Nousiainen et al. (eds), *The Responsible Selves, Women in the Nordic Legal Culture*, Ashgate, Aldershot, pp. 195–221.

Fürst, Gunilla (1997), 'När kvinnor utvecklar nya lönemodeller', in *Ledare, makt och kön, SOU*, no. 135, pp. 327–46.

Government Bill (1997/98), no. 177.

Hydén, Håkan (ed.) (1982), *Rätten som instrument för social förändring, Om legalstrategier*, Lund, Liber.

Johansson, Klas and Jessika Grahm (1975), *Vi är ju ändå bara städerskor*, Barrikaden, Göteborg.

Julkunen, Raija and Liisa Rantalaiho (1993), 'Women on Strike – Nonexistent or Silenced?', in Pauli Kettunen (ed.), *Strike and Social Change*, Turku Provincial Museum Publication Series 7, Turku, pp. 97–114.

Kjellberg, Anders (1999), 'Fagorganisering i Norge og Sverige i et internasjonalt perspektiv', in *Arbejderhistorie 1999, Årbok for Arbeiderbevegelsens Arkiv og Bibliotek*, Arbeiderbevegelsens Arkiv og Bibliotek, Oslo, pp. 57–83.

Knowles, K.G.J.C. (1952), *Strikes, A Study in Industrial Conflict*, Blackwell, Oxford.

Lane, Linda (1995), 'Unsuitable Work for Women? Women Employed as Trolley Conductors in Gothenburg, Sweden during World War II', BA thesis, Department of Economic History, Göteborg University, Göteborg.

Larsson, Lars-Evert (2001), 'Women's Wages within the Swedish Engineering Industry, A Historical Perspective', in Steve Jefferys, Frederik Mispelblom Beyer and Christer Thörnqvist (eds), *European Working Lives, Continuities and Change in Management and Industrial Relations in France, Scandinavia and the U.K.*, Edward Elgar, Cheltenham and Northampton, MA, pp. 147–56.

Nielsen, Ruth (1979), *Kvindearbejdsret*, Juristforbundets forlag, København.

Nilsson, Bengt (1996), *Kvinnor i statens tjänst – Från biträden till tjänstemän, En aktörsinriktad undersökning av kvinnliga statstjänstemäns organisering, strategier och kamp under 1900-talets första hälft*, Almqvist & Wiksell International, Stockholm.

Norrbottens-Kuriren (1975), 22 April.

Olsen, Anne (1984), 'Kvindeligt Arbejderforbund – Mellem kvindekrav og partikrav', in Anne Margrete Berg et al. (eds), *Kvindfolk, En danmarkshistorie fra 1600 til 1980, bind 2, 1900-1980*, Gyldendal, København, pp. 227–42.

Olsson, Åke (1996), *Nu eller aldrig! Om kvinnors kamp för rättvis lön*, Federativ, Stockholm.

Östberg, Kjell (1997), *Efter rösträtten, Kvinnornas utrymme efter det demokratiska genombrottet*, Bruno Östlings bokförl. Symposion, Eslöv.

Overud, Johanna (2000), 'I beredskap med Fru Lojal, Husmodern i nationens tjänst 1939–1945', *Arbetarhistoria*, no. 3–4 (95–96), pp. 18–25.

Pontusson, Jonas and Peter Swenson (1996), 'Labor Markets, Production Strategies, and Wage Bargaining Institutions, The Swedish Employer Offensive in Comparative Perspective', *Comparative Political Studies*, Vol. 29, pp. 223–50.

SAF (1990), *Marknad och mångfald – SAFs program för 90-talet*, SAFs förlag, Stockholm.

SAF–tidningen (1990), no. 33.

Shorter, Edward and Charles Tilly (1974), *Strikes in France, 1830-1968*, Cambridge University Press, London.

Stokke, Torgeir Aarvaag and Christer Thörnqvist (2001), 'Strikes and Collective Bargaining in the Nordic Countries', *European Journal of Industrial Relations*, Vol. 7, pp. 245–67.

Svensson, Lars (1996), 'Politics or Market Forces? The Determinants of the Relative Wage Movements of Female Industrial Workers in Sweden, 1960–1990', *Scandinavian Economic History Review*, Vol. 44, pp. 161–82.

Swenson, Peter (1992), 'Union Politics, the Welfare State, and Intraclass Conflict in Sweden and Germany', in Miriam Golden and Jonas Pontusson (eds), *Bargaining for Change, Union Politics in North America and Europe*, Cornell University Press, Ithaca, N.Y. & London, pp. 45–76.

Thörnqvist, Christer (1994), *Arbetarna lämnar fabriken, Strejkrörelser i Sverige under efterkrigstiden, deras bakgrund, förlopp och följder*, Avhandlingar från historiska institutionen i Göteborg 9, Göteborg.

Thörnqvist, Christer (1998), 'Hur trivialiteter blir ideologi, Vilda strejker i Arbetsdomstolen under 20 år', *Arkiv för studier i arbetarrörelsens historia*, no. 72, pp. 39–63.

Thörnqvist, Christer (2001), 'What Do Strikes Strike? The Impact of Strikes and Lockouts in Sweden 1975-1990', in Steve Jefferys, Frederik Mispelblom Beyer and Christer Thörnqvist (eds), *European Working Lives, Continuities and Change in Management and Industrial Relations in France, Scandinavia and the U.K.*, Edward Elgar, Cheltenham and Northampton, MA, pp. 157–71.

Tilly, Charles, Louise Tilly and Richard Tilly (1975), *The Rebellious Century, 1830-1930*, Harvard University Press, Cambridge, MA.

Traxler, Franz, Sabine Blaschke and Bernhard Kittel (2001), *National Labour Relations in Internationalized Markets, A Comparative Study of Institutions, Change, and Performance*, Oxford University Press, Oxford.

Waldemarson, Ylva (1996), 'Kön, klass och statens finanser – En historia om statligt arbetsgivarskap och statsanställda kvinnor 1870-1925', in Lasse Kvarnström, Ylva Waldemarson and Klas Åmark (eds), *I statens tjänst, Statlig arbetsgivarpolitik och fackliga strategier 1870-1930*, Arkiv, Lund.

Chapter 4

Promoting Equality in the Workplace: Legislative Intent and Reality

Karoliina Ahtela

Introduction[1]

It is widely agreed that the realization of equality between women and men cannot be based on the prohibition of discrimination alone. Active measures undertaken by the parties concerned are needed to promote equality. Since 1987, when the Act on Equality between Women and Men (the Equality Act[2]) was introduced, Finnish employers have been required by law to promote equality between men and women in the workplace. Now, after 16 years have passed, only meager promotional activity on the part of employers can be recognised. Why has it not been possible to initiate promotion of equality in the workplace to the extent promulgated by the Equality Act? This is the question addressed in this chapter. Answers to this question are sought by assessing the Equality Act from the point of view of law implementation research.[3]

Tala[4] (2001) proposes that the effects of a law reform be studied in relation to: 1) the objectives of the law reform, 2) the substance (strategy and means of regulation) of the law reform, 3) the implementation of the law reform, 4) the reaction of the objects of the law reform, especially reactions such as compliance or non-compliance. The model presented by Tala is used in this chapter to structure the discussion. However, Teubner has warned against evaluating law reforms using the causal logic of 'political goal – legal norm – social effects' (Teubner 1985a; Teubner 1985b). He presents a model based on circular interactions, where three basic types of failures of law are recognised. Thus, the law reform at issue in this chapter is also analysed from the angle proposed by Teubner.

The chapter is structured in the following way. First, the background of the Equality Act and its provisions concerning the promotion of equality are presented. Secondly, empirical evidence on the promotion of equality in the workplace in compliance with the Equality Act is analysed. Thirdly, the various reasons why the purpose of the legislation has not been realised to the fullest extent are analysed, using the framework of Tala: objectives for the law are discussed, the regulatory strategy and means of the law are analysed, problems of the implementation of the law are considered and reactions by the objects of the regulation are assessed. Fourthly, the Equality Act is analysed from the point of view of various failures of law, as defined by Teubner. Finally, conclusions are drawn regarding the future development of the provisions concerning the promotion of equality in the Equality Act.

Objectives and Provisions in the Finnish Equality Act

Background and Objectives

The starting point for the preparation of the Equality Act was the Convention on the Elimination of All Forms of Discrimination against Women (CEDAW), which Finland signed in 1980 but ratified only in 1986. It was held that legislative measures were needed before the convention could be ratified.[5] In this regard, the following passage in the preparatory work of the Equality Act (Government Bill, *HE*, 57/1985) is revealing: 'the starting point has been that Finland has generally endeavoured to realise the provisions of human right conventions as effectively as other European countries and especially as the Nordic countries'. Legislation relating to equality between sexes came into force in Finland, as the last Nordic country,[6] in 1987.

It is illuminating to compare the emergence of the equality legislation in Finland with that in Norway and Sweden, based on the analysis of Bacchi (1996). In Norway, the traditional image of women as carers and nurturers remained stronger than in neighbouring countries and the labour force participation rate lower. The feminist movement promoted the equality legislation in Norway. The women activists appealed to the common understanding that women see the world differently because they are nurturers and carers and, hence, their views need to be represented, especially in public life. On the other hand, in the 1970s there was a recognition in government and business circles that women needed to be encouraged to join the labour force. These were the driving forces behind Norway's equality act of 1978. The act contained the prohibition of discrimination based on sex, but no provisions for the promotion of equality by employers – except for the possibility of positive discrimination. The government, however, decided on successive Action Plans for promotion of equality, focusing on education and governmental organizations.

Women's labour force participation had already been an issue in Sweden long since and the participation rate of women was relatively high. As early as in the 1970s, the government had introduced various positive action schemes for promoting women (or the 'underrepresented sex'). During the long reign of the social democratic party, a corporatist governance model evolved in which collective agreements between trade unions and employers' organizations played a central role. In fact, the idea of equality legislation was opposed by trade unions and employers who anticipated interference in their joint decision-making. Thus, a bourgeois government managed to pass the equality act in 1980 and also a major amendment to it in 1992.

The law was a labour law. It was divided into two parts: the obligation of the employer to promote equality and the prohibition of discrimination.

To the contrary, relatively little of social debate and need for this legislation was observed in Finland. The women's movement and other social movements played only moderate roles in the gender equality process (Kjeldstad 2001). In comparison to other Nordic countries, women in Finland had already been integrated into the labour market prior to the emergence of the welfare state. The earlier agrarian society had been relatively egalitarian regarding gender (Julkunen). The gender gap in (total) earnings[7] between women and men was the lowest in Finland in comparison to other Nordic countries, Germany, the Netherlands and UK in the 1980s and 1990s (Sørensen 2001). In a similar vein, the economic independence (from their partner) of Finnish women was high in the 1980s, judging from the fact that it was the highest among the mentioned countries in the 1990s (Sørensen 2001).

Thus, even if the ideal state of full equality had certainly not been realised by the 1980s, the Finnish women enjoyed significant equality, which evidently led to the situation where feminist issues were not prominently on the political agenda. Also, as Nousiainen (2000) has argued, intense involvement by the labour market organizations in structuring the welfare state had perhaps reduced the question of gender equality to something secondary in the public mind. In fact, Finland lacked both of the two factors that had served to instigate equality legislation in many other countries, viz., an increased demand for a female labour force and a powerful women's movement (Ellilä et al. 1983). Thus, the need to ratify the CEDAW seems to have been the primary triggering factor for equality legislation in Finland, together with the model set by the neighbouring Scandinavian countries.

Provisions Regarding Promotion of Equality

The law reform in 1987 The Equality Act of 1987 obligates the employer to promote equality by encouraging both women and men to apply for vacancies, by promoting the assignment of women and men to different tasks, by creating equal opportunities for career advancement and by developing working conditions that suit both sexes. This obligation applied both to public and private employers. No sanctions were attached to a failure to comply. A related provision allowed for procedures of positive discrimination if they were based on a plan. For the implementation of the law, two authorities were created: Ombudsman for Equality and Equality Board. The Ombudsman has the task to supervise the observance of the act in private firms and in public administration and business. The Ombudsman shall especially provide advice and counselling to prevent the continuation or recurrence of unlawful practices. The Equality Board gives opinions to courts on such violations of the act for which compensation may be claimed.

The amendments of 1995 In the law reform of 1995, the obligation to promote equality was made more stringent. It was required that each employer promote equality systematically and purposefully (Section 6). Also, reconciliation of work and family, as well as prevention of sexual harassment in the workplace were added to the targets of promotion of equality. In addition, a provision (Section 6 a) was added, according to which an employer regularly employing at least 30 persons has to include measures for equality promotion in certain other annual planning that is legally required. The law contained no sanctions related to lack of compliance with this provision.[8] In the following, these provisions are presented, as well as the provision concerning plans as a justification for positive discrimination:

> Section 6 **Employer's duty to promote equality**
>
> Each employer shall promote equality between women and men within working life purposefully and systematically.
> In order to promote equality in working life, the employer shall, with due regard to the resources available and any other relevant factors,
> (1) act so that both women and men apply for vacancies;
> (2) promote an equitable recruitment of women and men in the various jobs and create for them equal opportunities for promotion;
> (3) develop working conditions so that they are suitable for both women and men, and facilitate the reconciliation of working life and family life for women and men; and
> (4) ensure, as far as possible, that an employee is not subjected to sexual harassment.
>
> Section 6a **Measures to promote equality**
>
> If an employer regularly employs a staff of at least 30, said employer shall include measures to further equality between women and men at the workplace in the annual personnel and training plan or the action programme for labour protection.
>
> Section 9 **Procedure that shall not be deemed to constitute discrimination**
>
> For the purposes of this Act, the following shall not be deemed to constitute discrimination based on sex:
> ...
> (4) procedure based on a plan aiming at practical fulfilment of the aim of this Act.

Impact of Equality Promotion Provisions

Impact on Employers

The original provision of the Equality Act, as enacted in 1987, concerning advancement of equality must be judged as having had only minimal impact. There is no empirical information on this matter, but the following passage in the government's proposal before the law reform in 1995 indicates this claim (Government Bill, *HE*, 90/1994): 'The regulations in the present section 6 about the employer's responsibilities for advancing equality have not led to such changes towards decrease of occupational segregation by sex and equal possibilities for promotion which were targeted when the law was decreed'.

And what impacts has the law reform in 1995 achieved in practice regarding the promotion of equality? None of the three surveys on the implementation of equality planning addressed the impacts of equality planning.

The Finnish Institute of Occupational Health carried out in 1996 an enquête study for investigating attitudes and competences in companies regarding promotion of equality (Kauppinen and Veikkola 1997). The study covered companies with over 30 employees. It came out that 15 percent of companies promoted equality actively. Likewise, 15 per cent of companies took equality into account, even if no specific measures had been carried out. In 40 per cent of companies, it was thought that equality would best be realised gradually, without any specific measures being implemented, and in 28 per cent of companies, other issues took priority.[9] An equality plan had been prepared, either as an independent document or as a part of the annual personnel and training plan or the action programme for labour protection, in 11 per cent of companies and 12 per cent of companies intended to prepare a plan. Thus, of the companies submitting answers to the enquête, 77 per cent of them had not or did not intend to prepare an equality plan. This study was conducted so soon after the enactment of the Equality Act, and before any guidelines from the Ombudsman for Equality could be promulgated, that it partly represents the starting point situation regarding the law reform in 1995.

In 1998, the trade union of clerical industrial workers in Finland (*Suomen Teollisuustoimihenkilöiden Liitto* 1999) organised a study on the views among its members on discrimination based on sex, the occurrence of sexual harassment and opportunities for the promotion of equality through equality planning. Of the respondents six per cent were at workplaces, where an equality plan had been prepared or its preparation underway. More than 60 per cent of the respondents did not know whether an equality plan had been made or whether it was under preparation.

In 1998, the Office of the Ombudsman for Equality conducted an investigation into the equality planning in the public and private sectors (Kaasinen 1998). From the respondents (105 organizations, mostly large ones) 78 per cent had prepared or intended to prepare an equality plan; more than half had already prepared one. From the companies investigated (large domestic or international companies), 52 per cent had an equality plan. From the ministries, ten out of 13 had an equality plan. However, the actual significance given to equality plans is manifested by the fact that only one ministry had mentioned an equality plan in its annual report. Regarding other governmental offices and institutions, 15 had prepared an equality plan, nine intended to prepare and 13 had not prepared and did not intend to prepare one.

To sum up, the studies indicate that several large and multinational companies have started equality planning after 1995; however, it is rare in smaller companies. In some companies equality planning has started before 1995 or even before 1987. Regarding public organizations, the situation seems similar: large organizations have been more active than smaller organizations. However, equality planning seems to cover only the minority of the employees nation-wide.

Impacts on Equality

In the following, we investigate whether statistical data would reveal such improvement in women's position that could be attributable to the Equality Act.

The share of women among the senior officials and upper management has increased from 17 per cent in 1988 to 23 per cent in 1998 (Haataja 1997; Women and Men in Finland 1999). However, this share was even higher in 1992, 25 per cent, and it has thus declined somewhat in the 1990s, apparently due to the recession. Thus, factors other than employers' promotion of equality appear to influence the share of women among the senior officials and upper management.

Regarding the highest levels of management, there is scanty information. It deals only with the present situation (Pulkkinen 2000). In the government, only three per cent of department managers and chief directors in Ministries are women. Of municipal directors, eight per cent are women, and of municipal department directors, ten per cent. Data on the share of women in the boards of companies is indicative only. Regarding the 150 companies listed on the Stock Exchange of Helsinki, only three per cent of board members are female. Another survey focused on 50 largest companies of Finland. Of board members, six per cent are female, and of managing team members, 11 per cent. In general, these figures are so low that hardly any progress regarding the participation of women at the highest levels of management seems to have taken place during the period when the Equality Act has been in force.

Regarding university professors in Finland, the share of women is the highest in Europe, 20.4 per cent in 2001 (Ministry of Education KOTA Database, *Opetusministeriö*). However, this achievement is mostly related to the high educational level of women, rather than any specific equality efforts by universities.

Neither has there been much impact regarding the pay gap between women and men. The pay gap has only slightly decreased during the period when the Equality Act has been in force. For full time employees, average monthly earnings of women were 80 per cent of men's earnings in 1987, and 82 per cent in 1998 (Women and Men in Finland 1999). This pay gap can primarily be explained through the vertical and horizontal segregation of jobs based on gender (Meyerson and Peterson 1997), the level of which has been one of the highest in the European Union (Finland's action plan for employment 1999). Segregation has not changed in any notable way between 1990 and 2000 (Finland's action plan for employment 2001).

To sum up, any impact of the promotion of equality by employers is hardly discerned from the statistical data concerning the very issues which were the original justification in the preparatory works for the enactment of the Equality Act (Government Bill, *HE* 57/1985): pay, occupational status and opportunities for career advancement.

Why the Promotion of Equality as Intended Has Not Been Realized

Thus, it can be said that the promotion of equality by employers, as prescribed by the Equality Act since 1987 and especially since the amendment in 1995, has gotten off to a slow start[10] and that impacts from such work are difficult to discern. Thus, the provisions concerning promotion of equality have had negligible impacts, even if 14 years have passed since the enactment of the Equality Act and six years since the last law reform where these provisions were clarified. Why has not the legislation been able to realise the intention of the legislator concerning promotion of equality by the employer? In the following, this will be discussed utilising Tala's (2001) framework, mentioned above, for analysing impacts of law reforms.

Objectives for the Law

The purpose of the Equality Act is to promote equality between men and women and to prevent discrimination based on gender[11] (Government Bill, *HE*, 57/1985). In the preparatory works, the government justified the law generally by referring to differences in the actual conditions of women and men, especially in the area of employment: pay, occupational status and opportunities for career advancement. The occupational segregation based on gender was emphasized as a problem. In a section of the preparatory work entitled 'The need for law reform', developments in other countries are described, as well as the intention of ratifying the CEDAW. Further, it is stated that the (then) current legislation does not sufficiently promote efforts towards equality and is not effective in preventing discrimination.

Thus, as discussed above, the main stimulus and motivation for the Equality Act came from outside sources, primarily from the need to ratify the CEDAW,[12] rather than from internal social and political forces. The real, but hidden, objective was to 'behave orderly among nations' and to ratify the convention when other countries had done so. Moreover, it can be said that the justification for the Equality Act, as discussed above, is quite far removed from the motivation of the CEDAW convention itself, expressed in its preamble: 'extensive discrimination against women continues to exist'.

Obviously, objectives and justification, which are not based on problems defined in domestic social and political debate but rather on an attempt to make problems defined outside the country fit to local conditions, may create difficulties relating to the interpretation of the objectives of the law. In such a situation, one would not wonder if the explicit objectives for the law became rhetorical or symbolic only. In fact, Nummijärvi (2000) argues that the provisions on equality promotion to a great extent are more symbolic than instrumental. Indeed, goal-setting for a law reform may influence how different actors commit to implement the provisions and to comply with them (Tala 2001). The influence of goal-setting of the Equality Act on regulatory strategy, implementation and reaction of employers is analysed in subsequent sections.

Strategy and Means of Regulation

Three kinds of failure regarding the strategy and means of regulation can be distinguished (Tala 2001). First, the problem of the law-drafter's lack of information: he/she does not know sufficiently the problem in question or means of regulation. Secondly, the problem of the law-drafter's lack of will: contradictory interests of actors participating in decision-making may prevent the utilization of the best means of regulation. Thirdly, the problem of the law-drafter's lack of regulatory ability: there simply are no such means of regulation that would produce the intended result.

Of these three types of failure, the problem of the lack of information can be recognised most clearly[13] in the case of the Equality Act, especially vis-à-vis two issues: deficient basis for decision-making and shallow notion of promotion of equality. In addition, there is type of failure not mentioned by Tala: technical problems related to the clarity and consistency of the law, in this case especially regarding the interrelation of promotion and planning as well as the nature of equality plans. These problems (the lack of information and technical problems) are presented below.

Deficient basis for decision-making One would expect that before the amendment in 1995 the situation in the field, regarding the promotion of equality, would have been carefully studied and different strategies evaluated. However, this was not the case. The amendment was not based on empirical studies or benchmarking with other countries. Rather it seems to have been based on vague assumptions on what was happening at workplaces and on how employers could be stimulated to promote equality. Especially regarding the strategy of implementation, the vagueness of thinking and the lack of knowledge about comparative studies were evident. This deficiency resulted in confusion about both the relation between promotion of equality and equality planning and about the nature of equality plans. These problems of regulatory strategy will be discussed in the following sections.

What is the promotion of equality by employers? There are two basic models of promotion of equality by employers: affirmative action and managing diversity. The American model of affirmative action (Skrentny 1996), which primarily targets a quantitatively balanced labour force in a company, can be seen as the historical starting point. The original motivation for affirmative action arose from the overt discrimination of coloured persons, especially of blacks, and the resultant exclusion of them from many areas of the society, including employment. However, in the legislation of the United States, gender discrimination, somewhat incidentally (Roseberry 1999), has been bundled with racial discrimination, the elimination of which has enjoyed a much wider political backing than gender discrimination alone. Thus, affirmative action was extended to cover also measures for overcoming inequality based on sex.

Affirmative action is characterised by a detailed procedural regulation that determines how a company must prepare an affirmative action programme (Reskin 1998). The obligation to practice affirmative action in a private company is contractual and is based on the power of the U.S. federal state as a customer: the federal state demands affirmative action from its contractors (providing products or services), except when the annual contract sum is small. If a company fails to practice affirmative action as specified, a sanction will follow. Another mode of obligation is encountered in the case of federal government as an employer. The President of the United States, using the highest executive power, commands federal organizations to implement affirmative action in their role as employers. In both cases, the obligation comes from outside the employer organization, and it is based on an ethical consideration.

In the other model, the model of managing diversity, the starting point is the strategy of the company (Advancing Women in Business 1998). The purpose of managing diversity is to benefit the whole organization and the whole personnel. Characteristically, managing diversity is tailored to the situation: on the one side, problems put forward by the personnel are tackled, and on the other side, managing diversity actions are linked to the strategy of the company. This model is implemented using the best practices and examples drawn from leading companies.

An important question is how the implementation of these two models can be advanced and stimulated. Regarding affirmative action, the crucial point is in the establishment of the obligation and in the creation of enforcement machinery that monitors the realization of the obligation. Here, the affirmative action programme prepared by the employer organization and its realization are in the focus. As mentioned above, the obligation may be based on the power of the customer to require contractually that some procedures be followed by its suppliers, on the executive power, but also on the legislative power, as in the case of Sweden, where equality plans are legally required from employers[14] and a lack of compliance with this provision is legally sanctioned.

Instead, in the case of managing diversity, there is no question of imposing any sort of obligation. First, it is not reasonable to oblige companies to act in their own best interest. Secondly, the situational differences within and among companies make it impossible to prepare such detailed procedural guidelines, on the basis of which it could be determined whether or not a company has fulfilled its obligation. However, the government is not fully without means for advancing the concept of managing diversity in companies. Research may provide empirical evidence for how useful managing diversity is from a business point of view. Also, it is possible to support benchmarking activities towards defining the best practices.

On which model is based the kind of promotion of equality between sexes, as required by the Equality Act? Not directly on either; it is rather a mixed model that contains elements from both. The starting point for the promotion of equality is ethical, and an obligation has been created through legislation. Regarding these features, the question is about the affirmative action (positive action) model. However, the law does not prescribe the procedure of promotion, and there are no enforcement mechanisms. These features suggest that the managing diversity model is in question.

This incoherence can be said to be one root cause for problems. There is an obligation for the employer, in the sense of affirmative action, but the procedural prescription and the enforcement mechanism are lacking, and thus the full functionality of the affirmative action model is not achieved. The type of promotion of equality wished is obviously similar to the managing diversity model, but the employer is not stimulated in ways that are in line with that model.

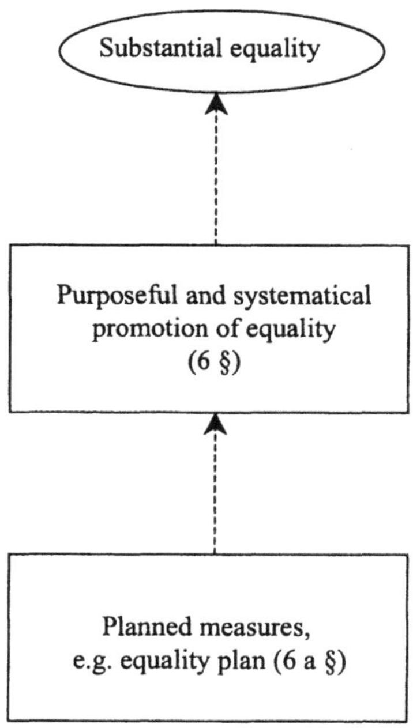

Figure 1. Equality plan, promotion of equality and substantial equality

Confusion over the relation between promotion of equality and equality planning. The Equality Act itself is clear regarding the distinction between promotion of equality (Section 6) and equality planning (Section 6 a). Both are required from an employer: promotion of equality is directly linked to substantial equality, one objective of the Act, and planning is a means for realising such promotion (Figure 1). However, this clarity is exceptional; both the preparatory work and the guidelines for employers (Toolkit for gender equality) mix up equality planning and promotion of equality. Thus, the erroneous view is conveyed that the obligation of the law is realised when an equality plan has been prepared. The fact that the measures to further equality have to be planned annually, whereas the obligation for promotion has been expressed in general terms, naturally adds to the possibility of this erroneous interpretation. This one-sided emphasis on equality planning directs attention away from any concrete promotion of equality and their results – even if the intention behind the law reform was exactly the opposite.

Confusion about equality plans In addition, the law reform of 1995 created confusion on the nature of equality plans. In fact, there are three different notions of plans in the Act:

1. As defined in Section 6: 'Each employer shall promote equality systematically' (the exact translation of the Finnish term used in the Act, '*suunnitelmallisesti*', is 'according to a plan'; however, according to the lexicon, the usual English equivalent is 'systematically').
2. As defined in Section 6a: Annual plan of measures, included in certain other, annual plans.
3. As defined in Section 9: Plans that allow positive action for the purposes of the Act.

Unfortunately, the preparatory work failed to define the mutual relationships among these notions of plans. Thus, for example, it remains open whether a company has fulfilled the obligation of the Act by preparing an independent Equality Plan (point 1 above) but neglecting the annual plans (point 2). The guidelines for employers, a publication prepared by the Ombudsman for Equality, let it be understood that this option would be possible, even if the wording of the Act is clear that only annual plans are explicitly required. Furthermore, in the preparatory work before the original law in 1987, it was held that plans of point 3 do not need to be written: even established practice will suffice. Whether the law reform of 1995 changed this interpretation, is open to debate.

Summary on regulatory strategy and means At the outset, the basis for law-drafting seems to have been deficient. This deficiency, evidently, has led, for its part, to an incoherent regulatory strategy and to problems of a lack of clarity and a lack of consistency of the law.

The Implementation of the Law Reform

From a number of central issues and results in implementation research, presented by Tala (2001), we will focus on those that are most relevant in this context. First, according to Tala implementation processes and implementation structures have a central role in implementation. Secondly, the front-line actor is in a key position regarding implementation. Thirdly, optional and diverse implementation strategies are available.

With regard to implementation structures, the Ombudsman for Equality and his/her Office is the only organization implementing the provisions on promotion of equality. The Act provides for no specific instruments for the Equality Ombudsman regarding the implementation of the provisions for the promotion of equality, but the general obligations of the Ombudsman to spread information and give advice cover also this aspect. However, the primary task of the Ombudsman is to monitor the compliance with the prohibition of discrimination and discriminating advertising; only as far as there are any resources left, the Ombudsman shall monitor the compliance with the provisions on promotion of equality (Government Bill, *HE* 57/1985). Thus, implementation of the provisions for the promotion of equality is clearly a secondary task for the Ombudsman.

In practice, four kinds of implementation processes can be identified. First, the Office of the Ombudsman has published guidelines for the employers on equality planning (Toolkit for gender equality). Secondly, since 1997, the office of the Equality Ombudsman has employed an official with the main task of supporting private companies and public organizations in equality planning. Thirdly, the Ombudsman has made visits to organizations, typically from five to ten annually, to discuss equality issues and to provide information on the Act. Fourth, the Office has conducted one survey on the extent of equality planning (Kaasinen 1998), as mentioned above.

Thus, the Office of the Ombudsman for Equality is clearly the front-line actor in implementation. Supposedly, the most significant of its activities has been the preparation of the guidelines (Toolkit for gender equality), published at the end of 1996. In contrast to other related activities, which reach a small number of employers annually, such guidelines (now on the World Wide Web) reach a much larger audience of employers.

Unfortunately, these guidelines contain a number of problems. Two of them have been treated already earlier: emphasis on planning at the cost of promotion itself and interpretation of the obligation for equality planning that is not based on the wording of the Act.[15] Thirdly, the guideline gives one understand that a fifty-fifty balance between sexes is the goal in every task, without taking the composition of the available labour pool into account. Of course, this measure may lead to unjustified positive discrimination.

The implementation option chosen by the implementing organization can be characterised as meek and amateurish – even taking into account the intentionally subordinated role that the monitoring of equality promotion has been granted in comparison with the other tasks of the Ombudsman. There has not been any focus on the public sector, even though it should be a forerunner according to the preparatory work, and even tough legal sanctions would be available. The support to employers, especially in the form of guidelines, has been amateurish – existing knowledge on these issues has not been used. Except for the one survey on the extent of the preparation of equality plans (Kaasinen 1998), there has been little efforts to define best practices from the equality work employers have been doing or to investigate impacts of that work.

In summary, the implementation structure has contained only one implementer that is simultaneously the front-line actor. Implementation of promotion of equality has been assigned to it as a secondary task. The actual implementation processes have been weak.[16] Here, it is interesting to refer to the early critical analysis of the Equality Act by Rowe (1988). He pinpointed several shortcomings in the Equality Act, but expressed the view that an intelligent, realistic interpretation of the law, which would utilise the law to the fullest, could make it to an effective tool against discrimination. It must be concluded that at least regarding promotion of equality this has not happened; implementation has not substituted for the shortcomings of the law but, rather, has amplified them.

Reaction by the Objects of the Regulation: Employers

According to the above-mentioned study initiated by the Ombudsman for Equality (Kaasinen 1998), a commonly held attitude in those organizations that had not prepared an equality plan was that there was no need for such plans because there were no problems regarding equality. However, even those organizations that had not prepared an equality plan viewed equality positively. The study also concluded that a clear majority of all respondents shun all bureaucratic monitoring and sanctioning regarding compliance with the Equality Act. It is viewed that work places are best approached in a positive, cooperative spirit. Furthermore, it was found that the Equality Act and what it requires is not known sufficiently.[17] Information on equality planning has been distributed enough, but the practical application of equality planning has been difficult, laborious and slow. Clearly, concrete templates of equality plans are wished.

A frequently repeating reaction to the Equality Act among employers,[18] but also by employees and the central trade union,[19] is that a more comprehensive view on equality is needed on the work place than equality between men and women. For example, age discrimination is mentioned. The related, underlying question might be why gender equality should be so much more important than other types of discrimination or lack of fairness that it deserves specific legal provisions or specific plans. Furthermore, equality is just one aspect of good working conditions – there is a need to develop all aspects in a balanced way (Otala 2000).

Private organizations To what extent have employers complied with the provision on promotion of equality? The mentioned studies above indicate that several large and multinational companies have carried out equality planning after 1995; however, it is more rare in smaller companies. For the majority of companies, the Equality Act has been the motivating force. On the other hand, in some companies equality planning started before 1995, or even before 1987. Even in those large companies that had not prepared an equality plan proper, equality issues had been taken into account in other planning or contexts. However, regarding larger companies, it is a troubling factor that the basic investigation into equality conditions has been made only by the minority of companies.

Public organizations As stated above, almost all of Ministries had prepared an equality plan by 1998.[20] Likewise, a majority of lower-level authorities had prepared or intended to prepare an equality plan by 1998. On the other hand, some authorities had started to promote equality already before 1995.[21] However, often a genuine commitment to promote equality seems to be missing. The following statement is revealing (Kaasinen 1998): 'The equality plan must be made, because the law prescribes it, but there are no expectations on it'.

Furthermore, the Government's follow-up report on Finland's equality programme 1997–1999 expressed a critical opinion especially concerning equality planning in the Ministries. One shortcoming cited was the general lack of participation by the top management in equality planning. Equality issues are seen as an area for specialists,[22] rather than a part of professional approach of a civil servant. Also it was observed that equality goals and equality talk substitute for action. The persons involved in the programme felt that emphasizing equality issues and speaking about them generates embarrassment among officials. The explanation put forward in the report is that it is commonly thought in Finland that equality has already been effectuated. Thus, it is difficult to see the need for any further action.

The *travaux preparatoires* for the law reform in 1995 held that public organizations (state or municipal) should be forerunners in the promotion of equality. Clearly, this noble ideal has not been realised.[23]

Summary on the reactions of employers A number of observations can be made regarding the reactions of employers. First, it can be noticed that larger organizations complied well regarding equality planning, part of them having started even earlier than 1995. Thus, there is no lack of positive attitude towards equality. However, smaller organizations had complied to a much lesser extent. Secondly, while there is very little data on the promotion proper, there are reasons to suspect that plans are made because they must be made and that they have little impact on the actual operations of the organization. Thirdly, there are misunderstandings among employers about what the Equality Act actually requires, and equality planning is experienced as difficult to implement. Templates of equality plans are wished. Fourthly, comments from both employers and employees reveal that there is a feeling of lack of balance regarding attention to gender discrimination in comparison to other forms of discrimination. Why is gender discrimination (and related promotion of equality) given a preferential treatment – in the sense of specific legislation – in comparison to other discrimination?

Referring to Tala's framework, we can see here the combined impacts of the deficiencies regarding objectives, regulatory strategy and implementation. The objectives of the law are recognised as rhetorical, and compliance with the law is largely on the rhetorical level, too. The regulatory strategy leads to equality planning for the law's sake rather than for equality's sake, and the shortcomings of implementation lead to employers experiencing confusion and difficulty.

The previous analysis, based on Tala's framework, suggests that there is no single primary reason for the failure of the Equality Act regarding promotion of equality. There are problematic features related to the background and purpose of the Equality Act, to the regulatory strategy of the Act, to its implementation and to the reaction by the objects of the regulation, which all together have led to a watering-down of the legislation's original intention.

Analysis Focusing on Interactions among Law, Politics and Society

Teubner (1985a) warns that the causal logic of the model 'political goal – legal norm – social effects', which can be seen as the basis of Tala's framework, even if he extends it, is limited to linear causality, and should be enriched for taking circular interactions into account. Regarding these interactions, Teubner (1985a; 1985b) recognises three ways in which regulation may fail. First, incongruence of law, politics and society: the regulatory action is incompatible with the self-producing interactions of the regulated system and the regulated system reacts by not reacting. The law is ineffective because it creates no change of behaviour. Secondly, over-legalization of society: the regulatory action influences the internal interaction of elements in the regulated field so strongly that their self-production is endangered. This leads to disintegrating effects in the regulated system. Thirdly, over-socialization of law: the law is captured by politics or the regulated system and the self-producing organization of the law is endangered. The result is disintegration of basic legal values and the unity of the legal system. In the following, the Finnish Equality Act is analysed in the light of the three failures of law as presented by Teubner.

Incongruence of Law, Politics and Society

First, there has been incongruence between law and politics. The Equality Act was not passed due to political pressure, but rather due to a perceived need to ratify an international convention, as discussed above.

Secondly, it can be argued that there has been incongruence between law and society. Even the overall template of the legislation had been taken from external sources. Even if imported to Finland from other Nordic countries, especially Sweden,[24] the equality legislation is based on the Anglo-Saxon legal system, incompatible with the Scandinavian system of labour law. This question has been discussed in terms of a conflict between individual and collective norms. It has been argued that the relation between the employer and the employee has been left as relatively unregulated in the Nordic legal system (Fransson 2000a; Fransson 2000b). The labour law is not as codified at the level of the individual as at the level of the collective (Bruun 1996). Pay and other conditions of employment are agreed on by organizations of employees and those of employers. Characteristically, there is a specific Labour Court, with representatives from both parties of the labour market. Nielsen (1996) argues that the employer's prerogatives have been accepted as a balancing factor to the right of forming trade unions; these prerogatives have not been expressed in law, but they have been an implicit clause in the collective agreements. Fransson (2000b) argues that the prohibition of pay discrimination can be seen as an intervening norm, as an intervention in the self-regulating collective system and market economy. She holds that there is a conflict between the law, putting forward an individual norm, and the collective norm as contained by collective agreements.[25]

Obviously, we have here a case of the first failure, namely incongruence of law, politics and society. The motivation and regulatory strategy of the provisions concerning promotion of equality have come from outside, and the regulated system has at least to some extent reacted by not reacting. The law remains symbolic.

Over-Legalization and Over-Socialization

There seems to be no over-legalization of the society, the second failure: it has been a guiding principle that the Equality Act be implemented in a soft manner in the working life and the obligations set to employers be modest.

However, there might be traces of the third type of failure, over-socialization of the law. It should be pointed out that just one major and a few minor amendments on the Equality Act have caused a mess from a legal point of view, as indicated by the many resulting internal inconsistencies of the Act discussed above. Obviously, in the law-drafting process, legal considerations have been somewhat set aside. As formulated by Teubner (1987), the successful attempts to increase the effectiveness of legal control have had repercussions on the internal structure of the law. At least to some extent, results of over-socialization of the law can be recognised. But has the Equality Act and its amendments been captured by politics or by the regulated system (actors as suggested by Teubner) or by the regulating system (this option is generally discussed by Tala)? Or was the law drafting process itself in some way insufficient, taking into account that the Equality Act has not been considered as important legislation?

Conclusions

Based on the presented analyses, the implementation of the provisions in the Finnish Equality Act prescribing promotion of equality at work places must be characterised as a failure, if we take the intention behind the Act literally. Judging by results, employers seem to have done little manifest promotion of equality and whether the employer is private or public makes no difference. On the other hand, it seems to be generally, even if silently accepted that these provisions of the Equality Act are just symbolic and there seems to be little dissatisfaction with this state of affairs.

What conclusions can be drawn from this analysis in view of the future development of the Equality Act regarding promotion of equality? First, the analysis based on Tala's framework provides direct guidelines. Obviously, rather than starting from externally defined problems, realistic objectives should be specified in relation to equality problems evident in the country. Goal-setting for the law reform should be based on relevant research and enlightened debate. Regulatory strategy and means should be selected based on in-depth knowledge of the phenomena in question, taking experiences in other countries into account. As Tala (2001) suggests, supported by a higher degree of knowledge, the margin of discretion of a law drafter can be broadened, and she/he can consequently prepare and use a more elaborate and appropriate set of regulatory strategies or means. Obviously, implementation of the law should be vigorous and professional, and its structures and processes should be thought carefully already in the law-drafting stage. Finally, there seems to be good-will towards equality among employers – the issue is how to motivate them to action. One possibility might be to search ways – legally based or otherwise initiated – of promoting gender equality as an integral part of other equality efforts and working condition programmes.

Secondly, the analysis based on Teubner's framework gives interesting hints. What is needed is a law that is congruent with politics and society: the significance of the gender issue on the political agenda and the equality situation at work places. Especially, it must be taken into account that gender discrimination in Finland seems to be primarily covert, and other measures are needed for promotion of equality than in the case of overt discrimination.[26] Finally, the symptoms of an over-socialization of the law must be avoided: as any other law, the Equality Act should be sound from a legal point of view.

Notes

1 This chapter is written under the auspices of a national research programme SYREENI funded by the Academy of Finland.

2 The expression 'Equality Act' in this paper refers to the equality act in Finland, in contrast to corresponding laws in other countries.

3 Here the objective is to assess to which extent general law implementation issues can explain observed shortcomings. Of course it is possible to adopt specific angles of analysis to the study of implementation of a particular law; such approaches are useful for illuminating

matters from that specific angle but may fail to pinpoint problems elsewhere. An example of an interdisciplinary, feminist analysis of lacking impacts of equality legislation is provided by *Schömer* (1999), regarding the Swedish case.

4 *Jyrki Tala*'s study *Lakien vaikutukset* (The effects of legislation, 2001) provides for a comprehensive overview on law implementation research.

5 The CEDAW convention requires in article 2, for example, that states adopt appropriate legislative and other measures, including sanctions where appropriate, prohibiting all discrimination against women, and take all appropriate measures to eliminate discrimination against women by any person, organization or enterprise.

6 An equality act came into force in Iceland in 1976, in Denmark in 1978, in Norway in 1979 and in Sweden in 1980. Thus, in all these countries the equality act came into force or was at least drafted before the CEDAW convention.

7 Surely, the pay gap in monthly wages for full time employees was greater in 1995 in Finland than in Sweden, Denmark and Belgium (*Nurmi* 1999). The difference is due to the fact that women are usually full time employed in Finland, whereas part-time employment is more common in Sweden, Denmark and Belgium.

8 However, by means of the legislation on civil servants, the failure of governmental offices and institutions to realise the obligations of the Equality Act could be sanctioned, but in practice this has never happened.

9 These results must be interpreted in the context of a deep recession, where many companies still struggled for survival.

10 It is interesting to compare, with regard to equality planning, the situation in Finland with that in Sweden, where equality planning has been obligatory for employers since 1991. According to a study organized by the Swedish Ombudsman for Equality (*JämOs Nyhetsbrev*), 22 per cent of private companies and 73 per cent of public employers had an equality plan in 2000. More than a third of private employers and 15 per cent of public employers expressed the opinion that equality planning had not made the work place more equal. Only five per cent of private and four per cent of public employers believed that there had been much or rather much impact on equality. Based on his inspection of equality plans (around 200 plans annually), the Ombudsman found that the majority of plans contain major shortcomings in comparison to the requirements of the law (*Årsredovisning* 2000). Taking into account that in Sweden, the provision is older, its enforcement is more stringent and more resources seems to be directed to its implementation than in Finland, the occurrence, quality and impact of equality planning can hardly be better in Finland than in Sweden.

11 This goal is also reflected in section 1 of the Equality Act: 'The aim of the Act is to prevent discrimination on the basis of sex and to promote equality between women and men, and, for this purpose, to improve the status of women, particularly in working life.'

12 It must be added that even the later amendments of the Equality Act, in 1992 and 1995, were partly motivated by the need to harmonise the Act with the regulations of the European Union. However, the influence of the community law was directed to redefining the prohibition of discrimination rather than the promotion of equality.

13 The experience of Sweden regarding the implementation of promotion of equality, presented above in footnote 10, leads one to ask whether the problem of a lack of regulatory ability also exists in this area. In Finland, however, the problem of a lack of information seems first and foremost to be the problem.

14 Swedish Equality Act, *Jämställdhetslag* (1991:433).

15 Also on the side of the prohibition of discrimination, the Office of the Ombudsman for

Equality is being criticised for issuing interpretations of the law not corresponding to the wording of the Act (Kajastie 2000).

16 It is interesting to note the explanations presented in Norway about the reduced effort in the implementation of equality measures in the beginning of the 1990s (Bacchi 1996), more than ten years after the enactment of the equality act. It was argued that those appointed (at that time point) to handle gender equality in the government were less likely to have a personal commitment to the issue of equality. It was also a concern that civil servants who took up this responsibility had no training for the task.

17 This problem of employers' lack of knowledge on equality legislation was also observed by Schömer (1999) in Sweden.

18 This kind of opinions have been presented by employers, as well as employees, during the visits of the Ombudsman for Equality (*Tasa-arvovaltuutetun vuosikertomus* 1999 and 2000).

19 *Kaasinen* 1998, p. 144.

20 However, this is not solely a merit of the implementation of the Equality Act. The preparation of equality plans in Ministries before the end of June 1997 was formulated as a project in the Government's Equality Programme 1997 – 1999 (*Pekingistä Suomeen: Suomen hallituksen tasa-arvo-ohjelma, 1997).*

21 An example of this is the Academy of Finland.

22 A quote from an interview, apparently with a leading official in a Ministry, is illuminating: 'We have professional people (for equality) here in the Ministry, who know and master the issue much better than we. And we can be utterly care-free and we can present us externally as an Eldorado of equality' (*Tasa-arvo valtavirtaan: Sukupuolten tasa-arvon tila vuosituhannen kynnyksellä,* 1999).

23 It should be mentioned that even the realization of the prohibition of discrimination based on sex varies in the public sector. This uneven result is reflected in the fact that the number of alleged discrimination cases presented to the Equality Ombudsman in both municipal organizations and governmental organizations far exceed the number presented in private organizations. However, one reason for this is that in the municipal sector a decision concerning appointment to an office may be cancelled if the Equality Act has been violated.

24 The example set by Sweden has been followed, for example, regarding equality planning that became compulsory for Swedish employers in 1992 and for Finnish employers in 1995.

25 Even if the argument presented deals with the prohibition of discrimination, it can be extended to cover the obligation of promoting equality. In Finland, however, the formulation of Section 6a of the Equality Act can be interpreted as an attempt to create a better fit with the existing labour legislation. In Finland, the employer has had to prepare annual personnel and training plans and action programmes for labour protection even before the Equality Act. Thus, the situation that an employer has a legal obligation of promoting some particular aspect of working conditions in a systematic way has been well established in the Finnish labour legislation, and equality planning was adapted to this practice.

26 A somewhat similar situation seems to exist in Denmark, where such strategies for promotion of equality have been chosen which take into account the popular opinion that equality has already been achieved (Nikell 2001).

References

Advancing Women in Business – The Catalyst Guide (1998), Jossey-Bass Publishers, San Francisco.

Bacchi, Carol Lee (1996), *The Politics of Affirmative Action*. Sage Publications.

Bruun, Niklas (1996), 'Tasa-arvo ja työmarkkinajärjestelmä' (Equality and labour market system). *Oikeus*, No. 2, pp. 152-157.

Ellilä, Heidi, Laakso, Heljä, Laiho, Ritva, Nousiainen, Kevät and Puoskari, Paula (1983) 'Meillekin tasa-arvolaki?' (To us an equality act?) Oikeus, No. 2, pp. 115-119.

Finland's National Action Plan for Employment 1999. Ministry of Labour.

Finland's National Action Plan for Employment, April 2001. Ministry of Labour.

Fransson, Susanne (2000a), 'Equal Pay for Equal and Comparable Work – a Question of Law or a Question of Labour Contract?' in: *Perspectives of Equality – Work, Women and Family in the Nordic Countries and EU*. Nord 2000:5. Nordic Council of Ministers. Copenhagen, pp 40-75.

Fransson, Susanne (2000b), *Lönediskriminering* (Pay discrimination). Iustus, Uppsala.

Haataja, Anita (1997), 'Nais- ja miestyövoima Suomessa' (Female and male labour force in Finland). Tasa-arvotoimisto. *Tasa-arvon työraportteja* 1/1997.

HE; Hallituksen esitys 57/1985. (Law proposition for the Finnish Equality Act)

HE; Hallituksen esitys 90/1994. (Law proposition for the amendment of the Finnish Equality Act)

Julkunen, Raija: *Women's rights in Finland – the ascendancy of citizen's rights*. Virtual Finland. Available from: http://virtual.finland.fi/finfo/english/women/women.html

JämOs Nyhetsbrev (2000) nr 1.

Kaasinen, Päivi (1998), 'Selvitys julkisen ja yksityisen sektorin työpaikkojen tasa-arvosuunnittelusta' (Investigation on equality planning on workplaces in the public and private sector). *Tasa-arvojulkaisuja* 1/1998. Sosiaali- ja terveysministeriö.

Kajastie, Hannele (2000), 'Women and Fixed-Term Employment' in: *Perspectives of Equality – Work, Women and Family in the Nordic Countries and EU*. Nord 2000:5. Nordic Council of Ministers. Copenhagen, pp. 143-164.

Kauppinen, Kaisa and Veikkola, Hanna-Kaisa (1997), *Tasa-arvoistuvat työyhteisöt* (Work communities getting more equal). Työterveyslaitos, Työsuojeluhallinto, Helsinki and Tampere.

Kjeldstad, Randi (2001), 'Gender policies and gender equality' in Mikko Kautto et al. (eds) *Nordic welfare states in the European context*. Routledge, London, pp. 66-97.

Meyerson, Eva and Petersen, Trond (1997), 'Lika lön för lika arbete: en studie av svenska förhållanden i internationell belysning' (Equal pay for equal work: a study on Swedish conditions in an international context) in *Styrsystem och jämställdhet, institutioner i förändring och könsmaktens framtid*. SOU 1997:114.

Nielsen, Ruth (1996), *Employers' Prerogatives in a European and Nordic Perspective*. 1996.

Nikell, Eva (2001), 'Är danskarna ett jämställt folk?' (Are the Danes an equal nation?) *Jämsides* No. 3, pp. 5-11.

Nousiainen, Kevät (2000), 'Women and Work in Today's Nordic Countries – Introducing the Themes' in *Perspectives of Equality – Work, Women and Family in the Nordic Countries and EU*. Nord 2000:5. Nordic Council of Ministers. Copenhagen, pp. 9-39.

Nummijärvi, Anja (2000), 'The Implementation of the Equal Pay Principle and Gendered Pay Structures' in *Perspectives of Equality – Work, Women and Family in the Nordic Countries and EU*. Nord 2000:5. Nordic Council of Ministers. Copenhagen, pp. 76-98.

Nurmi, Kaarina (1999), 'Sukupuolet EU:n työmarkkinoilla' (Gender on the EU labour market). *Sosiaali- ja terveysministeriön julkaisuja* 1999:2. Helsinki.

Otala, Leenamaija (2000), Hyvä ja tasa-arvoinen työyhteisö (Good and equal work community). Kansallisen työelämän kehittämisohjelma. *Työpapereita* 10, Helsinki.

Opetusministeriö. *KOTA tietokanta.* (Ministry of Education. KOTA data base on universities). Available at: http://www.csc.fi/kota/kota.html

Pekingistä Suomeen: Suomen hallituksen tasa-arvo-ohjelma (From Beijing to Finland: Finland's Government's equality programme). *Sosiaali- ja terveysministeriön julkaisuja* 1997:11. Helsinki.

Pulkkinen, Pia (toim.) (2000), 'Naiset ja miehet vallankahvassa' (Women and men at the top). Statistics Finland. *Gender Statistics* 2000:003.

Roseberry, Lynn (1999), *The Limits of Employment Discrimination Law in the United States and European Community.* DJÖF Publishing. 1999.

Rowe, Gerard C (1988), 'Suomen uusi tasa-arvolaki – oikeusvertailevia huomioita' (The new Finnish Equality Act – observations based on comparative law). *Oikeus*, pp. 41-55.

Schömer, Eva (1999), *Konstruktion av genus i rätten och samhället* (The construction av gender in law and society). Iustus Förlag, Uppsala, 1999.

Skrentny, John D. (1996), *The Ironies of Affirmative Action.* The University of Chicago Press, Chicago.

Suomen Teollisuustoimihenkilöiden Liitto (1999), *Työpaikkaposti* 3/99.

Sørensen, Annemette (2001), 'Gender equality in earnings at work and at home' in Mikko Kautto et al. (eds) *Nordic welfare states in the European context.* Routledge, London, 2001, pp. 98-115.

Tala, Jyrki (2001), *Lakien vaikutukset. Lakiuudistusten tavoitteet ja niiden toteutuminen lainsäädäntöteoreettisessa tarkastelussa* (The effects of legislation. Objectives for a law reform and their realization from the perspective of the theory on legislation). Oikeuspoliittinen tutkimuslaitos, Helsinki 2001.

Tasa-arvo valtavirtaan: Sukupuolten tasa-arvon tila vuosituhannen kynnyksellä. (1999), Loppuraportti Suomen hallituksen tasa-arvo-ohjelmasta 5.2.1997 – 28.2.1999. (Mainstreaming equality. The state of gender equality on the threshold of the new millennium. Final report on the Finnish Government's Equality Programme). Sosiaali- ja terveysministeriö.

Tasa-arvovaltuutetun vuosikertomus 1999 (Annual Report of the Equality Ombudsman 1999). *Tasa-arvojulkaisuja* 4/2000.

Tasa-arvovaltuutetun vuosikertomus 2000 (Annual Report of the Equality Ombudsman 2000). *Tasa-arvojulkaisuja* 4/2001.

Teubner, Günther (1985a), 'After Legal Instrumentalism?' in Günther Teubner (ed.) *Dilemmas of Law in the Welfare State.* Walter de Gruyter, Berlin, pp. 297-321.

Teubner, Günther (1985b), 'The Transformation of Law in the Welfare State' in Günther Teubner (ed.) *Dilemmas of Law in the Welfare State.* Walter de Gruyter, Berlin, pp. 3-10.

Teubner, Günther (1987), 'Juridification: Concepts, Aspects, Limits, Solutions' in: Günther Teubner (ed.) *Juridification of Social Spheres.* Walter de Gruyter, Berlin, 1987, pp. 3-48.

Toolkit of gender equality: Equality planning at workplaces. *Equality Brochures* 2000:1. Office of the Ombudsman for Equality. Helsinki.

Women and Men in Finland 1999. Statistics Finland. *Gender Statistics* 7.

Årsredovisning 2000 (2001) (Annual report 2000). JämO, februari.

Chapter 5

Care and Social Rights in Norway

Hege Brækhus

Introduction

Care is work. That premise is the starting point of this chapter. In other words, caregiving activities that hitherto might have been unassigned any value as compensable labour, do, in fact, constitute compensable labour. The methods of financing the provision of care often differ, however, from other types of work. Home care, the tending of the needs of family members, is still mainly financed within the family and, as such, is highly dependent upon the institution of marriage. More and more home care today receives its funding from public sources regulated by social security legislation.[1] The ways in which care is financed in different countries vary depending upon the culture and history of a particular country or region. Within the countries in the Scandinavian region, care issues are administered by a 'universal' welfare system which is based upon the independent economic status of each individual – whether gainfully employed or not – whereas in many European countries, it is assumed that there is just one breadwinner in a family through whom the caregiver may receive her or his economic security and social welfare.

A famous example of the latter model is the so-called Beveridge model created by Sir Willian Beveridge in the 1940s. He thought that men should ensure the social security of their wives and that women do not need social security of their own except in cases of widowhood or divorce (Beveridge 1942, 143). Pension schemes for widows and provisions for single parents may be seen as outgrowths of this thinking, although in many countries, such schemes have recently been abandoned in the name of sex equality.

In Scandinavia, the emphasis for a long time has been on economic independence, irrespective of maintenance and family status. Gainful employment has become a norm for both men and women. People providing care in the home are considered as being deviant from the norm, somehow performing lesser work. Care providers have been viewed as being 'ungainfully' employed. The work they give has been seen as diminishing in some way. However, the problems linked to the reconciliation of work and care have not been without consideration among policy makers. Unlike in Sweden, where private care is considered a subsidized occupation, in Norway, the independent livelihood of caregivers has been built on a 'welfare mix': funding drawn from both private maintenance and from a social security system that includes some special provisions for single parents and homemakers. The ways to finance care are multiple: private maintenance through a partner, subsidized care at home and subsidized public services. The fundamental hierarchy between waged labour and care, however, remains unresolved. The social security system still contains features that perpetuate the inequality and the dependency of caregivers. The system made up of various benefits forms a haphazardly planned patchwork of many gaps and contradictory elements. The main argument of this chapter is that even if the social security system in Norway has 'rescued' caregivers to a certain extent from being totally dependent upon a provider, a partner, such a system still largely relies on the existence of familial arrangements and private sources of maintenance.

Developments in the social security system raise questions about the foundational concepts of work and care underlying the same system. More worryingly, however, is the question how the system is gendered. Is the livelihood of the caregiver adequately secured? Are there gaps in the system that make the position of a caregiver vulnerable? How does the legislation influence the choices of women in life?

In the Scandinavian countries, most women are occupied in full-time or part-time paid work in a very sex-segregated labour market. Women's professional care-work in the public sector or in the market is low paid.[2] The levels of the benefits for caregivers are also low. The system is built on a notion that care does not need to be as highly remunerated as other types of work. In this chapter, my aim is to explore the outlines and systemic structures of financing care in the Norwegian social security legislation and their advantages and disadvantages from the perspective of caregivers. I will focus especially upon the issue of whether or not it is care itself or some other interest that is covered by the system.

My analysis focuses on three dimensions of the social security legislation: first, the coverage provided to caregivers in cases of sickness, maternity and old age (either through family or through independent social rights), secondly, the variety of methods to support care at home, *viz*., universal social security benefits, child benefit, home care allowance and, finally, the effects of these provisions on the position of women at large. The analysis will not cover the means-tested social assistance provision, which is available as the ultimate safety resort for everyone. As to the details of home care allowance, I refer to the chapter by Kristine Korsnes in this volume.

I will reflect on these provisions with regard to the social indicator, which in Norway constitutes the basis of eligibility. By defining a social indicator society assumes responsibility for some of the burdens resulting from such a need. Usually, the social indicator is quite obvious: illness, disability or unemployment. In case of home care, the social indicator is more difficult to define: is it the need of the caregiver or of the one being cared for, of the one suffering from the loss of income or something else? The conclusion that can be derived from my analysis is that the social need described in the legislation itself is usually not connected to the care work itself.

Even though the analysis easily leads to making a contrast between working women and caregivers, it must be emphasized that these regulations have effects on all women. Most women do care work at some point in their lives. Women may be indirectly discriminated against by the effects of a sex neutral social security legislation (Nygaard and Holgersen 1994, 90). The indirectly discriminatory effects are due to the fact that the best benefits are income-related. Most of the social benefits for caregivers in private homes are not bound to previous income, but, then, the level of the benefit is also very low. Even when the legislation is sex-neutral, with the exception of the so-called child benefit, which is paid to the mother if nothing else has been determined, the majority of social security recipients are women. Thus, the lower level of benefits adversely affects women more than men.[3] In short, women are dependent on social security when they do care work, but they do not enjoy as good a level of security as those persons who receive income related benefits. This fact can undoubtedly be regarded as a problem from the perspective of gender equity.

In recent years, there has been pressure on the social security system to become less generous. It is rather remarkable, therefore, that, at this juncture, some very important benefits designed specifically for women have increased. This phenomenon might be explainable by the supposition that the increased political influence of women generally has caused the underprivileged status of women to become recognized.

To conclude, I will discuss possible solutions to these problems. One choice would be to offer high-quality public care free of charge to everyone. But if public care is neither good nor cheap, families will continue to provide private care. Another possibility is to offer better rights for persons who provide in home care. The various social rights connected to private care in the social security legislation could be seen as a kind of salary for care-work. But is social security an adequate way to finance care-work? What qualities are needed for it to become adequate? Finally, I find it extremely important to raise the issue of the value of care. How can the eroded and devalued image of care be altered, be upgraded or improved in a society that prioritizes effectiveness and productivity?

The Social Rights of Housewives

When care in private homes is financed through family-based support, the carers' rights in cases of sickness, unemployment and old age easily become a problem. Housewives do not receive any compensation if they fall ill, neither are they entitled to unemployment benefits when the care responsibilities cease. The right to maintenance, however, still exists as long as the marriage lasts. But if sickness occurs at the same time as a divorce, a housewife will most certainly face an economic crisis. It is not customary that divorced housewives receive generous alimonies.

In case of pregnancy, a housewife is only entitled to the low maternity benefit for persons without previous income (Social Security Act, hereafter *Folketrygdloven* § 14-12). In some cases, housewives are insured against the loss of their spouse through death. This benefit is constructed in a way that makes widows more likely to be eligible than widowers. The level of the benefit is about half of what the deceased spouse would have received in case of old age or disability (*Folketrygdloven* Chapter 3 IV). This benefit is derivative from the rights earned by the spouse and its rationale is to compensate the loss of provider who otherwise would have secured the economic status of the caregiving spouse.

In cases of old age and permanent disability, however, housewives in Norway have some rights of their own. In the following text, I will describe the social rights earned independently by housewives.

Old Age Pensions

All residents in Norway are entitled to an old age pension at the age of 67, irrespective of previous income or work history (*Folketrygdloven* Chapter 19). The pension consists of a minimum benefit for everybody plus an additional benefit based on income earned at an earlier time which accrues pension points (*Folketrygdloven* Chapter 3 I-II). Since 1992, people who take care of children, the elderly or the sick, earn three pension points, which corresponds to a yearly income of 230 000 crowns (28 000 euros; Spring 2003), for their care work, even if they do not have an income. There are no other prerequisites, such as previous income or marital status (*Folketrygdloven* § 3-16). This additional benefit may be regarded as a benefit related to care work itself. The benefit, however, does not help the caregiver in the actual phase of caring because it is paid only after he or she is unable to provide care.

Disability Pensions

The 'disability benefits for housewives' rule (*Folketrygdloven* § 12-8) stipulates that if married persons working in the home become disabled, it is their reduced ability to perform domestic chores that is decisive when assessing their disability. For workers, it is the reduced ability to earn an income that defines eligibility. In both cases, the disability must rise over 50 percent before a claim can be raised. In practice, housewives have to be bedridden in order to be entitled to a pension. Even when ill, they are considered to be able to perform lighter household work like cooking and dishwashing, which, in many cases, makes them less than 50 per cent disabled. Illness or disability are not considered as complete hindrances to household work as they are with regard to gainful employment, which conceptualization again creates an unfavourable and indirectly discriminatory effect on housewives. The rule is applied only to persons performing care work in the home on a permanent basis. For part-time workers, the disability is assessed partly according to the general rule and partly according to 'disability for housewives rule'. The requirement of 'permanent basis' has had the consequence that the rule is seldom applied to persons doing care work. Those persons who provide care are often considered either as some kind of professionals or only as temporary housewives.

Like the old age pension, the disability pension consists of a minimum benefit for all and of an additional benefit based on earlier-earned income. People who take care of children, the old or the sick accrue three pension points and, consequently, are eligible for an additional pension.

Care Financed Through the Social Security System

What are the accepted social needs to make one eligible for social security benefits, apart from self-evident cases such as the inability to earn a living because of being either too young or too old. According to the prevalent ideology in our society, everybody has to earn his or her living and earn social security through independent income. In reality, society has to pay for several large groups of people who are not able to earn their own living. One such group is parents who may be entitled to social security benefits when they take care of their own children. In the following, I will describe three benefits designed for parents: the social security benefit for single parents, benefits to parents upon the birth of a baby and the universal child allowance. The benefits for the baby sitters of sick children and the home care allowance will not be discussed here. Finally, there are various benefits with regard to compassionate leave, such as the cash benefit for disabled people who need care and salary for carers which is paid through the social assistance scheme.

Social Security Benefit(s) for Single Parents

Since 1965, Norway has had a special social security benefit for single parents. The benefit is meant to cover living expenses for the single parent to make her or him able to take care of the child or children. The benefit, however, is quite low. In recent years, many single parents have been compelled to apply for social assistance as well. The history of the single parent benefit demonstrates that the single parent has always been considered a social problem rather than an 'ordinary' person in a different life situation.

Single parents may choose to stay at home and live on this benefit until the child is three years old. This choice means that even parents who could easily get a well-paying job and pay for somebody to look after the child may choose to stay at home and live on the benefit. The benefit may be paid for two additional years if the parent is in vocational education in order to get a paid job (*Folketrygdloven* § 15-6 (2)-(3)). In order to receive the full benefit, a person must not receive any income from paid work or, any such income earned must be very low (*Folketrygdloven* §15-9).

The basic precondition for receiving the benefit is that the parent is single, *i.e.*, not married to the other parent of the child or to anyone else. Social security legislation thus makes the spouse responsible for a partner's child, which is not presupposed in the general legislation on the maintenance of children (Child Act, *Barneloven* Chapter 7). Such responsibility, however, is based upon the regulation in the Marriage Act (Chapter 7), which requires shared responsibility for family maintenance. Since 1993, homosexual couples have been able to register their partnership, which means that the marriage act is applicable to them (Act on Registered Partnership, *Partnerskapsloven,* § 2). Consequently, they cannot be considered as single in the sense required in the single parent benefit scheme. Since 1999, cohabiting couples, both homo- and heterosexual, that have lived together for 12 of the last 18 months, are also no longer eligible for the benefit (*Folketrygdloven* §§ 15-4 – 15-5). In this case, maintenance is not regulated in any private law regulation on family relations, but the responsibility to provide for the partner's child is contained in the social legislation only. If the parent lives together with any other person such as her or his own mother or sister, or a friend, she or he is still a single parent and entitled to the benefit. In short, all sexual partners are supposed to finance the care of the child, but no one else. This arrangement shows that society also in our modern world gives value especially to female sexuality by stipulating that male partners are obligated to pay for her children regardless of whether they have legal responsibilities as parents or not.[4]

The political goal buttressing the single parent benefit has been said to be the welfare of the child. Most political parties, apart from the far right, seem to have accepted this rationale. On the other hand, there seems to be a moral pressure with regard to this particular benefit, which keeps its level low and maintains extensive limitations on its preconditions.

Why is the support for lone parents such a problematic issue requiring special measures but also evoking criticism? Why are single parents construed as a group of people for whom the society must provide because of their unfortunate fate and not because of the care they provide? To answer this question, it is best to look at the history. Norway passed a new Social Security Act in 1997 (*Folketrygdloven*) replacing the old one from 1966. The preamble to the old act stated that one of the objectives of the act was to combat the need arising from loss of providers (§ 1-1). It was considered a social wrong or an unfortunate fate to be deprived of a provider. In the new Act, the objective is no longer defined the same way. Only the needs of single parents are mentioned as the original reason for creating the benefit scheme. The actual rules, however, are identical to the old ones, so that the benefit is today as it was decades ago, built on care provided for within the family and on the existence of a provider. Benefits only come into question if the normal family-based system fails to meet the needs of family members.

The single parent benefit has many similarities with the maintenance it is supposed to replace. First, the level of the benefit is very low, corresponding to the low level of maintenance regulated in the marriage law (*Ekteskapsloven* § 38). Secondly, like caregivers who are provided for by their husbands, the recipients of this benefit are not entitled to social security benefits in cases of sickness, pregnancy and unemployment. As for disability and old age benefits, the situation is the same as the one for regular housewives described above.

In conclusion, this social security benefit is by now not much better than the regular social assistance because it is so low that many single parents have to apply for social assistance as well, for which they have to prove need. The advantage of the benefit is that it allows the needs of single parents to be discussed in terms of rights.

Maternity Benefits

Maternity benefits have improved a lot in recent years. Parents may now receive a benefit which is at the same level as their full salary for almost one year (*Folketrygdloven* § 14-6).[5] One can also prolong maternity leave by accepting a reduced benefit rate (*Folketrygdloven* § 14-7 (2); Chapter 14 III). Both the mother and the father are subject to the main precondition that they have earned an income for six of the last ten months prior to the period for which they are claiming the benefit. This requirement means that parents can even become employed after the woman has become pregnant and may even earn the right to the benefit during the pregnancy. Each of the parents is entitled to a benefit at the level of his or her own income up to a certain level.

The starting point is that mothers and fathers each enjoy the same rights, but there are also some differences. Only the mother can receive the benefit for a period before the birth. She is the sole receiver of the benefit for the first six weeks after the birth and she is actually forbidden to return to her paid job during these weeks (Work Environment Act, *Arbeidsmiljøloven* § 31 nr. 1 (2)). She is considered to need that time to recover and breast-feed the baby without any pressure from the employer.[6]

Since 1993, four weeks of the effective period of maternity benefit has been reserved for the father (*Folketrygdloven* § 14-10 (1)). This specification means that if the father does not want to use this opportunity, the total paid maternity leave will be one month shorter.

Since 1978, parents have been allowed to allocate the balance of the time as they prefer. It is then up to them to decide if the father or the mother would stay at home to take care of the baby and receive the benefit. In practice, mostly mothers have actually stayed home and received the benefit. In 1990, only 1.5 per cent of the entitled fathers used their right (Adresseavisa 1999). After the 'father's month' was introduced in 1993, the picture has changed. Among men becoming fathers in 1995, 78 per cent of those men who were entitled to the benefit stayed at home during these weeks and took care of their babies (Øverli 1999). This special month for fathers has actually become quite a success.

In the present system, the rights of mothers before and shortly after the birth as well as the 'father's month' are separate and independent of each other. They are understood as individual rights of each parent. Fathers can choose to take the paternity leave or they can choose to refrain from taking it. A mother cannot replace a father. There is, however, a significant difference in how rights can be enjoyed during parental leave. Mothers have the right to receive the benefit even if the father stays at home, while the father can only be entitled to the benefit if the mother actually goes out into paid work or receives a formal education (*Folketrygdloven* § 14-9 (4)). Thus, the mother can actually decide who is to receive the benefit.

In almost all countries, there have been difficulties in making fathers more responsible for the care of their children.[7] The Norwegian fathers' rights scheme shows that if fathers get rights of their own accompanied by adequate financial compensation, they are willing to stay at home. Once established, the system could perhaps later be extended to cover other situations such as compassionate leave.

The status as an earner of an income is crucial when receiving parental benefit. Marital status is of no significance because the rules are the same for married parents as for single parents. The income of a spouse neither reduces nor increases the benefit. The reasoning underlying this benefit is obviously very different from the single parent benefit because the parental benefit has nothing to do with an existence or non-existence of a provider. But what is the social indicator here? It is not the birth itself, because the unemployed mothers or fathers do not get this benefit of high value. The central precondition here is the loss of income, which is fully compensated by the benefit. The care of the newborn baby is understood as a hindrance to ordinary work, for which employed parents should be compensated. Care itself is almost invisible in this construction, even if it is required that the parents provide the care themselves and do not hire a nanny (*Folketrygdloven* § 14-4 (7)).

To evaluate the quality of the benefit, we also have to see what happens in cases of illness, unemployment or another pregnancy. Such risks are relatively well covered: if the mother falls ill during her period of maternity benefit, she can have her benefit postponed if the illness is serious (*Folketrygdloven* § 14-7 (5)) and receive sickness benefit instead (*Folketrygdloven* § 8-2 (2)). In most cases, the mother has a right to return to her job after maternity leave. If her last job was temporary and there is no job to return to, she is entitled to an unemployment benefit based on the maternity benefit itself. If the mother gets pregnant again, she will be entitled to a new period of maternity benefit. This arrangement means that maternity benefit has the same status as the income which it replaces. In all, parental leave benefits are designed to encourage parents to take on gainful employment and restrict their caring activities to the period of about a year that the benefit lasts, but they also secure the continuity of stable income level which practically no other benefits do.

Child Allowances

In Norway, all parents with children under the legal age receive child allowance regardless of whether they are single parents or whether they have an income or not.[8] However, the benefit is low, about 11 664 crowns (ca. 1400 euros) per child per year, so it cannot cover the living costs either for the child or for the caregiver. This benefit was introduced shortly after the Second World War, but the law-drafting process had started long before. In the early 20th century, some feminists had designed a scheme called a 'mother's salary' (Møller 1919), but when the benefit was finally introduced after the Second World War, it was called child allowance instead. Its aim was to improve the situation of families with children in general. Nonetheless, the special thing about this benefit is that, unless other arrangements are agreed, the benefit is paid to the mother (*Barnetrygdloven* § 11 (1)). According to the preamble to the law, it is stated that this provision is partly a recognition of her child-rearing work (*Socialdepartementet* 1934, 51). Because the benefit is only a kind of general support for families with children, it gives no additional rights in cases of sickness, old age or unemployment.

Cash Benefits for Disabled Persons

This benefit is not based on previously earned income, but is rather a compensation for such extra costs that disabled persons might incur if they are in need of help (*Folketrygdloven* Chapter 6). Extra costs signify here the salary of a personal assistant. To be entitled to the benefit, there must be a private care relationship (*Folketrygdloven* § 6-4 (1)), but it is not necessary that this relationship be formalized within an employment contract. The law is silent about whether and how the caregiver should obtain compensation for her or his services. The levels of the benefit are fixed according to a scale. An applicant will receive a benefit not to exceed the level of a normal salary for the assistance needed (*Folketrygdloven* § 6-4 (3)).

The social indicator, disability, is quite clear, as is the aim of the benefit: to help the disabled gain assistance at home. Nursing cannot be financed through this benefit. Strangely enough, the use of the money is not regulated at all. Nothing prevents the entitled person from making a formal employment contract with the person giving the assistance, but there is nothing that presupposes such an arrangement either. On the contrary, the level of the benefit seems to be too low to cover income, tax and other charges. Because this kind of assistance is mostly provided by family members, the payment for the work is probably meant to be transferred in the same way as maintenance, in an informal way inside the family. If there is no formal contract of employment, the carer does not have any social rights in cases of sickness, birth or unemployment. In short, the situation resembles the one of a married housewife without her own income.

Salary for Carers from the Social Assistance Scheme

One group of caregivers could be described as publicly employed while caring for relatives in private homes and doing normal household work on behalf of the disabled. Nursing is a public service not discussed further here. The Social Services Act (*Sosialtjenesteloven*) establishes a right to a salary for persons with particularly heavy caring responsibilities. It is not a very substantial right because it depends on the economy of the municipality and on the degree of necessity. On the other hand, the salary can be obtained for various kinds of care, whether it mean taking care of one's own disabled children or an elderly neighbour, but it cannot be used to finance the care of healthy children.[9] The benefit is regarded as an ordinary salary, which means that it is taxed and that all kinds of social rights automatically follow.

The Evaluation of the Benefits

Before the Second World War, all married women were supposed to provide almost all the care that was needed in the family without any salary or social security benefit, as a part of their maintenance obligation. Men were required to maintain them in return. On the other hand, the right to maintenance was not dependent on whether she actually did take care of anyone. She might have had no children or been too sick herself or she might have had female relatives or maids to do the care work. The big threat to this kind of life was the death of the man, the provider and head of the family. His death or disability was a social event that might require social insurance. The law concerning maintenance is very much the same today, but both the new social security legislation and the public care institutions have changed the situation for married women. However, the basic assumptions of private maintenance still exist.

The maintenance obligation is still as important a part of family law as ever before. Spouses must maintain each other either through unpaid labour at home or by providing for him or her economically (*Ekteskapsloven* § 38). Although the obligation to maintain a spouse is mutual, in my opinion, mutual maintenance is very much a fiction because the housewife seems to be much more dependent on the breadwinner than the breadwinner on the work of the housewife. The children, the sick or disabled are the ones being dependent on the work of the housewife, while the housewife might be totally dependent on the income of the husband. Even if the situation is much better today than it was before the war, women are still, to a certain extent, dependent on marriage. In our time of individual rights and independence, such patterns of dependency can be seen as undesirable. As I have been able to demonstrate above, women providing care are in many cases dependent on marriage because the benefits are very low or do not cover all social risks in a consequent way. How should the different benefits for care be organized in order to make the system fair for those persons providing care at home?

In an ideal situation, a starting point might be that the social benefits for care should enable the caregiver to be independent of the spouse, in most cases the husband, and of marriage in general. At best, benefits should be sufficiently generous, both in regard to the amount of the benefits and the period for which they are paid. The minimum level should be assessed according to the degree of responsibilities and other qualities of the care work. The benefit should last as long as the care requires and it should be independent of marriage and spouse's income. It would be

Table 1. The table shows the quality of each of the benefits mentioned above measured against indicators important to women as receivers of those benefits. Maintenance and ordinary salary are also included to make a better comparison.

	Amount paid	Period of payment	Payment on time	Independent of marital status	Proper social side benefits
Maintenance	Low / uncertain	Uncertain	Uncertain	Dependent on marriage	No
Single parent benefit	Low but enough for living	Three years for one child	Ok	Only persons without sexual partners	No
Child allowance for care	Very low	Long, longer than the need	Ok	Ok	No
Cash benefit for disabled	Recent value of care	Adequate	Ok	Ok	Possible but not practical
Salary from social assistance scheme	Recent value of care	Adequate	Ok	Ok	Yes
Maternity benefit	Mostly higher than the value of care	Short, approx. one year	Ok	Ok	Yes
Ordinary salary	Recent value of care	Adequate	Ok	Ok	Yes

important that the caregiver were able to rely on the accurate timing of the payment. In cases of illness, unemployment or birth, the caregiver should be eligible for full social benefits.

In Norway, the social security scheme contains a variety of ways to resolve some of these problems. In the following text, I shall evaluate how well the different benefits meet the criteria I just listed.

There are several rationales and, consequently, outcomes of the different benefit schemes, see table 1. For example, the single parent benefit compensates for the lack of maintenance from a spouse. Like maintenance, this benefit is also of low level and meant to cover just the minimum of living expenses. No rights can be derived of it in case of illness. However, it is less insecure than maintenance or alimony because it is always paid on time. When we turn to child allowance, a completely different goal is discernable: to establish universal supplement to all who are supposed to take care of children. It has never been meant to compensate the expenses fully or to alter a system based predominantly on private and unpaid care. The good thing is that it compensates for care itself, and that it is, of course, paid on time. It is also paid for a long period of time, probably longer than care actually takes.

Salaries for carers from the social assistance scheme might seem to fulfil most of the criteria. But obviously this benefit does not solve all problems relating to the economic compensation of care. First, it is strange that we find the rules for this salary in the law on social assistance. Secondly, the benefit is given only when there is an extraordinary cause – the need to look after one´s own healthy children does not entitle a person to this benefit. Thirdly, this salary is at the lower end of the pay scale of care occupations. Again, the low level is due to the market conditions for care, but it is also low because of the fact that municipalities are allowed to take their economic situation into consideration when they decide to whom and how much they pay. Fortunately, it is an ordinary salary generating automatically full income-related social rights.

Cash benefit for disabled people is paid to the disabled person in order to help him or her to pay somebody for providing care. The care work within the family, which otherwise would remain unpaid, is compensated, but the problem is that the caregiver her- or himself might not even see any of the money. The special quality of this benefit is that it is given where the social need lies, as social benefits are supposed to be. Thus, it does not turn the caregiver into a social 'case', but, at best, makes her or him a properly paid employee.

Maternity benefit is often more than a fair compensation for the care itself. Because of this fact, it actually 'hides' the value of care. The positive effect is that the high level of the benefit helps all kinds of people become caregivers and not only those persons whose market value is at the average low level for care-work. So far, this payment system has been the only compensation, which has brought men into care-work.

How Should Social Benefits for Care Be Organized?

Is an extended use of social benefits the answer to women's need for economic independence? One disadvantage of this kind of policy is that social benefits in many respects seem to be connected to unfortunate circumstances. As we have seen above, the two most common of these circumstances are lack of a spouse as a provider and a break from ordinary paid work. In this way, the benefits are linked either to problems in an ordinary family situation or in paid work. However, women should not be characterized as a social problem when they do important work.

Society seems hesitant about handing out generous social benefits for ordinary care. When there are no other preconditions for receiving benefits than just care, the amount of the benefit is too small to secure an adequate standard of living. Pension points are accrued on the basis of care but the pension is received only in cases of disability or old age. Only with respect to caring for the sick and elderly, does the amount awarded approach the level of an ordinary salary. The one exception to the low level of benefits, the maternity benefit, is not linked to care but to paid work and follows a completely different rationale.

If the care work itself and only the work entitles one to a benefit, it should be called a salary and not social security. It should be a salary for the sake of the status of the caregivers, but also in order to secure their rights in cases of sickness, unemployment, and so on. Accordingly, the best solution for caregivers would be an ordinary salary on regular preconditions. If this solution were to be adopted some time in the future, there would no longer be any housewives in the customary sense. Care giving housewives would all have turned into care-workers.

But who should pay their salaries? This question is of limited interest to the one who needs a salary, but it is still a difficult question for society. It could be the other parent of the child, but then the society would be required to guarantee the payment in order to eliminate both lack of ability and lack of will to pay. It could be ordinary employers. Before the war, employers paid salaries to husbands on a level that was meant to provide for a whole family. But not all caregivers or their spouses necessarily have an employer.

In Norway, a constant development towards more extensive social compensation schemes for care in the home has taken place in the 1990s, although there is still a long way to go before all care workers are given full economic compensation. In this respect, society already spends quite a lot of money on persons who perform care within the home, in addition to what is paid for care in public institutions. The most obvious exemption from this public responsibility is married mothers who take care of their own healthy children. But even they are supported, to some extent, by social security: maternity benefits, child allowances and cash benefits for parents with small children. Society also promises better and cheaper day care, which is the alternative to care at home, and which also costs a lot.[10] One could propose that the money allotted for day-care could be distributed in a more creative and satisfying ways for all women, allowing parents to choose between public or subsidized day care or earning decently subsidized care in the home.

If care in the home could most easily be financed through the social security scheme, the benefits should be considered as given to the ones in need of care – which is now the case for the cash benefit for disabled people. The weakness of this benefit, as it is today is that the recipient is not obliged to engage the carer on a formal employment contract to provide care for a decent salary.

Even if the salary for care were at a decent level, it would not be efficient in bringing highly qualified women and men into care-work. To the extent that we want this group to participate in care, we probably still have to give full compensation for the loss of their ordinary income. In the present situation, society already signals that high-qualified parents should participate in care by allocating them a substantial compensation in the form of parental benefits.

Care and the Problem of Equal Pay for Work of Equal Value

Women are rational beings. They choose to take care of relatives at home because other forms of care cost too much, they are not practical or they are not of decent quality. For many women, the options are either low-paid work combined with expenses for childcare or providing the care at home themselves without any regular pay. Women's responsibility for taking care of children and dependents in the home makes them accept almost nothing in return. One could even argue that they are dumping their working capacity. This system is mainly based on the marriage contract, which, so far, has not proved easy to remove.[11]

The development of social security rights connected to care modifies the marriage contract, but women's bargaining power is still quite low. This fact undermines the prioritized goal of social policy to enhance active participation of both men and women in all spheres of society. The principle of equal pay in the Sex Equality Act § 5 is an attempt to secure all women an equal opportunity to make choices irrespective of sex. However, it has been very difficult in practice to raise the level of salaries for occupations dominated by female employees, even if there were a serious motivation to do so. Public care is one of those occupations. Because the market forces are so dominant, laws and good intentions are not enough to increase the level of salaries for female-dominated occupations.

To improve women's salaries, I think it is necessary to co-operate with the market forces by raising women's bargaining power and their market value. To do so, it is necessary to eliminate the diminution of women's working capacity. The only effective way to do so is to pay properly for all the necessary work that women actually do, care included.

In my opinion, the problems of low pay in the market and unequal pay for work of the same value are closely linked to unpaid care work, which is provided in the marital home or for insufficient social security benefits.[12] If we can find ways to pay decent salaries for care wherever it takes place, women's market value and bargaining power as a group would gradually rise. To obtain this effect, improving the marriage contract, social security schemes and regular salaries for care should be considered. To get full recognition of the work the pay has to be acknowledged as a compensation for the care work itself. In such a situation, benefits would come close to wages. Utopian as such a scheme might sound, the issue is, nonetheless, of great significance: to give caregivers proper credit for what they do and value the care, which is an important function of the whole society, not just of the private sphere. In other words, the concept of social citizenship needs to be re-evaluated from the perspective of care, an argument also asserted by authors Gunnarsson, Burman and Wennberg in this volume.

Notes

1 Tove Stang Dahl has developed theories about the interrelated connection between the three recourses of women's economy: income in the market, social benefits and family support (Stang Dahl 1985).
2 In Norway, 68.1 per cent of all women were in paid work in 1998, but 45.2 per cent of them worked only part-time. (*Kvinner og menn i Norge* 2000, tables 6 and 8); in 1997 87 per cent of workers in health and social services were women (*Kvinner og menn i Norge* 2000, table 6.8). Average monthly income in health and social services was 18 566 crowns, while in banking the average was 24 739 crowns (*Statistisk årbok* 1999, table 210).
3 With regard to disability benefits, women received 73 per cent of what men did in 1998 (*Sjølvmeldingsstatistikk for folketrygdpensjonistar*, 1998, table 6), while 10.1 per cent of all women and 7.5 per cent of all men were receivers of disability benefit (*Statistiske publikasjoner fra Rikstrygdeverket*, S 08/98 *Nøkkeltall* pr. 30.6.1998, table 9).
4 The other parent of the child will normally pay maintenance for the child. The benefit will not be reduced because of this provision, but the social security agency will confiscate 70 per cent of any amount that exceeds the so-called minimum child maintenance (*Forskotteringsloven* § 5). Even if the entitled parent is receiving maintenance for herself (or himself) from the other parent of the child, the benefit will not be reduced; the social security agency will confiscate 70 per cent of it (*Folketrygdloven* § 15-10).
5 Full compensation for salary is only granted up to a certain level (*Folketrygdloven* § 14-5 (1)).
6 As mentioned above, there is also a benefit for mothers who have had no previous income, but this amount is very low (*Folketrygdloven* § 14-12). Fathers without income have no similar right.
7 The Canadian researcher Diane-Gabrielle Tremblay found out that when workplaces offered flexible working hours, fathers used this situation for pleasure, while mothers used it for care (Tremblay 2001).
8 However, single parents receive a higher level of benefit.
9 In England, since the late 1970s, there has been developed schemes for compassionate assistance. This kind of care is paid but only on a very low level and not given for care inside the family (Leat and Gay 1987).
10 This was one of the main electoral promises of the Labour Party in the electoral campaign of 2001.

11 We could imagine that some of those women would do care work on a salary paid by the spouse. The current understanding of the nature of a marriage contract seems to make this only a theoretical option. In Sweden it is not considered as an option at all (Agell 1998, 53).
12 Other feminist writers have also touched upon this issue (Estin 1996).

References

Agell, Anders (1998), *Äktenskap Samboende Partnerskap,* Iustus, Uppsala.
Arbeidsmiljøloven (Work Environment Act) 4 February Nr. 4 1977.
Barneloven (Child Act) 8 April Nr. 7 1981.
Barnetrygdloven (Child Security Act) 24 October Nr. 2 1946.
Beveridge, Sir William (1943), *Social Insurance and Allied Services,* Her Majesty's Stationery Office, London.
Dahl, Tove Stang (1985), 'Kvinners rett til penger' in Dahl (ed), *Kvinnerett II,* Universitetsforlaget, Oslo.
Editorial (1999), Mannsrolle og omsorg. *Adresseavisen, 8 January.*
Ekteskapsloven (Marriage Act) 4 July Nr. 47. 1991.
Estin, Ann Laquer (1996), 'Can Families be Efficient? A Feminist Appraisal' *Michigan Journal of Gender & Law* Vol 4 No 1.
Folketrygdloven (Social Security Act) 28 February Nr. 19 1997.
Folketrygdloven (Social Security Act) 17 June Nr. 12 1966.
Forskotteringsloven 17. februar Nr. 2 1989.
Innstilling fra den komité som blev nedsatt av Socialdepartementet 3. oktober 1934; Utkast til lov om barnetrygd med motiver.
Kontantstøtteloven (Home Care Allowance Act) 26 June Nr. 41 1998.
Leat, Diana and Gay, Pat (1987), *Paying for Care,* Research Report No. 661 Policy Studies Institute.
Likestillingsloven (Equality Act) 9 June Nr. 45 1978.
Møller, Katti Anker (1919), *Mødreløn.* Foredrag utarbeidet for N. K. N.s landsmøte 1919, Fredrikstad Dagblads Trykkeri.
Nygaard, Nils and Holgersen, Gudrun (1994), *Trygderett Lovforståelse – analysemetode og begrep,* Alma Mater forlag AS, Bergen.
Partnerskapsloven (Act on Registered Partnership) 30 April Nr 40 1993.
Sosialtjenesteloven (Social Services Act) 13 December Nr. 81 1991.
Trembay, Diane-Gabrielle (2001), *Work-family Balancing Measures: Results from Research Conducted in Canada with an Accent of Father's Participation in Family Issues.* Paper on IAFFE Conference in Oslo, June 2001.
Øverli, Bente (1999), Fedrekvote i fokus, *Mannsforskning nr. 1, 1999.*

Chapter 6

The Norwegian Home Care Allowance

Kristine Helen Korsnes

Introduction

In the recent policies of the European Union, a reconciliation between professional and family lives has been emphasized in order to enhance gender equality (McGlynn 2001). It is recognized that women and men have different roles in reproduction and, almost universally, women spend more time caring for young children than men do. While a participation in working life, in other words, the opting out of family life, has been seen as the key issue in Nordic feminist discourses, problems connected with care of young children have usually been framed from this vantage point. For example, discussions abound concerning women's rights to paid maternity leave, women's rights vis-à-vis returning to work or generally, women's rights in connection with the travails of combining family and work outside the home. In these discussions, some Nordic feminists easily overlook the desire of many women to take responsibility for their children and spend more time in caring for them.

Feminist politics, especially in Sweden, have encouraged women's labour market participation by promoting a rather extensive reliance on the communal day care system. In Finland and Norway, discourses have emerged about alternative forms of child care and different choices available to families, leading to the economic support of the home care of young children. *Kontantstøtte,* home care allowance (HCA) legislation, was introduced into Norwegian law in 1998. The HCA benefit system entitles families to receive state funds for their children, from one year to three years of age, who are not looked after in state-subsidized day-care centres. The Finnish system has many similarities and there are also parallels to the German and French systems, which will be discussed later in this chapter.[1] Still the system is quite exceptional and innovative from a comparative perspective.

From a feminist perspective, the home care allowance scheme is unavoidably a double-edged sword. In accordance with the traditions of Norwegian women's law, the starting point of any analysis of care is the real life problems and situations actually encountered by women. It is recognized that women have different relationships to paid work and care than men do. While not all phases of a woman's life are shaped by a steady working-life connection, it is argued that this fact should be taken into account when designing policies. However, it has also been pointed out that, at the same time, we must be aware of the risks of the home care law for women. In particular, it may reinforce a woman's already dependent position and may reduce their real choices. In this chapter, I will describe the political debates concerning HCA with a special emphasis on what implications the scheme may have vis-à-vis women's rights.

Background and Legislative History

The Norwegian Parliament, known in Norwegian as the *Storting*, began discussions about the HCA in 1996. The introduction of the HCA became the most essential issue when the three centre-bloc parties, *viz.*, the Christian Democratic Party, the Liberal Party and the Centre Party, negotiated the terms of their governmental pact in the autumn of 1997. After the election, these parties formed a coalition government and issued a proposal to the *Storting* to set aside funds for the introduction of the new HCA for one-year-old children as of 1 January 1998. The proposal also allowed for the arrangement to be extended to two-year olds as of 1 January 1999. The reform was adopted with the support of the Conservative Party and the far right Party of Progress. Later, these five parties entered into a written agreement, obligating them to retain the HCA for the rest of the *Storting* session. The Labour Party, the Socialist Left Party, several federations of trade unions and various other employees' organizations vigorously resisted the HCA. The reform evoked considerable debate, which also received intensive media attention. Nevertheless, in connection with the debate on the national budget for 1998, a majority of *Storting* representatives endorsed the introduction of the HCA for parents with small children and the HCA Act was passed on 26 June 1998 (The Home Care Allowance Act of June 26 1998, No. 41).

The main objective of the reform was to improve opportunities for parents with small children to spend more time on caring for their children themselves and less time distracted by financial worries and the pressures of a job by increasing the funds at their disposal vis-à-vis governmental cash support. This objective, however, was specified through different and partly contradictory principles.[2] According to the HCA Act § 1, the aim of the law is to provide families with more time to take care of their children at home, while, at the same time, not making such activity mandatory. The principle of the freedom of choice underlay the legislation, as evidenced by the variety of child-care arrangements, which qualified under the HCA legislation. Families are thus able to choose the best possible arrangement, which suits their individual preferences. Finally, the benefit scheme is designed to even out benefits to families by allocating to each family the same amount of national subsidies whether or not they choose municipal day-care.

These contradictory principles are probably due to the fact that neither within the three centre-bloc parties nor between these and the Conservative Party and the Party of Progress there existed a complete political unity of preferred policy. The

HCA scheme is therefore illustrative of how politics can be affected by compromises.

Apart from the above-mentioned aims, the law was expected to have non-intentional consequences for the following issues: the labour market, the process of establishing equality between men and women, the amount and quality of day-care centres and the demand for day-care provisions, and finally, for children with special needs.[3] With regard to the labour market, fears were expressed that the introduction of the HCA would make it difficult to recruit enough labour especially within the health- or care-related sectors. It was also feared that the HCA would slow down the expansion of public day-care facilities, having consequences for women who would probably experience greater problems in finding good day-care arrangements for their children. Consequently, they would experience a constrained freedom of choice when it comes to choosing whether to work or to stay home. Furthermore, the HCA was expected to curtail the career opportunities of women. The HCA was also believed to reverse the process of establishing equality between men and women by reinforcing the patriarchal family model. With regard to children with special needs, some people feared the government control of the quality of child-care services might deteriorate. The private day-care services would not be so exposed to scrutiny as the State subsidised day-care centres.

In fact, the debate concerned not only the actual effects of the scheme but also some of the most fundamental issues of social policy, i.e., employment strategy, gender equality and the best interests of the child. This interplay of so many complex issues and considerations in just one piece of legislation may explain why the HCA has been so controversial. Interestingly, evaluations of the effectiveness of the HCA after it had been in practice for some time revealed that few if any of the fears raised in the pre-enactment debate about the possible intended and unintended effects of the HCA had ever materialised. Up until the year 2000, 87 600 persons have received this allowance (St.prp. no.1, 1999-2000), but the alleged adversarial effects of their choice have remained insignificant. However, public debate has not yet come to an end.

Traditionally, our welfare system has been based on two types of compromises: the compromise between governmental control and the welfare or well-being of its citizenry and the compromise between labour and capital (Hovdum, Kuhnle and Stokke 1994). At the same time as the State increases the general well-being of its citizens, it also controls them, giving shape to and circumscribing their choices. Citizens are directed to make choices from within a framework of social benefits. The welfare State signifies both controlling paternalism and resource transfers from people who are better off to individuals without equally substantial means (Hovdum et al. 1994). Both of these compromises are manifest in the discussion about the HCA. While the first compromise seems to be connected to the public/private split, the compromise between labour and capital seems mostly attached to the boundaries between individual interests and collective interests or solutions emphasising either of these spheres.

Within the discussion about the HCA and its effects upon the occupational activity of parents and on the labour market in general, the compromise between control and welfare underlies governmental efforts to provide for day-care centres. Both incentives to work and quality control are at the core of developing public caring services. The introduction of the HCA scheme can be seen as another way to meet the demands of child-care and, hence, as an incentive to make people, especially mothers engage in waged labour, albeit with reduced hours. The HCA also returns the responsibility and control of caring back to parents, thus, enforcing the primary status of parents as caregivers.

The compromises made on the division of rights and responsibilities as well as of the tasks of the public sector have resulted in the modern 'transfer State' we have today. Social policy has accommodated itself to the needs of the labour market. Individuals with a strong labour force connection receive the best disbursements. This reality is of great importance to bear in mind with regard to the debate on the priorities: public services, or direct cash benefits to the families.[4] Subsidising day-care centres is more likely to encourage parents to work, which has beneficial effects for both themselves and for society. Parents 'pay back' society by working. The HCA, on the other hand, means that parents are being prevented from working which can be regarded as unfair since the parents are not 'paying back' society in a way that can easily be measured vis-à-vis the Gross Domestic Product. Waged labour has long been considered the main plank of welfare politics. The welfare State, however, has taken into account gaps in labour due to parental responsibilities by securing parents an access to social rights. However, this guarantee applies to short-time leaves only. In the long run, rights are bound to decrease. Because it is most often women who choose to work part-time or to refrain from working at all, the emphasis on a 'working plank' signifies a problem of justice and gender equality.

The HCA can be held as an answer to this problem, if considered a method by which to appreciate women's choices and prioritised values. When thinking of the low level of compensation, the picture grows quite dim. However, the allowance might have the potential for change in our conceptualisations of work. The discussion has introduced new substantive contents to the understandings of 'occupational passivity', 'idleness' and 'advantage'. Despite problems of economic unfairness, I would like to underline the importance of conceptual changes and critical reflections on what is understood to be 'work'.

The Legal Criteria of Receiving HCA

The home care allowance is provided for children between 1 and 3 years of age (The HCA Act § 8) who are resident in Norway (§ 2, section 2 and 3) and do not attend a day-care centre funded with government subsidies or who attend such a day-care centre only on a part-time basis (§ 2, section 1). The recipient is specified as the person with whom the child lives permanently (§ 3, section 1, cf. § 7, section 5 and § 9, section 2). Like the child, the recipient must be resident in Norway (§ 3, cf. § 2).

The *Storting* determines the amount of the payment (§ 7, section 1). Today, the grant amounts to 3 657 Norwegian crowns a month (460 euros), which means 43 884 crowns a year (ca. 5 500 euros).[5] This rate can be compared to an average Norwegian salary which may average approximately 230 000 Norwegian crowns a year (29 000 euros). If the family utilises a short time offer in a state-subsidised day care centre, the payment will be gradually reduced in proportion to the time spent in day-care: children spending less than eight hours a week in day-care receive a full allowance; 32 hours attendance reduces the allowance to zero (§ 7, section 2 and 3).

The Home Care Allowance Act is formally framed as sex neutral, but in reality, women are the ones most likely to opt for the HCA and, thereby, the ones most likely to suffer from the detrimental consequences of reduced working hours. Women in poorly paid, typically woman-dominated trades are likely to reduce their investments of time in waged labour. The legislative history shows that this outcome was an expected if not an intended implication of the HCA (St.prp. no.53, 1997-8, 31-2.). A recent evaluation has shown this result to be true; women do make up the majority of HCA recipients. This predominance of women as HCA recipients is why I often speak of women as the target group of the HCA legislation even if the official documents refer to both sexes or the family as a whole.

Attitudes may have been influenced by the legal characterisation of the HCA. Because of the form it has taken, the HCA is not to be regarded as a salary, or as a national insurance or social benefit.[6] The distinguishing characteristic of salaries is that they are earned; the characteristic of social benefits is that they are means-tested and meant to cover essential needs, regardless of whether they have been earned. Perhaps the HCA must be regarded as a grant in the middle between the earned income and the support for essential needs (see Brækhus 1999, 342). However, this characterisation is unlikely to be known to the majority of people. Also, it has some legal implications, as reflected in the way the HCA is co-ordinated with laws relating to taxes, working conditions, national insurance and social welfare.

To sum up the effects of the HCA on social security: receiving the HCA does not entitle to holidays; hence recipients do not earn holiday compensation. Laws relating to working environment do not protect recipients and their working hours are not regulated. Recipients have no rights to sickness benefit or sick pay, nor do they earn or keep rights to maternity allowance while receiving the HCA. Nor does the HCA usually give pension-points. Social security benefits are reduced as a result of the HCA. On the other hand, the HCA is not included in taxed income and, in contrast to many national insurance benefits, the allowance is granted regardless of previously earned income.

Supporters of the HCA scheme have pointed out that paying for work of a caring nature entails an enormous redistribution of social goods (see Brækhus 1999, 345). However, the HCA can be seen as the first step towards dedicating more value to unpaid work such as care-giving.

The Decrease in the Labour Market Supply

The aim of the HCA is to secure families more time to take care of their children themselves (according to the HCA Act § 1), which means reduced working hours to the least. If the intention of the law to lessen the total time spent on working and increase time spent on looking after children is realised, the HCA may lead to occupational passivity. The opponents of the HCA have expressed different opinions of what effect this change would have on the labour supply.

First, occupational passivity could lead to a shortage of manpower. This was pointed out in the proposal of the law (St.prp. no. 53, 1997-8), and the Labour Party and the Socialist Left Party highlighted it also, together with other different type of opponents. The Norwegian tax-system includes disincentives for parents to take paid work (see Lund 1998 and Thoresen et al. 1998, 16). Income taxes[7] and the cost of attending day-care centres reduce the parents' net profit from working compared with the alternative to staying at home and taking care of children themselves.

To counter this effect, the government subsidises places in day-care centres. This alternative results in a greater net profit from working as compared to staying at home, and is therefore likely to encourage more parents to prefer paid employment to occupational passivity.

The HCA cannot be regarded in the same way. In contrast to the subsidies provided for a place in a day-care centre, the HCA is likely to increase the effect of income taxes along with the cost of attending a day-care centre, that is, reducing the net profit from working, and thereby discouraging parents from gainful employment (see Strøm 1998, 7).

For this reason, the HCA can be said to influence parents' criteria of making choices relating to paid work. Work becomes less profitable. In other words, the HCA can be claimed to diminish the parents' freedom to choose to work. Taking another angle, the scheme can be esteemed as an attempt to increase incentives to care-giving.

The shortage of manpower could lead to difficulties in covering primary functions in Norwegian society in the years to come. The population is ageing.[8] This fact in and of itself will lead to a decline in the labour supply. The effects of the HCA are likely to reinforce this development. The shortage of manpower could further increase existing recruitment problems in trades that are already short-handed. Mostly at risk are the public and private health- and care sectors already experiencing great problems in recruitment,[9] due to the low income level in these sectors. Hypotheses based on economic theory suggest that there is a certain degree of correlation between wage levels and adjustments to the HCA (Sletvold 2000, 40).[10] Parents are likely to decide which one of them should stay at home after considering which solution will lead to the least reduction in income. Since women within the public sector often have lower income than their partner, they are most likely the ones to be staying home.

Nevertheless, these recruitment problems could also be explained by the fact that these trades seem especially well adapted to the HCA scheme. Employees often have untraditional working hours that are incompatible with the opening hours of day-care centres. These parents have to choose alternative child-care arrangements, which are not subsidised. For them, the HCA represents a direct contribution to the family income. For this reason, it seems reasonable to say that the need for a scheme like the HCA was very much present among these recipients. Furthermore, it would be possible for these parents to reduce their inconvenient working hours and spend more time with their children. However, both explanations result in withdrawing manpower from profitable work.

Career Terms

The occupational passivity promoted by the HCA has been claimed to cause parents great problems in terms of career (St.prp. no.1, 1999-2000). The ties to the labour market may weaken. As a result, parents might encounter problems returning to the labour market or finding work after being home. Being away from work for a period of three years may lead to the deterioration of competence and seniority, which in itself may lead to a decrease in income. Moreover, parents may experience a decrease in the amount of pension points accrued, causing them a reduction in future pension benefits.

Furthermore, fears have been expressed that parents, especially women, might stay at home longer than the period estimated, if they have more children either before the expiration of the first period of HCA, or shortly afterwards. This extension of time spent at home would enhance the effects pointed out above, and perhaps reinforce the views on women as unstable or shifty labour.

However, the break from occupational activities due to the HCA lasts mainly only for the period of the HCA. After that parents are expected to return to work. Two to three years (including the period of maternity leave), viewed in light of an entire working career, which extends over something like 30–40 years, might not be regarded as particularly substantial. Yet some parents may have problems returning to, or finding work after being home with their children and receiving the HCA, but this depends to a great extent on whether the parents were employed to start with.

According to the Working Environment Act § 31 no. 4 (the Working Environment Act is of 4 February 1977, No. 4), parents are entitled to a leave of absence from their occupational activities for a total of three years to take care of their own children. This entitlement means that parents, in principle, are guaranteed their old jobs back after having used the HCA scheme. The innovation represented by the HCA primarily entails an extension of the payment period.[11] Now parents can choose a three-year leave of absence, which they are entitled to in order to take care of their children and, to a certain extent, get paid for doing so. However, in order to be entitled to a full three years' leave, the last two years must be divided between the parents. This requirement means that the father has to exercise his right in order to entitle the family to full rights. The requirement may also encourage fathers to use the HCA scheme to a greater extent and thereby make them take more responsibility as carers in the upbringing of their children. In my opinion, these rights have been undercommunicated in the debate on the HCA.[12]

It may be true that parents might stay at home for more than three years if they have more children either before the expiration of the first period of HCA or shortly afterwards. Since the HCA does not give rights to maternity benefits (according to the National Insurance Act of 28 February 1997 No. 19, § 14-4), the financial risk of having to stay at home for a year without maternity benefit before being entitled to another HCA grant for the second child, seems likely to counter this. The same argument has been used by critics who argue that recipients of the HCA grant are not assured of a safe enough return to work, because having a second child within a three-year period must be considered as normal and expectable (see Brækhus 1999, 244).

In spite of this complexity, women's increased participation in the labour market and their investments in higher education seem likely to weaken the probability of them behaving differently than they generally would have done, as cash contribution would be considerably smaller than the wage they might lose (see Baklien, Ellingsæter and Gulbrandsen 2001, 30).[13]

Finally, it is my firm belief that focusing too much on the negative consequences of the HCA vis-à-vis women's careers or focusing on what losses women may suffer in terms of waged labour, might reduce the motivation for men to stay at home with their children. If men are given the impression that the upbringing of children is a duty without any good sides attached to it, while the life of men as full-time waged labourers is the desired norm, how can we expect any change? I believe it is important to visualise the good and rewarding sides of taking care of small children. After all, it is the work itself, i.e., the substance of the work, that matters which is probably why women so often choose to perform 'maternity work'. It is not likely that economic incentives are the only important ones. Focusing more on the rewarding sides of childcare we might also experience that a more equal allocation of this work becomes a heart issue for many fathers and perhaps some of the male dominated organisations within the labour market. This is not self-evident, though. Efficient anti-discrimination law is required to support the position of caregivers from not being discriminated against because of leaves due to parental responsibilities.

A Break in the Work Line

Occupational passivity stands in contrast to a long lasting policy pursued within welfare state politics, considering self-sufficiency by working as a main plank of welfare policy. 'Occupational passivity' is a negatively charged expression ignoring the inputs of caregivers. While public welfare benefits are usually decreasing at the transition from occupational passivity to occupational activity, the HCA then represents a pendant. Not surprisingly, this aspect has been brought into light in the debate[14] and may have seemed provocative to some of the participants.

Some opponents of the HCA seem to believe that it is a scheme that pays parents for leisure time, while taxpayers foot the bill. Or they consider the HCA scheme to promote a situation in which the agent (the parents) can exploit the employer (the child) and take an advantage of the child (Ekren 1998, 3).

The first belief correlates to standard understandings of the concept of work. Caring is not usually considered as work, but since anyone who has been involved in the upbringing of a child knows what hard work it actually is, a serious consideration of the nature of caring should not be so difficult. However, the fact that taking care of one's own children is also work, is often ignored in most arguments against the HCA. The HCA has been characterised as a scheme that pays people off from not buying a service, i.e., a place in a day-care centre (see Strøm 1998 and Lahnstein 2001). In my opinion, this characterisation stigmatises those persons entitled to the HCA as passive recipients of a grant they do not deserve.

Research shows that this stigmatisation is likely to affect the behaviour of recipients and potential recipients of the HCA (see Bungum, Brandt and Kvande 2001). Because many parents wish to take time off to care for their children even without receiving the HCA, the HCA could make them feel better about doing so – quite apart from what their financial situation would be – because of governmental approval. However, many parents have said they feel guilty for receiving the HCA, partly because they experience disapproval and gossip from colleagues and others (Bungum et al. 2001). No doubt, some of this guilt is due to the intensive debate that is going on. But feeling guilty is something working parents with small children need least of all (Kvande 2001).

Regarding the HCA, the key issue is childcare. The cost of attending day-care centres, combined with the considerable transformation of care from unpaid to paid work, which has been brought about by women's increasing participation in the labour force in recent decades, has made it discernible that child-care should be considered as work and costs money. Furthermore, the HCA is not meant to be a private benefit for parents, but rather a benefit for children. Although the HCA incitements affect parents' occupational status, the target group is children. This overlapping of effects provides an example of how different and conflicting political priorities can provide different signals to the same persons, i.e., everybody should work – people should spend more time making their children a priority.

What this scheme may entail for the future is an introduction on a lager scale of an extended understanding of the concept of work. The HCA may appear more accordant with the mentality of justice that the workfare rests upon. I would therefore like to ask what is 'work'?

From a micro-economic perspective, work can be defined as those human activities generating earnings. In most micro-economic models, individuals allocate their time between paid work and leisure. If anything is said about unpaid work, it is subsumed under leisure. From a macro-economic perspective, work is often seen as those activities that contribute to economic production and surplus value, measured by the Gross Domestic Product. Unpaid work such as child-care at home is labelled unproductive, while efforts brought forward by waged workers such as nurses in a day-care centre or hired private childminders will be regarded as working, and as such productive. Hence, obviously, both definitions are subjects to shortcomings and surrounded by inconsistencies and ambiguities. No matter what, I believe these understandings are distinctive in the HCA debate.

To define care giving as an occupation other than work just because it is unpaid does not seem completely obvious to me. Along with women's entry in the labour force, the work that previously took place within the households has been relocated to the market and the public sector. However, it is the same work that has to be done, and that is being done.

Historically, unpaid work was included within the Norwegian Gross Domestic Product during the first years after the second world war. The purpose was to present a more correct picture of the economic activity within the Norwegian society. However, the development of international standards for national accounts led to a change in which more weight was put into numbering goods and services merchandised within the market, than into the total real-economic assets making. Goods and services produced by unpaid work related to housekeeping were thereby excluded from the national accounts production idea. The requirement of internationally comparable numbers led to an exclusion of work related to housekeeping from the Norwegian Gross Domestic Product in 1950.

This history shows that it would not be inconceivable to include unpaid caring into the concept of work. An illustrative example of the practical application of the 'care as work' principle is the current National Pension Scheme, according to which pension points can be earned by care-giving (the National Insurance Act § 3-16). In 1997, a sickness benefit was introduced to comprise also the persons taking care of the child, i.e., the home-making husband or wife (the National Insurance Act § 9-5). This benefit was created to compensate families for the loss of income even in cases where sickness is preventing unpaid work such as childcare.

On the other hand, the HCA can also be understood as a break of the 'work line'. In my opinion, one should not overemphasise the priority of 'work'. Breaks are also important. In fact, underlining the 'work line' could be interpreted as a violation of the basic human right to choose work freely. Either way it implies paid work as the obvious standard of social organisation. Work should not be a must, especially if meaning that people are forced to low wage jobs without any prospects of improvement, instead of allowing them to devote their time for care giving at home.

With regard to the second belief, the risk of parents exploiting their children to their own advantage could be true when it comes to socially deprived parents' focusing only on the financial aspect of the HCA, especially if their children also have special needs, for instance, children with disabilities and children of immigrants who have needs relating to integration. In these cases it might be that the families do not see what is in their own long-term best interest, and therefore should be protected against short-term choices. In these cases, it is important to have a safety valve of the child welfare authorities who intervene whenever necessary to secure proper care for minors.

Care for Children: A Public or a Private Issue?

The HCA debate involves a possibility to choose between different kinds of child-care arrangements and to rank them. A common denominator of the critical attitudes towards the HCA, therefore, might be the underlying belief in day-care centres as the best caring alternative for children up to the age of three (see Lund 1998). Day-care centres seem to be increasingly regarded as part of the total educational system. In other words, it is considered wrong to deprive children of the right to attend day-care (see Josefsen 1999; Lund 1998).[15] However, because the HCA does not necessarily presuppose care at home, the HCA could lead to a reduced demand and, consequently, to a lessening supply of places in day-care centres, even closing many of them down. With regard to the freedom of choice, such a development could be unfortunate, as the demands for day-care places are not met. The government announced its goal to achieve complete covering of the demand by the year 2000, but so far, this aim has not been realised. Critics also fear that the number of private baby sitters will increase. Care would be provided by unskilled labour, which is also difficult to monitor.

On the other hand, there is professional disagreement as to whether day-care centres have positive effects on children's development.[16] As the negative effects seem to ease off as the child gets older, it means that it is more worrying if the youngest children spend long hours in the day-care centres than children closer to school age. Nonetheless, one might ask whether or not parents are the ones to choose the kind of child-care they prefer for their children.[17] Why deprive them of responsibility as regards child-care arrangements? We have compulsory school attendance in Norway, but day-care centres have always been voluntary, even if the demand has been increasing.

It has been argued that the HCA does not represent the targeted increase in parents' freedom of choice while parents who wish for a place in a day-care centre are rewarded financially for giving up this wish. This claim may be true and it shows the need for continuing the process of extending the provision of places in day-care centres. However, it cannot conceal the fact that the HCA represents a considerable financial support for families who do not want such a place and for families who have to use alternative child-care arrangements while waiting for a place.

Furthermore, there is no question that a place in a day-care centre for children up to the age of three is among the most expensive alternatives (see Wærness 1998, 5-11). This reality means that it could be socio-economically profitable to search for alternative child-care solutions. Considering the above-mentioned disagreements, it seems better to ensure places for children who are more certain to gain from having a place in a day-care centre than the youngest ones.

However, the introduction of the HCA has been assumed to make it more expensive for parents to choose a place in a day-care centre (see Strøm 1998, 2). The parents' choice is now between paying approximately 3 000 Norwegian crowns for a place in a day-care centre (for one child), or taking care of their children themselves, and seeking alternative child-care arrangements, such as private childminders (which in most cases are cheaper than a place in a day-care centre), while receiving the HCA. That is, they pay approximately 36 000 Norwegian crowns (4 400 euros) a year to attend a day-care centre, or receive 43 884 Norwegian crowns (5 500 euros) not to do so. The economical sacrifice by opting for a place in a day-care centre has, thus, increased after the introduction of the HCA and will certainly influence parents' choices. This effect has been criticised, in particular by Strøm (1998).

On the other hand, Ekren (1998, 4) criticises the opponents of the HCA (among these; Strøm) for ignoring the fact that cost analyses are also relevant for other child-care arrangements than day-care centres. He argues that there should be more focus on the fact that receiving the HCA also reduces the cost of choosing private child-minding (by parents or others) as opposed to working combined with letting children attend day-care centres.

Either way, as Ekren also points out, it's interesting that cost arguments are cited in the debate, and it's an essential point in this discussion that present users of day-care centres at least won't have their financial situation deteriorate.

Furthermore, I believe that the discussion must be considered in light of the fight for an off-privatisation of the reproductive sphere that started somewhere during the 1970s. Granting parents the right to decide the type of child-care they prefer for their children was feared to lead to unacceptable conditions under the façade of inviolable private life. The opponents of the HCA scheme have expressed fears that it is first of all parents who do not fulfil the norms/standards of good upbringing of children who will seek other alternative child care solutions than day-care centres. This tendency could be unfortunate for the children because of the lack of public control and because few other forms of social help are presumed capable of presenting a pedagogical competence on a par with day-care centres.

In my opinion, one cannot generalise parents as possible exploiters of their children. In particular, women within the four corners of their homes are not necessarily in a position to negotiate and may end up staying at home without wanting to do so. The structures of power and economy at home are gendered in many ways. Women's lower income, fear of violence and other corresponding factors may make it difficult to maintain their values and individual preferences.

Individual choices do not always coincide with choices of the families. Hence, the question can be posed whether the family or the individual should be the basic unit intersecting family and welfare politics. These problems are inherently linked with the discussion about effects of the HCA upon women and the process of establishing equality and a fair division of caring responsibilities between women, men (families) and the State. This part of the discussion will be discussed more in detail beneath.

Norwegian childcare politics have been a topic of heated disputes during the last decades. Some of the resistance of day-care centres is probably due to the fact that the governmental engagement regarding the upbringing of small children collides with a customary division of work between state and family. The government has invaded an area previously well attached within the sphere of privacy, in the families. Such childcare politics challenge the families' mandates to bring up their children themselves, and also the division of caring between the sexes. At the same time, a place in a day-care centre has been increasingly conceived as a part of children's democratic rights, which has softened the dominating place mothers have had in the daily care of small children. The new focus on children as independent subjects to rights seems to have led to a greater unity regarding day-care centres as important institutions for the well-being of children.

I would especially like to pay attention to the increasing intensity of governmental childcare policies that have taken place during this century. It has become almost impossible for a family to live on just one income and, therefore, even those women who would have preferred care-giving at home have been forced to take paid work. To overcome the disincentives to work, i.e., caring responsibilities, the government has had to intervene to a lager extent than before. Even if the picture is more complex, in my opinion, the governmental intervening must not be taken as sign of a good-will gesture. Especially the development programmes regarding child-care centres seem to be low prioritised, despite aims to meet the demand within the year 2000. Since the government can still rely on families to perform the necessary child-care in cases where public services are not provided, their level will never come close to what it might be if women had not felt that child-care was their personal responsibility.

This arrangement contributes to the double burden of women, at the same time as it makes it possible to constrain public welfare-budgets. Viewed from this perspective, the HCA could signify an acknowledgement of the government that a great deal of child-care still is performed in the private. By supporting families economically for child-care at home, the HCA can be held to establish the status quo as the social norm. Instead of looking at the HCA as an attempt to bring women 'back to the kitchen', one might say it represents a benefit that takes into consideration that women have never completely left it. This claim shows that Norway perhaps is not as modern as we like to think it is, but a politics that bases itself upon a society model more modern than it, in fact is, could mean that some groups would be left out by the government, when deciding who should be granted economic support. In Norway, there is a distinctive policy legacy from the early 20th century with strong emphasis on women's social rights and identities as mothers (Sainsbury 2001). Maybe this legacy still characterises some of the policy choices and neglects others.

Who should decide what is best for the children? I do not agree with an ideology that considers child-care as something we should always hand over to professionals. In my opinion, this means devaluating the worth of care-giving. It is likely to discourage men to take a greater responsibility of the upbringing of children, by depriving them of all faith they ever had in the possibility of succeeding in caring. Furthermore, the question of choice remains unresolved. If only places in public day-care centres are offered, the government is indirectly allowed to have the final say. The heavy subsidisation of some, but not all, families with young children must in my view be regarded as unfair especially when the demand for places in day-care centres still has not been satisfied. The explicitly expressed aim of the HCA to even out national subsidies to families with children, independent of their choice of day-care provision, seems to me to be highly valid.

Empirical Evaluation of the HCA

Recent evaluation reports on the HCA as regards its effects on labour supply, occupational participation and the labour market, give evidence of an insignificant readjustment (Baklien et al. 2001). As was assumed in the proposal to the *Storting*, mothers are the ones primarily affected by the HCA. Only one of thirty receivers of the HCA is a man (Øvrebø 2000). Hence, only the figures relating to the situations of mothers have been analysed in these reports.

The overall conclusion is that the reduction of working hours per week among mothers of 1–3 year-old children is relatively modest.[18] The evaluations bear no evidence of decreased participation in waged labour at large (Baklien et al. 2001, 25).

It was expected that low-paid women, women with a low net pay after reduced child-care costs are taken into account, or women with lower education would be those primarily considering the HCA as a substitute for earned income. The evaluations show this not to be the case.[19] Occupational participation has increased among full-time mothers within the group with the lowest educational level, while the increase in part-time working has been highest among mothers within the group with the highest educational level. Overall, the differences in occupational participation have been evened out among these groups (Baklien et al. 2001, 25).

Some of the reports showed changes in mothers' occupational behaviour exclusively due to the introduction of the HCA.[20] These reports found the HCA to have had a marked effect on the reduction of man-labour years amounting from 3500 up to 4500 compared to what the situation most likely would have been if the HCA had not been introduced.

Evaluations based on more recent[21] manpower studies by the National Bureau of Statistics found no changes as regards either the number of employed mothers or the proportions of full-time and part-time workers (Baklien et al. 2001, 28).[22] In terms of the number of working hours, they found an average reduction of 0–1.5 hours per week.[23]

With regard to the effect of the HCA upon all occupations, the reports found mothers in health- or care-related occupations to be less likely to stay home because of the HCA, while mothers in school or child-care jobs were most likely to stay at home because of the HCA. However, mothers within the health- and care-related sectors were more likely to reduce their working hours, so that no differences (in the average reduction of working hours per week) were found among the sectors when comparing those leaving work completely with those who only reduced their working hours.[24]

When comparing mothers in health- and care-related jobs with all other occupations or sectors, the reports found a reduction within the share *not working* among those within the first group, from 23 to 15 per cent (Baklien et al. 2001, 28-9). The full-timers were reduced from 23 to 18 per cent but this was compensated by the increase in the proportion of part-timers from 55 to 67 per cent. In all other sectors there was a weak, non-significant decrease in the proportion of those *working*, in both full-time and part-time jobs.

Among mothers receiving the HCA because of inconvenient working hours, i.e., ones incompatible with the opening hours of day-care centres, the reports found no reduction in maintaining inconvenient work (Baklien et al. 2001, 26). However, after the introduction of the HCA it seems as if fewer mothers among those working full-time choose to combine work with attending day-care centres, especially among women in the group with the second-highest educational level. And among these, women in the school and child-care sectors were found less likely to do so than women in the health and care sectors (Baklien et al. 2001, 25).

Comparing the proportions of recipients of the HCA in all jobs, the reports found no great differences (Baklien et al. 2001, 29). The measured changes, then, seem only to be connected to differences in occupational adjustments.

When measuring the HCA's effects upon families of children with special needs, the reports found nothing to indicate that the HCA has had negative effects upon functionally disabled children's access to and use of day-care centres (Baklien et al. 2001, 56). Furthermore, they found no alarming decrease in the use of day-care centres as a child welfare action (Baklien et al. 2001, 50). With regard to families with children of immigrants, the reports found ten per cent of these to let their children leave or to not apply for a place in a day-care centre after the introduction of the HCA (Baklien et. al. 2001, 51). Previous reports considering the attitudes of immigrant families toward day-care centres show that day-care centres are wanted primarily because children should learn Norwegian, rather than because of a need for supervision. Most immigrant families are traditionally oriented towards home-based childcare by mothers, who are generally believed to have little to gain within the Norwegian labour market. For them, the HCA represents an important economic transfer, which confirms and prizes choices based on traditional cultural values. Hence, the HCA have made culturally influenced choices more profitable. Considering this, the above-mentioned reduction has been held to be rather moderate (Baklien et al. 2001, 55).

Regarding the demand and supply for day-care centres, the report of Baklien et al. shows a decline in the actual use of day-care centres immediately after the introduction of the HCA, none the less this has risen later. Furthermore, they found no evidence of a decrease of day-care centres. The amount of parents demanding a place is still the same as before the HCA scheme. Even the rates of private childminders do not seem to have changed (Baklien et al. 2001, 46).

The HCA and Its Effects upon Women and Equality

One of the main issues in feminists' commitment to equality is women's need to achieve greater financial independence than they currently have. Simplifying slightly, this in many ways represents the key to making basic choices concerning one's life.

Caring is and has always been an important part of the services especially provided by women, and caring represents valuable work, because it is productive and costs money. The HCA can be seen as a first step in giving value to unpaid work such as child-care, but even so, the amount of the grant (up to 43 884 Norwegian crowns, ca. 5 500 euros, a year) is not enough to live on.

The downside of the HCA is a continuing expectation and acceptance of women to be provided for by their partners. This expectation reinforces the so-called tripartite providing system to (Dahl 1985)[25] according to which the choices of women often lead them to be having less money and being more dependent on a provider.

Receiving the HCA could lead to greater financial freedom and independence from provision in the short term because, in most cases, the HCA is paid out to mothers according to the Home Care Allowance Act, § 9. In addition, the HCA could be viewed as a step towards transferring more social resources to women as a group, which seems reasonable because women's entry into the labour market, together with oil, can be seen as the leading trends in the development of increased prosperity in Norway. But, because of the necessity for supplementary provision combined with the way the HCA is co-ordinated with criteria for receiving welfare rights, the HCA is likely to make women come off badly in the longer term.

Hence, some people have interpreted the aim of the HCA scheme as making mothers stay at home with their children, revitalising and preserving old gender role patterns of housewife mothers/male breadwinners, with further consequences for women's opportunities of taking or staying in paid work, their careers, the division of labour between the sexes and their rights to welfare benefits.

For this reason, it is interesting to ask why it is women rather than men who choose the HCA. The rational choices based upon the financial aspects have been cited as weighty explanations, since the concurrent effects of the tax system and the low wages of women can make it more difficult for women to insist on working. Or in any case, less worthwhile, while it is not necessary or of any great importance to their family's finances. Aspects relating to educational level, integration in working life, and conditions related to the workplace and its environment, are closely connected and likewise cited in the debate. However, research has shown that this is hardly the case.

Sletvold (2000, 74-87) finds wage differentials between parents to have no systematic influence on the decision as to which of them should stay at home or reduce their working hours. Nor were differences of integration in working life, measured by the extent of the working week and the levels of their positions, found to affect the choices. The same goes for differences in educational levels: mothers had higher educational achievement than fathers in more than half of the families. Education did not correlate to the choice of the HCA. However, conditions in the workplace were found to be explanatory to some extent. Mothers stated that they had better chances of reducing their working hours, but even in families where the fathers' employers were the most flexible, mothers were the ones who mostly reduced their working hours.

The conclusion seems to be that the experience of the HCA shows a tendency in public debate to exaggerate the meaning of social and financial conditions, and underestimate the continued weight of sex roles. The study of Baklien et al. (2001, 43) supports these findings, as they believe the use of the HCA to correspond to gender role patterns, in spite of its having been written in gender-neutral terms. However, Baklien et al. (2001) seem more willing to open the way for the explanations mentioned to have some effect upon the choices.

It does not look like the way the HCA is shaped correlates with women's occupational investments or adjustments. The choices seem to be made according to preference of values. Hege Brækhus (1999, 338) has argued that nobody chooses work of a caring nature because they do not earn money doing it. It is the work itself that matters. Other scholars, like Elisabeth Vigerust (1998, 214), have been more inclined to think that we cannot speak of free choice while society expect mothers to be the ones to stay home, according to traditional gender roles, rather than fathers.

In my view, we can never completely avoid such effects, without this meaning that choices made while such expectations exist need to be compulsory. And in the period when the children are small and very demanding, I do not necessarily find it strange that some women prefer to stay at home or reduce their working hours, even if such preferences do not result in fathers performing more child-care (see also Wærness 1998, 7).

What needs to be done is to ensure that these women's choices do not have such unfortunate effects for them. Granting them the same rights as workers, at least as regards pension points, maternity benefits and sickness benefits can do this. But also as regards wages, i.e., the amount of the HCA must be raised. To do so, I suppose society must overcome the view that work of a caring nature can not be characterised as work on a par with other work (see also, Brækhus 1999, 346). However, reaching this understanding might take some time and, presumably, these rights must be granted gradually (Brækhus 1999, 346).

Home Care Policies in Some EU Countries

Finland

In 1985, Finland introduced an allowance policy bearing a great deal of similarity to the Norwegian HCA.[26] Parents who take care of their children themselves receive so-called home care support, *hemvårdsstöd* in Swedish and *kotihoidontuki* in Finnish. The Finnish system differs in a fundamental way from the Norwegian system with regard to eligibility requirements and differentiated levels of the allowance. The Finnish *hemvårdsstöd* is granted to families with children between ten months and three years. The allowance consists of a statutory basic amount of 336 euros per month, an income- related supplement at a maximum of 134 euros per month and per child and a supplementary grant of 302 euros if the child has siblings below the age of seven who do not attend a day care centre.[27]

Some municipalities offer an extra amount to families who receive *hemvårdsstöd*. The amount of this extra contribution depends on the municipalities' budget and the number of available places in the day care centres. Parents with children in municipal day care centres are ineligible to receive the *hemvårdsstöd*. If the parents choose a private option, i.e., placing their child or children with a private babysitter or nanny or with a private day care center, the grant then is less generous and is paid directly to the private childminder, who, incidentally, must be registered as a childminder.[28] In these cases, the *hemvårdsstöd* is called *privatvårdsstöd*.[29] An allowance of 63 euros per month is paid to a parent who has a child under the age of three and who reduces working hours to a maximum of 30 hours a week.[30]

Unlike Norway, Finland guarantees a place in a day care centre for all claimants as a subjective social right. The choice between *hemvårdsstöd* and a place in a day care centre, therefore, has become more of a reality in Finland compared with the situation in Norway. Furthermore, the Finnish *hemvårdsstöd* is included in taxable income and affected by other social benefits. During the 1990s recession, eligibility was further curtailed. Up to 1993, one could receive both *hemvårdsstöd* and unemployment benefits. Between 1993 and 1995, it was possible for one parent to receive the *hemvårdsstöd* at the same time as the other one received unemployment benefits. Since 1995, it is no longer possible for one family to receive both types of benefits. The *hemvårdsstöd* would be deducted from any potential unemployment benefits paid out to the other parent (Knudsen 2001, 123). However, a family with one unemployed parent can receive the *hemvårdsstöd*, if the parent who is not unemployed looks after the child at home by her- or himself (Korpinen 2000, 180).

As in Norway, mothers make up the majority of the recipients of the benefits.[31] However, the proportion of men increased radically between 1993 and 1995.[32] The main reason for this increase was the adjustment of *hemvårdsstöd* and unemployment benefits, not men becoming more interested in looking after their children at home. This explanation is further supported by the fact that the amount of men receiving the benefits decreased radically when the above-mentioned restrictions came into force in 1996.[33]

The amount of the *hemvårdsstöd* was reduced in 1996 by approximately 23 per cent, which made many people afraid that the demand for municipal day care would increase and parents would stop opting for the allowance. This expectation proved to be correct: the number of children in municipal day care increased by 2 500 because of the cuts. Furthermore, some 4 000 families dropped out as users of the allowance because of its reduced level. At the same time, another 6 000 – 7 000 families with one spouse out of work saw the *hemvårdsstöd* being taken away from them because of the adjustments made correlating the *hemvårdsstöd* with unemployment benefits. As a result of these concurrent changes, the number of families receiving basic subsistence support – which is a constitutionally-secured subjective right – increased in 1997. The statistics for 1997 show that the use of the *hemvårdsstöd* increased again along with the proportion of children under three years covered by the system. In most of these cases, the families are taking care of their children themselves.

As in Norway, the allowance scheme has resulted in much heated political debate especially with regard to the effects upon the position of women in the labour market. Women's participation in the active labour force has declined as the system of the *hemvårdsstöd* has expanded (Sipilä and Korpinen 1998, 269; Salmi 2000, 191-92). But any leave from the active labour force is usually temporary, meaning that the labour force participation of mothers reverts back to high average figures after the youngest child has outgrown the age of receiving the *hemvårdsstöd* (Salmi 2000, 192-93). It has also been pointed out that the allowance seems to create a dependence on the income of the working spouse along with higher costs for employers with women employees. As in Norway, studies about the effects of the allowance have revealed women to be a heterogeneous group, with different values influencing their choices of how best to take care of their children.

It seems more difficult to measure changes in women's working patterns caused by the allowance and draw conclusions from them, because the introduction of *hemvårdsstöd* coincided with the economic decline in Finland in the early 1990s, with its concomitant high unemployment and scaling down of social benefits and services not to mention the complex composition of the allowance. It seems clear that the *hemvårdsstöd* has been an important source of livelihood for women and their families during periods where it has been difficult to get employment or stay employed. However, the proportion of recipients of the *hemvårdsstöd* has been rather stable also in periods with better economic and working conditions, which suggests that there is a certain quota of women who are interested in taking care of their young children themselves for a period of time.

In the late 1980s, about 50 per cent of the working mothers in Finland chose to stay home with unpaid leave or chose to stop working for a period of time because of the *hemvårdsstöd*. In Norway, we have experienced only minor adjustments when it comes to changes in the working hours of mothers.

The reasons are most certainly more complex than can be analyzed here. Suffice it to say that the Norwegian HCA seems to represents a more flexible way to reconcile work with the raising of children. The Norwegian solution detaching the requirements to receive the allowance from requirements addressing parents' adjustments in working hours seems to provide somewhat of an explanation. Nonetheless, in contrast to Norwegian women, the women in Finland have not been able to enjoy any sort of traditional reconciliation strategy, *viz.*, taking part-time jobs and working flexible hours. Therefore, adjustments in working patterns due to the *hemvårdsstöd* seem more innovative in Finland, than in Norway.

Despite the fact that free choice is more of a reality in Finland, where a place in a day care centre is guaranteed for all claimants, many women still prefer the *hemvårdsstöd*. This preference should also be expected to prevail in Norway and demonstrates the principle of freedom of choice as having value in and of itself.

France

The French system[34] has a rich array of child-related cash benefits, some of which bear similarities to the Norwegian and Finnish systems. In France, the Child-Rearing Allowance (*allocation parentale d'éducation*, APE) is paid to a parent who interrupts or reduces his or her professional activities. The allowance has its legal basis in the Social Security Code. It comes into play when the number of dependent children in a household rises to a minimum of two because of a birth, an adoption or the assumption of the responsibility of a child. It is granted to the person (housewife or househusband) who takes care of the child if she/he had previously been gainfully employed in a job generating pension benefits. The allowance is paid out until the child reaches the age of three. The allowance may be partially granted to a person working part-time. The total allowance amounts to 487 euros. The partial payout amounts to 322 euros if the part-time work does not make up more than 50 per cent of the legal working time; the payout falls to 243 euros if the employment takes up more than 50 per cent but less than 80 per cent of the working time.

The allowance may also be partially granted to both parents if they both work part-time. APE cannot be accumulated with other allowances managed by the National Family Allowance Office, such as the Young Child Allowance, the Adoption Allowance, the Family Complement, as well as with the payment of maternity or adoption leaves.

The APE – quite unintentionally – has been an incentive for non-qualified women to leave the labour market for as long as three years, with the risk of being unable to find a new job after the period of leave time. The activity rate of women with two young children has decreased from 74 per cent (1994) to 56 per cent (March 1998). The fact that 98 per cent of parents who take parental leave are women shows that the measure is far from being neutral in terms of encouraging a redistribution of roles between women and men. In the year 2000, in order to favour the return of caregivers to employment, it has been decided that when the parent resumes child care activities between the 18th and the 30th month of the child, he or she can retain the APE for two months even after going back to employment.[35]

Germany

Germany[36] has an arrangement called the childraising allowance, which, to some extent, resembles the Finnish and the French allowances. Since January 1986, parents have been able to claim the child-raising allowance or *Erziehungsgeld*, which is primarily understood as a recognition of the commitment it takes to look after children. Recently the arrangement has been altered. The legal basis is the Federal Child-raising Allowance Act, which has reformed the system of childraising allowances and has introduced a new parental leave. The allowance applies only to children born in or after 2002. With regard to children born prior to 2001, an earlier legislation continues to apply.

The childraising allowance is available from the day of childbirth until the child is 24 months old. The main requirement is that the mother or the father applying for the benefit not be gainfully employed on a full-time basis. Yet he or she may work up to 30 hours a week without losing the entitlement to the child-raising allowance. The maximum childraising allowance for each child is 307 euros per month. Alternatively, a budget of 460 euros a month is possible, but only up to the child's first birthday.

The childraising allowance is subject to income limits. In the first six months after childbirth, parents who have a single child can receive full parental benefits, provided that the household income is under 51 130 euros a year or 38 350 euros a year for single parents. When the child reaches seven months, the allowance is reduced in the case of married couples, who are not permanently separated and whose income exceeds 16 470 euros a year and in the case of other entitled claimants, whose income exceeds 13 498 euros a year. If the parents' annual income exceeds the stated limit, the allowance is reduced incrementally. Income limits increase for each additional child.

The new legislation entitles both parents to apply for parental leave or *Elternzeit* simultaneously for all or part of a maximum period of three years (for a child). With an employer's consent, up to one year of parental leave can be taken later, between the child's third and eighth birthdays. Each parent who takes parental leave may work up to 30 hours a week. An important provision includes the general right to part-time work if the employer has more than 15 employees and the right to have the number of working hours reinstated to pre-leave levels upon the termination of parental leave.

Two stated aims of the introduction of the new Federal Childraising Allowance Act have been to redress the traditional role division between the sexes whereby mothers typically stay at home to look after their children and to address the adverse effects this fact has had on the professional lives of women. In accordance with the Federal Childraising Allowance Act, Article 23, the Federal Government must collect annual statistics of the sex, nationality, status and employment status of the recipients. According to Article 24, the Federal Government is further required to submit a report by 1 July 2004 to the German *Bundestag* on the effects of the provisions on parental leave and part-time work during parental leave on employees and employers, as well as any necessary amendments. It is too early yet to say anything about the large-scale effects of the new Federal Childraising Allowance Act. However, given the track records of the Norwegian, Finnish and French legislation, there seems little reason to hope that the German allowance will have any particularly significant influence on redressing the traditional role division between the sexes.

Discussion and Concluding Remarks

One of the biggest issues of social policy and employment strategy today is the looming danger of occupational passivity. Any efforts to reconcile work and family are interpreted in light of decreasing labour force participation. In Norway, as everywhere else in Europe, the population is ageing and disincentives to work are increasing. Methods of adjusting the needs of the labour market – and consequently, the welfare system – to the care of children and ageing people must take into account the prospect of a decreasing amount of labour market participants.

However, the current policies are inconsistent in this respect. Norwegian trade unions have proposed a general reduction of working hours and the introduction of a six-hour working day. In addition, labour organisations would further activate early retirement schemes. Such a 'waste' of labour being seriously discussed, it seems unfair to allocate the whole burden of occupational activity to the parents of young children. Either way, it does not seem to make sense to exclude parents from an offer of state financial support on the grounds that there is such great demand for their labour market participation.

The original idea of enhancing the equality of families irrespective of their choice of childcare arrangement does seem to have been realized (see Baklien et al. 2001, 57-60). However, it also seems as though we cannot expect the amount of the HCA benefits to reach the level of the subsidies allocated to municipal day care centres in the near future. If the government is one day soon able to offer places in municipal day care centres to more families and at lower prices, we may, nevertheless, hope for further adjustments.

Then, the principle of freedom of choice in child-care arrangements should also become more of a reality. Now, the low level of wages in many woman-dominated trades, and, secondly, inadequate public day care curtail the choices of most families. Of course, it is possible that wages will increase and working conditions will improve due to the decreasing supply of labour and the increasing demand of qualified personnel because employers have to provide better offers to hold on to their employees. But, as Brox (1997) has pointed out, it cannot be just the people in the best-paying jobs who have the right to work, while people in low-paying jobs are the ones who have the duty to work. A political aim of merely securing cheap labour cannot be sustained in the long run. A decent level of income should be one of the priorities of employment policy.

An almost unanimous opinion prevails regarding the primary aim to secure the best interests of the child. However, this aim inevitably clashes with the goals of gender equality and the enforced occupational activities of women. According to the media interpretation of the evaluation reports, time spent with children has increased by only 1.5 hours per week on average. However, as Baklien, et al. have shown (2001), the 1.5 hours only signifies a reduction in the working hours of women, not necessarily the total time spent with children. Nevertheless, when considering the large amount of families who have received the HCA, it is fair to assume that there has been a considerable increase of 'parent-time'.

A problem yet to be resolved is to encourage men to assume a larger share of caring responsibilities. Equal wages would be one of the most important factors towards that end. The Christian Democrats have proposed that the Norwegian paternity leave, now four weeks, be extended up to ten weeks. The Norwegian Federation of Trade Unions, in its proposal, suggested eight weeks according to *Verdens Gang* 11 May and 15 June 2001.

The future of the Norwegian HCA scheme seems bright. Most parties would like to continue the scheme with slightly altered preconditions. The Centre Party would like to tie the allowance to the care provided by parents themselves at home, but would allow for an income of up to 100 000 crowns (ca. 12 000 euros) to complement the HCA (Lahnstein 2001). The Christian Democrats have proposed an augmentation of the level of the allowance. Both the Christian Democrats and the Conservative Party have suggested that the amount of the HCA should not necessarily have to correspond to the subsidies of a public day care place as was presupposed in the original proposal (Grimstad and Helleland 2001, see also St.prp no. 53, 1997-8). At the same time, the government has agreed to increase subsidies for day care centres by at least 240 000 000 crowns (ca. 30 000 000 euros) a year. This subsidy would mean price reductions amounting to approximately 2 000 crowns (ca. 240 euros) a year per one place in a day care centre (Orheim 2001).

Finally, the debate on the HCA seems to concern the issue of a just division of caring responsibilities. To what extent should families be expected to sort themselves out on their own? Is there any public or governmental responsibility to support the choices made by families either directly via allowance payments or indirectly, by providing subsidized services? Decisions on these issues are irrevocably dependent on the priorities and values of Norwegian society. So far, no ideal solution has been designed, but the current debates show a willingness at least to meet the needs and concerns in constructive ways.

Notes

1 In 1994, Sweden had a cash benefit plan, but it was repealed after only 6 months (see the law about *vårdnadsbidrag* or care benefits 1994:553, prop. 1993/94:148, and prop. 1994/95:61). Even before the passage of the Home Care Allowance Act, some municipalities in Norway had introduced various cash benefit schemes to parents with young children (see St.prp. no.53, 1997-8, 13-4).
2 These principles were first promulgated in St.prp no. 53, 1997-8.
3 These non-intentional effects were pointed out in St.prp. no. 53, 1997-8, but they have also been put forward by different kinds of opponents in various other connections.
4 Whether the government should supply services or give payments to the public is an old debate. It is not my intention to determine which choice is best. However, the HCA debate is special as it does not represent an either/or approach, but rather than a both/and approach.
5 The amount was raised from 3000 *crowns* 1 August 2003 due to a redistribution of public funds relating to day-care centres and the HCA. The increase of the HCA corresponds to the repeal of the *småbarnstillegg,* a fixed component within the children's allowance paid to families with children between one and three years of age. Families with children in day-care centres are compensated through reductions in price effectuated by increased governmental subsidies. Families whose children do not attend day-care centres are fully compensated through the raise of the HCA. The intention behind the redistribution of public funds is to increase the development of more day-care centres and reduce the price of attending day-care centres to an average of 2 500 crowns per month.
6 For more explicit explanations, see Brækhus 1999, 342 -6.
7 Increased income taxation will most likely lead to a too low labour supply (see Thoresen et al. 1998, p. 16). Besides, the regulation of tax allowances (see the Income Tax Act of 26 March 1999, § 15-4) could lead to that a family where one parent earns much money and the other does not, gets better off if the last one mentioned stops working and receives the HCA. This result is due to the fact that a husband or wife who supports both him/herself and his/her partner are granted a double family allowance from the tax authorities. Because of the head tax (the progressive taxation) the effect will be greater to tax payers who because of high incomes pay head tax. Besides, the head tax strikes into a higher income level for taxpayers within tax code 2. Together these benefits could amount to a lot of money if compared to the partner's alternative income after taxation. For further details, see Vigerust 1998, 215 and Thoresen et al. 1998, 14.
8 According to SSB [the National Bureau of Statistics], 1999.
9 This was pointed out in St.prp no. 53, 1997-8, 29-30.
10 Such hypotheses have also been presented in several (written) submissions on the HCA scheme.
11 From including only the period of paid maternity/paternity leave according to the National Insurance Act, to including nearly the entire leave of absence period according to the Working Environment Act.
12 Although they were pointed out in the proposal from the government to the Storting (St.prp. no.53, 1997-8).
13 A report present by The Research Council of Norway Feb. 2001, commissioned by and on behalf of the Norwegian Ministry of Children and Family Affairs. This report summarises a great number of reports published during the last three to four years. The following presentation builds consistently on the Baklien et al. (2001) report itself. Unless otherwise

stated, the report considers changes measured from 1998 to 1999.

14 For example by Vigerust, 1998.

15 See also 'Framework for day-care centres', regulation number 948 passed by the Norwegian Ministry of Children and Family Affairs, 1 December 1995.

16 Borge and Melhuish (1995) found negative effects upon small children and positive effects upon older children. Blau and Grossberg (1992) show negative effects upon children's cognitive development from mothers' entry into paid employment during the children's first year, while positive effects were found when they entered paid employment during the children's second or subsequent years. Hartmann (1992) and Andersson (1992) conclude that there are positive short- and long-term effects of day-care centres. Ulvund (1998) refers to somewhat contradictory results.

17 This is not necessarily valid for families at risk, such as socially deprived parents, or parents of children with special needs.

18 The average number of working hours per week was measured as having dropped from 23.9 to 22.4 hours per week, i.e,. a decrease of 1,5 hours (see Baklien et al. 2001, 24).

19 Measured by educational level. The evaluation reports did not have data of the mothers' actual or potential income (see Baklien et al. 2001, 25).

20 However, these changes appear only indirectly, since the reports restrict themselves to building on postulations concerning what the situation would have been like in 1999, if the HCA had not been introduced. And the changes measured are also based on different types of control or comparison parameters (see Baklien et al. 2001, 26). This way of measuring changes is also criticised (Baklien et al. 2001, 29).

21 These reports build on statistics for 1996–2000.

22 But the proportion of employed mothers varies somewhat within this period.

23 Some of the reports found no change, while others reported a reduction of 1.5 hours per week.

24 These reports were based on questioning mothers about whether they would have stayed at home regardless of the introduction of the HCA, or if the HCA was likely to be the cause of their staying at home (see Baklien et al. 2001, 28).

25 Dahl describes how women's and men's economic positions can be determined through the three providing poles; marriage, social security/benefits and income. She points out that women more often than men have difficulties achieving the stronger rights derived from income or social security, primarily because women commonly have a weaker position within the labour market and because of the close connections between income and social benefits. See also Burman et al. in this volume on the situation in Sweden.

26 With the adoption of the Children's Home Care Allowance Act 1985/24.

27 http://www.reform-monitor.org/index.php3?mode=status , 4 April 2003.

28 This requirement first appeared in 1997.

29 According to Governmental Proposal no. 53, 1997-8. I do not distinguish between the *hemvårdsstöd* and the *privatvårdsstöd* because the legal implications are the same.

30 http://www.reform-monitor.org/index.php3?mode=status , 4 April 2003.

31 During the 1980s, 97 per cent of the recipients were mothers (Knudsen 2001, 123). In 1996, 93 per cent of the beneficiaries were women (Korpinen 2000, 179).

32 The proportion increased from 6.3 per cent in 1992, to 15.2 per cent in 1993, 18.2 per cent in 1994 and 17.1 per cent in 1995 (Korpinen 2000, 179).

33 The proportion decreased to 7.3 per cent in 1996 (Korpinen 2000, 179).

34 The information about the France system draws on

http://www.europa.eu.int/comm/employment_social/missoc2001/f_part9_en.htm
http://www.childpolicyintl.org/countries/france.html
http://www.ilo.org/public/english/employment/gems/eeo/program/france/nfao.htm, 10 April 2003.

35 In addition to the APE, France has two allowances that subsidize the costs of home care for a child under the age of three, namely the Child Home care Allowance or *allocation de garde d'enfant à domicile*, AGED and the Private child care allowance or *aide à la famille pour l'emploi d'une assistante maternelle agree*, AFEAMA).

36 The information about the German system draws on
http://www.ilo.org/public/english/employment/gems/eeo/law/germany/l_ flcr.htm
http://www.germany-info.org/relaunch/info/facts/facts_about/life.html
http://www.europa.eu.int/comm/employment_social/missoc2001/d_part9_en.htm
http://www.bma.de/download/broschueren/a998.pdf, 10 April 2003.

References

Aftenposten (2001), '74 prosent av barna fikk kontantstøtte', *Aftenposten,* 22 January.

Andersson, Bengt-Erik (1992), 'Effects of Day-Care on Cognitive and Socioemotional Competence of Thirteen-Year-Old Swedish Schoolchildren', *Child Development 63 pp.* 20-36.

Baklien, Bergljot, Anne Lise Ellingsæter and Lars Guldbransen (2001), 'Evaluering av Kontantstøtteordningen', *Norsk Forskningsråd, Området for kultur og samfunn.*

BFD (1995), 'Forskrift om rammeplan for barnehagen', *FOR 1995-12-01 948.*

Blau, Francine D. and Adam. J. Grossberg (1992), 'Maternal Labor Supply and Children's Cognitive Development', *The Review of Economics and Statistics 74 pp.* 474-81.

Borge, Anne I. H. and Edward C. Melhuish (1995), 'A Longitudinal Study of Childhood Behaviour Problems, Maternal Employment, and Day Care in a Rural Norwegian Community', *International Journal of Behavioral Development 18 pp.* 23-42.

Brækhus, Hege (1999), 'Kontantstøtten for eller mot kvinnene?', *Kritisk Juss,* no.4 pp. 337-50.

Brox, Ottar (1997), 'Rolleforvirring i kontantstøttesaken?', *Aftenposten,* 17 November.

Bungum, Brita, Berit Brandth and Elin Kvande (2001), 'Ulik praksis – ulike konsekvenser. En evaluering av kontantstøttens konsekvenser for likestilling i arbeidsliv og familieliv', *SINTEF Teknologiledelse IFIM and Institutt for statsvitenskap og sosiologi,* NTNU.

Dahl, Tove Stang (1985), 'Kvinners rett til penger', in *Kvinnerett II*, ed. Tove Stang Dahl pp. 11-30.

Ekren, Steinar (1998), 'Kontantstøtten: En alternativ økonomisk vinkling', *Sosialøkonome,* no.6 pp. 2-6.

Grimstad, May Helen M. and Trond Helland (2001), 'Høyre og Kr.F. forlater Kontantstøtteprinsipper', *Aftenposten,* 15 March.

Hartman, Ellen, (1992), 'Mors og barnehagens betydning for barns skolegang, utdanning og utvikling av selvstendighet og autonom', *Tidsskrift for Norsk Psykologiforening* 29 pp. 716-30.

Hovdum, Anders Rosenhayn, Stein Kuhle and Liv Stokke (1994), 'Mot en ny velferdstat', in Tove Stang Dahl (ed.), *Pene piker haiker ikke*, pp. 331-6.

Josefsen, Laila-Brith (1999), 'Barnehagen – en del av utdanningssystemet', *Dagbladet,* 11 January.

Knudsen, Christin (2001), 'Kontantstøtten og mødres yrkesaktivitet i Finland og Norge. Likheter og ulikheter', *Søkelys på arbeidsmarkedet 2001,* no.2 pp. 121-127.

Korpinen, Johanna (2000), 'Child home care allowance – framing the finnish experience', in *Perspectives of Equality. Work, women and family in the Nordic Countries and EU,* Nord 2000 no.5 pp. 174-86.

Kvande, Elin (2001), 'Tar imot men liker det ikke', *Adresseavisa,* 15 February.

Lahnstein, Anne Enger (2001), '–En ny sentrumsregjering må reforhandle ordningen', *Aftenposten,* 16 March.

Lund, Diderik (1998), 'Kontantstøtte – en økonomisk analyse', *Dagens Næringsliv,* 31 January.

McGlynn, Clare (2001), 'Reclaiming a feminist vision: the reconciliation of paid work and family life in European Union law and policy', *The Columbia Journal of European Law,* vol.7, no 2 pp. 241-272.

Orheim, Karita (2001), 'Billigere Barnehager – en nødvendighet', *Dagsavisen,* 4 July.

Prop. 1993/94: 148 'Om lag om vårdnadsbidrag'.

Prop. 1994/95:61 'Socialutskottets betänkande om vårdnadsbidraget, garantidagarna og enskild Barneomsorg'.

Sainsbury, Diane (2001), 'Gender and the Making of Welfare States: Norway and Sweden', *Social Politics,* Spring 2001 pp. 113-141.

Salmi, Minna (2000), 'Analysing the Finnish Homecare Allowance System: challenges to research and problems of interpretation', in *Perspectives of Equality. Work, women and family in the Nordic Countries and EU,* Nord 2000 no.5 pp. 187-207.

Sipilä, Jorma and Korpinen, Johanna (1998), 'Cash versus Child Care Services in Finland', *Social Policy Administration 32*, no. 3, pp. 263-277.

Sletvold, Leif (2000), 'Kontantstøtteordningens konsekvenser for yrkesaktivitet og likestilling', *NOVA Rapport 15.*

SSB (1999), 'Fremskrivning av folkemengden 1999-2050. Nasjonale og regionale tall', *Ukens statistikk 48 pp.* 25-36.

St.prp. nr. 54 (1997-98), 'Innføring av kontantstøtte til småbarnsforeldre'.

Strøm, Steinar (1998), 'Kontantstøtten', *Sosialøkonomen nr.3 pp.* 2-7.

Thoresen, Thor O., Iulie Aslaksen, Charlotte Koren, and Kjetil Lund (1998), 'Kontantstøtte – noen betraktninger om effektivitet og fordeling', *Sosialøkonomen* no.4 *pp.* 12-21.

Ulvund, Stein Erik (1998), 'Barnehage eller hjemmeomsorg?', *Dagbladet,* 28 February.

VG (2001), 'Her er mitt LO', *VG,* 11 June.

VG (2001), 'Vil ha ti uker pappa-perm', *VG,* 15 June.

Vigerust, Elisabeth (1998), 'Kontantstøtte til småbarnsforeldre – et velbegrunnet sporskifte?', *Kritisk Juss nr.3 pp.* 205-21.

Wærness, Kari (1998), 'Barnet er viktigst', *Kvinneforskning nr.2 pp.* 5-11.

Øvrebø, Turid (2000), 'Spebarnsfedre vil ut av huset', *NIKK magasin: Maskuline mysterier,* no.1.

http://www.reform-monitor.org/index.php3?mode=status

http://www.ilo.org/public/english/employment/gems/eeo/law/germany/l_ flcr.htm

http://www.germany-info.org/relaunch/info/facts/facts_about/life.html

http://www.europa.eu.int/comm/employment_social/missoc2001/d_part9_en.htm

http://www.bma.de/download/broschueren/a998.pdf

http://www.europa.eu.int/comm/employment_social/missoc2001/f_part9_en.htm

http://www.childpolicyintl.org/countries/france.html

http://www.ilo.org/public/english/employment/gems/eeo/program/france/nfao.htm

Chapter 7

Economic Dependence and Self-Support in Family, Tax and Social Law

Åsa Gunnarsson, Monica Burman and Lena Wennberg

Introduction

Despite an actively promoted equality politics and a high rate of participation in the work force, family life and caring still shape the lives of women in Sweden today to a greater extent than such activities impact the lives of men.

To a large extent, women's living conditions are intertwined with family life. The normative and structural patterns shaping these living conditions emerge from traditionally gendered functions within the family in combination with how the family, as an institution, is organized in society. A general picture of the unequal distribution of power and resources between men and women shows that the economic dependence of women exists in the triangular relation among state, market and family, in which exchanges of time, care and money are processed (Stang Dahl 1985). In other words, family life constitutes economic and social subordination for women. According to mainstream social and legal science, however, knowledge about gender relations in the family can be best characterized by a black box (Gunnarsson 2001a; Nyman 2002).

Even in the Swedish welfare system, in which the independent economy of each individual, irrespective of family status, lies at the core of all legislation, family plays a role in defining the status of women – often to their detriment. Law and legal science mostly ignore this fact – as well as their own roles in creating overt and covert discriminatory patterns with regard to the family. As Frances Olsen has argued (Olsen 1985), the state constantly defines and redefines the family and adjusts and readjusts family roles. A task for feminist legal studies, therefore, is to challenge any biased conceptions of family life, any false neutrality or purported non-intervention.

The legal framework shaping the economic living conditions of a family can be described as an interplay of family law, tax law and social welfare law. All these fields of law are sex-neutral. However, since the structural relationship between men and women is ignored, it has become evident that the aims of Swedish sex equality politics to improve the status of women have not been achieved through sex-neutral legislation. By studying the structural relations between women and men and by studying how relations in the family are constituted, symbolized and processed in law, we aim to highlight the gap between official Swedish sex equality policy and what has been achieved through sex-neutral legislation.

We argue that the Swedish example of using sex-neutral law to promote equal opportunities in the labour market and the reconciliation of employment and family life, has reached a turning point. This assertion is important to make in the context of sex equality policy formations in the European Union.

In this chapter, we analyze the internal contradictions of family, tax and social welfare law with regard to their implicit assumptions of family and dependence. We argue that the dominant model of family life assumed by Swedish family, tax and social welfare law is a dual breadwinner family. A basic principle underlying these fields of law is a reliance on economic independence and self-support through work. The ideal two-income family, therefore, is when both parents work full-time and each has an income of his or her own, in about the same income group and above the poverty line. Families with just one parent do not fit into this model. According to a feminist approach to law, it is of special interest to ask whether law takes the specific problems of single, or 'solo', mothers into account.

The core of the normative problem that we want to explore is how legal reforms reflect and promote autonomy and self-support in relation to this two-income family model. When a family does not resemble the model, legal presumptions of economic dependence come into the picture. In reality, income and working-hours are unequally distributed between spouses and cohabitants, especially when they have small children (Nyberg 1997). Economic dependence and support of other family members is presumed in one way or another. The right to support during marriage, based on the concept of economic dependence, is still part of the Marriage Code. Legal reforms concerning needs-based public support to families often regard the family as a closed unit. For solo parents, economic self-support is seldom an option, which turns their household into some kind of defective family formation in relation to the model.

The dual breadwinner family model has created the norm for equality. Difference is any kind of deviance from this normative model. The model itself may become an obstacle to recognizing difference and finding solutions to problems, which are related to different life choices and family situations. Our analysis shows that there are also legal regulations, which are based on assumptions of economic dependence within the family. These legal regulations are not based, however, on the goals of official policies. In the Swedish sex-neutral context, the relationship between the concrete regulations and the underlying values of family models is far from explicit. In the following, we set out to explore these values vis-à-vis family, tax and social welfare law.

The methodological approach we used in this article can be best understood by referring to the significant role of preparatory works in the Swedish legal tradition.

The interpretation of law is functional and can only emanate from the use of certain specific sources of law, which are distinctively hierarchical. Preparatory works or *travaux préparatoires* are ranked second after statutory law and are rich in statements about the functional aims of the statutes. Often this material leading up to actual legislation include guiding principles according to which the law must be interpreted and applied. Judges as well as scholars are presumed to be very familiar with the texts and loyal to legislators' expectations about the function and aims of the legislation. In short, this legal tradition is expected to provide a high degree of predictability as to how a court may judge a case.

However, to fulfil the purpose of exploring how law can contribute to the resurrection of gender inequalities, an approach other than the traditional one is needed. We cannot rely on explicit aims of legislation. We also have to trace the implicit legal notions of family and dependence. A method deployed in this analysis has been to read the discourses in preparatory works with an eye to gaining a contextual understanding.

Sex Equality in the Workfare State

The changing scenery of the Nordic welfare countries has attracted plenty of research over the last years. By challenging the transitional phase of the Nordic welfare model, a deeper understanding of the distinctive Nordic qualities of social policy has been reached.[1] Empirical comparative studies show that the Nordic welfare countries are following a 'model-specific route', which has kept the distinctly characteristic features of the Nordic model relatively unchanged despite the political, economic and social upheavals of the 1990s. A high degree of universalism, in the sense that all residents are entitled to basic social security benefits and services regardless of their position in the labour market, is still one of the essential features of the Nordic model. Benefit levels and the ultimate safety net in the form of social assistance have been fairly high. Social insurance schemes, embodying earnings-related components for those persons with a work history, also uphold good standards of quality and are relatively generous. The structure of the benefit system is guided by an egalitarian principle and combined with a tax-based financing model. In comparison with the other members of the European Union, poverty rates are lower, income is more evenly distributed and sex equality policy is much more pronounced in the Nordic countries (Kautto et al. 1999; Kautto et al. 2001; SOU 2000:83).

This empirical evidence supports the image of the Nordic countries as women-friendly welfare states, an image developed not least by feminist scholars who have appreciated extensive programs providing welfare for women, families and children and extensive female participation both in the labour market and vis-à-vis policy making. In Sweden, the vision of a women-friendly welfare state has also been reflected in many legal reforms, which have made an important contribution to the progress of sex equality over the last three decades. The Government and the Parliament have both strongly emphasized that sex equality and the formation of the welfare state are closely connected (Burman and Gunnarsson 2001).

However, the vision of the women-friendly Nordic welfare state is now fading. Social citizenship, meaning the division of responsibilities between the individual and the state and among individuals within the community, is gendered and has become increasingly problematic from the gender perspective (Liebert 2001). The false conception of universalism in the Nordic welfare regimes has overlooked the existence of gendered diversity and difference in social citizenship, which arises from human functions connected to labour, care, responsibility and time (Sevenhuijsen 1998). The designation of social rights and duties can promote or undermine these human functional capabilities and a lack of capabilities is a problem of social justice (Nussbaum 1999).

Even the Swedish welfare system has left the economic power relations between women and men relatively unchanged. Women's unfavourable position is reflected in the way in which women are more dependent on the welfare state than men. In general, women have lower incomes than men, which, to a certain extent, is explained by a sex-segregated labour market where low-income work and part-time work are carried out mostly by women. The allocation of time to household and care work is also unequally shared between men and women.[2] Because the segregation of the labour market and work in the home is not sex neutral, the Swedish system obviously has a sex-related division of rights and duties.[3]

From a Swedish perspective, the core problem can be traced to a narrow concept of sex equality policies, according to which the dominant egalitarian idea is that women support themselves through labour market participation. The principle of independence via participation in the labour market has been an important goal of both socialists and liberal feminists. More importantly, however, it has also been supported by market interests. The principle promotes the interests of market actors who benefit from the increasing size of the domestic labour force. As a result, the percent age of married women working outside the home has increased. Substantial achievements in sex equality, therefore, should be analyzed primarily as a result of a labour market demand (Gunnarsson and Stattin 2001). Legal reforms implementing this narrow market-oriented gender policy have adopted a sex-neutral view of women as self-supporting individuals.

According to the Swedish welfare tradition, the so-called work principle has always been the leading principle. The main component of the Swedish social security system is social insurance. The right to benefits from social insurance funds is earned through paid labour and, thus, is geared towards the individual, and not towards the family. This workfare-based policy, with an earnings-related benefits system, pays no attention to the fact that individuals are gendered, live in different kinds of households and have different responsibilities vis-à-vis caring for children and the elderly. Two related underlying assumptions in tax law, social welfare law and family law are that every adult should work and that no one should be economically dependent upon any other individual. The distribution of welfare in Sweden has been a state-governed collective responsibility. Once employed, the individual's established position in the welfare system is well-protected, especially for those persons who have been employed full-time over a longer period.

The right and obligation of women to be self-supporting is articulated in the framework of a reconciliation ideology, promoting paid work and family life for both women and men. The Swedish framework for reconciliation is officially called the combination strategy, focusing on enforcing those legal, economic and social measures that have the potential to encourage women to combine paid work with family life. The combination strategy was aimed at eliminating the subordination of women in the family.

This strategy, however, has ignored an important normative dilemma by overlooking relational dependency within the household arising from the care work and household production traditionally performed by women. In sum, the combination strategy clearly shows that women's equality of rights starts and ends in the family. Earnings-related individual rights do not exist for women who do the work of a housewife (Burman and Gunnarsson 2001).

The ideology of equality, meaning that women and men should not only have formal equal rights, but also equal opportunities and equality of results, has strongly influenced Swedish legal reforms since the 1970s. According to the official statement in government documents, the policies of welfare and equality are mutually dependent. Equal rights for men and women are protected by the Constitution, which also includes a prohibition against legislation that is sex-discriminatory. The anti-discrimination principle is interpreted as requiring a formal sex-neutrality in law. Applied via a practice that is, itself, discriminatory, legal reforms have tended to maintain the status quo rather than to promote increased sex equality. Legal reforms also obscure the norm of the supremacy of the male and the presumed objectivity and universality of that norm. This result is not new for feminist legal studies around the world. The Swedish example, however, can contribute to theories about women as the particular other by revealing the large gap between the law and the progressive aims of sex equality politics. The conclusion is that the principles of sex equality expressed in the Swedish Constitution have become abstract because of a lack of constructive interpretation and efficient implementation (Svensson 2001).

Since the 1990s, the crisis of the welfare state has been a topic of great interest in the Nordic countries. In the early 1990s, after a long period of prosperity, Swedish unemployment increased. The restructuring of the public economy during the first half of the 1990s which was aimed at reducing the budget deficit and fighting inflation, actually had the result of undermining the general welfare system for which Sweden is well-known. Welfare-state induced impoverishment, for example, unemployment and poverty traps for low- and middle-income families, has escalated. Because these traps are said to create disincentives to work, a more consistent tax and benefit policy has been called for (Gunnarsson 2001a).

The contemporary Swedish debate about family policy and the welfare state's tax-benefit balance highlights the fact that single, or solo mothers are at the margin.

The term 'solo mother' refers to a mother not living with the person legally defined as the father to her children. Solo mothers are over-represented in poverty and unemployment traps. One part of this normative issue is about family identities. Another part is about women's dependence upon economic support. Despite the reality of individual-based social rights and fiscal obligations, nuclear family ideology is very much alive. Even if single parents are a group with specific needs and living conditions, they are not legally targeted as a group. In contrast to many other Western countries, this situation is not a symptom of a 'back to family values' crusade. It is more correctly seen as being rooted in a kind of hidden value, a conception of a model family, one which has never been systematically criticized and reflected upon.

The other part of the normative issue has to do with women's dependence on the welfare state for economic support. The workfare policy in the social democratic welfare model has not given women, particularly mothers, a strong platform for economic independence. Of course, the opportunity for women to seek paid work outside the home is a very important part of this process, but how this opportunity is made possible is very much related to the conditions of the market. When women shifted from working in the home to working in the market, men did not make a similar, reverse shift.[4] Instead, a partial institutionalization of care work has taken place. The goal of making sex equality politics compatible with the work-fare policy is a too narrow perspective. While the government has declared the importance of each parent's equal responsibility for the care of their children, very little action has been taken. Inequalities in how much time women and men devote to care work persist (Gunnarsson and Stattin 2001).

In the text that follows, we use a descriptive approach in order to identify how sex inequalities are resurrected in sex-neutral legislation. We show that an assumption of dependency between spouses still exists in family law, tax law and in work-related social security schemes, despite the dominant ideology of the self-support principle. We will also show how residence-related family support benefits and social assistance provisions are based on a presumption of maintenance obligations within the family.

The Liberalization of Family Law

Contemporary Swedish family law is characterized by secularism, individualism and equality. Economic independence for women is a central policy goal for sex equality. Since the 1960s, sexual politics have also been quite liberal, supporting neutrality regarding sexual behaviour and sexual orientation. As result of this tradition, a special concept of neutrality towards different family forms has been developed in family law, including the enactment of the Cohabitation Act in 1987.[5]

The liberal equality approach to family law began in the 19th century. During the period 1909–1929, the Scandinavian countries co-operated to harmonize their laws, which resulted in an almost identical constructions of egalitarian marriage, involving the liberalization of the family. Scandinavian laws differed from the laws in force in most other West European countries and are described as progressive for that time (Bradley 1996, 13).

In Sweden, the concepts of individualism and formal sex equality were introduced in a new Marriage Code in 1920. Married women were given the same legal subjecthood as men and the husband's right of guardianship was abolished. Each spouse also obtained an individual right to control and dispose of his or her marital property and each became responsible only for his or her own debts. However, the equality discourse of the 1920s was strongly connected to concerns about marriage as an institution and the country's demographic situation.[6] It was based on a notion of sex difference by which a traditional model of the family was maintained (Melby et al. 2000, 19-20). Married women's work outside the home was recognized as a possibility, but a rather exceptional one (Burman 2001, 76-77). A two-breadwinner model could fit into the new model, but, at the same time, it was based on a gendered division of work, an arrangement which supported reproductive and household work as women's areas. In addition, married women's economic dependence on their husbands was clearly articulated.

At the end of the 1960s, changing social structures and family patterns were used as core arguments for reviewing family law, but the reform process was not fully completed until the end of the 1980s. The aim was to reach beyond equal opportunities – to equality of result promoted by both family law and welfare policies (Bradley 1996, 73) – and to abolish old-fashioned conceptions of gender roles in family law. The notion of sex difference was replaced by a concept of equality based on likeness.

The most important change, in principal, was the articulation of economic independence, in addition to the existing norm of individualism, as a norm for sex equality in the family. The work principle and the combination strategy each played an important role in this shift. Sweden was described as moving towards a society in which each adult individual would be able to take responsibility for herself or himself. Individuals would not be economically dependent upon relatives. Equality between women and men would finally be a reality. Family law was one among many tools to be used in an effort to achieve such a society. Two important goals of the reform were to make it possible for each spouse during marriage to retain significant personal and economic independence and, because of decreasing economic dependence between the spouses, to limit the economic consequences of marriage, especially after divorce.[7]

Connections between private family law and welfare law were also clearly articulated[8] and used as arguments for the further liberalization of family law. The prevalent view was that welfare policies and institutions had replaced the previously important functions of the family and marriage as providers of social and economic security, especially after divorce.[9] It is less clear to what extent this development was considered relevant regarding the situation during marriage.

At the same time that the institution of marriage was being reformed, in order to adapt it to the combination strategy in the workfare state, the neutrality principle was introduced into family law. The principle states that the law should be morally neutral in relation to how individuals chose the form of cohabitation.[10] Despite the orientation towards a liberal view about informal and non-traditional relationships, marriage continued to be regarded as the 'normal and natural' family formation.[11] The central position of marriage as a family form was to be maintained by modernizing the institution of marriage, by increasing the independence between spouses and by abolishing the gender roles and moral dimensions of marriage.[12]

The neutrality principle should be interpreted only as signifying neutrality in relation to the choice of family form. The principle has nothing to do with equality. It only constitutes an acceptance of cohabitation as a morally respectable family form with its own function.[13] Constructing normative differences between marriage and cohabitation legitimates separate and different regulations of them in family law. The law on cohabitation has a more limited scope than the law on marriage, especially with regard to economic issues. The purpose of the Cohabitation Act is to regulate the economic relations of the cohabitants only. The rationale behind the law is to regulate only those issues which, from the practical perspective of everyday life, might require such a regulation in order to create a minimum of justice between the parties and to protect the economically weaker party, i.e. the female cohabitant.[14]

The special function attributed to cohabitation is 'freedom of choice'. Family law is based on the conception that individuals 'chose' cohabitation because they do not want to get married, principally in order to avoid the economic consequences of marriage. Marriage is defined as a voluntary agreement between two individuals who wish to apply a certain legal system to their relationship. This definition is meant to have the effect that cohabitation cannot be regulated in the same way as marriage. If it were, the law would impose regulations on the parties against their will.[15] Consequently, family law embodies two different systems. Individuals are expected to take into account the different legal implications connected to each type of family form.

It is argued that the limited purpose of the Cohabitation Act should not be understood as a disapproval of cohabitation as a family form. The fact that regulations in other legal areas, especially social welfare law, treat cohabitation and marriage similarly is seen as evidence of the state's neutrality.[16] Equal treatment of cohabitation and marriage in welfare law is regarded as important so that marriage would not be discriminated against as a family form.[17] If cohabitation and marriage were not treated in a similar way, a cohabiting couple would receive better benefits by being treated as two individuals instead of as one couple.

The 'freedom of choice' concept is reinforced by the possibility that parties can choose to contract out of the Cohabitation Act. In fact, this option creates one more legally accepted family form, free from all family law regulation. It has been considered important to give individuals the opportunity to 'release' themselves from the legal economic consequences of cohabitation, despite the fact that these consequences might be quite limited.[18]

In a liberal sex equality discourse, neutrality and freedom of choice presuppose equal economic power relations between men and women. The fact that such equality does not exist is acknowledged in the preparatory works, but the unequal consequences that follow from the decisions of individuals to cohabit are considered inevitable because of the concept of marriage as a voluntary agreement.[19] There is no possibility for cohabitants to contract 'up' to the legal and economic level of marriage. In the case that cohabitants would like to create a more complete legal framework for their relationship, marriage is indicated as the solution, the argument being that the marital property system and the equal division of marital property after divorce provide better protection to the economically weaker partner.[20]

In a framework of preserving marriage as an institution, the mixture of 'freedom of choice' with regard to family form, individualism, economic independence and sex equality together create an area within family law with contradictory messages. Despite the neutrality approach, the law indirectly creates strong messages that are gendered. The economically superior party, often a man, is given incentives to cohabit or even contract out of the cohabitation law. At the same time, the economically weaker party, most often the woman, is encouraged to get married.

Thus, Swedish marriage law addresses a woman's actual or supposed economic dependence on a man in a context of strong individualism and economic independence. Dependence was certainly recognized and occasionally given importance in the legislative process of the 1970s and 1980s, as was the fact that economic sex equality had not been reached. The lower income of women, owing, in part, to the fact that women more often work part-time and the distribution of roles within the family, which are slow to change, are identified as reasons why economic inequalities linger.[21]

Some provisions of marriage law take dependence into consideration and are especially constructed to protect women and provide for equal economic results. Other regulations mainly build upon the norm of economic independence, even if it is acknowledged that the norm is inconsistent with reality. Further, the idea of the family as a community sometimes breaks through the individualistic norm. There is no doubt, however, that economic independence – together with individualism – are upheld as the main principles of family law, based on the politically prioritized aim of liberating individuals.

Without a doubt, economic independence is an important step towards promoting sex equality in the family. On the negative side, a strong emphasis on economic independence makes it difficult to take existing dependence into consideration. The formally sex-neutral and sex-equal understanding in law makes actual female dependence invisible. By studying in a detailed way how economic independence and dependence are constructed and treated in family law, gender-related problems for women in relation to the independence principle might be revealed.

Support During Marriage – a Matter of Dependence

An obligation of mutual support between spouses was introduced in the 1920 marriage reform. Although formally equal, the law was based on different roles for men and women and on a conception of the wife as being economically dependent on her husband. The obligation to support a spouse could be fulfilled by work outside or in the home. One of the main purposes was to promote the independence of the wife and to give reproductive work a value.[22]

The conception of dependence within marriage is retained in the 1987 Marriage Code.[23] The fundamental right of spouses to the same economic standard within the marriage is explicitly stated in the preparatory works.[24] Spouses are obligated, according to their abilities, to provide economic support to cover their common and personal needs.[25] This 'right' to the same economic standard, however, is quite weak. In theory, the obligation can be enforced through court proceedings if one spouse does not fulfil his or her responsibility,[26] but such a construction, imported from civil law regulating market relations, is rather odd in a family context and, in all likelihood, has never been used (Nordborg 1999, 52).

Household work is no longer explicitly regarded as one of the optional ways to fulfil the support obligation. The male breadwinner model in the 1920 marriage law was regarded as outdated in the 1970s and at odds with the sex equality that ought to exist both in the home and in the labour market.[27] Instead, a new rule was introduced, outlining that each spouse was responsible for both the economy of the family and household work. Nonetheless, the support obligation can be understood as attributing to household work an economic value within marriage, albeit only indirectly (Nordborg 1999, 52).

The right of the spouses to the same economic standard is motivated in the preparatory works by a reference to a generally held support for this right. This right is not tantamount to abandoning the goals of increasing the opportunities for women to participate in the labour market and of equalizing the income of men and women. Instead, economic dependence during marriage is described in a sex-neutral way, as a fact of family life. The argument is that in the long-term, it is reasonable to assume that one of the spouses – the woman or the man – permanently or temporarily during the marriage will have a lower income than the other.[28] However, there is no discussion about why this result is so, or why and how men can also be expected to require and benefit from this mutual obligation. Furthermore, the sex-neutral approach hides the fact that parental leave is predominantly used by women and that mothers are over-represented in part-time work.

The support obligation is mainly discussed as a matter between spouses. Apart from a general statement that women's economic liberation has decreased their need to turn to their husbands for support,[29] there is no discussion in the preparatory works of the relationship between the support obligation in family law and the responsibility of the state for individual welfare. Clearly, the support obligation in family law is regarded as primary to social assistance and the other responsibilities of the welfare state.

Independence after Divorce

Maintenance after divorce was also introduced in 1920, mainly in connection with the new grounds for divorce known as incompatibility.[30] The male breadwinner was the primary provider of economic security for the divorced woman. Arguments about justice in relation to the value of the wife's work in the home were common.[31] Marriage was also regarded as limiting the opportunities of women to participate in the work force because their work in the home did not qualify them for work in the labour market.[32]

In the 1970s divorce reform, all the moral dimensions of divorce were abolished. The no-fault divorce was introduced. The meaning of the maintenance principle changed. Rather than compensating the wife for her unpaid work in the home and perpetuating female dependence on a male breadwinner, unpaid household work was ignored. Both men and women were assumed to be independent after divorce.

This shift in thinking was based mainly on three arguments. First, limited maintenance obligations are regarded as crucial to the no-fault divorce reform. Continuing legal consequences of marriage after divorce would make the (male) right to divorce incomplete.[33] Secondly, the state, rather than ex-partners, now assumed the secondary responsibility for the welfare of the individuals.[34] Finally, limited maintenance obligations were considered as crucial for the promotion of sex equality, at the time predominantly understood as being based on economic independence.

By articulating a principle of economic independence after a divorce, it was believed that spouses would be encouraged to set up their lives in such a way that they would be economically independent even within the marriage.[35] Women's economic independence, not as an existing reality, but as a goal, is used as a strong argument for reducing maintenance rights. The view that the law would contribute to social change has been proved false. Structural patterns of economic inequalities between divorced men and divorced women remain largely intact.

Some exceptions to the principle of economic independence after divorce have been accepted as necessary. Women are still expected to have a weak economic position after divorce due to the effect of marriage on their earning potential. Above all, older women, who are assumed to have lived in 'old-fashioned' marriages, are expected to be in need of maintenance. But, it is assumed that even in more 'modern' marriages, one spouse – obviously meaning the wife – might have taken care of the home and children for a long period of time and, therefore, might encounter difficulty entering the labour market.

A maintenance obligation is regard as motivated when the marriage has restricted the ability of one spouse to support herself. However, this matrimonial effect on women's labour-market opportunities is regarded as temporary, with the consequence that any maintenance is normally paid only during a 'recovery period' in order to enable the wife to secure employment or increase her income by further education or other employment-relevant activities.[36]

Similar concepts of 'recovery period' and 'rehabilitative purposes' can be found in the welfare law on survivor's benefits (Mannelqvist 2001). These remnants of openly expressed sex-related support needs can be understood as giving unpaid work in the home an indirect economic value. Nonetheless, arguments about 'recovering' and 'rehabilitation' portray women as problematic vis-à-vis the goal of economic independence, while failing to recognize existing power imbalances on a structural as well as an individual level.

Marital Property Law

The individualistic foundation of marital property law introduced in 1920 was described as a part of a project to give married women greater independence and equality. Individualism is still an important principle in marital property law, but without any particular discussions about its implications for sex equality. Each spouse owns and controls his or her property and is solely responsible for his or her own debts.[37] Important features of community and dependence, however, still exist with regard to assets, debts and the division of property after divorce.

Assets and Debts during Marriage A special kind of 'hidden' co-ownership between spouses and cohabitants has developed in case law.[38] Regardless of which spouse is identified as an owner according to economic principles in civil law, co-ownership can exist, especially regarding a common dwelling and household items.[39] One important argument for 'hidden' co-ownership has been that it is difficult to prove individual ownership in the family as a consequence of the economic and emotional community in a marriage (Teleman 1998, 31; Tottie 1990, 33). Another justification is based on the fairness of the consequences of the gendered use of money. In the preparatory works, the man is represented as the investor in the family and the woman as provider of goods for family consumption (Burman 2001, 78). Co-ownership is sometimes presented as a means to avoid the unfair consequences of the formal main ownership principle in civil law (Tottie 1990, 33), which tends to portray women as economically dependent on the 'investor.

During the discussions about marital property reform in the 1980s, some interest was paid to the tension between individual ownership and the economic community considered normal in a family. Although this tension was described as an issue of justice for women, these discussions did not result in any significant changes in law. The principle of the equal division of property after divorce was considered to accomplish justice between the spouses.[40]

An image of the family as a very special community is revealed in the ways in which the legal relationship between the family and creditors is constructed. Marital property law is imbued with considerations of the self-evident interests of creditors and with a special common interest within the family, which increases the risk of economic crime. The wife, as economically dependent, creates a risk that the husband will prioritize his family obligations ahead of his debts. This risk is also found in other areas of law, especially in the Enforcement Code. If a debtor is married, it is presumed that the debtor owns all the assets in the common home. The debtor's spouse who wants to claim ownership in the home has the burden of proof.[41] The individual legal rights of the debtor's spouse, generally assumed to be a woman, are subordinated. The family community is described as being so different from the labour market that it is impossible to uphold the individuality of the party not in debt, in favour of protecting market-related claims (Burman 2001).

Arguments about debt relief strengthen this image. According to the Debt Adjustment Act of 1994, it is possible to discharge individuals from the responsibility of paying their debts. If a debtor is married, the economic situation for the whole family is taken into consideration (Sörendal 2001). There is no freedom of choice when it comes to protection from either a partner's debts or his or her creditors (Burman 2001).

Divorce and the Division of Property In contrast to an individual understanding of ownership and responsibility for debt, the Swedish marital property system vis-à-vis divorce is largely based on a notion of community. The equal division of all marital property after divorce is the starting point. The spouses have the opportunity to contract out of the system, either partly or entirely.

The core argument behind the system in the 1920 Marriage Code was justice between the spouses. At that time, separate property in divorce was regarded as an unfair evaluation of the value of the wife's work in the home.[42] Regarding this system of division, the goal of limiting the economic consequences of marriage and divorce has not been fulfilled. The deferred universal community property system was preserved as the normal form of marital economic regime. The only major exception was introduced recently concerning short-lived marriages. With the no-fault divorce, such marriages seemed to have unfair consequences for the economically superior party.[43]

The main arguments for keeping the community system largely intact are similar to those arguments found in the 1920s reform. The system is regarded as the best way to create economic justice after a divorce. Here, the inconsistency between the independence principle and women's marginalized economic position in society is recognized, and sex equality, based on sex difference and female dependence, is given a prominent position in the preparatory works.[44] Property rules are not considered as suitable instruments for the promotion of economic independence and sex equality. Instead, it is important to take existing conditions into account.[45] Dependence undermines the independence principle and the law is not regarded as useful in promoting social change. Strikingly, the view is opposite to the attitudes towards maintenance.

The Nordic countries are once again co-operating in order to explore the possibilities for a future harmonization of their family laws. A strong reduction of the community property system has recently been suggested by a Swedish family law scholar (Agell 2003). The crucial arguments, high divorce rates and the frequency with which divorced individuals enter into new marriages, are treated in a gender-neutral way without reflections on gendered economic power imbalances. Perhaps the further harmonization process will show to what extent gendered dimensions of economic dependence and self-support in the family will be recognized and regarded as relevant.

Sex Equality in Welfare Support

The structure of welfare support for families has a crucial influence on the distribution of power, resources and organization within the family. Because most women are employed, they not only have the right to benefits based on social need,[46] but also the right to earnings-related benefits, such as social insurance, to cover loss of income, pensions and unemployment benefits. However, benefits based on earnings reproduce the income differences between men and women. On a structural level, these income differences can be explained by the fact that women account for a larger percentage of workers requiring parental leave and part-time work. But differences are also linked to the income differences that exist in the gender-segregated labour market. The earnings-related social benefits of women are relatively lower than the earnings-related social benefits of men, which is clearly revealed in the pension system. Many women will grow poorer as they grow older (Gunnarsson and Stattin 2001).

Direct economic support to families with children is given in the form of child allowance, housing allowance, advance maintenance allowance, parental insurance, paid maternity leave, children's pensions, care allowances for children with disabilities, allowances for international adoptions and financial aid to children attending gymnasia.[47] Subsidized childcare provided by municipalities and other approved providers is also a family benefit. Finally, social assistance is a last resort for families with children.

This wide range of benefits creates a complicated pattern of dependence between the household and the state and this pattern is gender-related. Until the 1980s, family support was clearly redistributive, mainly from childless households to families with children, with some emphasis on low-income families. The structural economic crisis of the early 1990s, however, shaped family support. Comprehensive welfare policy was abandoned. In the next sections, the tension between the individual's right and obligation to be self-supporting and family-based rights will be exposed.

Work Related Benefits and the Individual Income Tax

In the early 1990s, the tax system was redesigned in a comprehensive reform based on the principles of tax neutrality and horizontal fairness or equity. The idea of neutrality was to avoid unwanted welfare losses by adjusting taxation to promote what is understood to be an efficient allocation of resources in the market economy. Horizontal equity is an equality-oriented interpretation of the ability-to-pay-principle, implying horizontal equality of treatment. Both principles were invoked to justify broader income and consumption tax bases and a flattening of the income tax rate schedule. As an effect of these changes, more incomes and goods and services became taxable and the income tax became less progressive.

During the years after the implementation of the extensive tax reform, budget deficits and inflation escalated. Higher revenues and cut backs in social welfare replaced the old family policy. A personal social contribution was introduced at the same time as the tax bases for income taxes and consumption taxes were broadened, once again. So few deductions from an income from employment are allowed that taxation of employees came to resemble a gross income tax rather than a net income tax. Benefits, such as child and housing allowances and compensation levels for income losses due to sickness and parental leave were reduced. Municipalities increased fees for childcare (Gunnarsson and Stattin 2001).

The combined effects of these poorly co-ordinated reforms in tax and social law made the system as a whole more progressive, especially for families with low incomes. As a result, an increase in gross income leads, at best, to a very modest increase in disposal income, and sometimes even to a decrease for low-income families. The tax paid on the last crown of earned income and the loss of benefits that occurs directly or indirectly because of that crown consumes the increase in gross income.[48]

It is important to stress that these kinds of effects are a consequence of changes in both tax law and social security law. Through the reforms, a functional division of tax law and social welfare law has been realized. Social welfare for families falls under social welfare law. Tax law is only designed to fulfil money-raising objectives. Such a functional division between tax law and social welfare law makes it easy to use different principles for income distribution in the two systems. One consequence, however, is that the two systems contradict each other. The principle of independence is fully implemented in tax law. Family taxation, meaning the joint taxation of spouses and various tax reductions for the support of dependents in the household, is no longer part of the income tax system. Instead, the provisions of income support to families take the form of social benefits in cash and in-kind payments or reduced charges for public services.

Theoretically, the construction of entirely individual duties through income tax and individual social rights based on earnings-related social security schemes are rooted in an underlying assumption of the individual as autonomous. However, needs-based benefits rest on the assumption of the existence of an obligation to support and a corresponding dependence on support among family members. The individual who claims a social right is seen as a part of a larger unit, a family or a household (Gunnarsson 2001b).

Maternity Allowance and the Parental Insurance as Individual Rights Welfare support for families comes in two forms: as work-related and as residence-related benefits. Only maternity allowance and income-based parental insurance can be defined as work-related family benefits. Parental insurance covers both parental leave for the care of small children and temporary leave to care for sick children.[49] These benefits are individual, that is, the right to the benefit is based on one's right and obligation to support oneself, notwithstanding other private or public support obligations. These benefits are part of a social security scheme constructed as social insurance to cover income losses, rather than a fixed rate benefit aimed at guaranteeing subsistence level income. The definition of calculated income earnings per year is a central issue for the Swedish social insurance. Work-related income creates an obligation to pay social contributions and makes one eligible for benefits.

When claims on social insurance to cover income losses began to create budget difficulties, the strength of these individual rights were called into question. Due to budget constraints, the amount of compensation provided for the loss of income was limited. Only 80 per cent of earned income is covered and only up to a maximum of SEK 284 250 (ca. 30 000 euros) in annual income per year.[50] The idea of 'paying for your right' in order to eliminate a citizens' dependence on the state has been shown to be a rather weak concept. It creates the same relations of dependence between the citizen and the state as do other social benefits.

Parental leave insurance gives both parents the same legal right. When the reform was introduced in the 1970s, the goal was to improve sex equality, based on the belief that both parents want to combine work and the care of small children. Beyond this goal, the ideology of self support and benefits tied to earned income also requires parents to work.[51] This notion of parents as free agents, equally sharing the obligations of providing care to family members and contributing economically to the family household in addition to functioning within the labor market, turned out to be wrong. Women claim the right to parental leave much more often than men do, or the opposite, men do not claim the right to parental leave to the same extent that women do.[52]

In order to encourage fathers to assume a larger responsibility for the care of their small children, a new regulation was introduced in 1995. In a sex-neutral way, the reform gave mothers and fathers 30 days of parental leave each, a benefit which was non-transferable to the other parent. By increasing a father's responsibilities to care for his children, the reform was expected to reduce the 'family obstacles' diminishing the participation of women in the labour market. Measures to increase the role of fathers were declared to be a state responsibility.[53] Since 2002, the number of non-transferable parental leave days for each parent has been increased to sixty.[54]

The Tax Household The individual income tax structure is a result of a policy introduced in the 1970s. When the shift from joint taxation to individual taxation began, the main argument was that joint taxation in a progressive income tax system was an obstacle to a woman's ability to support herself. Joint taxation with the option of income splitting between man and wife, gave the bread-winner a favourable marginal tax rate.[55] After the introduction of the individual income tax, the effective marginal rate for married men increased. The generally lower marginal tax rate for women contributed to an increase in labour market participation by married women (Svensson 1997).

Whatever importance the individual income tax has had in promoting equality between men and women, the fact remains that the individual income tax is an anomaly when people continue to be dependent on each other in different family or household formations. The Swedish income tax system still has to define a unit larger than the individual in order to eliminate tax planning within the family. It seems that the protection of third party interest, in this case, the fiscal interest of the state, similar to the type of protection accorded to creditors in marital property law, gives rise to regulations that contradict the principle of independent, self-supporting individuals.

Since the introduction of an individual income tax, basic issues such as who is a taxable subject at certain income levels and who has a claim to certain deductions for professional expenses, have become more important. The tax law, therefore, includes regulations that treat transactions between family members – between husbands and wives and between children and parents – differently than transactions between other legal subjects. This special treatment of family transactions requires that definitions of spouses and children be added to the list of definitions in tax law.

In the past, the Income Tax Act contained a special definition of spouses, which emphasized the beginning and the end of a marriage. The tax law concept of marriage also governed other areas of law. This definition has since been abandoned. Today, the Income Tax Act relies on the definition of spouses found in marriage law. Registered partnership between persons of the same sex has been given the same status as marriage.[56] A special definition of children still exists in tax law. In this case, the definition of 'child' is broader than the one found in family law and includes stepchildren and foster children. Adult children are not included.[57]

Together, these definitions constitute a tax household. The tax household is not explicitly defined. The dominant tax law culture does not consider the tax household to be especially relevant in the individual income tax system. Some provisions, however, do presuppose the possibility of determining the taxable subject's relation to a household. Two significant examples are the deductions for additional living expenses in the case of double residence[58] and the deductions for periodic maintenance allowances.[59] Beyond these two types of deductions, the taxable subject's relation to a household is sometimes invoked in case law.[60]

Tax households are also relevant in the taxation of business income. Spouses can voluntarily divide a business income between themselves, provided that both are engaged in the enterprise as partners or one as an assistant to the other.[61] This division does not have to be based on a real transaction between the spouses. It is used only to assess taxable income.

The presumption of a fictive transaction between spouses has also been developed further in other areas of income tax law and shares similarities with the 'hidden' co-ownership in marital property law. The right to deduct interest from capital income is given to the spouse who has the liability and pays the interest. However, even when one spouse has a liability and the other spouse pays the interest, the right to the deduction rests with the spouse who has the liability. The right is awarded on the basis of an assumed transaction between the spouses (Lodin et al 2001, 475-476).

Deductions for family-related expenses are sometimes reduced, sometimes extended when compared to the general rule. Salaries to children under 16 years of age and to spouses are not deductible from the parent's income from business, capital or employment.[62] Deductions for additional living expenses and travel expenses to visit the family when the taxpayer has a double residence are extended as an exception to the general rule of non-deductibility for personal living expenses.[63] Expenses for childcare are always non-deductible.

Residence Related Benefits as a Social Right

Residence-based benefits are primarily based on the need for support. The common feature of these benefits is that they are supposed to provide basic welfare security for families with children. The child allowance, guaranteed levels for parental insurance, children's pension allowance, allowances for international adoptions and financial aid to children attending gymnasium, are all general in character. 'General' in this context means a fixed-rate benefit for a specified group of children, without means-testing based on parental income.

The other residence-based benefits are means-tested social rights. Means-tests are normally based on the income of the household. Residence-based benefits to families with children are tax-exempt, except for the care allowance for children with disabilities and guaranteed levels of parental insurance. The means-tested benefits are regulated by different social welfare laws and are not based on the same definitions of income and household. The income test and the benefit household are also wider concepts than tax household and taxable income. Part of the definition of a household or household income is related to the domicile of a child. The following sections provide examples of the differences between these concepts.

Subsidized Charges for Childcare The policy of subsidizing the costs of childcare is very much in line with Sweden's workfare approach to sex equality. Comprehensive, subsidized public childcare has been considered a basic condition for women's labour market participation. This shift of responsibility for the burden of childcare from the mothers to the public sector has not significantly changed the traditional patterns of responsibilities within the family. This situation has become more evident and was most recently acknowledged in a reform proposal aimed at limiting the rates for public day-care.[64] The need to limit the maximum rates charged is related to means-testing and the way childcare service is organized.

Municipalities have autonomy over the rates charged for public day-care, which, before the reform, led to a considerable variation in rates charges. Rates were based on different concepts of households and household incomes. In many municipalities they were also linked to the numbers of hours the child spent at the day-care centre. As a result, a large part of the problem of effective marginal tax rate (the so-called EMTR-problem) was caused by childcare fees.[65] If the family wanted to reduce their costs by consuming fewer hours of public childcare, one parent had to work part-time. Many women ended up working part-time because married or co-habiting mothers generally have lower incomes than their husbands or partners. One important objective expressed in the reform's preparatory works is to make decisions about part-time work gender-neutral. Setting a maximum for childcare fees and basing the rate on a single definition of household and household income are considered as useful instruments in this regard.[66]

The reform will not solve the EMTR problem, but it will make the EMTR more transparent and the same throughout the country. Another shortcoming in the reform is typical for legal reforms aimed at partial solutions to sex inequalities. To neutralize one source of inequality in women's and men's ability to support themselves, a new sex-related dependency is usually created. In this reform, the new inequality is rooted in the common definition of a household.[67] The definition includes stepparents, which leads to the conclusion that stepparents are presumed to help pay the cost of childcare. In most cases, the stepparent is a man co-habiting with a solo mother. The charges will be based on one income if the solo mother lives alone, but go up if she decides to live with a new partner, because his income will be included in the household income. The new regulations governing the rates for childcare thus create new forms of dependence, in which the disposal income of solo mothers decreases because the income-test is based on two incomes instead of one.

The Housing Allowance The housing allowance for households with children is divided into three parts. One reinforces the general child allowance and is related to the number of children in the family. The other two parts are means-tested. One is related to the cost of housing and the other to household income, calculated individually for each spouse. A child is a person under 18 years of age or a person entitled to a prolonged child allowance or to financial aid for education.[68] A person defined as a child due to his or her right to prolonged child allowance or financial aid for education must reside in the household of the parent or parents. That is, only a child above 16 years of age and registered as a resident of a parent's household may receive the benefit. The right expires if the student finishes or interrupts his or her studies.[69] Spouses are couples, men and women, who have or have had a child and are registered as living at the same address. The presumption with regard to spouses and couples defined as spouses is that they live together.[70]

The income limit for means-tested benefits is set separately for each spouse; the benefit declines if one of them has an income above the upper limit.[71] The housing allowance is based on estimated annual income. It is important to note that this figure is just a preliminary estimate. When the tax assessment is subsequently filed, a final decision is made based on actual income. This practice means that the recipient might be entitled to a higher housing allowance, in which case she or he will get additional money. Alternatively, if the final assessment reveals that the housing allowance was too high, it must be paid back. In both cases, the adjustment must be made within two years.[72] The benefit income base is defined, with reference to tax law, as the sum of all income from employment, self-employment and capital. Incomes from both self-employment and capital are adjusted when calculating the housing allowance. Income from capital is largely defined as gross income. In tax law, the assessment is based on net capital income. Income from self-employment is adjusted to neutralize tax measures used to equalise profits between financial years. Tax-free incomes such as study allowance and grants are also added to the benefit income base. Finally, 15 percent of the total wealth of the household above SEK 100 000 (11 000 euros) is added.[73]

The separate income limit for each spouse is justified in terms of encouraging labour market participation. That is, it is widely agreed that the social welfare system should be based on incentives that promote the willingness to work. An income limit based on the joint income of the spouses is undesirable because it allows the housing allowance to subsidize household work and thereby encourages one of the parents, usually the woman, to choose part-time work. Adopting a separate income limit, was intended to promote the participation of women in the labour market in keeping with the goals of sex equality policy.[74]

The Advance Maintenance Allowance When parents separate, the parent who does not live with the child is obligated to pay child support to the custodial parent. The advance maintenance allowance is an advance payment by the state of this child support entitlement. The allowance is a flat-rate benefit of SEK 1 173 (ca. 130 euros) per month per child.[75] The amount is half of the estimated cost of a child after the child allowance is deducted. The last time the policy was reformed, the cost of a child was estimated to be SEK 3 096 (350 euros) per month and the child allowance was SEK 750 (85 euros). Thus, the allowance was set by subtracting 750 from 3 096 and then dividing by two.[76] Every child eligible for support is guaranteed this amount notwithstanding the income of the contributing parent. In that respect, the benefit is partly seen to be a public support.

The advance maintenance allowance is constructed as a right of the child. It is a guarantee of a basic minimum standard for children who do not live with both parents. It is not a social right for the solo parent. However, the preparatory works in the legal reforms of the benefit have, over the years, largely focused on the dependent position of the solo mother. When the benefit was first introduced at the end of the 1930s, the primary goal was to prevent single mothers from becoming dependent on poor relief. Later on, the goal has been to prevent solo mothers from becoming dependent on social assistance.[77]

The household that receives the maintenance allowance is the one in which the child resides. The child is entitled to the benefit if the parents are not living together or if one of the parents is deceased.[78] The question of whether the parents are living together or not, therefore, is crucial. In determining entitlement, it is not necessary that the parents are living together permanently. That they actually live together is enough to make the child ineligible.[79]

Residence has become a more central issue than custody because, today, the primary rule governing custody is that parents are to retain joint custody after a divorce.[80] The parent with whom the child is registered and lives permanently is legally defined as the 'living-in-parent'.[81] To get the legal status of a 'living-in-parent', it is, of course, necessary to have custody of the child. Having custody of the child, however, does not exclude the other parent from also having custody. The benefit can be split between both parents if the child's home alternates between the households of the parents. It can also be reduced if the child has an annual income above SEK 48 000 (ca. 5 300 euros) a year.[82]

Social Assistance

Analyses and proposals in the preparatory works have repeatedly pronounced that access to the labour market is one way of preventing dependence on the welfare system. The Swedish emphasis on work manifests itself in social assistance policy, which was reinforced in the 1998 reform of the Social Services Act.

The original Act, which came into force in 1982, was epoch-making in many ways. Individual social rights were formulated within a framework of goals to be pursued by the social services system. The Act was meant to replace an old-fashioned and patriarchal legislation. Equal rights, a comprehensive view and the notion of free choice were the leading principles. From an historical perspective, state finances have affected the responses of the authorities to individual claims for centuries. The reform of 1998, however, partially withdrew a social right for the first time in 300 years.

An individual capable of working, who does not make 'himself' available for full-time work, is not entitled to social assistance. When the Act was reformed,[83] social assistance was declared to be a safety net of last resort for a person in a temporary financial crisis. The right to assistance is based on means-testing in each individual case. Social assistance is intended to ensure that people can maintain a reasonable standard of living and to increase the opportunities of individuals to live free from the support of others. The Act states that decisions concerning children shall primarily consider the best interests of the child.

The concept, 'reasonable standard of living', has its own section in the law, but is not defined in any more detail in the Act. It is supposed to be assessed by the municipalities on the bases of time and the circumstances under which the person in need of help is living. Municipalities have a great deal of latitude both vis-à-vis the distribution of benefits above the nationally-defined subsistence level and vis-à-vis administrative matters. The amount of assistance is to be determined on the bases of varying local conditions and needs.

Until 1998, all decisions regarding social assistance could be appealed. Evaluations of the dismantled right to appeal in court through the reform in 1998 revealed undesirable differences in the decisions made by the municipalities about the amount of income which constitutes a reasonable standard of living.

The new Social Services Act, which came into force in 2002, restored the right to appeal decisions in court, but did not change the fundamental power relations between individuals and the authorities, politics and law. The law is meant to be a welfare law for all citizens, though its status in the legal process (can be discussed) is subject to debate.[84] The new law retains the overall goals of the old. It can be characterized as a reform that dismantles the social rights ensuring that the fundamental needs of the individual are met by laying out rules giving municipalities autonomy and self-determination vis-à-vis means-testing.

The principle that every citizen has a duty to earn her or his own living is strongly emphasized. The legislation has undergone fundamental changes in the form of increased control and demands on the individual and the family. Entitlement to social assistance has been curtailed. The municipality is obligated to require that recipients of social assistance participate in trainee programmes; refusing to do so may lead to a loss of assistance.

The right of an individual to social assistance is evaluated in terms of the joint income of the cohabiters, even though there is no maintenance obligation in the Cohabiting Act as there is for married couples in the Marriage Code. Even any income a child might earn, for example, income from working during school holidays, is supposed to reduce or eliminate assistance, even though there is no obligation in the Parental Code for children to support their families.[85]

Solo Mothers as a Defective Family Formation

The model family or a 'normal family' in the legal model consists of a married, heterosexual couple, living together with their common children. Some feminist scholars have used solo mothers as an analytical category to reach an understanding of the gendered dimensions of the welfare state. A theory of gendered citizenship must consider not only the dependence of a woman on the labour market, but also opportunities for a woman to live independently of a male breadwinner. If one assumes that all married women, as well as cohabiting ones, are potential solo mothers, the state support that these mothers can receive may be used as a barometer of the strengths and weaknesses of the social rights of women with families irrespective of their level of education, culture, ethnicity or class (Hobson 1994).

Cutbacks in the public sector have had a negative impact on the economic circumstances of families. More households became dependent upon receiving regular income from the welfare office during the 1990s. At the end of the decade, approximately one-quarter of all children in Sweden lived in families with economic problems. About 120000 children lived in families receiving long-term social assistance (*Socialstyrelsen* 2001, 11). Three-quarters of these children had parents born outside of Sweden (Mossler et al. 1999).

Solo mothers were among the biggest losers when the general level of social security was cut in the 1990s. A report from the National Board for Health and Welfare calls attention to the fact that the situation of solo mothers deteriorated during the 1990s. Now, they have an even weaker position in the labour market. Low income and even poverty are common (*Socialstyrelsen* 2001, 231). This group, which accounts for one-fifth of all families in Sweden, is still, even after the economic recovery of recent years, the one that has the highest percentage of social assistance recipients, 35,2 per cent in 1990 and 32 per cent in 1998 (*Socialstyrelsen* 2001, 120). Together with their children, solo mothers live in greater poverty than any other group in Sweden today (Gähler 2001). In a recent study, 'lone' mothers in Sweden were assigned an almost 70 per cent higher risk of death than mothers with partners. The excess risk remained significantly higher even after adjustments were made for socio-economic status and history of severe somatic and psychiatric trouble (Ringbäck et al. 2000). The position of solo mothers in the welfare system is related to both gender and the absence of marriage (Björnberg 1994).

According to the preparatory works and political debate, one of the main goals of the welfare state is to prevent dependence upon social assistance (Wennberg 2001). In preparatory works, solo mothers are indirectly described as representatives of a defective family formation, revealing an underlying nuclear family ideology. Solo mothers are considered to be an economic threat to the municipalities of a dismantled welfare state. Instead of focusing on structure, gendered constructions of care and the difficult combination strategy for solo mothers, the recipients are highlighted as somehow defective human beings.

The large number of children on welfare is a big patriarchal concern, because these children are said to run the risk of inheriting certain values that might destabilize society, though any opinions as to the nature of these values never seems to be openly expressed.

The Social Services Act, therefore, contributes to the subordination of solo mothers and their children and makes them dependent upon the good will of the municipalities assessing the needs of the families. The national norm for social assistance is constructed to help a person in a temporary crisis. The national norm for assistance is unsuited for maintaining a reasonable standard of living over a longer period of time.

The notion of individual responsibility tends to hide gender constructions of care and power relations between men and women. As a result, solo mothers who are long-term recipients of social assistance and their children are socially excluded and constructed as second-rate citizens. Women in need of social assistance are now more dependent on political decisions rather than entitled to claim their rights as citizens. In this sense, public patriarchy has replaced a private patriarchy.

Sex Equality Begins and Ends in the Family

There is a widespread feminist critique calling for a new framework of social citizenship in the welfare state, one in which gender must be incorporated into the core concepts. Looking at welfare in the context of freedom can help feminists understand the changes which are happening within welfare reform and retrenchment and enable them to reconceptualize the welfare state in terms of woman-friendly principles that enhance a woman's freedom. A theory of gendered citizenship must consider not only the dependence of a woman on the labour market, but also the opportunities for a woman to live independently of a male breadwinner, irrespective of level of education, culture, ethnicity or class (Hobson 1994).

The theoretical framework used in this article argues that social citizenship encompasses both earning and caring (Lister 1997) and that human functions connected to labour, care, responsibility and time are gendered issues. In Swedish family law, tax law and social welfare law, this problem of social justice is expressed in the way autonomy is promoted in relation to the labour market, while dependence is promoted in relation to the family.

Citizens as Carers – a Feminist Critique

Hirschmann (2001) emphasizes social construction as important to the feminist approach to freedom and engages us in a reconsideration of the subject of welfare, of the individuals, predominantly women, who end up in the socially vulnerable role of caregiver. By challenging the conceptualization of women as caregivers, social construction allows us to call into question the fundamental assumptions about the sexual division of labour upon which welfare policies are based.

Tronto (2001) argues that care should be interpreted as a human activity, in which all people are engaged, both as givers of care and as receivers. This interpretation, she claims, should become a fundamental criterion for determining citizenship: a metaphor of citizens as carers, given a central role in the rethinking of the welfare state. Fineman (2001) focuses on the current dependence discourse, which stigmatizes certain individuals as pathological because they rely on welfare. Through a reconceptualization based on care, dependence would be recognized for what it is, an inevitable result of the human condition and caregivers would be compensated and respected for the valuable labour they provide (see Brækhus in this volume).

In the paradigm of the two income family model, solo mothers have been characterized as being well integrated in the labour market, enjoying the same individual and general rights as other citizens. Statistics show, however, that in the dismantled Swedish welfare system, solo mothers are becoming a socially-screened group located on the periphery of the labour market, poor and isolated from the public network and general public activities. A possible explanation for this exclusion is a false conception of the universalism of Swedish welfare regimes, one which overlooks the reality of gendered diversity and difference in citizenship. The importance of the social citizen as a gendered subject has to be emphasized.

Violations of citizen's rights in Sweden seem to occur as a consequence of structural conditions and de-gendered violation rules, which affect mothers and their children, especially solo mothers, through social constructions in legislation. Held (1993) offers an alternative vision of society and societal goals. She replaces the paradigm of the economic man as the dominant representation of humanity with the paradigm of the *relations* between mothers and children. What she seeks to elaborate is a conception of social relations based on the experience of women in terms of 'mothering', an activity performed by men as well as women. The phrase 'mothering person' is in place of 'mother' in the same gender-neutral way that various writers now speak of 'rational contractors'.

Instead of importing into the household, principles derived from the marketplace, perhaps we should export to a wider society the relations suitable for mothering persons and children. A household based upon concern and caring, rather than upon contracts, might then provide a model for society. This model of the relational *post-patriarchal family,* free from male dominance, provides insights into our notions of equality. It shows us that equality is not equivalent to having equal legal rights. A domain such as law, if built on no more than contractual foundations, can be recognized as just one limited domain among (many) others: law can be used to protect some rights when such rights would not be respected without the force of law.

European Integration and the Reconciliation of Work and Family Life

European integration highlights issues concerning a social citizenship. The development of social rights based on a liberal tradition of human rights instruments is reflected in European human rights documents.[86] The rights discourse is different from the ideals of a mutual solidarity and a mutual responsibility, characterizing the rights discourse in the Nordic countries. When social rights are characterized as a tradition of human rights or as a tradition of responsibilities, it leads to different perspectives about discrimination as a lack of equality. A human rights approach to social rights raises the basic legal question of discriminatory practices and anti-discrimination laws.

The extensive welfare policies of the Nordic states, based on solidarity and responsibility, have been interpreted as having created a universal, overall equality. Equality has come to mean non-discrimination, while collective and structural discriminatory practices have come to be invisible (Nousiainen et al 2001). Feminists have problematized the human rights discourse within the European Union, arguing that because it is based on the male as norm, it is not an obvious strategy for achieving sex equality (Kouvo, in this edition; Pentikäinen 1999; Shaw 2000).

Social citizenship in the EU is not easy to define. The attitude towards the basis for social rights is ambiguous. EU documents as well as case law from the European Court of Justice emphasize the family, a concept with different connotations and traditions across the union, as the fundamental unit for the distribution of welfare (McGlynn 2000). On the other hand, the labour market principle is fundamental in the concept of mobility of labour; the principle demands active citizenship, which has had a strong influence on the social dimension of the Union. Active citizenship includes the rights of migrant workers to transferable social benefits. Eligibility with regard to social rights is based on employment history. However, the rights of family members to family benefits are neither individual nor independent. The rights of family members are derived from the migrant worker.

From a Swedish perspective, European legal policy implies a conflict between residence-related and work-related social rights. Recently, the individual right to parental leave insurance was defined as an family benefit rather than as an individual one, exportable within the Union only if it can be derived linked to a bread-winner.[87]

The reconciliation strategy adopted by the EU is committed to promoting paid work and family life for both women and men.[88] Such a strategy is in line with the Swedish combination strategy for women's labour market participation and family life. On the surface, both the European reconciliation strategy and the Swedish policy are intended to eliminate gender differences with regard to activity in the labour market and household production. Introducing a combination strategy, which implies work-related individual obligations and rights, is an important step towards achieving gender equality. It is true that the reform of individual taxation was very important for the successful implementation of (the) sex equality policy. Sweden has even suggested that individual taxation should be used to improve sex equality in the European Union (Bergqvist and Jungar 2000).

However, no fault divorce and the notion of very limited maintenance rights after divorce are both based on strong conceptions of individuality and independence. On the other hand, the support obligation during marriage and the system of deferred universal community that rests on a notion of community and dependence might appear to be contradictory. One opinion is that the introduction of a system of separate property would have been a logical development in order to continue the liberalization of the family.[89] However, this kind of argumentation seems to presume that there is a causal connection between personal and economic independence, a presumption that must be challenged in light of the Swedish experience. Secondly, to understand of the whole picture, the analysis must include arguments based on different sex equality ideologies and the extent to which they take into consideration existing economic inequalities between men and women.

There is definitely a strong connection in family law ideology between sex equality and the work line principle as a way to promote economic independence. At the same time, however, a concept of sex equality also exists based upon the differences between women and men and their unequal economic positions. Perhaps the question should be asked the other way around – why has the notion of dependence not been given a more prominent position in the discourse, for example, with regard to maintenance rights?

As we have shown, strategies of combination in different areas of Swedish law are based on different principles of social protection with regard to the legal construction of the family. In particular, some are based on self-support and others on dependence. When the general national insurance system fails to operate during a cycle in a woman's life, she will become subordinated through discriminatory processes not only in the private sphere, but also in the public sphere vis-à-vis legislation. In sum, the combination strategies clearly show that the equality of rights for women starts and ends within the family. This statement is a deeply controversial one, but the contemporary debate about sex equality policies in Europe reveals the need for a comprehensive legal analysis of the position of women with regard to rights and duties in the Nordic welfare regimes and in the family.

Notes

1 In several projects connected to the extensive research program, *Norden och Europa*, launched by the Nordic Council of Ministers in 1995, new knowledge about the specifics of the Nordic welfare countries has been published. The empirically comparative studies presented in Kautto et al. 1999 and 2001 are of particular interest.

2 The Final report from the Government Commission on the Distribution of Economic Power and Resources between Women and Men (SOU 1998:6).

3 In Sweden, this diversity has been revealed by empirical studies. See Nyberg (1997).

4 Similar experiences are reported in comparative European studies. See for example Hantrais 2000.

5 SFS 1987:232. Homosexual Cohabitation Act (1987:813) was enacted the same year. In 1994, the Partnership Act (1994:117) was enacted, giving homosexual partners the right to register their partnership. A registered partnership and a homosexual cohabitation have almost the same legal and economical consequences as heterosexual marriage and heterosexual cohabitation, but some very important exceptions remain, regarding parenthood, especially adoption and custody.

6 LB 1918, p. 158.

7 See for example SOU 1972:41, pp. 57-58.

8 SOU 1972:41 pp. 63, 81-82, 112-114 and Prop. 1986/87:1, pp. 90-91.

9 See for example SOU 1977:37, p. 54.

10 SOU 1972:41, p. 58.

11 LU 1973:20, p. 74.

12 SOU 1972:41, p. 58 and LU 1973:20, p. 74.

13 SOU 1981:85, p. 116.

14 The principle guiding the relationship between cohabitation and marriage is maintained in the latest evaluation and review of the Cohabitation Act conducted by the Cohabitation Committee in 1999, SOU 1999:104, pp. 174-175.

15 Prop. 1973:32 , p. 85, LU 1973:20 p. 74, and prop. 1986/87:1, p. 40.
16 SOU 1972:41, p. 98.
17 LU 1973:20, pp. 73-74.
18 Prop. 1986/87:1, pp. 106-108.
19 Prop. 1973:32, p. 84.
20 See for example SOU 1999:104, p. 175.
21 SOU 1977:37, pp. 56-57 and SOU 1981:85, p. 100.
22 LB 1918, pp. 189-191.
23 SFS 1987:230.
24 SOU 1977:37, pp. 106-197 and prop. 1978/79:12, p. 135.
25 6 Chapter 1 § Marriage Code.
26 6 Chapter 5 § Marriage Code.
27 Prop. 1978/79:12, p. 136.
28 Prop 1978/79:12, p. 135.
29 Prop 1978/79:12, p. 75.
30 If the divorce was due to matrimonial fault, the party deemed responsible for causing it had no right to maintenance.
31 See for example LB 1913, p. 448.
32 LB 1913, pp. 448 – 449.
33 Prop 1978/79:12, p. 139.
34 SOU 1977:37, p. 109.
35 Prop 1978/79:12, p. 139.
36 Prop 1978/79:12, pp. 139-140.
37 1 Chapter 3 § Marriage Code.
38 The first Supreme Court cases were NJA 1980 p. 705, NJA 1981 p. 693 and NJA 1982 p. 589. One example from the 1990s is NJA 1992 p. 163.
39 For co-ownership to be assumed, the following conditions should be fulfilled: 1) the intention behind the acquisition of the asset was to acquire common property, 2) the spouses at least implicitly seem to have anticipated that the asset was a shared one and 3) the informal owner has made some kind of economic contribution to the acquisition. Taking care of children and the household have not yet been treaed as equal to economic contributions.
40 Prop. 1986/87:1, pp. 59-61. There were also other considerations, for example, the interests of the creditors. Some considerations were of a more practical nature or touched upon other ways in which justice could be achieved.
41 4 Chapter 19 § Enforcement Code. The presumption of ownership for a married debtor is applicable to cohabiters as well. In this respect, the similarity between marriage and cohabitation is emphasized. Almost identical rules for the purpose of protecting creditors and the market economy can be found in both the Cohabitation Act and the Marriage Code.
42 LB 1918, pp. 166 and 181.
43 Prop. 1986/87:1, p. 44-46
44 Prop. 1986/87:1, p. 42-44.
45 SOU 1981:85, p. 102.
46 The concept of benefits based on social need is used here to cover both means-tested and general benefits, which is a wider concept than how the concept is commonly understood in social welfare law.
47 SOU 2001:24, p. 44.
48 For a more extensive analyses of the Effective Marginal Tax Rate problem and family traps, see Gunnarsson, 2001 (b).

49 3 Chapter 4 § Social Insurance Act.
50 3 Chapter 2 § Social Insurance Act.
51 Prop. 1974:47.
52 See for example Prop. 1990/91:113.
53 Prop. 1993/94:147, pp. 17 and 66-70.
54 Prop. 2001/02:44.
55 Fi 1969:4, p. 60.
56 Prop. 1999/2000:2, part 2, pp. 38-39 and 651.
57 2 Chapter 21 § Income Tax Act.
58 12 Chapter 19 § Income Tax Act.
59 9 Chapter 3 § Income Tax Act.
60 One example is RÅ 1991 ref. 35.
61 60 Chapter 6 § Income Tax Act.
62 60 Chapter 2 and 3 §§ Income Tax Act.
63 12 Chapter 19 § in relation to 9 Chapter 2 § Income Tax Act.
64 Prop. 1999/2000:129, pp. 27-30.
65 Socialstyrelsen, 1997:5, Ds 1997:73, Ds 1999:53, SOU 1999:97 and SOU 2001:24.
66 Ds 1999:52, p. 57 and 1999/2000:127, p. 33.
67 4 § the State Subsidy for Pre-school and School Childcare Act.
68 2 § Housing Allowance Act.
69 1-3 §§ Prolonged Child Allowance Act and 2 Chapter Study Support Act.
70 3 § Housing Allowance Act.
71 5, 7, 13 and 14 §§ Housing Allowance.
72 4, 21 a and 21 b §§ Housing Allowance Act.
73 5 and 5 §§ Housing Allowance Act.
74 SOU 1995:133, pp. 158-159 and prop. 1995/96:186, p. 26.
75 8 § Advance Maintenance Allowance Act.
76 Prop. 1995/96:208, pp. 40-41.
77 Prop. 1964:70, pp. 104-108.
78 3 § Advance Maintenance Allowance Act.
79 RRV 1997:35, p. 35.
80 6 Chapter 3 § Parental Code.
81 3 § Advance Maintenance Allowance Act. The term 'living-in-parent' is directly translated. 'Custodial parent' is a more understandable term, but it cannot be used because it is an inadequate legal interpretation of the law.
82 8-10 §§ Advance Maintenance Allowance Act.
83 Prop. 1996/97:124.
84 Prop. 2000/01:80.
85 The right to benefits is stated in the Social Services Act (2001:453) Chapter 4, para. 1-6.
86 The European Convention for the Protection of Human Rights and Fundamental Freedoms of 1950 and the European Social Charter of 1961.
87 Kuusijärvi RÅ 2000 ref. 20, C 275/96.
88 See further Hantrais 2000.
89 For example Bradley 1996.

References

Governmental Bills

Prop 1964:70 Med förslag om bidragsförskott. (Advance maintenance allowance, Governments proposal)
Prop. 1973:32 Ändring i giftermålsbalken m.m. (Changes in the Marriage Code, Government proposal)
Prop 1974:47 Angående förbättrade familjeförmåner inom den allmänna försäkringen. (Improved Family Benefits, Government proposal).
Prop. 1978/79:12 Om underhåll till barn och frånskilda m.m. (Maintenance for children and divorced, Government proposal).
Prop. 1986/87:1 Om äktenskapsbalk m.m. (Marriage Code, Government proposal).
Prop. 1990/91:113 Om ny jämställdhetslag (New Sex Equality Law, Government proposal).
Prop 1993/94:147 Jämställdhetspolitiken. (Government Sex Equality Politics).
Prop. 1995/96:186 Nya regler för bostadsbidrag (Housing allowance, Government proposal).
Prop. 1995/96:208 Underhållsstöd till barn till särlevande förädlrar. (Advance maintenance allowance, Government proposal).
Prop. 1996/97:124, Ändring i socialtjänstlagen. (Social Services Act, Government proposal).
Prop. 1999/2000:2 Inkomstskattelagen. (Income Tax Act, Government proposal).
Prop. 1999/2000:129 Maxtaxa och allmän förskola. (Maximum Rate for day-care, Government proposal).
Prop. 2000/01:80 Ny socialtjänstlag m.m. (Social Services Act, Government proposal).
Prop.2001/02:44 Föräldraförsäkringen och föräldraledighet. (Parental Leave Insurances, Government proposal).

Government Committees and Other Official Documents

Lagberedningens förslag (LB 1913) till lag om äktenskaps ingående och upplösning m.m., Stockholm 1913. (Marriage and Divorce, Law Committee).
Lagberedningens förslag (LB 1918) till revision av giftermålsbalken och vissa delar av ärvdabalken m. m, Stockholm 1918. (Revision of Marriage Code, Law Committee).
SOU 1972:41 Familj och äktenskap 1. (Family and Marriage).
SOU 1977:37 Underhåll till barn och frånskilda. (Maintenance allowance).
SOU 1981:85 Äktenskapsbalk. (Marriage Code).
SOU 1995:133 Bostadsbidragen – effektivare inkomstprövning – besparingar. (Housing Allowances).
SOU 1998:6, Ty makten är din...Myten om det rationella arbetslivet och det jämställda Sverige. (The Final report from the Government Commission on the Distribution of Economic Power and Resources between Women and Men).
SOU 1999:97 Socialtjänst i utveckling. (Social Services).
SOU 1999:104 Nya samboregler. (Co-habitation Act).
SOU 2000:83 Two of a Kind? (Report from the Governments Commission on the Balance Sheet for Welfare of the 1990s).
SOU 2001:24 Ur fattigdomsfällan. (Report from Government Family Commission).
SOU 2001:54 Ofärd i välfärd. (Poverty in Welfare).
Fi 1969:4 Individuell beskattning. (Individual Taxation Commission).
Ds 1997:73 Lönar sig arbete? Rapport till ESO. Expertgruppen för studier i offentlig ekonomi.

Ds 1999:53 Maxtaxa och allmän förskola. Utbildningsdepartementet.
LU 1973:20 Lagutskottets betänkande. Ändring i giftermålsbalken m.m.
Socialstyrelsen, Social rapport, 2001.

Literature

Agell, Anders (2003), Nordisk äktenskapsrätt. En jämförande studie av dansk, finsk, isländsk, norsk och svensk rätt med diskussion av reformbehov och harmoniseringsmöjligheter, Copenhagen: Nordic Council of Ministers, Nord 2003:2 .

Björnberg, Ulla (1994), 'Ökad press på alltfler ensamstående mödrar', *Kvinnovetenskaplig tidskrift*, Nr 2, pp. 12-25.

Bradley, David (1996), *Family Law and Political Culture*, Sweet & Maxwell, London.

Burman, Monica (2001), 'Den farliga familjen och borgenärerna', in Monica Burman and Åsa Gunnarson (eds), *Familjeföreställningar. Om familjens betydelse inom juridik, ekonomi och forskning,* Iustus, Uppsala.

Fineman, Marta Albertson (2001), 'Dependencies', in Nancy J Hirschman and Ulrike Liebert (eds), *Women and Welfare. Theory and Practice in the United States and Europe*, Rutgers University Press, New Brunswick, New Jersey and London.

Gunnarsson, Åsa and Stattin, Chris, (2001), 'Jämställdhetsnormen i skatte- och socialrätten', in Monica Burman and Åsa Gunnarson (eds), *Familjeföreställningar. Om familjens betydelse inom juridik, ekonomi och forskning,* Iustus, Uppsala.

Gunnarsson, Åsa (2001a), 'Familjen – genusforskningens utmaning', in Monica Burman and Åsa Gunnarson (eds), *Familjeföreställningar. Om familjens betydelse inom juridik, ekonomi och forskning,* Iustus, Uppsala.

Gunnarsson, Åsa (2001b), 'The Autonomous Taxpayer an the Dependent Caregiver: The Effects of the Division Between Tax Law and Social Law', in Kevät Nousiainen, Åsa Gunnarsson, Karin Lundström, Karin and Johanna Niemi-Kiesiläinen (eds), *Responsible Selves. Women in the Nordic legal culture*, Ashgate Publishing, Aldershot.

Gähler, Micael (2001), 'Bara en mor – ensamstående mödrars ekonomiska levnadsvillkor i 1990-talets Sverige', in SOU 2001:54.

Hantrais, Linda (2000), *Gendered Policies in Europe. Reconciling Employment and Family Life,* Palgrave, Hampshire.

Held, Virginia (1993), *Feminist Morality. Transforming culture, Society and Politics*, The University of Chicago Press.

Hirchmann, Nancy J. (2001), 'A Question of Freedom. A Question of Rights? Woman and Welfare', in Nancy J Hirschman and Ulrike Liebert (eds), *Women and Welfare. Theory and Practice in the United States and Europe*, Rutgers University Press, New Brunswick, New Jersey and London.

Hobson, Barbara (1994), 'Solo Mothers, Social Policy Regimes and the Logics of Gender', In Diane Sainsbury (ed), *Gendering Welfare States.* Sage Publications,London.

Kautto, M., Heikkilä, M., Hvinden, B., Marklund, S. and Ploug, N. (eds), (1999), *Nordic Social Policy. Changing Welfare States*, Routledge, London.

Kautto, M. Fritzell, J., Hvinden, B., Kvist, J., Uusitalo, H. (eds), (2001), *Nordic Welfare States in the European Context,* Routledge, London.

Liebert, Ulrike (2001), 'Degendering Care and Engendering Freedom. Social Welfare in the European Union', in Nancy J Hirschman and Ulrike Liebert (eds), *Women and Welfare. Theory and Practice in the United States and Europe*, Rutgers University Press, New Brunswick, New Jersey and London.

Mannelqvist, Ruth (2001), 'Efterlevandepensioner och familjen – tillbaka till framtiden?' in Monica Burman and Åsa Gunnarson (eds), *Familjeföreställningar. Om familjens betydelse inom juridik, ekonomi och forskning,* Iustus, Uppsala.
Melby, Kari, Pylkkänen, Anu, Rosenbeck, Bente, and Christina Carlsson Wetterberg (eds), (2000), *The Nordic Model of Marriage and the Welfare State,* Copenhagen: Nordic Council of Ministers, Nord 2000:27 .
Mossler, Karin, Torége, Jan and Öström, Anna (1999), '120.000 barn berörs av långvarigt socialbidrag', *SCB Välfärdsbulletinen*, Nr 2, pp. 16-19.
Nordborg, Gudrun (1999), 'Kärlek och ekonomi – juridiskt undantagstillstånd?', *Kvinnovetenskaplig tidskrift*, Nr 1, pp. 49-63.
Nussbaum, Martha (1999), *Sex and Social Justice.* Oxford University Press, Oxford.
Nyberg, Anita (1997), *Women, men and incomes. Gender equality and economic independence*, SOU 1997:87.
Nyman, Charlott, (2002), *Mine, yours or ours? Sharing in Swedish couples,* Doctoral theses at the Department of Sociology, Umeå University, No 24.
Olsen, Frances (1995), *Feminist legal theory*, Aldershot, Dartmouth.
Pentikäinen, Merja (1999), *The Applicability of the Human Rights Model to Adress Concerns and the Status of Women,* Forum IURIS, Publications of the Faculty of Law University of Helsinki.
Ringbäck, Gunilla, et al. (2000), 'Mortality among lone mothers in Sweden: a population study', *The Lancet*, Vol. 355 2000, pp. 1215-1219.
Sevenhuijsen, Selma (1998), *Citizenship and the Ethics of Care. Feminist Considerations on Justice, Morality and Politics*, Routledge, London.
Shaw, Jo (2000), 'The problem of Membership in European Union Citizenship', in Laura Kallioma-Puha (ed), *Perspectives of equality: work, women and family in the Nordic countries and EU,* The Research Program 'Norden och Europa', Nordic Council of Ministers, 2000:5, Copenhagen.
Svensson, Eva-Maria (2001), 'Sex Equality: Changes in Politics, Jurisprudence and Feminist Legal Studies', in Kevät Nousiainen, Åsa Gunnarsson, Karin Lundström, Karin and Johanna Niemi-Kiesiläinen (eds), *Responsible Selves. Women in the Nordic legal culture*, Ashgate Publishing, Aldershot.
Svensson, Lars (1997), 'En historia om löneutjämning – kvinnors och mäns löner i långsiktigt perspektiv', in SOU 1997:136.
Sörendal, Hanna (2001), 'Skuldsanering och kön', in Monica Burman and Åsa Gunnarson (eds), *Familjeföreställningar. Om familjens betydelse inom juridik, ekonomi och forskning,* Iustus, Uppsala.
Teleman, Örjan (1998), *Bodelning under äktenskap och vid skilsmässa*, 3rd edition, Norstedts, Stockholm.
Tottie, Lars (1990), *Äktenskapsbalken och promulgationslag m. m*, Norstedts, Stockholm.
Tronto, Joan C. (2001), 'Who Cares? Public and Private Caring and the Rethinking of Citizenship', in Nancy J Hirschman and Ulrike Liebert (eds), *Women and Welfare. Theory and Practice in the United States and Europe*, Rutgers University Press, New Brunswick, New Jersey and London.
Wennberg Lena (2001), 'Ensamstående mödrar – rätt till välfärd eller försörjda av män?', in Monica Burman and Åsa Gunnarson (eds), *Familjeföreställningar. Om familjens betydelse inom juridik, ekonomi och forskning,* Iustus, Uppsala.

Chapter 8

The Reform of Sex Crime Law and the Gender-Neutral Subject

Johanna Niemi-Kiesiläinen

Introduction

Reforms of the laws on sexual crimes are taking place both in Sweden and Finland around the turn of the millennium. The Chapter on Sexual Crimes in the Finnish Criminal Code was completely reformed in 1998. In Sweden, a Committee report, proposing important reforms, was presented in 2001 (SOU 2001:14). In addition, the purchase of sex was made a criminal offence in Sweden in 1998.[1] In Finland a working group set up by the Ministry of Justice made a similar proposal in 2003 (OM 2003:5).

While these reform efforts coincide, the discussions in the respective two countries have been quite different. The Finnish reform proposals have a liberal undertone, emphasizing sexual liberalization, non-intervention into sexual mores and freedom of choice. In the Finnish working group memorandum, prostitution and the purchase of sex are, in addition to a liberal freedom of choice discourse, discussed in the context of trafficking as organized crime. To the contrary, the Swedish discussion is permeated by a feminist discourse, exploring the possibilities of improved protection against sexual violations and abuse and setting violence against women into a structural analysis of the power relations between the sexes in society.

These different approaches to sexual crimes cannot be explained by the differences in legal traditions or social policies in these two countries. Due to a shared history (Finland was part of Sweden until 1809)[2] and continuous cooperation in the legal field, the legal systems of Finland and Sweden share common legal principles and many laws resemble the respective laws of the other country. The social policies are also quite similar. Until recently, most social services were provided by state and municipal authorities. The Swedes have more faith in public policies and state intervention as instruments of change than the Finns, but the difference is a matter of degree, not one of kind. For example, the policies against substance abuse have been quite controlling in both countries, including a repressive criminal policy against drugs, high taxes and a state monopoly on alcohol, social programmes for alcoholics and tardiness in providing medical help for drug users.

Because the legal tradition or social policies do not offer an explanation, the different approaches to sexual crimes might be explained by different understandings of equality between the sexes. While in Finland equality is understood as an already existing state of affairs, the Swedes seem to be much more conscious about the inequalities that exist. Especially the political parties have been active in incorporating equality politics into the programmes and many politicians, including Prime Minister Göran Persson have declared themselves to be feminists.

In this setting, it is interesting to look how different discourses construct the central notions of sex crime law, such as sexuality, subjectivity, force or consent. In this chapter, I will take a constructionist look at the legal regulations and discourses, especially in the official documents about sexual crimes. I think that law plays a crucial role in the construction of social phenomena. Law not only regulates something that exists prior to law, in a pre-law reality, but law itself is also a part of the social construction of that same reality.[3] Actually, law is a particularly powerful tool in the social construction of reality because it is the only discourse that is backed by the legalized use of force. Legal discourse defines what is allowed and what is prohibited. Its definitions are endorsed both by social condemnation and by official sanctions. The most powerful legal discourse is criminal law because it carries with it the threat of the severest legal sanctions. In addition, the discourse of criminal law affects other ethical and moral discourses about right and wrong, as well as social practices that are not of immediate relevance to criminal courts.

Contemporary feminist writing on criminal law has discussed the constructions of female and male sexuality in the context of rape law (Estrich 1987; Lacey 1998, 105; Naffine 1997, 99; Andersson 2001; Lacey, Wells and Meure 1990, 305). But laws on sexual crimes in a broader sense, including laws on statutory rape, sexual abuse, prostitution and sexual harassment, are also important in constructing the sexuality and the gendered subjectivity. Rape has been a serious and heavily punished crime throughout history, but the regulation of other above-mentioned issues has undergone through drastic changes. While the changes in sexual ideology are reflected in rape law and its implementation, the ruptures in the liberal discourse on sex crimes have become even more evident in the changes of regulation of these other issues. Therefore, I will explore the constructions of sexuality and subjectivity in the sex crime law in a broader context than just forcible rape law.

Such constructions are also culturally and historically grounded. History may also make us more alert in recognizing the underlying assumptions of contemporary discourses. I will therefore start this chapter by analyzing the construction of sexuality in the historical development of Finnish sex crime law.

Four phases are distinguished. First, sexual relations are regulated as property and as a means of exchange between the families. In the second phase, illustrated by the Code of 1734, law was a tool for defining chastity and the regulation of patriarchal power. In the next phase, in early 19th century liberal society, the protection of morals took on a new form in which the patriarchal double standard played a crucial role. Fourth, modern liberal regulation is represented by the new Finnish sex crime law of 1998. The historical periodization in this chapter follows the development of Finnish criminal law and is summarized in Table 2. The laws often include different elements dating from different times and ideologies. It turns out, however, that changes in contemporary conceptions of sexuality are reflected in the respective law with surprising accuracy.

The historical account makes it explicit that law has been a powerful tool in the social construction of sexuality and of female and male subjectivity. Sex crime law not only reflects contemporary constructions of gender and sex, sexuality, sexual crimes, subjectivity and the relation between the body and the mind, but it also participates in the construction of these concepts (Lacey, Wells and Meure 1990).

The contemporary discourses, the liberal and the feminist, are then discussed more thoroughly. These two discourses give quite a different account of the central notions of sex crime law, such as violence or force, sexuality, sex and subjectivity. In this chapter, I will look at the sex crime reforms in both of these countries from a constructionist perspective.

The liberal discourse in the *travaux preparatiores* of the Finnish 1998 reform presupposes specific constructions of sexuality and subjectivity in which the subject of law is assumed as sex neutral and detached. Sexuality is depicted as a liberal exchange between two equal subjects, in the absence of any qualities or power relations.[4] The 'good' that the law is intended to protect is defined as sexual self-determination. In a critical account, however, this liberal discourse turns out to be very problematic when any difficult issue of sexual crimes, such as sexual abuse of minors or prostitution, is discussed. Out of these texts, a counter-discourse of protection emerged whenever sexual encounters between unequals, especially with underaged persons, was discussed, but it was suppressed by the dominant liberal discourse.

The starting point of the Swedish law drafting in the mid-1990s was quite different. The Women's Peace Committee understood violence against women, as it stands in contemporary society, as a consequence of the power imbalance between women and men. The Committee on sexual crimes recognized this starting point, but was less explicit about it. Nevertheless, this committee was concerned that regulation of rape law had not been successful in bringing about justice for the many victims who did not fulfil the requirements of the law. The aim was an improved protection of victims of sexual crimes. The outcome of this, as I call it, feminist discourse is discussed as a means of incorporating the power imbalances into the legal regulation.

I will explore the possibilities of gaining a new understanding of sexuality as relation, the recognition of power relations in sex crimes and the construction of subjectivity as related and attached. More specifically, I will explore some topics that have been particularly difficult to encompass within a liberal discussion. I will argue that issues, such as consent, the protection of minors and others in a vulnerable position, prostitution and sexual harassment, can be better dealt with when the emphasis in the discussion is shifted from autonomous subjects to relations.

The First Historical Construction: The Regulation of Sexuality as an Exchange between Families

The regulation of sexuality during the Middle Ages and in early modernity was connected with the arrangements of economic relations among families. In the event of a marriage, property and labour were transferred from one family to another (Pylkkänen 1990, 91) in an exchange transaction. The property arrangements for marriage were, partly, made to secure the economic position of the bride, while, after the marriage, the responsibility for the daughter was handed over to the husband's family. In some cases, her economic position was protected with something known as a morning gift. And, of course, the regulation emphasized the need to guarantee marital birth to the children.

The legal framework in which the control of sexuality took place was marriage law. Criminal law was less significant (Aalto 1996, 92) and it supported the marriage law. In particular, the crime, 'maiden violation', protected the authority of the custodian, that is, of the father or of other male relatives to arrange a maiden's marriage by making the seduction of an unmarried girl a crime (Kristoffer's land law 1442, the Book of Marriage 1.1). In maiden violation, the male relative in charge was the party whose right had been infringed upon, not the young woman herself. Consequently, the young woman, who was seduced or forced into the extra-marital relationship, was not punished for it (Pylkkänen 1990, 83, 105; Aalto 1996, 91).

Thus, the control of sexuality was a male prerogative. A number of researchers discuss the gender system of this era in terms of ownership (Table 2). Not only were the perpetrators explicitly men, the objects of protection were also men, as owners of women's sexuality (Brownmiller 1975). The object of both the crime of rape and 'maiden violation' was the husband or the custodian (usually male) (Utriainen 1994, 124). An important criterion for punishment was the status of the woman violated. Women with the status of maiden or wife were of greater value than other women. Violations of these types of women were punished more severely than the violations of women who were neither maidens nor wives. Another status differentiation was made between maidens of marital and extra-marital birth. The seduction of a maiden of extra-marital birth was punished with a fine that was only half of what the perpetrator had to pay for the seduction of a maiden of marital birth (Kristoffer's land law 1442, the Book of Marriage 3.1).

In order to be protected by criminal law, a woman had to be under the protection of a man – either a husband or male custodian who acted as the head and representative of the family or clan. The stronger the social position of the family, the more effective the protection afforded to the woman. In practice, a woman who belonged to the lower strata of society or who was on her own could not expect the criminal law to protect her very effectively.

This asymmetrical protection is exemplified by the regulation of adultery. According to medieval law, a married woman was punished and lost her status and any economic benefits which had been conferred upon her by marriage if she committed adultery (Magnus Eriksson's (1350) and Kristoffer's land law (1442) the Book of Marriage 11; Utriainen 1994, 124). For men, adultery was not prohibited by law. In fact, it was rather widely practised, while women with lower social status were nearly unprotected in the face of sexual harassment and abuse by their masters (Aalto 1996, 181).

The Second Construction: The Church and the Struggle to Define Sexual Morality

The emergence of a central authority, the growing influence of the Church, and the Reformation marked the development in the Kingdom of Sweden and Finland in the 16th and 17th centuries. The church and the state actively pursued a policy to establish an 'absolute' sexual morality according to which sexual intercourse was reserved for the realm of marriage, which had been blessed by the church. Trials for sexual crimes were transferred to secular courts, away from the jurisdiction of the church and from the control of the peasant community itself. The peasant community, however, was unwilling to change its traditional mores. In fact, a tolerance of practices, such as premarital sexual relations survived a long time, especially in the countryside (Aalto 1996; Nieminen 1951, 76).

Since the Middle Ages, the church had imposed a legal ban on sexual relations between unmarried men and women, that is, fornication, and on extramarital sex, that is, adultery. After Reformation, this quest was invigorated through different regulations in the course of the 16th and 17th centuries, which were finally codified in the Code of 1734.

Instead of maiden's violation, which only punished the seducer, the regulation of fornication made pre-marital sex a criminal act for both parties (Nieminen 1951, 78-81). Yet, the fines for a woman were generally only half of the man's fines (1734 Book on Crimes 53.1). And those fines were costly; poor women often had to suffer some type of humiliating public reprisal for the crime if they could not afford to pay the money to satisfy the judgement (Aalto 1996, 121-123, Telste 1994, 135).

Invocation of the Mosaic law in the mid-16th century contributed to a change in the views on adultery. A relation between an unmarried woman and a married man became a serious, even capital, offence (the Code of 1734; see Aalto 1996, 95-97, 103). In practice, the penalties were less severe (Aalto 1996, 99-101). The absolute sexual morality established by the Code of 1734[5] could never be fully implemented in practice and the control of premarital relations by the community persisted into the next century.

Through this development, both the Church and the State tried to shift the regulation and control of sexuality away from families into the public realm. From a woman's point of view, the development was ambivalent. While the former regime had failed to protect lower class women from sexual abuse and to guarantee support for their illegitimate children, the attempt by the Church to rein in such relations and to settle the issue of support for the children by treating the crime of adultery severely can indeed be seen as a radical and even emancipatory measure.[6]

At the same time, the legal development meant stricter control of women's sexual conduct, which is most obvious in the regulation of fornication. Formerly, it was not considered necessary to punish a woman for an illicit relationship because the very visibility of her pregnancy made the relationship public for her part. In this respect, the crime of infanticide was a way to control women's morality (Pylkkänen 1990, 108; Telste 1994, 128). In the new context, a woman was guilty of fornication or, if the man was married, of adultery, a crime with a severe punishment. Consequently, the new regulation meant a harsher treatment of these 'fallen' women (Aalto 1996, 105).

During this period, from the Middle Ages to the early modernity, what I call the traditional regulation of sexuality and sexual crimes was constructed (Table 2). In Sweden and Finland, the regulation was codified in the Code of 1734. Traditional values, protection of sexual morality, marriage, sexuality tied to the status as a wife and patriarchal social structures were protected by the church.

The Protection of Sexual Morality and the Construction of a Double Standard

The Enlightenment produced a lively exchange of ideas which influenced the criminal law of the late 18th century Sweden and Finland. Punishments were made more lenient. In particular, capital punishment was systematically mitigated by the Courts of Appeal (Anners 1965, 150). In 1779, Gustav III abolished capital punishment for rape, bigamy and adultery. The criminal policy discussion of this period was concerned with infanticide. Illegitimate births had become more common and they were still condemned by the Church. Capital punishment for infanticide was criticized as too severe a measure for desperate women. Its use was restricted in the 1779 reform but it was not abolished (Anners 1965, 1, 166; Blomstedt 1964).

After Finland became part of the Russian Empire in 1809, legal reform was halted for several decades. The Code of 1734 remained in force almost unchanged until the Criminal Code of 1889 was enacted. The regulation of sexual relations in the 1889 Criminal Code was still based on the principle of absolute sexual morality. The 1889 Criminal Code reflected the same traditional values and conceptions as the Code of 1734, the protection of sexual morality, marriage and patriarchal social structures. Thus, also the 1889 Criminal Code can be characterized as 'traditional' as in Table 2. When we look at the Criminal Code more in detail, we soon notice, however, that besides the official absolute sexual morality, there exists a sexed regulation, which can be conceptualized as the 'double standard'.

In principle, sexual intercourse was still restricted to marriage within which it was the duty of the spouses to procreate. The wife was presumed to have given permanent consent for intercourse with her husband and, therefore, rape in marriage could not be thought of as a criminal act.[7]

Other forms of sexuality were forbidden with some degree of subtlety. Homosexuality and sodomy were forbidden. Also, sexual relations between persons of the same kin were regulated in some detail. Likewise, the protection age for minors included several categories. Fornication and adultery were still forbidden and objects of a prodigiously detailed regulation. The ideas of Enlightenment were expressed in the level of sanctions, which was much more lenient than before.

The new social circumstances and sexual practices are reflected, albeit indirectly, in the double standard that can be read from the provisions of the 1889 Criminal Code. While absolute sexual morality was the official ideology of this era, among the prevalent practices, different social norms were applied to male and female sexuality. In practical life, premarital and extramarital relations of men were tolerated, but both abstention from sexual relations prior to marriage and fidelity during marriage were required of women. Most obviously, middle and upper class women were the standard bearers of the sexual morality and their behaviour was most cautiously guarded. In lower classes, mores were more relaxed in the countryside. In cities, a visible sign of the double standard was prostitution in its various forms. Public morals did not especially favour men's patronage of prostitutes but, nevertheless, it was accepted as a fact of life and definitely not condemned the way women's extramarital relations would have been. In practice, the double standard in upper and middle classes meant that women were divided into two kinds: those who were chaste and those who were prostitutes or otherwise fallen (Nieminen 1951, 91).

While this short description of the moral double standard of this period may seem self-evident, it clearly was in contradiction with the publicly promoted morality. While later legal research has characterized the legal regulation of the period as representing this so-called absolute sexual morality, my reading of the criminal law shows that the double standard, if not explicit, is at least distinguishable in many provisions. Certain legal provisions set explicitly different standards for women and men. The distinction between good and bad, or deserving and undeserving, women is equally visible in many regulations. Furthermore, many sex-neutral provisions had different effects on women and men depending upon the social position of the accused.

This bi-partite division of women is discernible in the interpretation of the provisions on rape. In early Swedish jurisprudence, a view had been expressed that the rape of a woman who had already lost her virtue could not be punished as rape. This view was later abandoned by the jurisprudence, but as late as the early 20th century, we find an opinion that the quality of the woman who had been raped 'naturally' affected the punishment to be meted out (Forsman I 1917, 121-122, 124).[8]

The double standard practically required an institutionalized system of prostitution.[9] Prostitution was explicitly forbidden.[10] What was punishable was prostitution by women.[11] Men could be punished for a number of activities that included leading, tempting or forcing a woman into prostitution or into comparable depravity.[12] There was no prohibition in the Criminal Code against the patronage of prostitution, but such sexual activity was, as a matter of fact, a criminal deed either as fornication or as adultery. In practice, clients were not punished (Häkkinen 1995, 101-103).

In the 19th century, prostitution was an essential feature of the sexual culture in towns. Prostitution in its various forms, such as brothels, streetwalkers and kept women, was common. Men in different social classes, especially students and upper class men, had experiences of patronage (Häkkinen 1995, 78-85). Prostitution was controlled through administrative orders. From the mid-19th century on, its practitioners were required to have a license and to undergo regular medical check-ups (Häkkinen 1995, 163-166; Järvinen 1990, 71). The control measures were directed at prostitutes, their clients were hardly ever targeted. The purpose was to prevent the transmission of venereal diseases and, therefore, the regulation was oriented more towards the protection of health and sanitation than the maintenance of public morality (Forsman II 73; Häkkinen 1995, 166; Järvinen 1990, 72).

The double standard setting different standards for deserving and undeserving women is also reflected in the provisions relating to the ages of consent. The regulation of ages of consent was a novelty. In earlier times, sexual intercourse with a person under twelve was punishable as rape.[13] The absolute age of consent under the Criminal Code of 1889 continued to be twelve. In addition, two new ages of consent were introduced: fifteen and seventeen. These age restrictions were applied to protect girls who had no experience of sexual intercourse.[14] If a girl had a sexual experience and had thereby stepped off the path of chastity, her morality could no longer be protected. Instead, she could be held accountable for prostitution, which, in this situation, might prove to be the only way to earn a living.

Legislation relating to fornication (pre-marital sex) and adultery (extra-marital sex) had both symbolic and actual importance for the control of the sexuality of middle class women. The regulation was sex-neutral. Because the social norms for pre-marital and extra-marital sex were gendered, these regulations did little to prevent men of the same social standing from visiting brothels or mistresses. Public control was weakened when an indictment for adultery was made dependent upon the wish of the aggrieved party.[15] If the adultery had led to divorce, the prosecutor, however, was obliged to file charges. In a society where economic rights were in the hands of men, this regulation reinforced the control of wives who risked not only losing their status within the marriage but also risked gaining public condemnation for adultery.

The requirement of chastity for middle and upper class women is illustrated by the discussion on the abolishment of any punishment for fornication by women. An one-sided decriminalization had been enacted in Sweden in 1810 because the often visible pregnancy put the responsibility on women clearly enough. On somewhat contradictory grounds, decriminalization was not considered possible in Finland. On one hand, decriminalization was thought to refute the idea that a woman had a will of her own. On the other hand, however, it was essential to preserve a free choice for her because the respectability of the family depended on the woman and the welfare of society depended on the family (Forsman II 1917, 50). Consequently, the woman was seen as having a free will, which she had the right to exercise as long as she did so in the interests of the family and society.

The protection of public sexual morality turned out to be a system by which to control women's sexuality through the legislation relating to ages of consent, prostitution, fornication and adultery. Either there was no willingness to control men's sexuality, indicated by the lack of willingness to make the patronage of prostitution criminal and by excluding them from the ages of consent, or the provisions, such as fornication and adultery, were not applied to men. The system was based on two double standards, a different standard on men and women and the idea that women were of two kinds for whom two different standards existed. Honourable women received protection through marriage or as eligible daughters – actually, a provision against seduction equal to maiden violation was retained in the Criminal Code of 1889[16] – whereas fallen women could hardly expect protection from the criminal law. Instead, they might be charged with prostitution.

The female subjectivity we encounter here is divided. On the one hand, we have protected women, with few rights, but also with little responsibility in the face of the law. Their responsibility is to refrain from adulterous relationships. On the other hand, we have the women with no rights at all, but full responsibility for extramarital sex, be it paid or not. And then we have men, with all rights and very little risk of ever having to take responsibility for their sexual activities.

The Liberal Construction of Sexual Self-Determination

The Finnish reforms of sex crimes law during the 20th century have been a liberal project. As I will argue in the following text, the reforms have been guided by certain basic assumptions of the liberal political ideology. At the core of liberalism is the individualization of actions and moral choices. Accordingly, the conception of the autonomous subject, neutrality towards moral convictions and the conception of sexuality as deliberate and distinct acts have been the undercurrent of the reform projects. Even if some of these assumptions have been explicit in the *travaux preparatoires,* their most powerful effect on the reform work derives from the presence – unquestioned and taken for granted – of the liberal ideas in contemporary thinking. Thus, it is important to deconstruct the liberal thinking in the formulations of sex crime law.

The most explicit aim of the reforms has been not to use criminal law as a control or guide to sexual morals any more (Government Bills 52/1970, 1 and 6/1997, 163-164; Rautio 1999, 383). While the old regulation was designed to protect general sexual morality, an important goal of the reform was to attain neutrality in relation to different expressions of sexuality and to ensure the right of sexual self-determination of each person. The law should be neutral regarding different expressions of sexuality and different relations. In the 1998 reform,[17] sex-neutral language was used to underline the law's neutrality. The neutrality towards moral convictions is reflected by the change of the Chapter's title from the value-laden, 'Crimes against Chastity' to the neutral-sounding, 'Sexual Offences'.

In many ways, the 1998 total reform of Chapter 20 of the Criminal Code completed a reform project that had been under way for several decades. Several provisions of the 1889 Criminal Code, such as the prohibition of fornication, adultery and prostitution, had been repealed early on.[18] The struggle over the 'sexual revolution' was reflected in the Finnish Parliament in 1970 when, in a close vote in the Parliamentary Committee, the Parliament decided that rape in marriage should remain unpunished to protect the sanctity of marriage.[19] Thus, neutrality concerning sexual partners did not go as far as including married women as autonomous subjects with a right to sexual self-determination. The liberalization project regarding homosexuals was more successful with the reform of 1970, while homosexuality between consenting adults was legalized, but the age of consent was higher than the age of consent for heterosexuals and a specific ban on spreading information about homosexuality was stipulated, in the form of a prohibition against instigation to homosexual deeds (Hiltunen 1998).

According to the *travaux preparatoires* of the 1998 reform, the key purpose of the law is the protection of sexual self-determination (Government Bill 6/1997, 2, 161, 170). The *travaux preparatioires* also explicitly relinquished the protection of sexual morality as an aim of the sex crime law. It was no longer necessary to influence the contents of individuals' sexuality and sexual orientation through legislation relating to sexual crimes because these matters should be assigned to the sphere of an individual's sexual self-determination (Government Bill 6/1997, 163-164). The purpose of the law is to protect 'the right to self determine one's sexual conduct' (Government Bill 6/1997, 161), irrespective of the concrete contents of the manifestation of sexuality, as long as it does not violate the right of other people to sexual self-determination. In an enlightened spirit, the above- mentioned provisions concerning homosexuals were abolished. By introducing sex neutral language, homosexual and heterosexual rape are to be treated in the same way.

The choice of sexual self-determination as the basic protected good of sex crime law seems to be connected to a specific construction of other basic concepts of criminal law, most notably the concepts of autonomous subject, sexuality and the private/public dichotomy. Obviously, sexual self-determination is an important dimension of an individual's autonomy, a central premise of the concept of the human subject both in the modern social theory and in the modern legal systems. And no doubt, the protection of physical safety, guaranteed by the State, is an essential requirement for the existence of an autonomous subject and for the freedom to exercise self-determination in any field of life.

The central position of self-determination in modern liberal criminal law is bound up with the concept of the autonomous subject, which is one of the basic concepts that form the foundation of modern law (Tuori 1997, 321). The modern subject is conceived as a self-governing, independent, detached and rational entity, capable of autonomous decision-making. It has no characteristics, such as sex, age, (other than legal majority) colour or ethnicity (Davies 1994, 182; Naffine 1990, 100; Svensson 1997). The legal entity has the rights guaranteed by the legal system: the right of ownership, the right to enter into contracts, the right to decide on the use of her or his labour contribution, the right to opinions and convictions and the right to express them, and the right to sexual expression and self-determination.

When the law on sexual crimes takes the protection of sexual self-determination as its point of departure, it also assumes the above-described subject of law. The relationship between the protection of women from violence and the protection of women's right to self-determination has been ambiguous all along, however. In domestic crimes against women, the concern has not been to protect women against violent interference. Rather, women's self-determination has been acknowledged only when it comes to the rescue of the domestic perpetrator from prosecution and punishment (Niemi-Kiesiläinen 2001). The ambivalence is also illustrated by the systematization of rape law, which has been classified at different times as violent crime, as a crime against liberty or as a sexual crime. The ambivalence is also present in the feminist discourse on rape law, with its debate on whether rape is a violent crime or a sexual crime (Estrich 1987).

The concept of subject is particularly powerful in criminal law, where responsibility for criminal acts is allocated. Thus, criminal law discourse is necessarily focused on the perpetrator and it is the perpetrator whose autonomy and will are discussed. Since the perpetrators are most often men, the male perspective has been dominant also in criminal law theory (Naffine 1997). Victims have seldom been discussed as subjects but, rather, as objects of crimes in criminal law. When the sex crime law assumes two autonomous subjects as representatives of sexual normality, its focus of protection is on autonomous, self-determining women, that is, on adult, middle-class, white, economically self-supporting women.

As I will try to show with the following examples, a discussion involving these assumptions necessarily leads to trouble when it encounters situations of sexual abuse in which the victims do not correspond to the subjectivity described above. Clearly, many victims of sexual crime are minors, mentally or physically handicapped, intoxicated or otherwise in some kind of vulnerable situation. Often, they are dependent on the perpetrator because of family ties, employment or institutional affiliation or for other reasons. Sex crime law includes a number of specific provisions to protect some of these victims. Thus, in the analysis the underlying assumptions of sex crime law, it is important to analyze such other forms of sexual abuse than rape that are on the fringes of sex crime law and where concepts of subject, agency, and victimization are less obvious.

Before going on to concrete examples, the construction of the sexuality connected to the concepts of autonomy and subjectivity has to be examined. In the *travaux preparatoires* of the new sex crime act, normal sexuality was depicted as a liberal exchange between two equal subjects, in the absence of any qualities or power relations. Furthermore, the construction of sexuality in the new law is act-centred, sex being an act defined by time and place. The new legal definitions of the most important elements of crime – sexual intercourse and sexual act[20] – reflect both the act-centred construction of sexuality and the perpetrator's perspective. The most serious crime, rape, requires an element of sexual intercourse, which is defined as a penetration of the body.[21] Other forms of sexual violations do not constitute rape, notwithstanding the amount of violence or sexual content of the acts or the depth of the violation of integrity. These other acts of sexual nature may be punished as sexual abuse[22] or as coercion into a sexual deed.[23] A sexual deed is defined from a perpetrator's perspective as an act of an essentially sexual nature by which one is seeking sexual arousal or satisfaction (sic!).

In the following text, the new Finnish sex crime law is used as an example to examine the limits of liberal discussion. With its one-sided emphasis on self-determination and its rather enlightened spirit, the law gives plenty of examples of how the liberal discourse on most crucial legal issues is necessarily simplified and distorted.

Critical Examples of the Use of Sexual Self-Determination

Degrees of rape

In rape, the sexual self-determination of the victim is basically denied by the use of force. The denial of self-determination is reflected in the construction of the elements of rape. The crime of rape is divided into three categories according to the severity of the violence and using similar criteria as in earlier reforms of the Criminal Code for other crimes, such as assault and robbery. The focus of the act is on violence, whereas consent is not mentioned as an element of rape. An essential substantive amendment was that the use of coercion other than violence to force a person into sexual intercourse became explicitly punishable as a lesser grade of rape.

The differentiation of rape into different degrees was justified by the seriousness of the violation of sexual self-determination (Government Bill 6/1997, 164). The most important element in qualifying a rape as aggravated is the amount of violence used. Most of us agree that this differentiation is a sound policy, but can it logically be justified by arguments concerning the degree of the violation of self-determination? We probably agree upon that a case where a person is forced into sexual intercourse with a knife on her throat is more serious than a case where she is forced to have sex under threat of losing her job. The former case is punishable as an aggravated rape, carrying a maximum punishment of ten years imprisonment, and the latter case as a coercion into sexual intercourse with the maximum of three years.[24] Both are repugnant acts and making a comparison of their respective gravity may be experienced as a rather strange and uncomfortable exercise. But seen from the perspective of sexual self-determination, the outcome is almost the same. In one way, the violation of sexual self-determination implicit in the threat of the loss of a job may be even more serious than in violent rape because such a threat may be repeated and the threat may restrict sexual self-determination continuously – unless the victim resigns from the job. From the point of the protection of physical integrity, the matter is less complicated: severe violence violates physical integrity more seriously than do acts constituting the crime of coercion into sexual intercourse.

Age of consent

The Government Bill recognized the problems from the point of sexual self-determination related to ages of consent (Government Bill 6/1997, 167). The age of consent, paradoxically, restricts young people's opportunities of having sexual relationships and, thereby, indirectly their right to self-determination, even though the threat of punishment is directed at the adult party, not at the child.

When the prohibition against the sexual abuse of children is induced from the protection of sexual self-determination, the protected 'good' is actually their right to sound development towards sexual and other self-determination. This construction, however, requires a great deal of developmental psychology and knowledge that certain acts are harmful to children's development. Logically, Section 20(6) of the Criminal Code states that, in order to be punishable as the sexual abuse of a child, an act must be conducive to harming the development of the child. But how do we judge such harm? Should not an act which violates the sexual integrity of a child be punishable irrespective of its effects? The purpose of the Code's language has not been to let acts concerning very young children go unpunished just because we may have insufficient knowledge about the harm such acts cause.

Protection of persons in vulnerable situations

The provisions aimed at protecting persons who are in dependent or vulnerable positions or in need of special protection are similarly problematic from the perspective of sexual self-determination. The special provisions protect students under eighteen, inmates in hospitals and at institutions and persons in other especially dependent positions from sexual relations with the persons upon whom they are dependent. In addition, protection is afforded to young, immature persons under eighteen against sexual abuse.[25] Again, there are good grounds to provide special protection to these groups, but it is difficult to justify these provisions by the protection of sexual self-determination. A romantic and sexual relationship with a teacher, for example, may be exactly what a student aims at and wants. To prohibit such a relationship indirectly restricts the student's self-determination, even though it is the teacher who is punished and not the student. The justification for the prohibition is that, by virtue of his or her position of authority, the teacher has the opportunity and means to subject the student to repercussions, if things do not go the way the teacher wishes. The student is not capable of envisioning such a situation, while the teacher is aware of such risks. For these reasons, the special provisions are justified, despite their patronising element and the restriction of self-determination.

The focus on sexual self-determination has led to certain limitations of liability that will make the implementation of the provisions difficult and, most likely, considerably restrict the protection offered by the provisions. The act at issue has to be qualified as an abuse of position and it also has to include an element of persuasion. The purpose of these qualifications is to allow for the possibility of normal sexual relations even for persons in such hierarchical relationships (Government Bill 6/1997, 178). Even if one believes that such normal sexual relations are possible, one has to ask whether they have to be protected at the cost of making a very important protective regulation almost impossible to implement.

Prostitution

The greatest problems for a liberal thinker lie in the provisions relating to prostitution (Svensson 2000). Prostitution has not been a crime in Finland since 1936 and its patronage has never been defined a crime as such.[26] In the 1998 reform, a prohibition to buy sex from persons under eighteen was enacted.[27] The Government Bill addresses the legal regulation of prostitution from the perspective of self-determination (Government Bill 6/1997, 168). When prostitution is examined as a financial transaction between two adults exercising their sexual self-determination, it is difficult to see in it anything that deserves criticism (Träskman 1998). However, a prostitute's limited opportunity in choosing her clients is considered a typical feature of prostitution (Järvinen 1990, 96). In other words, a prostitute's sexual self-determination is *de facto* restricted.[28] This *de facto* restriction may be the one of the reasons why the treatment of sexuality as a commodity is so offensive to many people.

The mere fact that the human body is regarded as a commodity can be seen as a degradation of human dignity. In addition, sexuality contains a particular dimension of personal integrity. This important element of sexuality is violated by the use of the human body as a commodity, despite the fact that such a violation is difficult to conceptualize. Prostitution is not a popular profession, and its practitioners are recruited from the most vulnerable and economically and socially excluded members of society (Häkkinen 1995, 210) and for whom, according to Järvinen, all the safety nets of society have failed (Järvinen 1990, 52). The sex trade is also deeply entangled with organized crime, drug abuse, extortion, and violence, with all their concomitant risks.

The liberal and sex-neutral discourse of the Finnish *travaux preparatoires* omitted one important argument against the criminalization of prostitution, viz., that previous experiences of defining prostitution as a crime and the prosecution of prostitutes were directed at women prostitutes, who were socially excluded to start with. This criminalization had led to the repressive control of persons who also were otherwise exploited and abused.

The *travaux preparatoires* diligently discussed the negative effects of the criminalization of prostitution. The discussion was sex-neutral and did not assess the effects separately for each party. The negative consequences of criminalization, such as any increases in the power of a procurer, in the level of violence and in the prevalence of sexually transmitted diseases, were carefully enumerated.[29] These risks seem quite obvious if a prostitute's acts are made into crimes. It is less obvious, however, that the same risks are connected with the criminalization of the acts of the client. In Sweden, the patronage of prostitutes was made a crime in 1999, but not the actions of prostitutes, and the above-mentioned risks have not realized.[30]

The example shows that liberal and sex neutral language may be used to hide the sex specific reality and consequences of a legal regulation. Under the pretext of neutrality, only the control of women was actually discussed. Obviously, there was no intention to restrict men's sexual self-determination over purchased sex. Had the law's premise been to strengthen the sexual self-determination of socially and economically excluded women, the discussion would have taken on a different tone.

In Sweden, for example, the discussion has focused on the harm caused to those who prostitute themselves and to the whole society, including the effect on equality (SOU 1995:15). Especially, the role of the clients in the process of becoming a prostitute was emphasized. In a broader view, prostitution was seen as a manifestation of the inequality between the sexes.

Sexual harassment

The last example, which will be discussed further below, is the explicit position that it was inappropriate to use the Criminal Code to protect women against sexual harassment (Government Bill 6/1997, 162). The Bill also discussed sexual harassment as a violation of sexual self-determination. Everyone should have the right to decide who touches his or her body and where, as well as the right not to be addressed in sexually coloured and intimidating language. Other measures, especially those concerning equality in the labour market were considered more appropriate means of combating sexual harassment.

It is a matter of definition, however, whether this kind of sexual harassment is a violation of sexual self-determination. No doubt, a function of sexual harassment is to show women their place and role as objects of male sexual desire and, thus, restrict their freedom of sexual expression and their exercise of self-determination. While this function operates at a structural level, it is more difficult to assess at the level of actions taken. Most often women experience violations of their physical integrity, such as touching, patting, groping, or violations of sexual integrity, such as name-calling. However, there seems to be a danger of victimizing women when we say that this kind of behaviour *per se* is a violation of sexual self-determination. Most Finnish women, I think, would say that they are fully capable of retaining their sexual self-determination, even if they find that being called a 'whore' and other like communications are serious violations of integrity.

New Constructions: Sexuality as a Relationship and Integrity as the Protected Good

These examples from the new Finnish sex crime law suggest that if we choose sexual self-determination as the point of departure in the discussion of sex crime law, we do not get very far. It limits the way we can conceptualize subjectivity and sexuality and, thus, it limits the way we can discuss a variety of sexual violations directed at differently situated women, children and men. We need to reconsider the protected good of sexual crimes.

Nicola Lacey (1998, 112) has argued that the problem with sexual autonomy, as the protected good of sexual crimes, is that it presupposes a dichotomy between the mind and the body and, in fact, posits the mind over the body. In this context, both the harm of the sexual crimes, as a violation of a person's authority over the access to his or her own body and the wrong committed, understood as a failure to control one's own body, reflect a hierarchical relationship between the mind and the body (Lacey 1998, 113). Therefore, sexual autonomy or self-determination as the protected good of sex crimes necessarily encompasses the harm caused by these crimes in a narrow way. It may not even wholly encompass the physical harm done, but it is especially unable to grasp the psychological component involved.

Today, we have plenty of research on the psychological trauma caused by rape, incest and other sexual abuse. Consequences are often serious and sometimes long-lasting. There may even be a component of the violation that is difficult to describe in diagnostic terms. Describing the effect of sexual violence, Sari Näre writes that it '...threatens the realm of fantasies and images, hopes and expectations, in which one's identity is vulnerable, and the transitional state of the mind...' (Näre 2000, 3). The discussion of the legal regulation of sexual crimes leaves something unsaid if it fails to reach out for the elusive: to examine how the provisions can be used to protect sexual integrity, understood as both physical and psychological inviolability.

As Nicola Lacey does, I also suggest a shift in the discussion about the protected good of sex crimes law towards protection of integrity. This shift is not radical at all. In fact, it might be even called reactionary. The protection against violence and sexual inviolability has been the protected good of sexual crimes law throughout the history. I believe, however, that, by trying to include the psychological component of harm, we will reach a deeper understanding of the violation of sexual integrity.

The concepts of sexual self-determination and physical and psychological integrity are not mutually exclusive. Rather, sexual self-determination may be understood as one facet of integrity. Nevertheless, my argument is that a different focus is significant for the content and interpretation of the law. At the theoretical level, when the emphasis is shifted towards the protection of integrity, we have the chance of reconsidering the concepts of legal subject and sexuality, both concepts paramount in sex crime law.

While the concept of self-determination excludes the relational aspects of subjecthood from the analysis, the concept of integrity allows us to recognize that the subject is always in a relation with the other. The subjectivity is not a pre-existing entity. Instead, it is continuously constituted in interaction with the other.

The modern concept of subject is the construction of the social and political theory of the 19th century. While it disregards the relational aspects of human life, it is also blind to its own gendered quality. In the 19th century political theory, political and civil rights belonged to a male subject in the public sphere (Møller Okin 1979, 278). The public sphere, however, assumed a private sphere for reproduction and maintenance and a private female subject with no similar rights, not even any rights relating to her own body. From an historical perspective, gender may also be understood as a relationship instead of as a preconceived category (O'Donovan 1997, 62; Hirdman 1990; Heinämaa 1996; Svensson 1997). Thus, the focus on integrity and gender as relation may be helpful when we want to view the victim as a subject.

In the Finnish liberal discussion, the parties of a sexual exchange are considered autonomous and equal. In violent rape, the agency of the victim is all but denied, making violent rape an easy case for a liberal thinker. Other forms of sexual abuse are more complex because they include victims who are able to express their views or to resist to some extent, though not fully. The focus on sexual self-determination easily leads to logic according to which the victims of sexual crime are expected either to be fully able to protect themselves or completely incapable to express their views.

This problem has been discussed in the context of domestic violence. Both empirical and theoretical studies on domestic violence have challenged the ambiguous requirement that the female victim either has to leave the relationship altogether or accept the role of a passive object of crime (Mahoney 1991; Gordon 1987; Naffine 1997; Ruuskanen 2001). Most women, even if they stay in their relationships, use several tactics to avoid danger, to protect and defend themselves and their kin and to mitigate the consequences (Fischer, Vidmar & Ellis 1993). In a similar vein, the victims of sexual crimes should be seen as actors and yet worthy of protection when their sexual self-determination is constrained.

Furthermore, while a focus on self-determination is bound up with a certain view on sexuality, the shift towards the protection of integrity opens up to a more relational view on sexuality. The shift of perspective from autonomous subjects to the relations between subjects seems logical since sexuality is naturally inter-subjective. Sexuality as a phenomenon, separated and isolated from other people, can cover only a small portion of what can be understood to as sexuality.

A lawyer with a feminist approach may instinctively be suspicious of a conception of sexuality as a relationship for the very reason that any relationship between the victim and the perpetrator has so often been a reason to minimize the gravity of the sexual crime. For example, the marital relationship has served to remove the punishment of the act; any interaction between victim and perpetrator before the act has been used to induce guilt feelings in the victim and to minimize the act, and so on. The explanatory note to the new Finnish law on sexual crimes is not without similar references. Although it states that '...the relationship between the perpetrator and the victim should not be mentioned as a extenuating circumstance...', a little later, it makes a full turn, stating that '...interaction between perpetrator and victim prior to the act together with other circumstances of the act...' could be an extenuating circumstance (Government Bill 6/1997, 175). A fine line is drawn here between relationship and interaction. For me, it is quite difficult to see the difference. According to the same text, marriage is a relationship and, thus, not considered an extenuating circumstance. But being married necessarily includes interaction. To confuse matters even more, marriage is a fact that is specifically mentioned as a reason for which the victim may withdraw a complaint and for the prosecutor to drop the charges (Government Bill 6/1997). In the worst case scenario, the mention of interaction in this context carries with it the serious danger of widening the scope of mitigating circumstances to different kinds of interactions between a boyfriend and a girlfriend, between two acquaintances, between ex-spouses, between ex girl/boyfriends and so on.[31]

Reference to relation, therefore, should necessarily include an analysis of the power relations between the parties and within the gender system of the society. In violent rape, the abuse of physical force always means imposing one's power on the victim (MacKinnon 1987, 50, 88). In other sexual crimes, the abuse of power is structural and contextual. Thus, provisions concerning the special protection of dependent or helpless persons refer to structural power between generations, in the family and in social institutions. The suggested shift in analysis will open up the discussion to include differences among the victims and their positions of dependency, capacities and cultural circumstance.

In light of contemporary knowledge, the consequences of sexual abuse seem to be opposite to that of common knowledge, according to which the most dangerous

Table 2. Law on Sexual Crimes: Background Ideology and Object of Protection

	Archaic	Traditional	Modern	Postmodern
Ideology	Family/ Clan	Patriarchal	Liberal individualism	Sense of community, Feminist
Protected good	Property	Sexual morality	Sexual self-determination	Integrity
Subject/ Sexuality	Family/Man Property	Man Status	Perpetrator Act	Perpetrator, victim Relationship
Context	Relations between families	Marriage	Freedom of individual	Abuse of power

sex crime is an attack by a stranger in an isolated place. According to Sari Näre, the stronger the emotional bond between perpetrator and victim and the more serious the violation of the relationship of trust, the greater the consequences of sexual violence seem to be (Näre 2000, 6). This result is opposite to the understanding of the relationship from the perpetrator's perspective, according to which the sexual violation has been interpreted as less serious if the perpetrator believes that he has a right to have sex with the victim, be it a spouse, a partner, a date from a restaurant or a prostitute.

To admit that power relations are gendered not only imbues the discussion with a feminist flavour, it also gives a new content to the morality of the regulation. Unlike in the 19th century discussion, the issue is not the moral character of the individual sex acts, but rather the ethical dimension connected to the exploitation of the existing inequality between the parties. The inequality may be institutional as between patient and staff, generational as among family members or structural as between the sexes. In any case, the protection has both individual and structural dimensions.

Sexual Crimes Revisited

In the following text, I will explore how the shift of the focus from the protection of self-determination to the protection of integrity, from sexuality as an exchange to sexuality as a relation, and from sex as category to sex and gender as a power relationship would change the discourse on selected issues of sex crime law. In addition to the new Finnish law, I will also use examples from a new Swedish report on sexual crimes published in 2001. The vantage point of this report seems to correspond to the critique presented above, since the report defines sexual integrity and sexual self-determination as the protected goods of the proposed legal reform (SOU 2001:14, 108). Vis-à-vis sexual abuse, even sexual self-determination is held irrelevant and the only protected good should be the sexual integrity of the child (ibid. 110).

Other than this emphasis on sexual integrity, the Committee was not very explicit in its theoretical or ideological foundations. It is definitely not openly feminist or concerned with a woman's perspective, which is surprising because the Committee was appointed as a consequence of the work of the Commission on Violence Against Women. This Commission worked from a woman's perspective and recognized a power imbalance between the sexes (SOU 1995:60; Nordborg & Niemi-Kiesiläinen 2001). The instructions to the Committee on Sex Crimes had a more narrow view on equality. It was instructed to research whether sexual crimes against men and women are treated the same in the court practice (Dir 1998:48). Instead of an openly articulated feminist perspective, the victim's perspective in the report follows from a series of rape cases that had evoked considerable public outrage and scholarly discussion during the 1990s. Two of the cases concerned the abuse of a child and two other cases the gang rape of a young intoxicated girl. The core issue in all the cases was whether the element of force in the rape law had been met. The public discussion was concerned about the insufficient protection that rape law afforded to victims.

The Swedish and Finnish provisions on rape do not mention the concept of consent as an independent element of rape. The crucial element is violence or threat of violence (Andersson 2001). It is argued that the focus of the crime, thus, is placed on the actions of the perpetrator instead of on the behaviour of the victim as easily happens if the central element of the crime is consent. In any case, consent takes away the coercive element of the crime, thus requiring that the victim manifest her non-consent or resistance to the perpetrator(s). Besides violence and the threat of violence, rape can be committed by causing the victim to be unconscious or otherwise unable to protect herself. Other sexual abuse of intoxicated or disabled persons is punishable as the lesser crime of sexual abuse.

The most problematic cases in the application of these provisions are the ones where no violence or explicit threat of violence has occurred. In two infamous Swedish cases,[32] the perpetrators, a group of young men in each case who had sexual intercourse with a young intoxicated girl were convicted of sexual abuse. The implicit threat in the situation was insufficient to fulfil the elements of rape but, on the other hand, it was asked whether the helplessness required for the sexual abuse of an adult – the girls were not under legal age (which is 15 in Sweden) – was present since each girl was clearly able to understand the situation. The concept of subjectivity these provisions and cases require is something a victim either has fully or has not at all. It is an on/off switch. Yet, in many cases fear, intoxication, mental disease, exhaustion, and so on, impair the ability to defend oneself rather than eliminate it, and this impairment makes exploitation possible.

The Swedish Commission proposes that the crime of rape should include situations in which the perpetrator coerces another person into a sexual act by abusing her intoxication or similar incapacitation. Thus, the requirement that the perpetrator himself has caused the intoxication of the victim should be omitted from the definitional element of rape. The purpose is to eradicate the distinctive elements in rape respective to sexual abuse.

According to the new Finnish law, rape can be accomplished by causing in the other person unconsciousness, fear or another state of mind in which she is unable to defend herself. In contrast to the former law, it is no longer required that the victim defend herself with every conceivable means.[33] This difference is a welcome acknowledgement of the realities of such situations as described above and it allows for the interpretation of such situation from a standard that recognizes the victim's fear, despair and bewilderment. However, the wording of the law is: the inability to defend herself. Similarly, the provisions relating to sexual exploitation of persons with mental disease or in a self-induced state of intoxication[34] place the focus on the requirement that the victim be unable to defend herself or to express her will. With these wordings, the distinction between full autonomy and no autonomy at all (as a full control over the body) seems to be reinforced.

Moreover, these provisions seem to reveal an underlying idea of sexuality according to which a woman is supposed to defend herself against sexual assault and advances by physical means. According to this idea, the male perpetrator is not supposed to nor required to understand any other language. As the definition of rape makes force used by the perpetrator the decisive criteria, instead of consent, the legal interpretation should focus on the actions of the perpetrator, not on the actions of the victim. But suddenly, law and practice seem to turn this upside down by requiring the victims either full ability to self-determination or no ability defend herself at all.

Is such perception of sexuality that before embarking on a sexual act everyone should inquire about the other person's consent and ability to give consent much too radical? As Kevät Nousiainen comments, in the legislative process to reform the law on rape, the extent to which the parties should be required to ascertain each other's consent was not even discussed (Nousiainen 1999, 20). This issue has to be addressed if we think that one of the most important tasks of the law is to protect those who are in a vulnerable position.

Both the Finnish and the Swedish reforms aim at the improvement of the protection of minors. The difference between the liberal ideology in the Finnish law and the more protective approach of the Swedish law is evident in the regulation of ages of consent. The ages of consent are sixteen in Finland and fifteen in Sweden; sexual intercourse and sexual acts with persons under those ages are punishable. Significantly in Finland, the restrictions which age limits impose on sexual relations between consenting young persons are seriously discussed. Since no abuse of power is involved in such relations, the act is not punishable, if there is no great difference in the ages or in the degrees of psychological and physical maturity of the parties.[35] The regulation is logical from the perspective of self-determination. From the perspective of a violation of integrity, the immaturity of the adult does not suffice as an excuse. A relationship between an immature adult and an immature young person is likely to harm the latter – whether they are on the same level or not.

A number of feminists have relied on Foucault's concept of power, adding to it analyses of the distribution of power in society between the sexes. In some feminist analyses, rape is regarded as the manifestation and regenerator of that distribution (Brownmiller 1974; MacKinnon 1987, 50). While, from the Nordic perspective of sex equality, the radical feminist analysis appears to ignore the progress that has been made, some cultural practices supporting sexual violence may, indeed, be seen as manifestations of male power. Sexual harassment may be understood as such a practice. Even in the Nordic countries, more than half of the women have been subjected to name-calling, touching, comments about the female parts of their body, and other type of sexual harassment (Heiskanen & Piispa 1998, 54) and, according to Päivi Honkatukia, young girls also experience it continually (Honkatukia 1998). Men and boys can engage in this kind behaviour without any social sanctions.

Studies by Sari Näre and Päivi Honkatukia revealed the positive sides of Finnish sexual culture. Young women felt that they were capable of negotiating the terms of sexual interaction. Honkatukia found, however, that this feeling was attached to the fact that at a very early age girls are socialized to assume responsibility for handling harassment by boys and men as quietly as possible. Young women are supposed to maintain the gender system. Unless they do so, they are considered deviants and risk being ostracized and called names (Honkatukia 1998).

If the discourse is concerned with self-determination and individual acts, sexual harassment is obviously not a matter for criminal law. Individual acts may be slight, and imposing sanctions for such acts might lead to an unwanted expansion of control. An individual act imposes a negligible violation on another person's self-determination. It is only when examined in context – repetition, work, school or institutional setting, difference in the structural power of the parties – that the real meaning of the harassment is revealed. During the Finnish legislative process, the view was adopted that disturbing, sexually-loaded behaviour is an offence against the public peace and safety (Government Bill 6/76, 162) and is punishable when it happens in a public place.[36] This view overlooks the fact that harassment is mostly done by individual men to individual women and it rarely takes place in public places. In general, the acts are not exactly indecent (as is exhibitionism), but they may be fairly ordinary, such as patting and speaking with sexual innuendo.

While the violation of sexual autonomy may be ambiguous, the violation on sexual integrity is often obvious. To conceptualize it, however, we need to abandon an act-centred view of sexuality and understand the context in which the actions are taken, context here meaning the relative power between the parties. This restructuring is not designed to downplay the problems of contextualization. Alain Norrie has pointed out that criminal acts are always interpreted in a context and that the relevant contextualization is the key issue in imposing responsibility. One of the tasks of feminist legal research is to make women's experiences part of a relevant context. In Sweden, the new law on crimes against a woman's peace addresses contextuality – the continuous, often aggravating and culturally-rooted nature – of domestic violence (Nordborg and Niemi-Kiesiläinen 2001). Sexual harassment can hardly be discussed without taking into account the context of individual acts, the relationship between the parties and the continuous violation of the integrity of the victim.

Conclusion

Law is a powerful tool in defining and constructing sexuality. The historical account provided in this article was both unexpected and yet familiar. Not surprisingly, the different phases of regulation – sexuality as property, the absolute sexual morality, double standard sexual morality and liberalization – were distinguished in the history of Finnish sex crime law. What I did not expect to find, however, was how well the law corresponded to the sexual ideologies of the respective periods, and especially how much the double standard of the 19th century was reflected in the law.

In the late 20th century Finnish sex crime law, we encounter a completed liberal project. Sexual crimes are made sex-neutral and neutral in relation to expressions of sexuality. The aim of the sex crime law is to protect sexual self-determination. In the liberal *travaux preparatoires,* we find a discourse about the sexuality between two featureless, detached and equal individuals, fully capable of exercising their self-determination in their sexual relations. In rape, this ideal is broken down by the use of force or the threat of force. This depiction is different than we have found in feminist studies of rape law, which have revealed constructions of female and male sexuality in which the male sexuality has been depicted as the active, initiating and striving and the female sexuality as responsive, passive and submissive (Naffine 1997; Lacey 1998; Andersson 2001). The new law seemed to require a high standard of self-determination of its subjects and, thus, drew my interest to those situations when the subject would fall short of attaining this high standard of self-determination.

With its aim of protecting sexual self-determination, the law takes the side of those persons whose capabilities of exercising self-determination are not questioned, that is, of an adult, empowered, middle-class, white woman. If you can define a rape and cry rape, you will get protection. But the vantage point of self-determination was found to be insufficient when any hard issues of sex crime law, such as consent, legal age, impaired capacity, abuse of dependency or sexual harassment were discussed. It was suggested that the focus of the discussion should be shifted towards the conception of integrity as the protected good of sex crime law and understanding sex, sexuality and subjectivity in relational terms in a context of a structural gendered system.

The liberal project is derived from the era of sexual liberation in the 1960s and 1970s. While the emancipatory power of sexual liberation should not be abandoned, we have to admit that in the beginning of the 21st century, we know a lot more about sexual abuse and exploitation. This exploitation includes elements of the abuse of power, which a liberal discourse can hardly reach. Therefore, a shift in discourse is inevitable.

Notes

1 Law on the prohibition of purchase of sexual services 1998:408.

2 Although Finland was under Russian rule (1809–1917) before independence, the Swedish-Finnish legal tradition survived during this period. After 1917, judicial cooperation has taken both official and informal forms.

3 I owe thanks to a number of people who have commented on various drafts of this article. Special thanks for the constructionist understanding of law are addressed to my colleagues in the research project VISE: Violence in the Shadow of Equality: Gendered Structures in Finnish Legal Discourse and Päivi Honkatukia, PhD, in particular as our tutor.

4 I have developed these themes in two articles, written in Finnish, in which I first challenge the sex neutrality of the language (Niemi-Kiesiläinen 1998) and then the liberal notion of sexuality (ibid. 2000).

5 The Code of 1734 was a comprehensive codification of the Swedish law, covering both Sweden and Finland. Finland was a province of the Kingdom of Sweden until 1809.

6 Finland, as part of the Kingdom of Sweden, took part in the 30-year war of the 17th century and in many other wars of the 18th century. The wars apparently added to the large-scale

problem of illicit births. Generally, the fathers of these children were married and were of higher social standing than the unmarried mothers (Aalto 1996).
7 The law did not explicitly mention marriage. It prohibited illegal intercourse, which, of course, did not refer to marital intercourse.
8 Apparently, a lot of rape went undetected. Therefore, it might have been rather an academic question how the rape of a 'fallen' woman should be punished. In this undetected crime, the victims of sexual offences were usually women from social classes lower than the social class of the perpetrators. For example, crimes against servant girls on farms by owners and relatives did not, as a rule, lead to criminal proceedings (Aalto 1998).
9 See Häkkinen 1995, 226, who links prostitution with strict norms of sexual morality.
10 Criminal Code of 1889, Chapter 20, Section 9.
11 Presumably, such activity by men was beyond anyone's imagination at the time.
12 Criminal Code of 1889, Chapter 20, Sections 10 and 11, Chapter 25, Sections 7 and 8.
13 The Code of 1734, Chapter XXII, Section 1(1).
14 Criminal Code of 1889, Chapter 20, Section 7.
15 The rationale of the regulation of adultery was to protect the family. Forsman II 1917, 37-39, Alamaiset ehdotukset 1884, 176.
16 Chapter 25, Section 8.
17 Act 24.7.1998/563 came into force 1.1.1999.
18 The prohibition of fornication was repealed in 1926 (5.2.1926/24), adultery in 1948 (23.9.1948/683) and prostitution in 1936. Prostitutes, however, were subjected to repressive health and social control measures until 1986 (Law on flagrants 57/17.1.1936).
19 As legal scholars were diligent to point out, rape in marriage included elements for which punishment could follow as undue coercion or assault (Rautio 1999, 382). These crimes, however, carry a far lesser punishment than rape. The provision of rape was changed in 1994 to include rape in marriage. Here, as in many others respects as well, Finland has been far more conservative than other Nordic countries. In Sweden, for example, rape in marriage was made a crime in the reform of the Penal Code of 1965.
20 Criminal Code, Chapter 20, Section 10.
21 Criminal Code, Chapter 20, Section 10.
22 Criminal Code, Chapter 20 Section 5.
23 Criminal Code, Chapter 20, Section 4.
24 Criminal Code, Chapter 20, Sections 2 and 3.
25 Criminal Code, Chapter 20, Section 5. The protection of immature persons was added to the text in Parliament, see Parliamentary Committee, LaVM 3/1998, 22. Even though the Committee Report does not specifically mention it, it was probably thought that this provision would replace the repealed special age of consent for homosexuals, Rautio1999, 383.
26 Patronage fulfilled the elements of either fornication, if the patron was not married, or of adultery, if he was married, in the 19th century, but the criminal justice system was not interested in prosecution of these crimes. See p. 175.
27 Criminal Code, Chapter 20, Section 8.
28 This view is also recognised in Government Bill 6/1997, 168.
29 Report of the Committee for Ordinary Law 3/1998, 8-9.
30 Lag (1998:408) om förbud mot köp av sexuella tjänster (Law against Buying Sexual Services) came into force 1.1.1999 in Sweden. About the experience, see SOU 2001:14, 307. Olsson and Svensson 2000.
31 See, about such development in femicides, Nourse 1996.
32 The cases are known by the name of the place where the crimes took place, such as the

Södertälje case (NJA 1997 s. 538) and the *Rissne* case (*Svea hovrätt* B 3935-00, 13.7.2000).
33 Government Bill 6/1997, 172, for earlier requirement, Honkasalo 1970, 100.
34 Criminal Code, Chapter 20, Section 5(2).
35 Criminal Code, Chapter 20, Section 6.
36 Criminal Code, Chapter 17, Section 21.

References

Aalto, Jari (1998), *Tager man qvinno med våld.* Naisiin kohdistunut seksuaalinen väkivalta 1840-64 Turun ja Vaasan hovioikeuspiirien oikeustapauksissa. (Sexual Violence in Finnish Courts 1840-64) Suomen ja Skandinavian historian tutkielma. Stencile. Helsinki: University of Helsinki.

Aalto, Seppo (1996), *Kirkko ja kruunu siveellisyyden vartijoina. Seksuaalirikollisuus, esivalta ja yhteisö Porvoon kihlakunnassa 1621–1700*, Suomen historiallinen seura, Helsinki.

Alamaiset ehdotukset Suomen Suuriruhtinaanmaan Rikoslaiksi. Komitea, määrätty tarkastamaan vuonna 1875 painettuja alamaisia ehdotuksia. (Proposal for the Criminal Code) 1884. Helsinki: Suomalaisen Kirjallisuuden Seura.

Andersson, Ulrika (2001), 'The Unbounded Body of the Law of Rape: The Intrusive Criterion of Non–Consent', in K. Nousiainen, Å. Gunnarsson, K. Lundström and J. Niemi-Kiesiläinen (eds) *Responsible Selves. Women in Nordic Legal Culture*, Ashgate, London.

Anners, Erik (1965), *Humanitet och rationalism. Studier i upplysningstidens strafflagsreformer – särskilt med hänsyn till Gustav III:s reformlagstiftning*, Rättshistorisk Bibliotek 10, Stockholm.

Anttila, Inkeri (1994), 'Två reformer av lagstiftningen om sexualbrott', *Nordisk Tidsskrift för Kriminalvidenskab*; Vol. 81, pp. 15-24.

Bell, Vikki (1995), 'Beyond the "Thorny Question": Feminism, Foucault and the Desexualization of Rape', in J. Temkin (ed.), *Rape and the Criminal Justice System*, Dartmouth, Aldershot. Original edition (1991) *International Journal of the Sociology of Law*; Vol. 19, pp. 83-100.

Blomstedt, Yrjö (1964), 'Rikoslakireformin ensimmäiset vaiheet vuoden 1866 osittaisuudistuksiin saakka', *Historiallinen arkisto*, Vol. 59; pp. 421-518.

Brownmiller, Susan (1974), *Against Our Will*, Simon & Schuster, New York.

Davies, Margaret (1994), *Asking the law question*, Sweet & Maxwell, Melbourne.

Duncan, Sheila (1996), 'The Mirror Tells: Constructions of Gender in Criminal Law', in A. Bottomley (ed.), *Feminist Perspectives on the Foundational Subjects of Law*, Cavendish, London.

Estrich, Susan (1987), *Real Rape*, Harvard Univ. Press, Cambridge.

Fischer, Karla, Vidmar, Neil and Rene, Ellis (1993), 'The Culture of Battering and the Role of Mediation in Domestic Violence Cases', *Southern Methodist University Law Review* ,Vol.46, p. 2117.

Forsman, Jaakko (1917a), *De särskilda brotten enligt strafflagen af den 19 december 1889, Anteckningar enligt föreläsningar. Första afdelningen: Brotten mot individens rättsgebit.* (Crimes against Individuals) Juridiska studentfakultetens förlag, Helsinki. 2-3 uppl.

Forsman, Jaakko (1917b), *De särskilda brotten enligt strafflagen af den 19 december 1889, Anteckningar enligt föreläsningar. Andra afdelningen: Brotten mot det medborgerliga samhällets rättigheter*, Juridiska studentfakultetens förlag, Helsinki. 2-3 uppl.

Gordon, Linda (1989) *Heroes of their own lives: The politics and history of family violence Boston 1880-1960*, Virago, London.

Government Bill 50/1970 *Hallituksen esitys Eduskunnalle siveellisyyteen kohdistuvien rikosten rankaisemista koskevan lainsäädännön uudistamisesta.* (Sexual Crimes, Finland)

Government Bill 6/1997 *Hallituksen esitys oikeudenkäyttöä, viranomaisia ja yleistä järjestystä vastaan kohdistuvia rikoksia sekä seksuaalirikoksia koskevien säännösten uudistamiseksi.* (Crimes against Justice System, Authorities, General Order and Sexual Crimes, Finland)

Heinämaa, Sara (1996), *Ele, tyyli ja sukupuoli: Merleau-Pontyn ja Beauvoirin ruumiinfenomenologia ja sen merkitys sukupuolikysymykselle*, Gaudeamus, Helsinki.

Heiskanen, Markku and Piispa, Minna (1998), *Faith, Hope and battering: a survey of men's violence against women in Finland,* Statistics, Helsinki.

Hiltunen, Rainer (1998), 'Rikoksesta kohti tasa-arvoa. Homoseksuaalien oikeudellisen aseman tarkastelua', *Oikeus*; Vol. 2/1998, pp. 51-64.

Hirdman, Yvonne (1990), Genussystemet. Chapter 3 in *Demokrati och Makt i Sverige*. SOU 1990:44.

Honkasalo, Brynolf (1970), Suomen Rikosoikeus. Erityinen osa I 1. Henkilöön kohdistuvat rikokset. *Suomalaisen lakimiesyhdistyksen julkaisuja* B:107. Helsinki.

Honkatukia, Päivi (1999), 'Gender, Social Identity and Delinquent Behaviour', *Retfærd*, Vol. 86; pp. 41-52.

Honkatukia, Päivi (2000), '"Lähentelijöitä riittää" – tyttöjen kokemuksia sukupuolisesta ahdistelusta' ("There Are Lots of Those Men..." Girls' Experiences of Sexual Harassment), in Päivi Honkatukia, Johanna Niemi-Kiesiläinen and Sari Näre (eds), *Lähentelyistä raiskauksiin: tyttöjen kokemuksia häirinnästä ja seksuaalisesta väkivallasta*, Nuorisotutkimusverkosto, Helsinki.

Honkatukia, Päivi, Luukkainen, Tuula, Mikkonen, Tanja, Mäkelä, Kaisa, Niemi-Kiesiläinen, Johanna and Ruuskanen, Minna (2001), 'Pricilla – aavikon kuningatar' (Queen of the Desert: Gender and Subject), *Oikeus*, Vol. 1/2001, pp. 136-142.

Häkkinen, Antti (1995), *Rahasta – vaan ei rakkaudesta. Prostituutio Helsingissä 1867-1939*, Otava, Helsinki.

Järvinen, Margaretha (1990), *Prostitution i Helsingfors – en studie i kvinnokontroll*, Åbo Akademis förlag, Turku.

Kimpimäki, Minna (1998), 'Seksuaalinen itsemääräämisoikeus, oikeushyväajattelu ja moraalisen närkästyksen aika', *Oikeus*; Vol. 2/1998, pp. 20-29.

Lacey, Nicola (1998), *Unspeakable Subjects. Feminist Essays in Legal and Social Theory*, Hart Publisher, Oxford.

Lacey, Nicola, Wells, Celia and Meure, Dirk (1990), *Reconstructing Criminal Law. Texts and Materials*, Weidenfeld and Nicolson, London.

MacKinnon, Catharine (1987), *Feminism Unmodified. Discourses on Life and Law*, Harvard University Press, Cambridge MA.

Mahoney, Martha (1991), 'Legal Images of Battered Women: Redefining the Issue of Separation', *Michigan Law Review*, Vol 90, pp. 1-94.

Møller Okin, Susan (1992), *Women in Western Political Thought*, Princeton University Press, Princeton. (Original edition, 1979).

Naffine, Ngaire (1990) *Law & the Sexes. Explorations in feminist jurisprudence*, Allen & Unwin, Sydney.

Naffine, Ngaire (1997), *Feminism and Criminology,* Polity Press, London.

Niemi-Kiesiläinen, Johanna (1998), 'Naisia, miehiä vai henkilöitä: Seksuaalirikokset ja sukupuoli', *Oikeus*, Vol. 2/1998, pp. 4-19.

Niemi-Kiesiläinen, Johanna (2000), Mitä seksuaalirikoslailla halutaan suojella? (What Are We Trying to Protect with Laws against Sexual Crimes?), in Päivi Honkatukia, Johanna

Niemi-Kiesiläinen and Sari Näre (eds), *Lähentelyistä raiskauksiin: tyttöjen kokemuksia häirinnästä ja seksuaalisesta väkivallasta*, Nuorisotutkimusverkosto, Helsinki, pp. 137-168.

Niemi-Kiesiläinen, Johanna (2001), Criminal Law or Social Policy as Protection Against Violence, in Kevät Nousiainen, Åsa Gunnarsson, Karin Lundström and Johanna Niemi-Kiesiläinen (eds), *Responsible Selves. Women in Nordic Legal Culture*, Ashgate, Dartmouth.

Nieminen, Armas (1951), *Taistelu sukupuolimoraalista. Avioliitto- ja seksuaalikysymyksiä suomalaisen hengenelämän ja yhteiskunnan murroksessa sääty-yhteiskunnan ajoilta 1910-luvulle*, WSOY, Porvoo.

Nordborg, Gudrun and Niemi-Kiesiläinen, Johanna (2001), 'Women's Peace: A Criminal Law Reform in Sweden', in Kevät Nousiainen, Åsa Gunnarsson, Karin Lundström and Johanna Niemi-Kiesiläinen (eds), *Responsible Selves. Women in Nordic Legal Culture*, Ashgate, Dartmouth.

Nourse, Victoria (1996-7), 'Passion's progress: Modern Law Reform and the Provocation Defence', *Yale Law Review*, Vol. 106, pp. 1331-1448.

Nousiainen, Kevät (1990), 'Miten vapauden poluilla kompastutaan: naisista ja eräistä vapauteen liittyvistä yhteiskuntateoreettisista näkemyksistä', *Oikeus*, Vol.1/1990, pp. 11-28.

Nousiainen, Kevät (1999), 'Equalizing Images? Gendered Imagery in Criminal Law', *Suomen Antropologi*; Vol. 24, pp. 7-24.

Olsson, Hanna (2000), 'Männen, lagen och prostitutionen' in Nordborg, Gudrun, Ågren, Karin and Nilsson, Eva (eds), *Strategier och kontrakt för ekonomi och kärlek*, Rapport från 10:e Nordiska KvinnoJuristmötet. Iustus, Uppsala, pp. 135-148.

Näre, Sari (2000), 'Nuorten tyttöjen kohtaama seksuaalinen väkivalta ja loukattu luottamus tunnetaloudessa', (Sexual Violence against Adolescant Girls: Hurt Confidence in the Economy of Emontions), in Päivi Honkatukia, Johanna Niemi-Kiesiläinen and Sari Näre (eds), *Lähentelyistä raiskauksiin: tyttöjen kokemuksia häirinnästä ja seksuaalisesta väkivallasta*, Nuorisotutkimusverkosto, Helsinki, pp. 77-136.

O'Donovan, Katherine (1997), 'With sense, consent, or just a con? Legal subjects in the discourse of autonomy', in Ngaire Naffine and Rosemary Owens (eds), *Sexing the Subject of Law*, Sweet & Maxwell, London.

OM 2003:5. Ihmiskauppa, paritus ja prostituutio. Oikeusministeriö. Työryhmämietintö. (Trafficking, soliciting and prostitution. Ministry of Justice. Working Group)

Parliamentary Committee LaVM 3/1998 Lakivaliokunnan mietintö 3/1998 Hallituksen esitys oikeudenkäyttöä, viranomaisia ja yleistä järjestystä vastaan kohdistuvia rikoksia sekä seksuaalirikoksia koskevien säännösten uudistamiseksi.

Parliamentary Committee LaVM 50/1970 Lakivaliokunnan mietintö n:o 11 Esitys 50/1970 Hallituksen esityksen johdosta siveellisyyteen kohdistuvien rikosten rankaisemista koskevan lainsäädännön uudistamisesta.

Pateman, Carol (1988), *The Sexual Contract*. Stanford University Press, Stanford.

Pylkkänen, Anu (1990), *Puoli vuodetta, lukot ja avaimet. Nainen ja maalaistalous oikeuskäytännön valossa 1660-1710*, Lakimiesliiton kustannus, Helsinki.

Rautio, Ilkka (1999), 'Seksuaalirikokset', in Olavi Heinonen, Pekka Koskinen, Tapio Lappi-Seppälä, Martti Majanen and Kimmo Nuotio (eds), *Rikosoikeus. WSLT*, Helsinki.

Smart, Carol (1998), 'The Woman of Legal Discourse', in Kathleen Daly and Lisa Maher (eds), *Criminology at the Crossroad, Feminist Readings in Crime and Justice*, Oxford University Press, Oxford.

SOU 1995:15 Könshandeln.

SOU 1995:60 Kvinnofrid.

SOU 2001:14 Sexualbrotten. Ett ökat skydd för den sexuella integriteten och angränsande frågor. (Sexual Crimes, Including English Summary)

Svensson, Eva-Maria (1997), *Genus och rätt. En problematisering av föreställningen om rätten*, Iustus förlag, Uppsala.

Svensson, Eva-Maria (2000), 'Kritik av en juridisk argumentation – det krävs två för att dansa en tango', in Gudrum Nordborg, Karin Ågren and Eva Nilsson (eds), *Rapport från 10:e Nordiska Kvinnojuristmötet*, Iustus förlag, Uppsala.

Telste, Kari (1994), '"Hun torde icke aabenbare det..." Seksualitet, kjønn og kropp i norsk rettsmateriale på 1600- og 1700-tallet', in Marianne Liljeström, Pirjo Markkola and Sari Mäenpää (eds), *Kvinnohistoriens nya utmaningar: från sexualitet till världshistoria: konferensrapport från det IV Nordiska Kvinnohistorikermötet 27-30 maj 1993, Tammerfors*, University of Tampere, Department of History 17.

Träskman, Per Ole (1998), 'Går det att tygla lusten? Om straffbar pornografi, pedofili och prostitution' *Tidskrift utgiven av Juridiska Föreningen i Finland* pp. 352-373.

Tuori Kaarlo (1997), 'Ideologiakritiikistä kriittiseen positivismiin', in Juha Häyhä (ed.), *Minun metodini*, WLST, Helsinki, pp. 311-329.

Utriainen, Terttu (1994), 'Hur har sexualbrottens normer förändrats i Finland?', *Nordisk Tidsskrift for Kriminalvidenskab*, Vol. 81(1), pp. 122-129.

Utriainen, Terttu (1996) 'Inkeri Anttila ja seksuaalipolitiikka', in Raimo Lahti (ed.), *Kohti rationaalista ja humaania kriminaalipolitiikkaa*, Helsingin yliopisto (Kriminologian julkaisuja 2), Helsinki, pp. 222-226.

Chapter 9

On the Limits of the Concept of Equality: Arguments for a Dynamic Reading

Kevät Nousiainen

Focus on Conceptual Change

For several decades now, equality has had a bad name in feminist research. Carol Smart, in her *Feminism and the Power of Law*, published in 1989, presents a critique in a nutshell that is, I think, representative for many feminists. To cite Smart: '[t]he growth of modern feminism...corresponds both to notions of equality and the idea that equality of opportunity can be achieved through law in the form of legal rights. Law may remain oppressive to women, but the form it takes is no longer the denial of *formal rights* which are preserved to men... while it might have been appropriate for early feminists to demand legal rights...the rhetoric of rights has become exhausted, and may even be detrimental... especially ...where the demand is for a "special" *right...for which there has been no masculine equivalent...*'. Also, '... the liberal notion of equality is *too limited to affect structural inequalities...*' (Smart 1989, 139. Italics KN).

According to Smart, feminists in the late 20th century have had to face the dilemma of outdated notions of equality and legal rights as a means to equality of opportunity. In the past, rights have been an intrinsic and useful part of feminist claims. It has been possible to couch feminist claims in terms of rights and, thus, promote women's interests and get social wrongs recognized. Feminists should notice, however, that the language of equality and rights has become even counterproductive. Resorting to the language of rights gives a false impression of the power difference between men and women as having been resolved, which is not the case. To engage in the discourse of rights opens the door to competing rights. The male Empire strikes back with the same means, using the rights of men against the rights of women. Although rights are often formulated to deal with *a social wrong*, they are always, or at least in the UK, Smart adds, *focused on the individual* who must prove that her rights have been violated. Rights are devised to give protection against the state, but rights may be also used by some individuals against some other, less powerful individuals. Legislation on gender equality may be used by men just as much as it is used by women. Because rights are based on an *androcentric standard,* 'in order to have any impact on law one has to talk law's language, use legal methods, and accept legal procedures. All these are fundamentally anti-feminist.'[1]

Interestingly, Smart and many other feminists seem to focus on a rather static understanding of equality, of the type represented by lawyers devoted to the tenets of classical liberalism and focused on equality as a state already arrived at rather than a goal yet to be achieved.[2] Equality is treated as a concept necessarily connoting the formal equality of individuals. Formal justice is often connected to the principle of equality according to the Aristotelian formulation found in the Nicomachean ethics, that is 'like cases should be treated alike and unlike cases unlike'. Such a principle provides no answer to questions of what cases should be regarded as alike or unlike or which differences are morally and legally relevant. The formal principles of justice and equality only demand that once classes and categories are defined, their members should be treated alike. A moral criticism of substantial justice is not possible on the basis of such formally equal justice (Westerman 2001, 2-3).

Such an idea of equality is clearly separate from considerations connected to distributive, collective justice and its outcome, an equality of results or 'actual' equality. Hilary Charlesworth and Christine Chinkin, two feminist scholars of international law, describe equality in liberal legal theory thus: '[t]he liberal idea of equality...is limited to procedural rather than to substantive equality. Formally, it requires equal treatment of people or states, but without reference to their actual situation. Consequently liberal equality is a very blunt tool when dealing with cases of long-term, structural disadvantage and inequality both as between states and within them' (Charlesworth and Chinkin 2000, 32). Discrimination is seen as a static and relativistic concept, which, under EC law, provides a remedy only for those persons in situations which can be likened to situations experienced by the members of the opposite sex. Non-discrimination is not dynamic redistribution (Ellis 1998, 332).

Many feminists also assume that to demand a similarity of person and situation as a basis for *equality cannot accommodate feminine difference.*[3] This assumption becomes apparent in the demand that there has to be a male comparator in order that sex discrimination can be proven. This requirement involves comparing 'like with unlike' or 'a woman needs to be like a real or hypothetical man in order to substantiate a complaint' (Thornton 1990, 1).

No doubt equality is connected to rights and law, although it is also an important normative concept in modern societies in general. Social practices and institutions are often legitimized by exalting their egalitarian nature also in more general contexts. The relation of rights to (social) justice is ambivalent. For many liberal theorists, rights and justice coincide. Even among those persons who affirm this claim, there is considerable latitude between those persons who identify 'natural rights' with a narrow set of rights often connected to a proprietor's entitlements and those persons who allow for a more expansive list of social, economic and cultural rights (Campbell 2001, 56). In any case, equality certainly is the pivot upon which the declarations of human rights turn and the leading principle of modern constitutions.

Social justice and equality, rather than formal equality, are '*acquis de notre modernité*'. Social justice and equality are what modernity has had to offer. Even the critique of the welfare state is localized around the idea of equality.[4]

Equality as *non-discrimination* is often understood as a concept or principle that has been the invariant basis of justice since ancient times. When the Aristotelian maxim is referred to, the citation rhetorically implies that the principle of equality, as such, has been a basis for the Western understanding of justice since time immemorial. This implication is false.[5] Today's concept of equality is based on a very different understanding of what things are similar and what things are not than previous understandings have been. This change concerns both equality as a legal principle, connected to societal practices, and equality as a concept.

The aim of this chapter is to plead for an understanding of equality as a dynamic concept, one that has been subject to change over time. By turning to a *conceptual history of equality,*[6] I draw attention to the changes that have taken place. I also discuss different connotations of the concept of equality in different contexts. This exercise should show something of the dynamics involved in the concept. The concepts certainly change in the context of historical struggles or the societal praxis in general, but social history remains outside the scope of this study.

I attempt to show that the concept of equality has undergone at least *two profound changes*. The first change made the *principle of universal equality*[7] the basis for all legislation. The latter of these changes has brought the *concept of discrimination* to bear in the legal practices connected with the concept of equality.

I propose that the *notion of slavery* was a relevant context for discussions about equality until the first part of the 20th century and that this context was replaced by the *notion of discrimination* by the end of that century. There is continuity between the two contexts, however. The discourse on slavery as a *social practice*, rather than as an *individual state*, brought the collective deprivation of a group of people to the foreground. Equality understood as non-discrimination also turned the focus of the discourse on equality towards collective abuses and the detrimental treatment of groups. This change has also blurred the dividing line between formal and substantive equality or between the equality of opportunity and the equality of results. The inherent contingency of which elements should be considered 'like' about situations or persons is accentuated. Contingency is an element in all politics. In a sense, even justice as equality is contingent in that different judgments can be made about what things are to be considered 'like'.

Universal Equality and Natural Difference

The first of the major changes of the use of the concept of equality in European law took place in the early modern time. This change was expressed in the classical declarations of the universal rights of men. A line of theoretical thought runs through the debates on subjective rights and freedoms, beginning in the late Middle Ages, gains momentum in the 17th and 18th centuries and finally takes form in the declarations of rights of men and citizens. Consequently, the principle of equality was included in the constitutions of modern nation states. The change consisted of a new recognition of the normative equality of all men. There had been no such assumption in pre-modern law.

Up until the 17th and 18th centuries, European laws had paid little attention to those proponents of natural law who denied the relevance of the natural differences inherent in human beings to their legal position. The differences considered legally relevant criss-crossed European societies in numerous ways – differential treatment was considered just because people were different as to their religious beliefs, estate, status, locality, origin, sex, etc. Accordingly, to give anyone his or her equal rights had to be considered in the context of the relevant social group – a group that often in no way excluded the person in question from simultaneously belonging to other groups.

From the Greek philosophers of the 5th century BC to Rousseau and from Hugo Grotius to modern human right conventions, natural human equality was defended by some philosophers and lawyers, but denied by the majority of them. The topic of natural equality was often discussed in connection with slavery. This linkage of slavery with equality was true of ancient Greece and Rome. While, according to Aristotle, similar things should be treated similarly, all human beings were not naturally similar. In *Politics,* Aristotle defends slavery and says that it is 'clear that, just as some are by nature free, so others are by nature slaves; and for these latter the condition of slavery is both beneficial and just' (Aristotle 1988). There already were opponents of this assumption among the Greeks by that time, as Aristotle himself remarks in his *Rhetoric*.[8] The proponents of the early modern natural law could condemn slavery or condone it on the ground that a human being is free by nature – a person could, according to the proponents of slavery, also freely relinquish his or her freedom.

In Europe, slavery proper became rare in the Middle Ages and was often replaced by less comprehensive forms of servitude. Europeans took part in the slave trade in other parts of the world, however, and slavery was an important feature in the European colonies outside Europe. Slavery became an issue of international law with the Peace of Utrecht in 1713 when Great Britain obtained a monopoly on the importation of slaves. The English abolition movement started during the second half of the 18th century. By this time, the abolition of slavery seems to have become primarily connected to groups of non-European 'others', people of African origin, in particular.[9]

When the equality of men was seen as the opposite of slavery, slavery referred to a lack of freedom and autonomy, which was a denial of the universal human attributes of rationality and freedom. Slavery, as a term, covers many types of bondage, but the understanding of early modernity referred to slaves as human beings treated as pieces of chattel, as the property of another person, obeying not law but the will of their master, and, thus, devoid of rights. Universal human attributes, similar in all men, should make such bondage not only immoral, but also against the law of nature. This very assumption lay behind the universal rights of men declared by the Enlightenment.

Neither the Declaration of the rights of men of the French Revolution nor the US Constitution of 1787 with the amendments of 1791 was based on an assumption of an *actual, literal similarity* of all men, however. These documents were an outcome of the understanding arrived at by the 17th and 18th century theory of inalienable human rights. Equality of men, according to that theory, is an abstraction which reduces into irrelevance human differences that, in themselves, are self-evident. However, individual and social differences are irrelevant when it comes to the recognition of all men as legal subjects.

The theory of social contract was based on a double definition of subjecthood. Legal subjects, on one hand, are treated as subjects because they are subjected to necessary, unavoidable political rule, but, on the other hand, legal subjects also have the status of ontological and epistemological subjects upon whom acts and attributes can be predicated and whose autonomy entitles them to legislate for themselves. Loyal subjects under legal state sovereignty (*imperium*) were represented simultaneously as persons with rights, or subjects entitled to dominate their private possessions (*dominium*). The limits of both *imperium* and *dominium* were set by the equal rights of other subjects. State sovereignty was acceptable as long as it allowed for the equal entitlement of every citizen. No legal subject was to be dominated by another subject, however, because all legal subjects were naturally equal. All men were *represented* as 'naturally' similar in relevant respects, in what was needed for subjecthood, although, for all other purposes, they could differ considerably – for historical or other contingent reasons.

Such a representation of legal equality, declared fundamental for the creation of society, has performative power, as Christine Fauré has pointed out in her study on the history of the declarations of human rights. A declaration of rights is not something to be verified or falsified, but performative: it creates the representation of legal capacities invested in 'man' and the representation of man invested with legal capacities. When the Bill of Rights of Virginia declared rights as the basis of government, this enunciation had illocutionary power that declared men free and equal. Many philosophers have declared the empirical equality and freedom of all men a fallacy. It is 'absurd and miserable nonsense' to claim that all men are born free, as Jeremy Bentham remarked. This truism does not make equality null and void. The declarations of human rights have a self-referentiality that makes them effective in spite of their claims being easily shown to be empirically false (Fauré 1997, 8-24).

If we believe what Michel Foucault claims in his *Les Mots et les choses*, the epistemology of the 'classical age', i.e., the 17th and 18th centuries, consisted of a theory of representation. The concepts of nature and human nature, according to Foucault, guaranteed the basis of representation. Representation relied on the human ability to conceive of similarities and of the natural structure of all things that appears as similarities to the human faculties. Imagination, one of the properties of human nature, can discern similarities that the mind arranges into knowledge. There are inherent resemblances in things, which are presented as similarities to the human mind. Nature and human nature, thus, were thought to permit the reconciliation of resemblance and imagination, which provided a foundation for, and made possible, all the empirical sciences of order (Foucault 1989, 67-71).

The basis of knowledge in that type of an *episteme* was something that could also be called *discrimination*. In the 17th and 18th century context, the term, discrimination, was understood as the action or faculty of the human mind to distinguish or differentiate, or the power of observing similarities and differences accurately. A dictionary example for the word, discrimination, from the time of the 'classical' *episteme* is 'to make a discrimination between the Good and the Bad'.[10] Discrimination as a faculty of a discerning mind seems to have referred to something akin to the faculty of judgement – and judgement again was often assumed to rely on the imagination. To discriminate was to make a difference, to differentiate, to perceive differences, to distinguish and to make a distinction.

Foucault does not discuss political philosophy or the theory of inalienable human rights of the 'classical age' explicitly in this connection. Yet, one can easily claim that the social contract theory of the 17th and 18th centuries is based on the theory of representation or on an analysis of man as the basic element in the representation of a society. The image of man and the natural similitude of all men were the basic elements of the social contract theory. Society was represented as consisting of men or as consisting of individuals whose foundational similarities were to be noticed by anyone in possession of the faculty of discrimination.

When discrimination in the sense of differentiating between men as foundational subjects – legal or political – is forbidden by a performative declaration of the universal rights of man, it becomes possible to understand discrimination as making an adverse distinction with regard to a person, *discriminating against* someone. I think it is important to stress that the idea of discrimination at the time of the birth of the modern legal and political order consisted of making a difference. The principle of equality was based on the assumption that to make a difference between men as foundational beings or subjects was to make an irrelevant and false distinction, based on what is different in men in a historically or socially contingent manner.[11] To discriminate against someone is to lack discrimination or to give consequence to such differences that are not relevant.

One facet of the representation of men as naturally equal in the first declarations of the universal rights of man is a deeper differentiation and exclusion on the basis of certain differences that were singled out: especially differentiations based on sex and race. It has been argued that, although women were certainly devalued in pre-modern Europe, they were considered a type of 'lesser men' rather than an absolute 'other', something qualitatively quite different from men. The pre-modern definition of 'women', even in medicine, relied on a rather quantitative devaluation.[12] The devaluating discourse on women ran among several other devaluations that defined different and unequal rights for different groups of people.

The political rights that women had enjoyed as members of the nobility or some other status group were removed by the French revolution. Women were explicitly excluded from judicial power in 1789. Radical or grass root movements during the revolution often made use of protests by women. *Sansculottes* allowed women to protest in favour of the Constitution and to take part in voting by acclamation. Political action, including individual voting, of the roll-call type of balloting was denied to women, however (Fauré 1991). The Jacobins excluded women from all public representation, even by preventing their unofficial public appearance by giving a double connotation to the phrase 'public woman'. For a woman to be 'public' connoted for the Jacobins a breaking of the rules of sexual morality.

Gender emerged as a political category when the principle of equality gained social and political importance (Gerhard 2001, 28). The 17th and 18th century theories of natural law often presented the family as the only natural association. Families were the actual smallest units of societies, instead of individuals that are usually taken as the basic components of proto-liberal theories. Ute Gerhard has pointed out that the explanations given for marriage underwent a change in the latter part of 18th century. The positions of Christian Wolff in the mid-eighteenth century and that of J.G. Fichte at the end of the century are very different. Between these two theorists is the contribution of Jean-Jacques Rousseu to gender philosophy.

For Wolff, the traditional hierarchy within the family could be justified by custom. Fichte presented a philosophy of the ego and woman as a non-ego who is only able to rise to the level of a man in marriage by the love shown to her husband's particularity (Gerhard 2001, 29-30). Law is reserved for self-determined, free subjects, but marriage is not a legal association, because its basis is unequal, if mutual, love. Modern marriage was not seen entirely as a function of generation or procreation. Sexual intercourse was described accordingly in terms of love on the side of the woman whose impulse is to satisfy the man. The male sex was 'purely active', the female sex 'purely passive'. This line of thinking follows the typology presented by Rousseau, who presented a cultural significance of femininity in a way that has evoked enthusiasm among women and feminists – making woman socially the opposite of man provides a theory of sex based on difference rather than devaluation. The difference in the 'very essence' of the sexes was referred to as a basis of legal inequality, however.

The French revolutionaries, engaged in drafting the Constitution, excluded servants and other non-owners among men and all women from citizenship. This exclusion was based on a theory of political and legal representation that differentiated those persons entitled to be represented in and as the nation, or capable of self-representation, from those persons who were to be represented by others (Scott 1996, 34-35).

When the Jacobin rule consolidated and drew law, order, masculine virtue and sexual difference together in a tighter way, attacks on women's political role became more vehement. In this context, an extension of their sex was seen in every part of the bodies of women, not only in their primary sexual organs. A natural mental differentiation of the sexes was read from bodily difference.[13] The characteristics considered relevant for the successful performance of legal subjecthood were claimed to be lacking in women. Women were represented as anti-citizens, lacking in rationality, sense, individuality, egotism – lacking in everything that was included in the abstraction of relevant properties for legal subjecthood. The analysis of sex was affirmed as a fundamental difference, the study of which was to be excluded from the scope of political philosophy and law and included in the disciplines of biology, medicine, and anthropology. Biology and medicine took over the job of differentiating, of perceiving and constituting the difference between the sexes.

The crime of Olympe de Gouges, the writer of the *Declaration of the Rights of Woman*, was that she argued that nature provided no model for the distinctions that men invent. Her writings sought the grounds for active citizenship for women. In doing so, her texts erased the difference of sex in many ways. After de Gouges had been executed as a traitor and her death was officially reported, she was described as having been born with 'an exalted imagination'. She had wanted to be a man of state, forgetting the virtues that belong to her sex (Scott 1996, 51-52) – and, by doing so, she showed a lack of discrimination.

I think it might be more fruitful to consider the modern qualitative dichotomy of the sexes as a result of the declaration of the universal and equal rights of men, rather than a denial of rights as a result of differentiation on the basis of sex, understood in a biological sense. In other words, the genesis of biological sex, perhaps, is rather to be found in the Enlightenment equality principle than in the genesis of inequality in biological sex. The same claim could be made of race, which came to be understood in a biological and anthropological sense at the time when the idea of universal human rights was promoted with the claim that all men are similar in such respects that are relevant for human rights. During the historical processes of early modernization, when legal and political focus was on the principle of equality, women were pronounced incapable of successfully performing legal and political subjecthood, because their 'difference' was conceived in a qualitative, biologically defined manner.

From Slavery to Discrimination

An important conceptual change takes place when the former context of discussing equality as opposite to the condition of slavery is replaced by a new opposition, setting equality against discrimination and giving equality the primary connotation of non-discrimination.

The discourse on slavery continued in the 19th century, first as a matter of the abolition of slaves in a concrete sense. The practice of slavery continued even where the universal rights of men had been declared. The abolition of slavery in the French colonies took place after the Revolution, but not without controversy. By this time, the issue of slavery was clearly presented as one concerning the justification of 'us' enslaving the 'others'. The latter were usually thought of collectively as black Africans. There still were cases in British and US courts affirming the legality of the slave trade the first decades of the 19th century, but, after 1825, such arguments were no longer presented. The abolition of slavery was a more difficult issue. In the United States, abolition was effected as a result of the Civil War. The anti-discrimination legislation adopted after the Civil War concentrated on 'race' and was based on racial categories prevailing in the 1860s (Minow 1993, 222). The nineteenth century American legal system recognized three races, 'white', 'Negro' and 'Indian', which were made to cover all ethnic groups (Minow op. cit. 231-232).

International law of the 19th century also became engaged in the abolition of slavery and in putting an end to the slave trade in particular. At the Vienna Congress in 1814-15, the slave trade was condemned in general terms. Great Britain, by that time, had become the leader of international efforts to abolish slavery and slave trade. Slavery took place in sovereign states, while the slave trade had often been international and, thus, a more suitable target for international intervention than slavery *per se*. By 1890, both slavery and the slave trade had been prohibited and declared to be crimes by the legislations of the European and American members of the society of States. International commitments against slavery were proclaimed, the most important among them being the General Antislavery Act of the Brussels Conference in 1890, aimed at ending the traffic in African slaves. There was a general consensus regarding the unlawfulness of the international slave trade. The prohibition had the nature of *jus cogens* already by the end of the 19th century (Hannikainen 1988, 75-87).

The League of Nations acted as the central organ of international law after World War I. The International Labour Organisation, ILO, was established through the peace treaty of Versailles. The ILO was the only part of the League of Nations to survive after World War II. The organization dealt with the modern conditions of work and, from the beginning, housed not only governments but representatives of labour market organizations in each of the member states. This corporatist element of the ILO, in a sense, was an early example of the later development of international law, including non-governmental organizations as *de facto,* if not always formally recognized, actors in the field.

The ILO was also an important scene for the turning away from slavery towards discrimination as a significant conceptual context for a discourse on equality in matters connected with working conditions. The League of Nations continued the abolition via a series of conventions against slavery. The 1926 Slavery Convention obligated the parties to the convention to prevent and suppress the slave trade and to bring about the abolition of slavery. The obligation regarding the abolition of slavery did not attain a peremptory nature in the time between the World Wars, however. Slaves, according to the Slavery Convention, were defined as things rather than as persons.[14]

The situation changed after World War II. Article 4 of the Universal Declaration of Human Rights, 1948 prohibits 'slavery or servitude', as well as a slave trade 'in all forms'. The UN modernized international anti-slavery rules in the Supplementary Slavery Convention in 1956.[15] New institutions and practices, by that time, had been drawn up under the term slavery, however. The Supplementary Slavery

Convention names such practices as debt bondage, land serfdom, and traffic in women and children.[16] The term, slavery, is used here to describe a situation where one person has a comprehensive type of power over another person. The term also refers to 'institutions and practices similar to slavery'.

In this context, slavery receives connotations that differ from the classical one. In classical philosophical, political and legal discourse, slavery is the opposite of freedom. The laws against slavery consist of emancipation in the sense of extending individual autonomy and rights to the enslaved person. From the time of the abolition movements, national and international, the focus was on collective groups. The continuing slavery-like practices drew attention to the collective deprivation of whole groups of people. Such groups were set aside, segregated and distinguished from others in everyday practices. The discussion about slavery *vis-à-vis* such groups became less concerned with individual freedom and decisions and more centred on their collective experience of deprivation. Categories of people were represented as having been mistreated and abused, even subjugated under circumstances resembling slavery.

The use of the concept of discrimination in international law expanded first during the era following World War II. During this period, the work of the ILO and in the United Nations in general ran parallel in many ways. The Charter of the United Nations (1945) refers to 'universal respect for, and observance of, human rights and fundamental freedoms for all *without distinction as to race, sex, language or religion*' (Italics KN). The terminology referring to discrimination, at that point, was still not stable. What we now conceptually understand as discrimination is already present in international law. The concept was referred to by using different terms, such as distinction, segregation and discrimination. All these terms connote setting apart, distinguishing and making a difference in the treatment of a group of people on such collective grounds as race or sex.

The expansion of the use of the term, discrimination, and the development of its conceptual use can be followed in the ILO instruments of the 1940s and 1950s. The term, discrimination, begins to appear in conventions typically in the context of working conditions that could previously easily have been described as slave work, for groups of people set apart from the rest of the national population. The first mention of the term, discrimination, seems to appear in Convention C 82 in 1947.[17] The convention concerns the problems of rural areas, often economically backward, with large amounts of migratory workers, many of them with inadequate housing, health care, social security, education and conditions of employment. Part IV of the convention forbids discrimination on grounds of race, colour, sex, belief, tribal association or trade union affiliation. Wage discrimination is one of the forms of discrimination mentioned in this context.

ILO Convention C 98 of 1949[18] concentrates on the protection of organized workers against 'acts of anti-union discrimination'. Convention C 104[19] abolishes penal sanctions in the contractual relations between employers and workers. Such sanctions were still in use against groups of indigenous workers, but not against other workers employed by the same plantation or other enterprise. This differential treatment was seen as discrimination (Art. 5 of the Convention). Indigenous groups and tribal populations were also living under worse conditions than other national groups. Convention C 107[20] includes schemes for the protection of these groups and for their integration into national societies. Another ILO convention concerned with agricultural workers recruited to work on tropical large-scale agricultural enterprises or plantations is Convention C 110,[21] aimed at a definition of the terms of employment in many material ways. By the beginning of the 1960s, the term, discrimination, seems to have received its current connotation in international law.

The stabilization of the concept of discrimination connected to equality is demonstrated by its lexical use, as reported in two dictionaries I have in my home library. The Oxford Dictionary, 1944 edition, gives discrimination the primary meaning of discernment or judgement. The Collins Cobuild English Dictionary, 1995 edition, gives three meanings for the word, discrimination.[22] The sense of the word known in the 18th century, *viz.*, the ability to recognize and understand the differences between two things, comes only third in number in the list of the meanings offered for the word. The primary sense offered is 'the practice of treating one person or group of people less fairly or less well than other people or groups'. Examples given of the use of the word in this sense are: '[s]he is exempt from sex discrimination laws' or 'discrimination against immigrants' or 'measures to counteract racial discrimination'. This current primary sense of the word, discrimination, found in the 1995 dictionary, compiled from a database of different contemporary texts and spoken language,[23] was not mentioned at all in the 1944 dictionary; that is, the older dictionary did not record the use of discrimination as 'a practice of treating one person or group of people less fairly or less well than other people or groups'.

The turn from slavery to discrimination did not mean that equality would have been understood in a more individualistic manner than previously. The term, discrimination, lost some of its original connotation, i.e., of making a difference, of distinguishing. The term then gained a connotation connected to the treatment of groups. This conceptual change seems to be related to the change that had already taken place in the discourse of slavery itself. In the modern era, slavery had become the bondage of non-Europeans, of alien groups engaged in 'slave work' under conditions that differed from those conditions of the main populations. Also, 'practices similar to slavery' often referred to forms of servitude of such groups. Already from the beginning, equality, as non-discrimination, *related to the differential treatment of groups of people*, rather than of individuals. 'Special measures' that ran against the traditional formal treatment of the principle of equality were recognized in this context. In practice, affirmative action was introduced.[24]

Race and Sex

The abolition of slavery, in many ways, was connected to the emancipation of women. Both in national and international contexts, women's movements became involved in the movement against slavery. Women were refused the right to participate in the World Anti-Slavery Convention in London in 1840, but they organized outside the formal meetings (Stienstra 1994, 47-48). Similarly, the exclusion of women from the organized movement against slavery was the incentive for establishing a movement for the rights of women in the US.

The League of Nations took on the responsibility of supervising agreements on trafficking in women and children. Four conventions for the protection of women were made in 1904, 1910, 1921 and 1933. Forced marriages and the treatment of a wife as chattel as a piece of property along with sexual slavery or the forcing of a woman into prostitution have been understood in this way as forms of slavery. The sexual slavery of women or the exploitation of children does not oppose the state of freedom with the condition of slavery. Rather, slavery connotes economic exploitation and moral deprivation. The UN Convention for the Suppression of the Traffic in Persons[25] seeks to protect the women exploited in prostitution, even when the women in question have given their consent to this state 'similar to slavery'. Freedom, autonomy and self-determination here are not the opposites of slavery. Slavery, in this context, reflects the protective nature of early international law addressing the wrongs committed against women (Hevener 1983). Emancipation from such forms of slavery would not necessarily make the emancipated girls or women autonomous persons entitled to self-determination, considering that the rights of women were in many ways restricted.

The protective intent of first international law instruments concerned with women has been noted by feminist scholars a long time ago.[26] Such protection was both approved of and disapproved of by early feminists according to how much emphasis they put on sexual difference and especially motherhood as a constitutive feature of femininity. From the beginning, women acted as NGOs in the ILO. Women's deputations to the Paris Peace Conference in 1919 had helped to include the principle of equal remuneration for work of equal value in the ILO Constitution. Yet, many ILO instruments made it difficult for women to engage in labour. Many of the treaties express an attempt to protect women because they are physically different from men and more vulnerable. Women were seen to be in moral danger and their roles as wives and mothers endangered by many circumstances. ILO's Convention Concerning Night Work of Women Employed in Industry[27] limits the work women can do on the ground that it is not suitable for women to work at night. Early international law instruments concerned with the legal position of women have a strong resemblance to the early modern naturalization of the sex difference.

The revival of the idea of inalienable human rights after the second World War also included a revival of the idea of the family as a natural rather than a legal community.[28] That political governments should not interfere with families is a point of view presented in many international law instruments. The relations between private persons were also usually considered outside the scope of state responsibility in international law, although slavery was never seen in this light. The conventions concerned with women reflect the naturalization of the sexual difference in 18th century discourse, with its emphasis on women's natural propensity to nurture.

The women-specific post-World War II international law instruments are typically concerned with discrimination against women. Discourse on equality as non-discrimination followed the earlier discourse on equality as non-slavery in the sense that, once again, race was the first issue to be addressed, followed by sex. The UN International Convention on the Elimination of All Forms of Racial Discrimination (1965)[29] gave a definition of discrimination later followed by the UN Women's Convention, CEDAW (1979).[30] Similarly, national legislation on racial discrimination has often been proposed and also put into place before laws on sex discrimination. The principle of equality as non-discrimination, however, involved a new operationalization of the principle in both cases.

The Operationalization of Equality as Non-Discrimination

The equality principle had certainly been adopted into most European constitutions by the early decades of the last century. Many of the constitutions even included a list of prohibited detrimental treatment on such grounds as religion, ethical origin, or sex.[31]

Up until quite recently, equality as a 'formal' principle was, indeed, more of a *principle* than of a rule and, thus, of relative rather than of absolute importance. A difference between these two designations is often made in contemporary legal argumentation. When two rules conflict, a rule is either valid and has to be applied or is not valid and should not be applied whereas a conflict of principles should be solved by finding a solution that optimalizes the weight of the principles involved (Alexy 1986). It would seem that operationalization in form of secondary legislation makes equality more often a *rule*. If equality is treated mainly as a principle of law, other principles may be balanced against it. Anti-discrimination laws and other forms of secondary legislation based on the equality principle often express clear rules that, if they are applied to a case, are to be applied as such, not in a manner modified by considerations due to other legal principles.

All through the first half of the 20th century, the equality principle was thought to demand in most European states that the courts and administrations treat individual legal subjects according to law in an equal, i.e., in a *non-arbitrary manner*. Today, the idea of popular sovereignty is limited by the demand that the equality principle should be respected by the legislator.

According to a post-World War II interpretation, states are responsible for upholding the equality principle also as a principle of international law. Most states have ratified the most important international human rights conventions. Some human rights instruments such as the UN Declaration of Human Rights, are considered binding upon states as conventional international law, although there has been no formal commitment by the states.

Early international human rights instruments understood state responsibility for upholding the equality principle to consist only of the *state itself respecting* the principle. The interpretation has changed, however. The state has a responsibility of *ensuring* that the citizens or 'all individuals' can enjoy the rights they are entitled to. When, in the language of human rights conventions, it is said that 'the law shall prohibit any discrimination and guarantee to all persons equal and effective protection against discrimination on any ground such as race, colour, sex, etc.' (UN International Covenant on Civil and Political Rights, 1966, Art. 26), this provision means that the state may have the responsibility of *interfering in the affairs between individuals* in order to guarantee the enjoyment of rights. In these cases, human rights instruments wield what is known as horizontal effect. The UN Race Convention of 1965, the paradigmatic convention in matters of discrimination, imposes upon states parties immediately binding obligations of removing racial discrimination.

The equality principle also covers many new areas. Respecting traditional political and civil rights usually demands that the state powers do not prevent the use of the rights, which are centred on the idea of 'negative freedom'. According to many human rights documents, as well as many late 20th century constitutions, the state is responsible for guaranteeing an *equal distribution of the basic necessities of life.* Thus, the state is made responsible for socially mediated production and its outcome. Economic, social and cultural rights[32] increase state responsibility for 'positive freedom'. Economic and social rights require resources, continuous monitoring and spending on social protection. The difference among regimes more or less committed to social welfare is reflected in this area.

A focus on economic, social and cultural rights has turned the interest of human rights law to persistent cultural practices, economic inequalities and social differentiation. Such phenomena were bypassed by the conceptualization of equality in the first generation of human rights. This new focus makes it easier to take the gendered dualism of early modern citizenship into consideration. When the discrimination of women includes their 'rights and freedoms in the political, economic, social, cultural, civil or any other field', the *structures that separate the public and private spheres become visible.*

In the area of economic rights, there is a long tradition of international labour rights concerned with equality, culminating in the principle of equal pay. Even the ILO Constitution, elaborated upon at the Paris Peace Conference in 1919, had already included the principle of equal remuneration for work of equal value. The principle was specified by ILO Convention 100 which covered equal pay for both 'equal work' and 'work of equal value'.

The equality legislation of the European communities originally consisted of Article 119 of the Treaty of Rome, later Article 141 of the Treaty of Amsterdam, on equal pay, which mentions sex as a forbidden ground of differential treatment. The article was a reduction of Article 2(1) of ILO Convention 100 on equal pay. Art. 119 of the Treaty of Rome had very little if any practical effect until the 1970s. The development of EC legislation on sex discrimination started with changes in court practice, which were adopted in a series of directives, such as EC directives on Equal Pay in 1975 and on Equal Treatment in 1976, revised in 2002. An attempt to operationalize equality as non-discrimination was thus evident in EC law.

The definition of discrimination has become more subtle. The definition used in the UN International Convention on the Elimination of All Forms of Racial Discrimination (1965),[33] Article 1, has been adapted to other contexts. The UN Women's Convention, CEDAW, of 1979[34] includes a non-discrimination approach, which was translated from the Race Convention of 1965. The definition of discrimination is similarly worded in both these conventions as 'any distinction, exclusion or restriction made on the basis of sex (or race) which has the effect or purpose of impairing or nullifying the recognition, enjoyment or exercise by women...of human rights and fundamental freedoms...' (CEDAW Article 1). The words 'the effect or purpose' refer to a distinction of two forms of discrimination, *direct* and *indirect discrimination*.

Direct and indirect discrimination are difficult concepts. They are given a slightly different interpretation in different jurisdictions. Direct, 'original' form of discrimination excludes individuals directly on the basis of sex. According to many national laws, such discrimination is forbidden also when it is made on the bases of marital status, pregnancy and family responsibilities. On the other hand, cultural attributes such as a relatively stronger practical obligation to family responsibilities can be a ground for indirect discrimination. For example, an age requirement that appears to be neutral as to sex can discriminate indirectly if women, because of gendered division of labour in child care, less seldom fulfil the requirement. Because women are assumed to be natural nurturers, they also tend to be the child carers; their working life may be interrupted and they may start working later in life than men. This overload of caring is the origin of many forms of indirect discrimination (Easteal 2001, 55-56).

When trying to show direct discrimination, the claimant must show that something happened because the claimant is a woman, is pregnant or has family responsibilities. In order to show indirect discrimination, the claimant has to show that apparently neutral rules exist which one group can comply with and another group cannot and that these rules, policies or practices have no real relationship to the job. One must prove a group-based harm, not an individual disadvantage.[35] National legislations that have adopted the idea of indirect discrimination do not guarantee that the huge field of cultural practices that can be described as indirectly discriminatory would actually be brought under critical survey. At least in Finland, the use of the concept of indirect discrimination in courts has been rare, and here as well as in Australia, 'popular conceptions of discrimination do not yet encompass the notion of indirect discrimination'.[36] Indirect discrimination can be rather difficult to detect.

Often, it has to be discovered and evidenced by statistics or some other form of systematic monitoring, rather than by looking at individual acts or behaviour.

When discrimination is understood as 'harm' caused to women or another group that is discriminated against, the emphasis is not on purposive action on the part of the person considered responsible for the wrong, but on 'careless' or negligent behaviour, inattention to the social processes that cause 'adverse impact'. The distribution of 'harm' has a social dimension because our vulnerability to particular kinds of harm derives not only from individual circumstances, but also from our membership in a particular class, race or group (Graycar and Morgan 1990, 272-276).

A major change in understanding 'harm' as socially produced has to do with the *development of a 'risk society'* where risks can be calculated and the *responsibility for risks shifts to include negligence* rather than purpose: preventing people from taking forbidden risks becomes one of the important aims of legislation. When we say that someone is taking a risk, this statement implies that the risk taker does not want the risk to occur. Taking a risk happens in order to reach some other objective. The person in question is willing to disregard the eventuality of the risk in order to realize that aim. Legal intervention in risk-taking necessarily concentrates less on purposive acts and more on negligent behaviour.

Typically, intentions are not relevant considerations in discrimination cases. Both direct and indirect discrimination, according to the anti-discrimination laws of today, can be present without there being any intention to discriminate. In this respect, compensation of the damage caused by discrimination does not even require the element of negligence. The emphasis is on discrimination as unintentional adverse treatment.

To describe harm as 'gendered' is to identify the gender dimension in its incidence and distribution. Women suffer particular harms and injuries as women (Conaghan 1998, 134). A gendered harm, such as harassment, may well be caused by behaviour that is not very intentional or purposive. Sensitivity to the risks of gendered harm in this respect perhaps resembles an increased sensitivity to many other types of socially produced harms.

The CEDAW also contains a broader definition of discrimination than that contained in the earlier treaties, covering both equality of opportunity, i.e., formal equality and the equality of outcome or *de facto* equality (Charlesworth and Chinkin 2000, 217). According to the CEDAW, 'temporary special measures aimed at accelerating de facto equality between men and women' is not to be considered discrimination (Article 4 (1)). The States parties are allowed to take affirmative action in order to diminish or eliminate conditions which cause or help to perpetuate discrimination. Affirmative action or positive measures are limited for the purposes of upholding formal equality in certain ways, however. Differentiation of treatment does not constitute discrimination, if the criteria for differentiation are 'reasonable and objective and if the aim is to achieve a purpose which is legitimate', as the UN Human Rights Committee states in connection with the International Covenant on Civil and Political Rights (ICCPR).[37] The criteria used by the Human Rights Committee were originally developed by the European Court of Human Rights ostensibly to measure discriminatory national laws since the *Belgian Linguistic Case* (cit. Charlesworth and Chinkin 2000, 214-215).

Pregnancy is, so far at least, a *uniquely feminine state*. A narrow interpretation claims that discrimination on the ground of pregnancy is not sex discrimination because sex discrimination can only exist where women can be compared to men. Strictly speaking, an androcentric model of equality does not allow for the treatment of pregnancy as a ground of discrimination. This controversy has now been settled by both national courts and European Court of Justice in favour of treating pregnancy discrimination as a form of sex discrimination. The issue of pregnancy is paradigmatic for the claim that the notion of equality is androcentric and does not allow for sex difference or for the feminine. The cases which have been decided in favour of treating discrimination on the basis of pregnancy as sex discrimination reduce the force of the claim of the fundamental androcentricity of the concept of equality.

The UN CEDAW convention, in some ways, has gone further than EC law in presenting discrimination in a gynocentric way. This gynocentrism is especially evident in the CEDAW Recommendation on violence against women which treats gendered violence without any comparisons between the forms of harm typically suffered by women and the forms of harms typically suffered by men.

Both EC/EU law and the UN CEDAW Convention seem to be based on separating sex from gender, that is biologically understood dimensions of sex versus socially defined sex. To my mind, equality law in these documents and the practice based on them present a new epistemology. It constitutes a different level of legally recognized subjectivity because it seems to concentrate on gender instead of sex. This does not remove the problems of difference. Martha Minow analyses versions of the dilemma of difference on the basis of US law. We may create difference either by noticing it or by ignoring it. Decisions should not be based on discriminatory grounds, but if these grounds are not acknowledged, they effectively continue to matter. Focusing on these differences, however, can reinforce the stereotypes they consist of. Governmental neutrality, on the other hand, can eternalize the past consequences of differences (Minow 1993, 218). According to Minow, there are unuttered assumptions underlying the dilemma of difference. Categorization is the means used for treating difference, but the distinguishing features behind the categories appear natural rather than chosen. One has to make the unexpressed points of reference and comparison visible. Preconceptions frame our perspectives. Judges tend to assume their own perspective as universal and superior to others, preferring the status quo as natural and free from coercion (op. cit., 227-230).

It is important to consider the performative power of this type of subject representation. It is, by no means, unproblematic to present women as a socially constructed group, especially as a group violated against, suffering from maltreatment and consisting of individuals that are similar to each other in all legally relevant respects. Politics based on such an identification of a group is not devoid of adverse effects. It can create categories of people which are considered less capable and, therefore, less deserving than others. The legislation that discriminates in favour of such a group is easily considered as privileging instead of as correcting gendered, socially engendered harm (Bacchi 1996).

Yet, I think that equality as non-discrimination has become a *collective rather than individual concept*, with a focus on *societal structured problems* rather than on personal grievances. When discrimination is detected in a manner involving statistics on groups of people, what is in question is something that has to do with *distributive justice as well as formal equality*. A powerful critique of the anti-discrimination legislation continues to be that it does not produce equality of results. A monitoring of the equality of results becomes necessary, however, and makes the inequalities visible and, thus, possible targets of anti-discrimination law.

Conclusion

As Carol Smart so clearly presents, the grievances of today's feminists against the notions of equality and 'rights discourse' seem to arise from an understanding that claims based on equality and rights produced positive results while *formal inequality* was the rule, but not in a regime based on formal equality. By the 1980s, formal equality of the sexes had become the norm in Western jurisdictions. Equality as a notion seemed to prevent all attempts to go 'beyond equality and difference'; to paraphrase the title of a much-cited collection of feminist texts (Bock and James 1992). Yet, feminist politics would demand that equality based on similarity could accommodate difference.

The assumption that there is no way beyond equality and difference is one I wish to reconsider. It is true that modernity has understood justice in terms of law and rights, in a legalistic and universalistic manner. Yet, neither rights nor the notion of equality are something that can be shaken off easily. Nor is there reason to assume that the notion of equality invariably has its modern, formal sense or liberal connotations. Rather, the *modus operandi* of the equality principle has changed, as well as the context in which the principle is evoked.

Recent feminist philosophy has opened the notion of sex to a dynamic understanding which may avoid both the denial of difference and the denial of sameness. Sex can be thought of as existing as performative acts, as a style or as 'adverbial unity' with a dynamic manner of being, where a feminine or masculine style is not tied to static essential structures (Gatens 1991; Butler 1990; Butler 1993; Heinämaa 1996). It would be strange to have an understanding of law based on legal positivism, essentialist legalism or an acceptance of static foundational subjects of law, combined with a phenomenological understanding of how sex 'is'. To believe that law – legal methods and concepts – are 'fundamentally anti-feminist' is to accept an understanding of law that denies any dynamic changes in how law 'is'.

I believe Carol Smart is right when she demands that the feminist approach to law should be focused on redefining wrongs. I understand her to mean that she actually wishes to provoke justice in law or to find a way of redefining equality in a way that reflects socially-structured wrongs and interests, while avoiding the androcentric bias of modern law.

I have not attempted an explication here of what that kind of opening up in law could be, speaking in a more general way. Rather, I have argued that justice as equality is not necessarily inimical to feminism. Adopting the role of devil's advocate in defence of a dynamic understanding of how law 'is', I have discussed changes in the definition of the notion of (sex) equality as well as changes in the context and *modus operandi* of the equality principle. It is striking to me that the concept of *equality as non-discrimination* is a late development. On basis of the changes I describe, there seems to be reason to question the accuracy of the pejorative aura surrounding 'equality' as a concept and 'equality feminism' or 'research on equality' have received in feminist literature since the 1980s. There can hardly be a total denial or even neglect of the principle of equality by feminists or indeed any other group representing 'difference' in the late modern world. A violation of such formal rights as the right to equal protection of personal integrity certainly cannot be suffered by feminists of any description.

I wish to repeat that the power involved in the faculty of discriminating, observing differences accurately, is what the concept of equality is about. What is similar and what is different is by no means a given. In our late modern societies, justice consists of making correct discriminations about what is and what is not equal. A failure to make such determinations, such discernments, is wrong. Such a wrong is Lyotard's '*différend*', which resides in the inability to recognize harm and such is Derrida's account of justice, ever becoming and never there.

Carol Smart concludes her book on feminists and the power of law by demanding that 'law's power to define and disqualify...should become the focus of feminist strategy rather than law reform as such. Feminism has an ability to redefine the wrongs of women which law too often confines to insignificance. Feminism can redefine harmless practice as harm. The legal forum provides an excellent place to engage in this process of redefinition. Law cannot be ignored precisely because of its power to define, but feminism's strategy should be focused on this power rather than on constructing legal policies. It is important to resist the temptation that law offers, namely the promise of a solution.' (Smart 1989, 165-166). Amen to that – what a dynamic concept of equality may indeed offer is a contestation rather than a solution.

This chapter is written under the auspices of the national research programme, SYREENI, funded by the Academy of Finland.

Notes

1 Smart (1989) pp. 145- 146. Italics KN. Smart uses, among other things, the presentation of the Norwegian feminist lawyer Tove Stang Dahl when arguing about the androcentric standard of law.

2 Sirkku Hellsten (1996) forcefully presents the strong tendency in liberal philosophy to revert to a discourse on equality as an existing state of affairs, instead of as a goal to be achieved. Hellsten also discusses (Hellsten 1997) some problems inherent in contemporary liberal political theory and points out the importance of paying attention to the differences between Continental humanistic traditions and Anglo-American liberal economics when making general pronouncements about what 'liberal equality' consists of.

3 See e.g. O'Donovan and Szyszczak 1989 pp. 44-45, where the authors sum up anti-discrimination legislation thus: '[i]t merely asks that men move over to make a little room for the women who can conform to the male norm'.

4 Lenoble and Berten (1990) describe the crisis of law and politics at the end of the 20th century. They belong to those philosophers who have helped me to seek the dynamics in equality from the recourse to discerning judgments.

5 I am, of course, far from being the first one to point this thought out. See e.g. MacKinnon 1989, where the Aristotelian concepts on race and nationality are claimed to be limited and the concept of sex to be quite inappropriate. MacKinnon demands a radical change.

6 Conceptual history differs from the history of ideas by concentrating on the genealogy of a concept and its uses, instead of by showing the 'historical roots' of today's ideology. When working on a conceptual history, the researcher traces changes in the use of a concept or clusters of concepts. Many political historians have pointed out that having a term, phrase or name for something differs from having a concept. A concept can consist of different words, combinations of words and can be expressed in different languages. The changes in the concept of equality, for example, can be traced by paying attention to the synonyms used for equality or to the different contexts of the use of the term. The literature on conceptual history by political scientists is by now extensive; see e.g. Ball et al. 1996 and Lehmann and Richter 1996.

7 By a legal principle, I understand a concept with legal normative power. Concepts are never purely descriptive or without a prescriptive dimension. Our conceptual framework is intertwined with power relations. A description of a state of affairs takes place at the price of the preclusion of other descriptions and established concepts certainly exclude other conceptualizations. Modern legal discourse consists of a conceptual framework that relates to valid norms. Among such norms, a distinction between rules and principles is often made. I use the term 'principle of equality' when referring to the positive, normative use of the notion of equality and to the term 'concept of equality' when discussing the general, conceptual understanding of equality.

8 Aristotle makes a short comment on such an opposition by remarking that the Sophist Alcidimas, a pupil of Gorgias, defends the view that slavery is against nature. The issue of to what extent slavery was disputed in ancient Greece has been discussed extensively in political philosophy and history. The Marxist view has been that a critique of slavery in the ancient world was inconceivable, see Karl Marx: *Capital, Vol. 3.* The opposite view has been defended by, among others, Karl Popper, who, in his *The Open Society and Its Enemies* (Popper 1963, 70) claims that there was a strong anti-slavery movement in Athens in the fifth century BC.

9 The issue of slavery was framed in this way even by the 18th century. Slaves clearly connoted black Africans, e.g., for Montesquieu. In The Spirit of Laws, published in 1742, Montesquieu writes in a chapter 'Of the Slavery of the Negroes' thus: 'Were I to vindicate our right to make slaves of the negroes, these should be my arguments'... and continues with an ironical explication of why African slaves are needed on plantations and how their colour makes a great impact on their treatment. Montesquieu 1752, XV, 5. The text is based

on a clear opposition of 'the Negroes' and 'us', and constitutes an exclusion based on race while it argues for abolition.

10 The example is taken from a text of 1705. Shorter Oxford English Dictionary, Third Edition 1944.

11 Although some political philosophers had affirmed the natural equality of men much earlier, there was a 'thickening' of the theme of natural equality in the 18th century philosophy. Jean-Jacques Rousseau is the philosopher *par excellence* who wishes to eliminate the social history of men from a consideration of their natural equality. In his text on inequality, *Discours sur l'origine et les fondements de l'inégalité parmi les hommes*, written in 1754, he argues that inequality and slavery are the outcome of socialization and deepening differentiation. He radicalizes the assumptions of natural equality presented by Hobbes and Locke. The reasons of inequality were under debate at the time *Discours* was published – Rousseau wrote the text in order to participate in a competition for texts on 'the origin of inequality', held by the Academy of Dijon in 1753.

12 According to Thomas Laqueur, medicine was late in discovering the different functions of the male and female organs of reproduction. Lacquer claims that effectively, medicine, until the 'classical age', only recognized the male sex and considered the female sex as a less potent and inverted form of it, see Laqueur 1990.

13 Michèle LeDoeuff describes the interrelated account of medicine and philosophy and shows how the theory of Jean-Jacques Rousseau of the profound difference of women was reflected in the medical account of women's bodies, written by the French doctor, Roussel. Roussel turned Rousseau's account of feminine altruism and softness into medical terms, describing the female body. Such an account of the body was again taken by the revolutionaries and the post-Revolution's politicians to affirm the political, social and legal alterity of women. See LeDoeuff 1989.

14 League of Nations Slavery Convention, 1926, Article 1 gives a traditional definition on slavery: '[s]lavery is the status or condition of a person over whom any or all of the powers attaching to the rights of ownership are exercized'.

15 UN Supplementary Convention on the Abolition of Slavery, the Slave Trade, and Institutions and Practices similar to Slavery, 1956.

16 Article 1, UN Suplementary Convention on the Abolition of Slavery.

17 Social Policy (Non-Metropolitan Territories) Convention (1947).

18 Right to Organise and Collective Bargaining Convention (1949).

19 (Shelved) Abolition of Penal Sanctions (Indigenous Workers) Convention (1955).

20 Indigenous and Tribal Populations Convention (1957).

21 Plantations Convention (1958).

22 First sense: discrimination is the practice of treating one person or group of people less fairly or less well than other people or groups. Example: *She is exempt from sex discrimination laws...discrimination against immigrants...measures to counteract racial discrimination.*

Second sense: discrimination is awareness of what is good or of high quality. Example: *They cooked without skill and ate without discrimination.*

Third sense: discrimination is the ability to recognize and understand the differences between two things. Examples: *We will then have an objective measure of how colour discrimination and visual acuity develop at the level of the brain...the system that allows a mother to make the discrimination between her own and alien lambs.* Collins Cobuild English Dictionary (first ed. 1987, new edition 1995).

23 Collins Cobuild English Dictionary, 1995. This edition has been drawn from a database of

different types of writing and speech, mostly from 1990 onwards. It should reflect the actual contemporary use of the word. I assume that the conceptual use of the word in this respect follows the actual popular use.

24 For example, the Indigeneous and Tribal Populations Convention of 1957, Art. 3 permits 'special measures...for the protection of the institutions, persons, property and labour' of these groups, but warns against using such special measures 'as a means of creating or prolonging a state of segregation'.

25 Convention for the Suppression of the Traffic in Persons and of the Exploitation of the Prostitution of Others (1950). 53 UNTS 39.

26 See e.g. Hevener 1983 and Hevener 1986.

27 Revised 1948. 81 UNTS 285.

28 Universal Declaration of Human Rights, Art. 16(3) describes the family as 'the natural and fundamental group unit of society', which is 'entitled to protection by society and the State'.

29 International Convention on the Elimination of All Forms of Racial Discrimination, 21 December 1965, 660 UNTS 195.

30 United Nations Convention on the Elimination of All Forms of Discrimination against Women, 18 December 1979, 1249 UNTS 13.

31 The Finnish Constitution of 1919 did not include such a list. A list had been proposed in connection with the *travaux préparatoires* leading to the Constitution, but it was removed during the approval of the law in the Parliament. A reference to sex, also included in the proposal, was removed from the final text of the Finnish Constitution of 1919. A list of forbidden grounds for discrimination was introduced by a reform in 1995.

32 UN Covenant on Economic, Social and Cultural Rights 1966, European Social Charter 1969.

33 International Convention on the Elimination of All Forms of Racial Discrimination, 21 December 1965, 660 UNTS 195.

34 Convention on the Elimination of all Forms of Discrimination against Women, 18 December 1979, 1249 UNTS 13.

35 This description of the differences of evidence required in order to prove direct and indirect discrimination is given by Esteal 2001, 66-67 and follow Australian law, the Sex Discrimination Law 1984, and the State and Territory equivalents valid in Australia. For EC law, see Ellis 1997.

36 Esteal 2001, 67, citing Hunter 1992.

37 International Covenant on Civil and Political Rights, 16 December 1966, 999 UNTS 171.

References

Aristotle (1975), *The Nicomachean Ethics*, Oxford University Press, London.

Aristotle (1988), *The Politics*, Cambridge University Press, Cambridge.

Bacchi, Carol (1996), *The Politics of Affirmative Action: 'Women', Equality and Category Politics*, Sage, London.

Ball, T., J. Farr and L. Hanson (eds) (1996), *Political Innovation and Conceptual Change*, Cambridge.

Bock, Gisela and Susan James (eds) (1992), *Beyond Equality and Difference: Citizenship, Feminist Politics and Female Subjectivity*, Routledge, London and New York.

Butler, Judith (1990), *Gender Trouble. Feminism and the Subversion of Identity*, Routledge, New York.

Butler, Judith (1993) *Bodies that Matter: On the Discursive Limits of 'Sex'*, Routledge, New York.
Charlesworth, Hilary and Christine Chinkin (2000), *The boundaries of international law. A feminist analysis,* Manchester University Press, Manchester.
Conaghan, Joanne (1998), Tort Litigation in the Context of Intrafamilial Abuse. '*Modern Law Review*' pp. 127- 139.
Easteal, P. (2001), 'A Kaleidoscope View of Law and Culture. The Australian Sex Discrimination Act 1984'. *International Journal of the Sociology of Law* 29:1, pp. 51-74.
Ellis, Evelyn (1998), *EC Sex Equality Law.* 2nd Edition. Clarendon Press, Oxford.
Fauré, Christine (1991), *Democracy Without Women. Feminism and the Rise of Liberal Individualism in France*, Indiana University Press.
Fauré, Christine (1997), *Ce que déclarer des droits veut dire: histories*, Presses universitaires de France.
Foucault, Michel (1989), *The Order of Things*, Tavistock/Routledge, London and New York.
Gatens, Moira (1991), 'A Critique of the Sex/Gender distinction' in S. Gunew (ed.), *A Reader in Feminist Knowledge*, Routledge, London.
Gerhard, Ute (2001), *Debating Women's Equality. Toward a Feminist Theory of Law from a European Perspective*, Rutgers University Press, New Brunswick and London.
Graycar, Regina and Jenny Morgan (1990), *The Hidden Gender of Law*, The Federation Press, Sydney.
Hannikainen, Lauri (1988), *Peremptory Norms (Jus Cogens) in International Law*, Finnish Lawyers' Publishing Company, Helsinki.
Heinämaa, Sara (1996), *Ele, tyyli ja sukupuoli: Merleau-Pontyn ja Beauvoirin ruumiinfenomenologia ja sen merkitys sukupuolikysymykselle,* Gaudeamus, Helsinki.
Hellsten, Sirkku (1996), *Oikeutta ilman kohtuutta. Modernin oikeudenmukaisuuskäsityksen kritiikkiä,* Gaudeamus, Helsinki.
Hellsten, Sirkku (1997), *In Defense of Moral Individualism*, Philosophical Society of Finland, Helsinki.
Hevener, Natalie (1983), *International Law and the Status of Women*, Westview Press, Boulder, Colo.
Laqueur, Thomas (1990), *Making Sex. Body and Gender from the Greeks to Freud*, Harvard University Press.
LeDoeuff, Michèle (1989), *The Philosophical Imaginary*, The Athlone Press, London.
Lehmann, H. and M. Richter (eds) (1996), *The Meaning of Historical Terms and Concepts: New studies on Begriffsgeschichte*, Washington.
Lenoble, Jacques and André Berten (1990), *Dire la norme. Droit, politique et enunciation*, E.Story-Scientia, Bruxelles.
MacKinnon, Catherine (1989), *Towards a Feminist Theory of the State*, Harvard University Press, Cambridge Mass.
Marx, Karl (1971), *Capital: A Critical Analysis of Capitalist Production. Vol.3, The Process of Capitalist Production as a Whole*, Allen & Unwin, London.
Montesquieu, Charles de Secondat (1752), *The Spirit of Laws* . L'Ésprit des Lois, 1742, translated into English by Thomas Nugent, revised by J.V. Prichard.
O'Donovan, Katherine and Erika Szyszczak (1989), *Equality and Sex Discrimination Law*, Basil Blackwell, Oxford.
Popper, Karl (1963), *The Open Society and Its Enemies. Vol 2 The High Tide of Prophecy: Hegel, Marx and the Aftermath*, Routledge & Kegan Paul, London.

Rousseau, Jean-Jacques (1994), *Discourse on the Origin of Inequality*, Oxford University Press, Oxford.
Scott, Joan Wallace (1996), *Only Paradoxes to Offer. French Feminists and the Rights of Men*, Harvard University Press, Cambridge Mass and London.
Smart, Carol (1989), *Feminism and the Power of Law*, Routledge, London.
Stienstra, D. (1994), *Women's Movements and International Organisations*, Macmillan, London.
Thornton, Margaret (1990), *The Liberal Promise: Anti-Discrimination Legislation in Australia*, Oxford University Press, Melbourne.
Westerman, Pauline (2001), 'Formal Justice as a Common Language', in Arend Soeteman (ed.), *Pluralism and Law*, Kluwer Academic Publisher, Dordrecht, Boston and London.

Reference Books

Shorter Oxford English Dictionary, Third Edition, 1944.
Collins Cobuild English Dictionary, 1995 Edition.

Chapter 10

Equality through Human Rights: Nordic and International Feminist Perspectives on Rights

Sari Kouvo

Introduction

During the 1990s, feminist scholars and activists have increasingly engaged in international human rights discourses. The unifying slogan for this feminist and women's advocacy movement is: *Women's Rights are Human Rights.* The questions dealt with by 'international' feminists under this slogan have related to the refocusing and reshaping of the international human rights discourse in order to better accommodate it and to make it correspond to 'women's' experiences and needs.[1] The international human rights community, to some extent, has accepted the feminist critique.[2] The relative openness of the international human rights community towards feminist demands has led to human rights optimism amongst feminists. Some feminist scholars, such as Dianne Otto and Anne Orford from Australia, however, have raised the question whether the changes undertaken by the international human rights community, to a sufficient extent, have changed the fundamental principles or the internal logic of international human rights law (Orford 1999; Orford 2002; Otto 1997a; Otto 1997b).

Nordic feminist scholars have not engaged themselves in the international human rights discourse to the same extent as feminists in the English-speaking world. In the Nordic context, matters relating to the advancement of women and the equality between the sexes, to a large extent, have been dealt with through the sex equality project of the democratic welfare state. The focus has been less on the promotion of individual rights than on economic and social policies for re-adjusting structural sex inequalities. However, in line with the downsizing of the public sector and an increased attention to the heterogeneity of and the prevailing differences within the Nordic women's community, there is a growing interest in rights-based approaches.

The aim of this chapter is to discuss the relationship, interconnections and differences between Nordic feminist legal studies and the so-called international feminist legal scholarship. The focus will be on the debate about rights and on the way in which Nordic feminist legal scholarship can contribute to the international feminist human rights debate. Finally, I will ask what Nordic feminist legal scholars could learn from the international debates.

Inter-Humanness, the Generic Core and the Reluctant Periphery

In her article, 'Forgoing New Identities in the Global Family?', Hanne Petersen (2000) introduces the concept of inter-human law. According to Petersen, inter-human law is related to world law or to the law of an emerging world society, but it focuses more on inter-human relations than on territorial boundaries and connections (Petersen 2000, 52). In other words, inter-human law is less like international law and more like what law would be if it were built on knowledge on relationality between and among human beings and groups of human beings.

I am fond of Petersen's concept of inter-human law and of her writing promoting an inter-human law. Petersen's emphasis on inter-humanness corresponds well with contemporary feminist and other critical scholarship that attempts to move beyond a *simple* emphasis on difference and diversity by using empathic and relational approaches (see for example Braidotti 1994; Cornell 1998; Svensson 2001). The inter-human approach can also serve as a means for redirecting our thinking about international human rights law. An inter-human approach can contribute to downplaying the European legacy and male bias in international human rights law and allow alternative perspectives to affect the core of human rights (Petersen 2000; Petersen and Vindeløv 2000).

The 1990s was marked by an increased focus on diversity and difference within academic feminisms. Many frontiers were transgressed concerning racial, ethnic, class and other gender-based differences among women. Regional, national and local differences among women were also reviewed. Using the word 'feminisms' in plural and books with titles such as 'Feminisms or '*Feminismer*' are examples of the increased importance given to the acknowledgement of differences (Kemp and Squires, eds 1997; Larsson ed. 1996). During the 1990s, Western or Euro-centred feminists learned to make distinctions and to draw epistemological dividing lines between and within Mediterranean, French, German, Anglophone and Nordic feminisms. The work of the European women's studies network, ATHENA, and its forefront figure Rosi Braidotti have been important in the rearranging of our knowledge about European feminisms (Braidotti and Vonk, eds 2000).

However, acknowledging historical, cultural and language differences, when engaging in trans-European feminist dialogues, does not equal an understanding of 'Europe' as heterogeneous. In feminist debates about international or global issues, the Occident or Euro-centred world tends still to be treated as an epistemologically and ontologically coherent entity, defined by the core countries in Europe and North America and delimited from the developing world, defined by the African, Asian and South or Latin American context. The difficulties for feminists to integrate new distinctions or differences into their thinking have been succinctly expressed by Donna Haraway:

> It has seemed very rare for feminist theory to hold race, sex/gender and class analytically together – all the best intentions, hues of authors, and remarks in prefaces notwithstanding. /.../ threes will always reduce to twos, which quickly become lonely ones in the vanguard. And no one learns to count to four. These things matter politically. (Haraway 1991, 129).

Today, the traditional tools and analytical models deployed in the Nordic context no longer provide us with sufficient explanations. We are aware of the fact that the notions of universal welfare and equality no longer hold. There are increasing numbers of people who do not sense the belonging to the communities or who fall in between the welfare systems. To tackle these issues, Nordic feminist legal scholars have now begun to turn to other than legal feminist scholarship and to the international human rights model in search of explanations and solutions. Feminist scholarship has always been rather keen on travelling throughout the academic world, as well as in and out of it. However, increasingly, scholars have started to pose questions about, not only the intended, but also the unintended and sometimes unwanted consequences of such travels, as well as about the contextual meaning and reasoning behind concepts and epistemologies.

Acknowledging differences, of course, is not an end in itself, but its value is dependent on how it contributes to the issues that are being dealt with. Petersen suggests that acknowledging difference should aim at a more profound knowledge about life and law. For her, difference is not a problem but an asset. In much feminist scholarship, especially feminist scholarship regarding the 1980s debates on sameness and difference and the 1990s debates on diversity, making distinctions became an end in itself. The focus shifted from making distinctions and acknowledging differences to theorizing about differences. The feminist epistemological and the political projects are no longer intertwined as they used to be, but today, theorizing about differences is understood as *the* feminist epistemological project, which exists irrespective of any political projects.

Nordic Feminisms and Other Feminisms

The Nordic countries tend to be represented as historically, culturally and politically fairly coherent: they have intertwined histories with similar legal systems, welfare state systems and similar approaches to sex equality issues. This sameness, however, is more dependent on the Nordic people perceiving themselves as unified in their difference from the rest of Europe and the world, than on an actual unity and coherence. Much of the perceived coherence and unity of 'the Nordic people' and the Nordic countries are being renegotiated. This renegotiation results from fractures caused by several developments. Denmark, Finland and Sweden are member states of the European Union, whereas Norway and Iceland have remained outside. The Nordic welfare states have experienced a radical down-sizing process. There are increased demands for action to fight discrimination against non-European first, second and even third generation immigrants. Finally, there is a growing concern for the rights of the indigenous peoples, the Inuit and the *Sámi* populations, who live in the northern parts of Norway, Sweden and Finland and in the territories governed by Denmark. These developments, among others, have led to disillusionment of the 'universal Nordic Model' and to a need to search for new approaches.

The relative difference of the 'North' from the rest of Europe has led to the development of 'Nordic feminist' schools of thought. The Nordic 'women's law' tradition, for example, has evolved since the 1970s, emphasizing and believing in the importance of the state as a motor for sex equality and equal opportunities schemes, as well as in the importance of women's collective processes.[3] The Nordic women's law tradition has not engaged in international women's and human rights discourses to any considerable extent. Nordic women were given civil and political rights fairly early in the 20th century. The well-developed public welfare sector, as it seems, has made it unnecessary to use rights-based approaches when dealing with economic and social issues.

Nordic feminisms and Nordic women's law scholars have a conflictive relationship to English language feminisms and feminist jurisprudence. English language feminisms hold a special position within international academia because English is increasingly becoming the globally accepted academic language. English-language feminist concepts and theories have had a remarkable capacity to travel.[4] In the Nordic context, the hegemonic position of English language feminisms is boosted because French, German, Italian and Spanish feminisms reach the Nordic countries via English language translations and interpretations and because Nordic feminists need to write and publish in English to become part of international academia.[5]

However, although Nordic feminisms might academically perceive themselves as marginal, on the political level *we* perceive that we have participated in building what is often considered to be the most sex equal systems in the world (Svensson 2001). Speaking from a Swedish perspective, Eva-Maria Svensson explains what being Swedish and Nordic has meant for Swedes and more specifically, for Swedish feminists. According to Svensson, the self-image of Sweden is that it is the most equal country in the world. The Swedish self-image corresponds to the image that the international community now has of the country. However, both the self-image and the image outside Sweden are inaccurate. 'Sweden has deluded itself and the world' (Svensson 2001, 71). While Nordic feminist legal scholars are increasingly questioning the Nordic equality model and discussing especially its failures, they, nevertheless, remain loyal to the Nordic model. Alternatives seem seldom to be looked for elsewhere. Hence, Nordic feminists engage in international feminist discourses both from a marginal and a superior position. They strive for participation in the international debates while at the same time perceiving themselves as forerunners in the advancement of women's issues and sex equality matters.

Prevailing Feminist Approaches on Human Rights

While Nordic feminists perceive of themselves as Nordic both while taking marginal and dominant positions, English language feminisms seldom call themselves English language or Anglo-feminisms.[6] Hence, the feminist scholarship that I will present below as international feminism is the dominant form of feminist international human rights law scholarship, which tends to be Anglo-American, liberal, individual and rights-centred as well as oriented to the empowerment of women. The English language and especially Anglo-American feminists' *right* to perceive themselves as generic tends to hide their situatedness or the context from which they speak. For example, in the edited volumes on women and international human rights law, the authors are mainly scholars from universities in Canada and the US, including some from Australia and the UK. All of them write from a 'universal' perspective. The contributors from African, Asian and South and Latin American contexts tend to situate their work in their national or regional contexts (see for example Cook 1994; Askin and Koenig 1999). Nordic scholars are not represented in any of the works. In Haraway's words, this lack of representation does matter politically.

Amongst the earliest well-disseminated feminist writing on international human rights law are the work of Hilary Charlesworth, Christine Chinkin and Shelley Wright, 'Feminist Perspectives on International Human Rights Law' (1991) and that of Karen Engle, 'International Human Rights and Feminism: Where Discourses Meet' (1992). Charlesworth, Chinkin and Wright claim that international law is male both in form and content and argue for a feminist engagement in international law. Karen Engle notes also that international law and its institutions give preference to a male norm and that academic interpreters have tended to support this norm. However, Engle is more cautious than Charlesworth, Chinkin and Wright when discussing the potential of a feminist or women's human rights discourse. She notes that, in her experience, arguing for women's human rights signified suppressing doubts about the grand human rights project. Moreover, she notes that the feminist engagement in the grand human rights project would probably change feminism as much or more than it would change human rights (Engle 1992, 603-606).

The 1990s feminist international law has been more influenced by the pragmatic project of Charlesworth, Chinkin and Wright and less by the more ambivalent approach of Engle. The early 1990s feminist international and human rights law scholarship became very woman-centred and empowerment-oriented and it served as a counter-hegemonic discourse with respect to both the old schools of international and human rights law scholarship and to international and human rights law structures. This feminist project is well-framed in the book by Hilary Charlesworth and Christine Chinkin, 'The Boundaries of International Law' (2000). According to Charlesworth and Chinkin, the feminist international law project has two major roles: (1) the deconstruction of the explicit and implicit values of the international legal system, and (2) the reconstruction of another international law (Charlesworth and Chinkin 2000, 60-61). The term, deconstruction, is not used with reference to Derridean or post-structural notions of deconstruction, but with reference to a more popular understanding of deconstruction as merely seeing beyond the evident and detecting the underlying values. The definition of the feminist international law project is also framed in the terms of the dual commitment of feminism, on the one hand, to produce new and relevant knowledge about women and women's situations and, on the other hand, to promote changes for women and in women's situations.

During the first decade of feminist knowledge production about international and human rights law the main approaches have been:

- Critique of international human rights as male-biased because few efforts have been made to reconstruct the male-centred human rights framework by other means than by creating alternative discourses for women; and because the international human rights system is male-dominated and prioritizes male-centred issues on its agendas.
- Critique of specific international human rights norms or practices on similar grounds as the above, that is, an analysis of how international human rights law addresses issues such as violence against women or gendered war crimes.
- Critique of national or cultural practices such as female gender mutilation, women's lacking economic and social rights in specific national contexts and so on by using international human rights norms as standards and point of reference.
- Critique of the general and woman-centred initiatives by the UN and in the international human rights law for their tendencies to stereotype women and for their inability to integrate perspectives of differences amongst women.

However, as noted above, the consequence of the feminist strategic deconstruction of international law has been (is) that international law cannot be deconstructed so much that the deconstruction would put the potential of the reconstructive project into question. Hence, much of the feminist deconstruction has targeted only the more or less, at least for feminists, explicit values of international law. Moreover, only narrow themes have been approached. Thus, the legal paradigm defining the tasks for international law scholars has been broadened but slightly. As a consequence, the feminist strategic deconstructive international law project has developed into a dominant form of feminist international law scholarship.

The dominant scholarship is written in native English language and it can be characterized as very strategic, a bit too dogmatic, yet fairly liberal and with a strong women's empowerment component (Charlesworth, Chinkin and Wright 1999;

Dallmeyer 1993; Peters and Wolper, eds 1995). This dominant discourse, in fact, is very much like the UN discourses on women's human rights. The academic feminist human rights project and the sex equality project of the UN and the international human rights community have increasingly come to use the same language, to promote the same strategies and to share the same goals. Feminist international law scholarship focuses on women, uses gendered language and promotes ideas of both targeted and specific action for gender equality. The UN and its human rights community emphasize the importance of women's human rights and equality between the sexes. They stress that the full enjoyment of human rights for all and equality between the sexes is dependent on targeted action for the advancement of women and gender mainstreaming action that builds on partnership between and attention to both women and men.

The commonality between the feminist and the institutional human rights discourses can be explained by several positive factors. The overall awareness of sex inequality has increased due to strong lobbying by women's advocates and others, especially within the Vienna process. The unifying effects have led to considerable success of the global violence against women campaign. There is increasing pressure from certain UN Member States to focus on sex equality and the advancement of women. Within the UN system itself, the position of women has strengthened through the promotion of women and the establishment of new procedures. Such new procedures facilitate inter-institutional dialogues between, for example, the Office of the High Commissioner for Human Rights and the Division for the Advancement of Women.

The fore-mentioned reasons for the similarity of the feminist and institutional human rights discourses focus on the impact of the feminisms, the women's advocates and the NGOs on international human rights system. Feminist international human rights scholarship has presumably also been affected by the human rights rhetoric of the UN and its human rights community. The increasing institutionalization and depolitization of feminism and feminist theory both in academia and via extra-ordinary mechanisms in the UN has led feminist international law scholars increasingly to accept the ways and means implemented within the UN system for sex equality and women's advancement. Karen Engle claims that any attempt to integrate the margins into the core will probably be disruptive for both the margins and the core. However, given the hierarchical relationship between the margins and the centre, these disruptions might not be equally perceived by the margins and the centre.

Nordic Feminist Legal Studies Approaching the International

As I noted above, in the Nordic countries the engagement in 'rights' debates has been limited, because it is customary to deal with rights through distributive justice schemes. The construction of the Nordic democratic welfare states has been perceived of as a common project engaging the people, their political representatives and the institutional settings of the state. The Nordic states tend to be perceived of as well meaning and attentive to the needs of the citizen/human being. These representations of the Nordic states have been deconstructed during the past decade. However, there are tendencies amongst Nordic scholars that integrate political and institutional dimensions into their human rights analysis and view the democratic state project or civil and political rights as intertwined with the social welfare state project or economic and social rights. An example of this tendency is the work of Martin Scheinin. He sees rights as multi-party structures or bundles of binary relationships. According to Scheinin '[u]nderstanding human rights as multi-party structures helps to overcome the narrow conception of human rights as related *only* to the vertical relationship between the State and the individual' (Scheinin 1999, 8). Integral to Scheinin's view of international human rights as multi-party structures is his consistent attempt to take a holistic approach to the rights field and to give equal attention and equal legal *value* to civil and political rights and economic, social and cultural rights.

When Nordic scholars engage in the international human rights discourse, they tend to promote the idea of international human rights elsewhere. The 'rights debates' in the Nordic countries have largely dealt with fundamental rights and democratic governance. The Nordic countries, however, are all members in the major international human rights instruments and each of the Nordic countries has one human rights centre. On the other hand, though, the signing and ratification of the human rights treaties have not been subject to any broader public debates about substantive rights. Relatively little of the work of the human rights centres actually deals with Nordic circumstances.[7] Non-Nordic rights debates tend to concern the European Convention on Human Rights or human rights in the European Union. The main exception is the discussion about the rights of indigenous peoples, in which the Nordic countries take actively part in a wider international context.

There is a similar divide within Nordic feminist legal studies concerning the approach to rights. Nordic feminist legal scholars approach rights in a different way than international law scholars working with international human and women's human rights discourses. Nordic feminist legal studies scholars engage with rights mainly through the Nordic constitutional and social rights debates and very few Nordic feminist legal scholars have worked on international human rights.[8]

Liisa Nieminen analyzed in her thesis '*Perusoikeuksien emansipatoriset mahdollisuudet?*' (The Emancipatory Potential of Fundamental Rights? 1990) the potential of using constitutional or fundamental rights in women's emancipatory struggles. Her thesis is a thorough historical and comparative study of fundamental rights from a feminist perspective, but she only briefly touches upon international human rights law and its potential in stating that '[m]aybe the possibilities of international human rights bodies to succeed in this regard are better than are the possibilities of the authorities of the state, which are tied with the national traditions (e.g., with religious ideas)' (Nieminen 1990, 492). Hence, Nieminen shows us the black box of international human rights law, but does not yet, in 1990, attempt to open it.

Nevertheless, the aforementioned distinction is not clear-cut and the Nordic rights discourse has also developed since the early 1990s. For example, Nousiainen and Niemi-Kiesiläinen argue that '[i]n legal reform, women's issues have been articulated as enhancements of certain policies rather than as issues of rights or discrimination', but at the same time Nousiainen and Niemi-Kiesiläinen claim that '[p]olicies have been most effective in promoting women's position when they have been articulated as individual and universal rights...' (Nousiainen and Niemi-Kiesiläinen 2001, 21-22). The use of 'rights' and 'rights' in this seemingly contradictory manner is probably a lapse resulting from, on the one hand, the special focus of Nordic legal feminism on the welfare state and welfare state schemes for promoting equal opportunities and gender equality and, on the other hand, the many and often rather unspecific ways in which the concept of rights is currently used. That is, in feminist discourse, the concept of rights is used both to define a generic conception of women's rights that changes its form and content dependent on which subject matter is currently being analyzed.

The increased internationalization of both academia and law, however, has also led to increased feminist knowledge travelling, not the least within the framework of international human rights. Nordic feminists have not yet developed their own approach to international human rights, but they show an increased interest in both international human rights and in the dominant feminist international human rights law scholarship.

Conclusions

The aim of this chapter has been to shed light on the relationship between different feminisms with a special focus on how Nordic feminist legal scholars can contribute to the international feminist debate about rights, and vice versa. To conclude, I will outline what I perceive as the potential contributions of Nordic feminist legal scholarship. Finally, I will point out some of *our* shortcomings.

When addressing Nordic feminist legal scholarship I noted that *we* perceived ourselves as marginal vis-à-vis dominant English language feminist legal scholarship. This perception of ourselves as marginal is substantiated by the fact that English language feminisms reach the Nordic context in a greater extent than Nordic feminisms have an impact beyond the Nordic context. As English language feminisms travel so well, English language feminisms have become decontextualized and dislocated, as opposed to other language feminisms that seem less generic. The fact that English language feminisms seem generic has contributed to a rather uncritical appropriation of English language feminist conceptual and analytical frameworks and undermined critical questioning about whether certain concepts are translatable or whether certain analysis can be borrowed. During recent years, Nordic feminist legal scholars have increasingly begun to question their perception of themselves as marginal and to critically analyze the Nordic model in relationship to other feminist epistemologies and equality models.

The specificities that Nordic feminist legal scholars tend to highlight as positive aspects of Nordic feminist legal thought include emphasis on collective processes and distributive justice. While Nordic feminist legal scholarship does not promote what Petersen outlined as an inter-human approach, Nordic feminist legal scholars do emphasise a decentring of the individual scholar and view knowledge production as a collective process. Nordic feminist legal scholars have not utilized individual rights rhetoric to support their claims for equality and societal change. Rather, feminists have supported the Nordic distributive justice model. Distributive justice is viewed as a means to move beyond formal equality and to ensure that all individuals in society are given equal opportunities to empower themselves. Hence, by using the socio-legal knowledge base of Nordic women's law traditions and by developing the contemporary Nordic human rights scholarship, Nordic feminist human rights law scholarship could contribute to the feminist international human rights law scholarship by decentralizing civil and political rights and promoting economic, social and cultural rights, by re-defining the public/private distinction and by promoting new conceptions of individual and community by using experiences from the Nordic welfare states as models.

Hence, Nordic feminist legal scholarship can contribute to the ongoing international feminist debates about rights. At the same time, Nordic feminist legal scholars might become more culturally aware of the Nordic constructions of gendered subject by engaging in the feminist international human rights law.

I will exemplify some of *our* shortcomings through the Swedish debate regarding the murder of Fadime Sahindal. In 2002, Fadime Sahindal was killed by her father because she had defied her father's will through her choice of partner and life style. The father had repeatedly threatened to kill her. Fadime's answer to the threats had been to go public, to lecture in schools, in public institutions and elsewhere about the situation of immigrant women in Sweden. The death of Fadime Sahindal (known to the Swedish public by her first name) resulted in horrified outcries about 'honour killings', but also in a public debate among politicians and feminist academics about why she had been killed. The debate concerned also the epistemological blind spots in Swedish (and Nordic) feminisms.

The feminist debate was spurred in a speech by the Chair of the Socialist Party, Gudrun Schyman who argued that Fadime was a victim of a patriarchal manifestation of power at its worst and that ethnicity and cultural background were irrelevant for such manifestations (Schyman 2002a and 2002b). As a result, some members of the Socialist Party argued that although they, as members of the left wing party, were feminists they were not feminists in the extreme Schymanian sense. They were feminists in the sense that they acknowledged that women were discriminated against, but not in the sense that they would acknowledge patriarchal structures as an explanation for a daughter murder.[9] Swedish feminists reacted against Schyman's old-fashioned feminism according to which everything can be explained by class and sex and according to which ethnicity, sexuality or re-interpretations of or fractures in identities do not exist.

The Swedish women's historian Yvonne Hirdman argued in an article in Sweden's largest daily newspaper *Dagens Nyheter* (30 January 2002) that Schyman betrayed Fadime by claiming that culture had nothing to do with her death. Fadime had spent her life contesting her father's culture and trying to become part of Swedish culture.[10] According to Hirdman, it should be recognized that the Swedish gender system, as the result of educational processes for the promotion of equality between women and men during many decades, was different from the gender systems that resulted in daughter murders.

Irene Molina, and a few other feminists, who have tried to promote the inclusion of racial and ethnic dimensions into Swedish and Nordic feminist epistemology and awareness about the situation of immigrant women in Sweden, reacted strongly to Hirdman's article. They tried to publish a reply to Hirdman in *Dagens Nyheter*, but the newspaper was not interested in publishing their reply. Hence, Irene Molina and her colleagues published their reply in the Swedish Electronic Gender Studies List. In their reply, they accused Hirdman of being flagrantly ethnocentric when claiming that Fadime had died defending the Swedish gender order and that hardly any patriarchal manifestations of power comparable to a daughter murder existed in Sweden.

The article of Molina and others led to one of the most heated debates in the history of the gender studies list. Most of the respondents agreed that Swedish feminism had problems when dealing with other categories than sex and class and that the Swedish model had given priority to class and sex in its non-discrimination work. However, agreement was not reached about how to approach other analytical categories such as race and ethnicity or about how the Swedish model 'deals with' its immigrant population and its indigenous *Sámi* population through social welfare schemes. Fadime remained at the centre of these debates, not as a person, but rather as an icon or a symbol through which analytical categories and their fractures could be exemplified.

The case of Fadime was dissected into race, sex, culture and class components and a human rights perspective was evoked only to underline the point that what happened to Fadime should not happen. A human rights perspective was not evoked to criticize the inability of the Swedish state to protect Fadime.

The debate showed that in Sweden, and possibly also in other Nordic countries (maybe this is a universal habit), there is a preference for seeking simple explanations for cases such as the murder of Fadime, explanations that reduce a person to a piece in a complex, but still explainable, puzzle of sex, class, race and culture. The lack of inter-humanness and the need for structural explanations is understandable because the Swedish equality model has been constructed by giving preference to ideas and community on behalf of the individual and through dealing with what could be called human rights violations through educational and social welfare schemes. This model has been a successful one, but it is becoming rather dangerous when fewer and fewer people see themselves as belonging to 'the community' and when the system fails a growing number of persons and groups of people.

I would like to conclude that some of the challenges of the contemporary Nordic feminist legal studies lie in the necessity to re-interpret our own position, on the one hand, as marginal or even marginalized and, on the other hand, as the foremost and prioritized interpreters of 'Nordic women' and their relationship to and their uses of law. However, in the face of these challenges, easy solutions, such as the use of the dominant, international feminist emphasis on and interpretations of human rights, should be avoided. Such an emphasis does not make women into human beings, but rather supports our tendencies to create icons and to see only by way of constructed categories.

Notes

1 For overviews of feminist analysis of international human rights law see Askin and Koenig 1999, 2000 and 2001.

2 The World Conference on Human Rights (Vienna 1993) came to emphasize that women's human rights are human rights. The following World Conference on Women (Beijing 1995) underlined the integration of a gender perspective and the importance of promoting women's human rights.

3 Some of the main publications in Nordic legal feminism are Stang Dahl (1988), Nordborg, ed. (1995) Nousianen et al., eds (2001), and Nousiainen and Pylkkänen (2001) and Svensson (2001).

4 The success of the sex/gender distinction is an interesting example of how well English language concepts can travel. See the Athena study on the uses and abuses of the sex/gender distinction in Braidotti and Vonk, eds (2000).

5 Nousiainen et al., eds (2001) is an example of a trans-Nordic publication in English that aims at contributing to a wider knowledge about Nordic legal feminism outside Nordic academia and to an increased inter-action between Nordic and other feminisms.

6 Braidotti and Spivak define feminisms in their work, including Anglo-feminisms by way of their nationality, locality or other special features. See Braidotti (1994) and Spivak (1999).

7 There are also exceptions. The European Convention on Human Rights has been much debated in Finland and much effort has been put into analyzing whether the Finnish legislation is in accordance with the provisions of the Convention. Similarly, the Child Convention has been much discussed in Sweden. The debate was instigated by the Swedish Children's ombudsman and amongst the NGO *Rädda Barnen* (Save the Children).

8 In this chapter, I analyze mainly Nordic feminist legal studies because I am mostly interested in the interaction between 'Nordic' and 'international' feminisms. However, there are several works of Nordic (woman) international lawyers dealing with human rights and women's human rights: Hellum and Stewart (1999); Kirilova Eriksson (1990); Kirilova Eriksson (2000); Pentikäinen (1999); Pentikäinen, ed. (2000); Pietilä and Vickers (1990); Tomasevski (1998).

9 *Vänsterpartiet* (The Socialist Party in Sweden), in accordance with its statute, is a feminist party. *Vänsterpartiet* was the first party to proclaim itself a feminist party and, thereafter, most other political parties have done the same. The critique against the feministification of the Swedish political scene has been that mere naming does not make anybody, let alone political parties, feminists.

10 Hirdman (2002) and the debate on *Dagens Nyheter's* website 02-01-30. Hirdman is one of the most well-known Swedish feminists, and her *genus* system theory formulated in the beginning of the 1990s forms the foundation of most Swedish sex equality work during the 1990s.

References

Askin, Kelly and Koenig, Dorean (eds) (1999), *Women and International Human Rights Law, Vol. 1.*, Transnational Publishers Inc., New York.

Askin, Kelly D. and Koenig Dorean M.(eds) (2000), *Women and International Human Rights Law. Volume II. International Courts, Instruments, and Organizations and Select Regional Issues Affecting Women,* Transnational Publishers, Inc., New York.

Askin, Kelly D. and Koenig Dorean M.(eds) (2001), *Women and International Human Rights Law. Volume III. Toward Empowerment,* Transnational Publishers, Inc., New York.

Braidotti, Rosi (1994), *Nomadic Subjects. Embodiment and Sexual Difference in Contemporary Feminist Theory*, Columbia University Press, New York.

Braidotti, Rosi and Vonk, Esther (eds) (2000), *The Making of European Women's Studies, Volumes I-II*, Utrecht University, Utrecht.

Charlesworth, Hilary and Chinkin, Christine (2000), *The Boundaries of International Law. A Feminist Analysis*, Manchester University Press, Manchester.

Charlesworth, Hilary, Chinkin, Christine and Wright, Shelley (1991), 'Feminist Approaches to International Law', *American Journal of International Law*, Vol. 85(4), pp. 613-45.

Cook, Rebecca (ed.) (1994), *Human Rights of Women. National and International Perspectives*, University of Pennsylvania Press, Philadelphia.

Coomaraswamy, Radhika (1994), 'To Bellow Like a Cow: Women, Ethnicity, and the Discourse of Rights' in R.J. Cook (ed.), *Human Rights of Women. National and International Perspectives*, University of Pennsylvania Press, Philadelphia.

Cornell, Drucilla (1998), *At the Heart of Feminism. Feminism, Sex and Equality.* Chichester: Princeton UP.

Dallmeyer, Dorinda G. (ed.) (1993), *Reconceiving Reality: Women and International Law. Studies. (Transnational Legal Policy no. 25)*, The American Society of International Law, Washington D.C.

Engle, Karen (1992), 'International Human Rights and Feminism: When Discourses Meet', *Michigan Journal of International Law*, Vol. 13, pp. 517-610.

Haraway, Donna (1991), '"Gender" for a Marxist Dictionary: The Sexual Politics of a Word', in D. Haraway (ed.), *Simians, Cyborgs, and Women. The Reinvention of Nature*, Routledge, New York.

Hellum, Anne and Stewart, Julie (1999), *Women's Human Rights and Legal Pluralism on Africa. Mixed Norms and Identities in Infertility Management in Zimbabwe*, Tano Aschehoug, Oslo.

Hirdman, Yvonne (2002), 'Hon sviker det som Fadime stod för', *Dagens Nyheter, 30. January,* (and the debate on *Dagens Nyheter's* website 30. January).

Kemp, Sandra and Squires, Judith (eds) (1997), *Feminisms*, Oxford University Press, Oxford and New York.

Kirilova Eriksson, Maja (2000), *Reproductive Freedom. In the Context of International Human Rights and Humanitarian Law*, Kluwer Law International, The Hague, Boston and London.

Kirilova Eriksson, Maja (1990), *The Rights to Marry and Found a Family. A World-Wide Human Right*, Iustus förlag, Uppsala.

Larsson, Lisbeth (ed.) (1996), *Feminismer*, Studentlitteratur, Lund.

Nieminen, Liisa (1990), *Perusoikeuksien emansipatoriset mahdollisuudet?*, Lakimiesliiton kustannus, Helsinki.

Norborg, Gudrun (ed.) (1995), *13 kvinnoperspektiv på rätten*, Iustus förlag, Uppsala.

Nousiainen, Kevät (1993), 'Juridiskt språk och nationalitet', *Retfærd*, Vol. 16(4), pp. 60-72.

Nousiainen, Kevät and Niemi-Kiesiläinen, Johanna (2001), 'Introductory Remarks on Nordic Law and Gender Identities', in Kevät Nousiainen, Åsa Gunnarsson, Karin Lundström, and Johanna Niemi-Kiesiläinen (eds), *Responsible Selves. Women in the Nordic Legal Culture*, Ashgate Publishing Ltd, Aldershot.

Nousiainen, Kevät and Pylkkänen, Anu (2001), *Sukupuoli ja oikeuden yhdenvertaisuus*, Forum Iuris, Helsinki.

Nousiainen, Kevät, Gunnarsson, Åsa, Lundström, Karin and Niemi-Kiesiläinen, Johanna (eds) (2001), *Responsible Selves. Women in the Nordic Legal Culture*, Ashgate Publishing Ltd, Aldershot.

Orford, Anne (1999), 'Muscular Humanitarianism: Reading the Narratives of the New Interventionism', *European Journal of International Law*, Vol. 10(4), pp. 679-711.

Orford, Anne (2002), 'Feminism, Imperialism and the Mission of International Law', *NJIL* vol. 71, pp. 275-296.

Otto, Dianne (1997a), 'Rethinking the Universality of Human Rights Law', *Columbia Human Rights Law Review*, Vol. 29(1), pp. 1-46.

Otto, Dianne (1997b), 'Rethinking Universals: Opening Transformative Possibilities in International Human Rights Law', *The Australian Yearbook of International Law*, Vol. 18, pp. 1-36.

Pentikäinen, Merja (1999), *The Applicability of the Human Rights Model to Address Concerns and the Status of Women*, Forum Iuris, Helsinki.

Pentikäinen, Merja (ed.) (2000), *EU-China Dialogue. Perspectives on Human Rights – With Special Reference to Women*, Lapland's University Press, Rovaniemi.

Peters, Julia and Wolper, Andrea (eds) (1995), *Women's Rights Human Rights. International Feminist Perspectives*, Routledge, New York and London.

Petersen, Hanne (2000), 'Forgoing New Identities in the Global Family? Challenges for Prescriptive and Descriptive Normative Knowledge', *Retfærd*, Vol. 23(3), pp. 46-54.

Petersen, Hanne and Vindeløv, Vibeke (2000), 'En samtale om ret i Bevægelse', in Peter Blume (ed.), *Grundrettigheder – Årsskrift*, Jurist og Økonomforbundets Forlag, Copenhagen, pp. 283-91.

Pietilä, Hilkka and Vickers, Jeanne (1990), *Making Women Matter. The Role of the United Nations, 3rd Edition*, Zed Books Ltd, London and New Jersey.

Scheinin, Martin (1999), 'Human Rights of Women as Human Rights', in Lauri Hannikainen and Eeva Nykänen (eds), *New Trends in Discrimination Law – International Perspectives*, Publications of Turku Law School, Turku.

Schyman, Gudrun (2002a), Kongresstal, Vänsterpartiets kongress 2002, (http://www.helgo.net/enar/politik/talibantalet.html).

Schyman, Gudrun (2002b), 'Fadime offer för mäns förtryck', *Dagens Nyheter, 26. January* (and the debate on *Dagens Nyheter's* website 26. January).

Spivak, Gayatri Chakravorty (1999), *A Critique of Postcolonial Reason. Toward a History of the Vanishing Present*, Harvard University Press, Massachusetts.

Stang Dahl, Tove (1988), *Women's Law*, Norwegian University Press, Oslo.

Svensson, Eva-Maria (2001), 'Sex Equality: Changes in Politics, Jurisprudence and Feminist Legal Studies', in Kevät Nousiainen, Åsa Gunnarsson, Karin Lundström, and Johanna Niemi-Kiesiläinen (eds), *Responsible Selves. Women in the Nordic Legal Culture*, Ashgate Publishing Ltd, Aldershot.

Tomasevski, Katarina (1998), *A Primer on CEDAW for International Development Co-operation Personne*, SIDA, Stockholm.

Chapter 11

Bringing Difference into the Classroom: Cross-Cultural Experiences in Teaching

Hanne Petersen

'...in so far as people still believe in the ideal that moral education and general tolerance may make humanity happier, humanity owes much to Erasmus.' (Huizinga 1957, 192)

Erasmus, a Dutchman, who lived from 1466 to 1536, was a great cosmopolitan and reputedly the greatest scholar in the Northern Renaissance. He was a humanist, an idealist, a pioneer of the modern spirit. According to Johan Huizinga, the twentieth century Dutch historian who published a biography of Erasmus in 1957, Erasmus seemed, at times, as though he were not strong enough for the age in which he lived. Erasmus lived during the Reformation, a time when protests were raised against the power of the Catholic Church and the road was paved for the emerging state order, which would rule Europe for the next centuries to come.

During this age, '*...Catholics regarded him in the heat of the struggle as the corrupter of the Church, and the Protestants as the betrayer of the Gospel, yet his words of moderation and kindliness did not pass by unheard or unheeded on either side*' writes Huizinga (1957, 192).

Erasmus was a restless travelling scholar, who studied, taught and wrote in many European countries. The European Union has named its exchange programme for students after this recognized European scholar; a programme which now requires that universities in EU countries offer opportunities for students from other parts of the European Union – and the world – to come and study.

The Erasmus Course

As a consequence of the Erasmus programme, in a small country and language area, such as Denmark, all courses are now offered in the global *lingua franca*, English. These English courses are often attended by a few Danish students and a varying number of students from other countries. Thus, teaching an Erasmus course at the

University of Copenhagen means teaching a cosmopolitan group of students about topics which also have some regional or general relevance.

During the autumn semester of 2001, I taught a course entitled 'Global Perspectives on Gendered Law' to a small group of 13 students from at least six different nations and with links to the three monotheistic religions, Christianity, Judaism and Islam. The majority were female students and not Danish citizens, but the three men attending the class were all Danish citizens. The only woman who was a Danish *citizeness* was of non-EU origin and married to a man from the Maghreb. Another of the participating women was an EU immigrant married to a Dane. The nations represented in the course were Danish, Dutch, German, Italian, Finnish and Australian.

This diversity in background is unusual for an 'ordinary Danish' class of law students, where the overwhelming majority of students are Danish and Lutheran Christians, although the number of students with an Islamic and immigrant background is growing. The number of female law students at the University of Copenhagen is now over 60 per cent.

The difficulties encountered when addressing such a broad topic to a rather diverse group of young people are reflected in the structure and organization of the course itself. The course covered an emerging field of knowledge, which at the moment has a rather vague outline. I was a bit unsure whether it would be premature to offer a course of this kind. The experimental character was reflected both in the course outline and in the small number of participants.

The course was presented as follows in the course catalogue of the Law Faculty of the University of Copenhagen:

> *Course objective*: The aim of this course is to contribute to the development of an emerging field of learning, which may be called world law or global law. The course will focus on globally oriented processes, concepts, issues and perspectives concerning law. The aspiration is to be able to transcend a discussion on Western (human) rights and equality discourse, and to proceed to a discussion and understanding of law and legal phenomena on a transnational and global level. In this course law is understood not as an objective and neutral entity, and not as a body of rules but as a cultural and normative dynamic process. Rules are understood as having meaning only in the context of institutions and procedures, values and ways of thought. The course will address issues of both practical and theoretical relevance with an aspiration to link them. Both socio-legal, jurisprudential and what might be called psycho-political juridical perspectives will be important.
>
> *Course outline*: The course takes the global process, which has put issues concerning the relation between gender and law on its agenda during the last quarter of a century, as its starting point. This process has been supported by international institutions, trans-national movements, and technological developments. Through this process a number of concepts have been developed or

have gained attention. The course attempts to deal with global perspectives on gendered law through an investigation of some of these concepts rather than through a primary focus upon positive legal texts. In this way, it is hoped also to find new constructive ways to deal with what has been called the 'traffic jam of conventions'.

Some of the concepts, which are suggested as a starting point for reflection and understanding of the globalized normative process:

- *diversity* (difference, discrimination, pluralism)
- *justice* (economic, creative, cultural, social)
- *relations* (dependence, dominance, friendship, generations, marriage)
- *resources* (human, material, physical, spiritual)
- *values* (care, dignity, equity, love, responsibility, service, solidarity)
- *survival* (maintenance, poverty, security, sustainability, work)

Relating these concepts to international law and examples of national law, we hope to be better equipped to bring together and to discuss different perspectives of the global discourse on law and gender. This discourse is especially well developed by feminist epistemology and feminist jurisprudence, but the intention is also to include emerging views on relationships between the European/Western world (sometimes also called the minority world) and the majority (non-Western) world.

Over the last quarter of a century, Nordic women's law has attempted to develop a new conceptual approach to jurisprudence. This new conceptual approach entails money law, housewife's law, caring maintenance and birth work (Dahl 1983). This approach has been taken further by the 'Women and Law in Southern Africa' (WLSA) research project, which has dealt with issues such as maintenance, inheritance and access to resources (Hellum 1999).

This course is inspired by and, to a certain extent, based upon this heritage as well as upon the teacher's experiences with issues of law and gender in the Nordic countries, Africa, Pakistan and Greenland.

Examinations: Students are required to deliver a written synopsis of maximum 10 pages about 3-4 weeks before the oral examination. The oral examination is based upon the synopsis, but will cover all the relevant required reading.

Reading: Required reading covers approximately 450 pages. Final texts will be presented at the beginning of the course in order to be able to include recent literature. Check my personal website for information.

In the following, I shall try to describe some of the reflections and experiences I had while preparing, teaching and giving examinations in this course. My hope is that this approach may give some insight into the challenges that coping with differences pose.

An Experience Based and Experimental Approach

To a large degree, my wish to develop a course dealing with both global and feminist/gendered legal issues stems from my cooperation in the 1990s with the WLSA (Women and Law in Southern Africa). From 1992 and over the following decade, I worked as a facilitator with members of this enthusiastic group of researchers. Their empirical research has made a considerable impact on education, political agendas and legislation in the region. I also participated in courses in Pakistan in 1996 and 1998 on Women's Law and Women's Law Methodology. These courses were organized by Rubya Mehdi, a Pakistani lawyer, who has lived in Denmark. She has developed courses in Islamic law at the University of Copenhagen and has researched and written about legal issues both in Pakistan and Denmark (Mehdi 2001). Further, for four years, from 1995 to 1999, I worked at the University of Greenland in an Arctic environment where global perspectives were embraced by motivated students. On a more personal level, in December 2000, I traveled with my parents, sisters and brothers, spouses, nieces and nephews to Argentina, to visit with the descendants of my own maternal great grandparents, who left Denmark for Argentina in 1885. These South American relatives have maintained a familiarity with the Danish language and with a number of Danish cultural traditions. This experience underlined the importance of the 'extended' family as a globalized 'institution' and resource to me.

During the course, we made use of personal experience – understood as experiential data – which was abundant among the students in the class. Such experiences serve to exemplify and concretize abstract theories and approaches and allow for combinations of fields of study, which may otherwise seem unrelated or even disconnected. However, this approach is not a usual approach in the curricula of European law programmes. It should be underlined clearly at the outset that a presentation of personal experience must serve the purpose of linking the diversity of 'individual' and 'personal' experiences with a more general theoretical approach – in this case, to issues of globalization, multiculturalism and legal pluralism (Bentzon et al. 1998).

The gendered and normative aspects of these contributions related to mixtures of modern, feminist, religious identity, immigration, cross-cultural and cross-religious marriages, military background, etc., in a globalized context, in a world after 11 September 2001. I was neither sufficiently aware nor experienced enough to know that the general perspectives of this biographical data should have been highlighted more clearly during the classes, even though some of these general aspects and patterns emerged gradually.

A Conceptual Approach and a Kaleidoscopic Method

Presenting a 'non-black-letter-law' course like this one at a Faculty of Law is always difficult. It was only possible because the committee which approves optional courses for the law school curriculum is less concerned with controlling the dogmatic positivist content of 'international' or Erasmus courses than with controlling the substance of courses offered in Danish. This course could probably not have been offered in Danish under the circumstances, but there is greater license – and necessity – for the interpretation of what is legally relevant when the audience is global or international. The existence of Erasmus courses could lead to a greater inclination to infuse legal teaching with more international and global issues. Difference and diversity in the student group, thus, will also have an impact on the outline of the course content itself.

As already mentioned, the diversity of the group also influenced the organization of the course. Facing a diverse audience, it is necessary to address common issues, shared by participants to attract interest and attention. Instead of focusing on international conventions, which to my view would not have sufficiently addressed the global nature and aspirations of the course, I chose to address a number of concepts, which I had previously discussed via e-mail with my Nordic and African colleagues.

In hindsight, this approach also presents difficulties because most Western European law students are trained in legal positivism and state-centred thinking. Thus, thinking of 'law without the state', that is, of norms produced by entities and institutions other than the state is unfamiliar and requires some rethinking and unlearning. In an effort to begin our process of thinking differently, we watched a film, 'Ancestors on-line', about the search of two young Zimbabwean actors for their cultural roots and background. The director of the film is a Danish woman, who shot the footage in Zimbabwe along with a Zimbabwean female film director. Thus, both directors had the same material with which they produced different films. Unfortunately, we were not able to see the film produced by the Zimbabwean director, but the choice of producing material cooperatively may serve as an inspiration for other forms of cooperation based on differences in background but commonality of professional experience.

It is generally my experience that visualizations, such as films, videos, images, stories, serve well as a tool for association, reflection and rethinking when the aim is to teach law in inter- or cross-cultural contexts. Images allow for a very wide range of simultaneous reflections and reactions.

Working with the key concepts of diversity, justice, relations, resources, values and survival would perhaps have required some kind of written or oral presentation at the beginning or end of each class, outlining the thinking that went into the choice of the key concepts. These are vast concepts, and ones that are also frequently the subjects of debate.

The concepts were chosen because I considered them important. I made the choice based upon my own reading and experiences and after consultation with colleagues. To a certain extent, the presentation of this 'fan of concepts' is related to a kaleidoscopic approach or method, which I have dealt with elsewhere (Petersen 1996). This method is not based on systematic analysis or broad empirical studies but, rather, on an impression, perhaps even an intuition of which issues, topics or concepts may be useful when dealing with the development of cross-cultural globalized knowledge about law. The etymology of the originally Greek word 'kaleidoscopic' refers to the viewing of beautiful forms. To my view, one contribution of the female/feminist scholar would be to participate in the construction of an 'ethics of aesthetics' - to highlight legal or normative forms which might contribute to a 'good and beautiful life' of both men and women of the 'family of mankind' or 'world society'.

We do not yet understand the interrelations between these concepts, as we do not yet understand the complex interrelations between the global processes and discourses in the fields of economics, (state) politics, culture, ecology and the emerging socio-critical 'anti-globalization' politics. We do not yet fully understand the implications of these interrelations for the way we perceive 'law' and for how we have to teach law under circumstances very different from the circumstances to which we have been accustomed.

Global Concepts?

I shall briefly present some of the insights vis-à-vis the broad key concepts that have cropped up in connection with dealing with a number of different texts. These broad concepts, upon which volume after volume have been written, necessarily allow only for a superficial view of changing patterns. Many of these concepts have usually been discussed, understood and interpreted in a specific context – typically in the context of the state order. When they are discussed in another context or at another 'level', i.e., in a global context, this other usage has implications for understanding, interpretation and prioritizing.

The concept of *diversity* was initially been discussed within the ecological discourse. This discourse is itself a globally oriented discourse, where ecological problems are understood as global problems, which need to be solved through globally-oriented initiatives, actors and norms. *Diversity* is understood as a positive attribute within this discourse. This concept is in contrast to the high value placed on *equality* in liberal modern uniform state orders. More positive evaluations of diversity and difference are gradually gaining ground in the social and cultural fields, where societies, which are gradually becoming more pluralist and multicultural, like the European societies, construct their new values. A changing worldview also seems, to some extent, to lead to a development of a 'planetary consciousness'. Diversity, however, is also met with reactions of xenophobia, discrimination and what has been called 'cultural fundamentalism'. Thus, dealing with diversity and difference often gives rise to very strong emotional and conflictual tensions and reactions.

The 'clash' between equality and diversity is often intense when it comes to issues concerning women. The modern feminist movement of the 20th century has been strongly attached to enlightenment values of equality and liberty and has constantly struggled with the dilemma of the recognition of female and feminine difference. Perhaps it would be easier – and perhaps more dangerous – to live with this dilemma under global conditions.

This dilemma is also encountered in discussions about *justice* in a globalized world. In an article entitled 'Towards an integrated concept of justice', Nancy Fraser advocates an understanding of justice as a *redistribution,* relating to socio-economic conditions and as *recognition* of cultural and other significant differences. The development of such a 'diverse' concept of justice might be helpful both from a gendered and a global perspective.

That *relations* are important from a gendered and female perspective is beyond a doubt. It was also clear for the student from the personal experience about immigration, trans-national marriages and religious and cross-religious family life. Identities were clearly relational on both personal and public levels.

The relationships, which have been given special legal attention in the state order, are the relations between the individual 'citizens' and the state. The relations, attention to which is given in the globalized world, are largely contract relations between or among formally equal contract partners. Non-contractual and non-state relations, however, are of great importance for women, children, the weak and the aged. A lot of feminist scholarship has underscored the – normative – importance of other types of relations governed by custom, tradition and religion, especially in family and inter-generational relations. When gendered relations are viewed from a global perspective, rather than from a state perspective, it becomes even clearer that non-state normativity, non-state or trans-state relations and non-market relations are of important significance. Perhaps globalization may lead to an even stronger emergence of the type of norms, which Berman calls 'world law' and which are created by and govern non-state actors and relations. In a globalized world, the role of customs, tradition and religion undoubtedly gains greater importance as guidelines for actions and decisions not least in gendered matters are seen from a socio-legal point of view. The role of state law in no way becomes obsolete, but it has always been less hegemonic in women's lives than in men's lives. This imbalance is underlined by the processes of globalization.

When earlier important institutions, norms and values lose importance, validity and practical and convincing power, the need for 'new' or neo-traditional or neo-conservative normative points of orientation becomes stronger. Another important global discourse of great significance for jurisprudence is the discourse on 'state impotence' as Therborn calls it (2000). With a weaker state and, thus, also with weaker – sometimes perhaps even mainly symbolical – regulation, other perhaps stronger or equally strong forms of normativity and normative orientation may gain greater influence.

Religious norms can offer transnational, transmaterial, or spiritual worldviews, the need of which seems to become stronger in younger generations as well. The reinvention, reinterpretation and remaking of traditions is another sign of the need for normative guidelines under globalizing conditions. Perhaps paradoxically, the existence of diversity and difference may lead to 'traditionalization' in matters concerning gender roles and gender relations and to the enforcement of traditional values in morality and law. Tradition, customs and religion, even in reinterpreted ways, become tools that secure a sense of order in times of change, confusion and insecurity and in situations where states are weak.

In a way, these non-state normativities might even be considered *resources* of importance from both a gendered and a global perspective. When states become less able to deliver security, access to other types of relations, networks and resources become important. This dependence upon other types of relations is probably more clearly recognizable and researched by women of the South than by Northern Euro-American women, but we may see an increasing acknowledgment of inter-dependence in the North as well.

The most dominant global discourse over the last few years without doubt has been the economic discourse of neo-liberalism, the free market economy and economic competition. During much of the 20th century, the dominant – almost hegemonic – discourse on *values* has been concerned with economic values. The critical discourse on globalization has given much attention to this restricted approach and its many destructive consequences. Again, the religious 'wisdom-traditions' have been focusing on those limitations, not least because the world religions all have long ethical traditions of dealing with *non-economic values*. The so-called 'global ethics-movement' underlines the role of non-state norms in global society, as well as the role of 'universal responsibility' and duties described by the Dalai Lama in his book, 'Ethics for the New Millenium'.

The 'rediscovery' of non-economic or post-materialist values seems especially relevant from a gendered perspective. The development of the protection and the preservation of such values must go together with a more just and equitable distribution of economic values on a global scale. Such development is also necessary for peace, justice and solidarity.

The unequal distribution and the appalling poverty in many parts of the world threaten *survival*. The importance of this concept has grown during the 20th century. For a long time, this concept has been linked to the ecological discourse, especially to the concept of *sustainability*. This concept, with its focus upon inter-generational relations, is very well-suited for reflections from a gendered perspective. State orders may have difficulties providing norms with a long-term perspective because of short election periods. Norms and traditions relating to family and kinship institutions include a long-term perspective as a condition of survival as well as maintenance in many parts of the world where security in old age is not guaranteed by states and pensions.

I hope that this sketchy treatment of the reflections about the concepts around which the course was organized gives some idea about the challenges arising from the interfaces among globalization, gender and the changing perceptions of law and legal concepts. Evidently this account is only a beginning. Much more focus and work are needed on this issue by future generations of students and researchers.

Gendered and Professional Identities under Conditions of Globalization

The majority of Danish and Finnish students go to other EU countries to study. I have no information on EU exchange of students and I have no figures concerning the percentage of female students attending the Erasmus programme. I would not be surprised, however, if the percentage of female students was higher than for male students. Going abroad or to another country to study for a semester or two could perhaps be seen as part of contemporary female 'Bildung' or general education. One could also speculate about whether the nomadic female student goes abroad in search of the knowledge, experience and insights she cannot find at home, perhaps much as the restless Erasmus, who moved from country to country in the Europe of the pre-Reformation era to find scope for his need for free studies.

It is not an exaggeration to claim that hardly any university or law faculty in Europe has so far reacted to the challenges which have arisen owing to the internal and external changes they have been undergoing over the last few decades. Among the internal changes is the 'gender' shift in the student body, which is becoming increasingly feminized. I assume that such a shift leads to a 'silent reorientation' of the female students and to an as-yet unacknowledged demand for new courses and approaches to law and to what it means to be 'a lawyer'. The female lawyer of 'the new age' has other expectations vis-à-vis her future professional and personal life than a male lawyer of the old century or a female lawyer of her mother's generation. This shift in expectations is furthered by the changes in the environment of the European law faculties. This environment is becoming more European, more global, more post-industrial, more post-modern and more of an information and service society. The challenges of incorporating global issues into university teaching seem to remain rather general for most faculties (Bateman et al. 2001).

On the basis of my limited experience with Erasmus courses and with the participating female students, I dare to claim that the personal and professional identities of a number of female law students in Europe and Australia are undergoing transformations. Perhaps a 'new' form of 'post-modern' global feminine orientation is emerging and it may also interest many men. This orientation is concerned with the reconciliation of modern and post-modern values and with global injustices and their gendered, though not necessarily personal, implications. This orientation is also, perhaps, concerned with constructing and recovering a 'feminine identity' supported by a critical embracement, examination and reinterpretation of traditions, including religious wisdom traditions. The claims for gender equality alone do not seem sufficient for this generation who have seen the deficiencies and the costs of these claims in their mother's generation. However, from a global perspective, issues of social and economic inequality again become important in a broader sense.

The context and the outlook of the present generation of students, especially of Erasmus students, differ from the modern feminist movement and the regional outlook of, for instance, the Nordic Women's Law of the mid-70s. It comes as no surprise, but it implies that the points of orientation for the contemporary law student in a globalized world differ from the points of orientation of students a generation ago. Citizenship, family relations, traditions, customs, religions and education have other meanings in cross-cultural marriages, immigrant lives and contemporary nomadic lives than they had a quarter of a century ago. This change of meaning is perhaps especially significant for the 'cosmopolitan elite' to which the Erasmus students belong, but it is of even broader significance.

Dealing with Differences in 'Moral Education'

Attempting to develop a curriculum for a cosmopolitan/global Erasmus course and trying to evaluate the insights achieved by students by means of an examination entail various problems. In the long run, we need to develop teaching and examination processes and materials, which reflect global legal issues that differ from national issues and should be taught and tested accordingly.

One of the lessons to be learned from this teaching process is that expectations or reactions should not be taken for granted and that as much as possible be verbalized and spelled out clearly by the teacher. This articulation requires continuous, conscious and self-conscious reflections on the part of the teacher. Diversity in student background means diversity in expectations, in experience, in study traditions and in examination experience and grade expectations. It also means differences in the mental and psychological make-up of students. Insecurity is necessarily greater where many traditions and different expectations meet and awareness of this insecurity should ideally be accounted for by every student in the class, but, of course, especially taken very seriously by the teacher. In an experimental class, where a new subject is being developed, all things cannot be foreseen. Some insights and clarifications emerge only gradually. In this situation, it is probably very important for the teacher – and perhaps also for the students – to keep track of the subtle and often psychological and emotional strains and processes, which form part of every culture shock. This culture shock is, perhaps, intensified in a group with a very varied background, but it is part of most multicultural contexts, including the educational context.

Perhaps an explicit concern with and reflection upon the impact of culture shock and its role in education would be useful in the cultivation of the ability to cope with the differences which are part of globalized, multicultural and moral education.

So far, I know of very little literature on the teaching process of this kind. An article entitled 'The Perils to Pluralistic Teaching and How to Reduce Them' written by an Australian economist indicates a certain resistance from students towards 'new' ways of teaching which should be addressed directly at an early stage. He writes that universities have become places '*at which one receives the present state of knowledge in neatly packaged form without any diversions into the history of the discipline or the personalities and politics that shaped it'*. This description is also quite apt for many law students who are not used to other ways of teaching. However, *'if one explains to students what is going on, they seem to be far more receptive, particularly when they can see that in other parts of their lives they do tolerate, even enjoy, debate and ambiguity and can argue cases.'* (Earl 2002).

Dealing with a combination of global and gendered perspectives mixes the diversity of global processes and discourses with issues concerning personal and gendered identities, which are often very emotional and sensitive. This mixture is quite a complex cocktail, which has also proven to be more difficult to handle than I had expected. I was especially surprised by some of the very emotional reactions by some of the students after examinations. The students were generally satisfied with the evaluations given during the class. The examinations, however, caused some frustration for some of the Danish-based students, who typically attach great importance to the grades they receive. Thus differences, difficulties and options in career expectations in a multicultural world may also have to be dealt with. Opening up for a personal and individual approach to teaching and examination may, perhaps, lead to greater disappointment when misunderstandings arise.

More knowledge about inter-cultural communication and teaching is important both for teacher and students if we want contribute to the Erasmian ideal 'that moral education and general tolerance may make humanity happier', as Huizinga wrote. The Dalai Lama seems to share this ideal with Erasmus. Education is not only a great moral force, but also a great normative force of long-lasting consequence and power. So, perhaps the development of cosmopolitan courses would be a fruitful way for globalized and Nordic feminist legal studies to deal with and become inspired by diversity and difference.

References

Bateman, Catherine, Baker, Tim, Hoomenborg, Elske and Ericsson, Ulrika (2001), 'Bringing global issues to medical teaching', *The Lancet*, Vol. 358, pp.1539-1542.

Bentzon, A. W (1998), 'Legal Pluralism' in A. Hellum and J. Stewart (eds.) *Pursuing Grounded Theory in Law. South-North Experiences in Developing Women's Law*. Mond Books & Tane-Aschehoug, Harare & Oslo, pp. 30-47.

Berman, Harold (1995), 'World Law', *Fordham International Law Journal*, Vol. 18(5), pp. 1617 – 1622.

Earl, Peter E. (2002), 'The Perils of Pluralistic Teaching and How to Reduce Them', *Post-autistic economics review* (formerly newsletter), Issue 11, article 1.

Dahl, T. S. (1995), *Kvinnerett I and II*, Universitetsforlaget, Oslo.

Dalai Lama (1999), *Ethics for the New Millenium,* Riverhead Books, New York.

Fraser, Nancy (2000), 'Redistribution, recognition, and participation: towards an integrated concept of justice', *UNESCO's World Culture Report 2000 on Cultural Diversity, Conflict and Pluralism*, pp. 48-57.

Hellum, Anne (1999), 'Traditional Healing' in Anne Hellum, *Women's Human Rights and Legal Pluralism in Africa. Mixed Norms and Identities in Infertility Management in Zimbabwe.* Mond Books & Tane-Aschehoug, Harare & Oslo, pp. 187-205.

Huizinga, Johan (1957), *Erasmus and the Age of the Reformation,* New York: Harper.

Mehdi, Rubya (2001), *Gender and Property Law in Pakistan: Resources and Discourses*, Jurist- & Økonomforbundets Forlag, Copenhagen.

Petersen, Hanne (1996), 'Grasping kaleidoscopic circumstances – Methodological Considerations for Animating Legal Sensibility' in S. Arnfred and H. Petersen (eds), *Legal Change in North/South Perspective*, Occasional Paper no. 18. International Development Studies, Roskilde University, pp. 136-146.

Thernborn, Göran (2000), 'Globalizations. Dimensions, Historical Waves, Regional Effects, Normative Governance' *International sociology*, Vol. 15(2), pp. 151-179.

Appendix 1

Course plan and literature:
GLOBAL PERSPECTIVES ON GENDERED LAW
Course plan:
Thursdays 13.00-16.00, Fall 2001

6.9. NO CLASS, *SUGGESTIONS*

Visit the exhibiton at Kongens Nytorv 'Earth Seen From Above'. Photos by French photographer Yann Arthus-Bertrand. http://www.yannarthusbertrand.com. The exhibition is open until September 12 and well worth seeing. Visit the following websites: www.unhchr.ch/html/racism/index.htm Discussions on the UN conference on 'Equality, Justice, Dignity', August 31 to September 7, 2001, (follow the news about the conference)

http://www.generationterrorists.com/quotes/mlk.html. Read the text by Martin Luther King: *I have a Dream.*

13.9. *Introduction - input and ideas from students; discussion about course format and student activity. Introduction on law and globalization.*

Suggested texts:

Harold Berman (1995): World Law. In Fordham International Law Journal,

Göran Therborn (2000): Globalizations. Dimensions, Historical Waves, Regional Effects, Normative Governance. In International sociology, June, Vol 15(2), pp. 151-179.

Saskia Sassen (2000): Whose City is it? Globalization and the Formation of New Claims. In Lechner & Boli (eds) (2000): The Globalization Reader. Blackwell Publishers p. 70-76.

Richard Falk (1993): The Making of Global Citizenship. In Brecher et al.: Global Visions. Beyond the New World order. South End Press, Boston, pp. 39-50.
Samuel P. Huntington: *The Clash of Civilizations?* In Lechner & Boli (eds) (2000): The Globalization Reader. Blackwell Publishers p. 27-33.

15.9. *Relations (dependence, dominance, friendship, generations, marriage) suggested texts:*
Virginia Held (1993): Feminist Morality. Transforming Culture, Society and Politics. Chapter on *Non Contractual Society. The Post-Patriarchal Family as a Model in Feminist Morality*. The University of Chicago Press. pp. 192-214.
Anne Hellum (1999): *Traditional Healing*. Chapter 11 in Women's Human Rights and Legal Pluralism in Africa. Mixed Norms and Identities in Infertility Management in Zimbabwe. Mond books & Tano Aschehoug, pp. 187-205.
Film on family relations in Zimbabwe: Ancestors on line.

20.9. NO teacher in CLASS – but students are free to meet in the classroom for own discussions, suggested reading: William Twining (2000): Globalisation & Legal Theory. Chapter 1, *Introduction*, pp.1-14.

27.9. *Gendered law suggested texts:*
Kevät Nousiainen (1999): *Interfaces of Law*. In Eriksson & Hurri (eds) Dialectic of Law and Reality. Readings in Finnish Legal Theory Publications of the Faculty of Law. University of Helsinki pp. 237-254.
Farida Shaheed (1997): *The Interface of Culture, Customs and Law – Implications for Women and Activism*. In Rubya Mehdi & Farida Shaheed (eds): Women's Law in Legal Education and Practice in Pakistan pp. 47-62.
J. Oloka-Onyango and Sylvia Tamale (1995): *'The Personal is Political' or Why Women's Rights are Indeed Human Rights: An African Perspective on International Feminism*. In Human Rights Quarterly, pp. 691-731.

4.10. *Diversity (difference, discrimination, pluralism) suggested texts:* Our Creative Diversity. Report of the World Commission on Culture and Development. UNESCO Publishing. 1996. http://www.unesco.org/culture_and_development/ocd/ocd.html (choose what you find most interesting)
UNESCO's World Culture Report 2000 on Cultural Diversity, Conflict and Pluralism. *Part One. Cultural diversity, conflict and pluralism*, pp. 24-42.
Bentzon et al. (1998): *Legal Pluralism*. Chapter 2 in Pursuing Grounded Theory in Law. South-North Experiences in Developing Women's Law. Mond Books & Tano Aschehoug pp. 30-47.
Ali A. Mazrui (1989): *Post-Colonial Society and Africa's Triple Heritage of Law: Indigenous, Islamic and Western Tendencies*. Chapter 12 in MacCormick & Bankowski (eds): Enlightenment, Rights and Revolution. Essays in Social and Legal Philosophy. pp. 252-268.

11.10. *Justice (economic, creative, cultural, social) suggested texts:*
Julie Stewart et al. (2000): In the Shadow of the Law. Women and justice delivery in Zimbabwe. Chapters 1 & 2, pp.13-38.
www.unhchr.ch/html/racism/index.htm. – Material on UN conference against Racism on *Equality, Justice, Dignity*, August 31 to September 7, 2001.

Nancy Fraser (2000): *Redistribution, recognition, and participation: towards an integrated concept of justice*. Chapter two in UNESCO's World Culture Report 2000 on Cultural Diversity, Conflict and Pluralism, pp. 48-57.
Upendra Baxi (2001): *Globalisation. Human Rights Amidst Risk and Regression*. In IDS Bulletin Vol 32, No 1, 2001, pp. 94-102.

25.10. *Resources (human, material, physical, spiritual)*
Alice K. Armstrong (1992): Struggling over Scarce Resources. Women and Maintenance in Southern Africa. Chapter 1, *Introduction* pp. 1-7, & 3, *The obligation to maintain* pp. 31-56.
Nitza Berkovitch (2000): *The Emergence and Transformation of the International Women's Movement*. In Lechner & Boli (eds) (2000): The Globalization Reader. Blackwell Publishers pp. 255-258.
Agnete Weis Bentzon: *Negotiated Law – The Use and Study of Law Data in International Development Research*. In Lund & Marcussen (eds): Access, Control and Management of Natural Resources in Sub-Saharan Africa. Methodological Considerations. Occasional Paper no. 13/1994, International Development Studies, Roskilde University pp. 92-108.

1.11. *Values (care, dignity, equity, love, responsibility, service, solidarity)*
Roland Robertson and JoAnn Chirico: *Humanity, Globalization, and Worldwide Religious Resurgence*. In Lechner & Boli (eds) (2000): The Globalization Reader. Blackwell Publishers pp. 93-98.
Sassen, Saskia (1998): Globalization and its Discontents. *Section II Women under Fire. Chapter 5 Toward a Feminist Analytics of the Global Economy, Chapter 6, Notes on the Incorporation of Third World Women into Wage Labour Through Immigration and Offshore Production*. The New Press, New York. pp. 79-131.
Hanne Petersen (1994) *'On Love and Law in European Community Building'*. Journal of Behavioral and Social Studies, Tokai University. Tokai University Press, 1994, pp. 217-224.

8.11. *Survival (maintenance, poverty, security, sustainability, work)*
Hanne Petersen (1997): *Gender and Nature in Comparative Legal Cultures*. In David Nelken (ed): Comparing Legal Cultures. Dartmouth. Socio-legal Studies Series, 1997, pp. 135-154.
Rodolfo Stavenhagen (2000): *Culture and Poverty*. Chapter 6 in UNESCO's World Culture Report 2000 on Cultural Diversity, Conflict and Pluralism, pp. 101-110.
Arjun Appadurai & Katerina Stenou (2000): *Sustainable pluralism and the future of belonging*. Chapter 7 in UNESCO's World Culture Report 2000 om Cultural Diversity, Conflict and Pluralism, pp. 111-123.

5.11. *Integrating values and norms – global ethics? suggested texts:*
Mehdi, Rubya (1996): *Fundamentalism and Flexibility in the Islamic Law*. In Signe Arnfred & Hanne Petersen (eds): Legal Change in North/South Perspective. Occasional Paper no. 18, International Development Studies, Roskilde University, pp. 147-158.
Hans Küng: *A Global Ethic as a Foundation for Global Society*. In Lechner & Boli (eds) (2000): The Globalization Reader. Blackwell Publishers pp. 39-45.
Dalai Lama (1999): Ethics for the New Millenium, *Part III, Ethics and Society*, Chap-

ters 11-14, Universal Responsibility, Levels of Commitment, Ethics in society, Peace and Disarmament. Riverhead Books, New York, pp. 161-217.

22.11. *Project discussions*

30.11. 12.00 – deadline for synopsis deliverance

End of Week 49 – oral examinations

Index

For Product Safety Concerns and Information please contact our EU
representative GPSR@taylorandfrancis.com
Taylor & Francis Verlag GmbH, Kaufingerstraße 24, 80331 München, Germany

www.ingramcontent.com/pod-product-compliance
Ingram Content Group UK Ltd.
Pitfield, Milton Keynes, MK11 3LW, UK
UKHW021832260926
475702UK00049B/491

* 9 7 8 0 8 1 5 3 9 0 7 3 2 *